Praise for

Eisenhower and Cambodia: Diplomacy, Covert Action, and the Origins of the Second Indochina War

"Rust's brilliant account of the Eisenhower and Kennedy administrations' attempts to leverage a recalcitrant Cambodian leader into a cold war alliance reveals much about American diplomacy then and now. Extensively researched and exceptionally readable, this groundbreaking book discloses the often shadowy realities of what occurs when government officials from dissimilar cultures endeavor to bend each other to their will."

—Walter E. Kretchik, author of *US Army Doctrine: From the American Revolution to the War on Terror*

"William J. Rust's engaging book contributes significantly to our understanding of US–Cambodian relations, the origins of the Vietnam War, and the role of covert operations in American foreign policy during the Cold War. As in his other books, Rust relies on extensive archival research to craft a gripping and accessible narrative that brings to life the characters on all sides of this complex story."

—Jessica Elkind, author of *Aid Under Fire: Nation Building and the Vietnam War*

"Rust's books on the early years in Vietnam and Laos established him as the preeminent scholar of the period. Cambodia during this time frame remains overlooked. Thus the author's best book to date fills an important place in the literature. It is excellent scholarship, written as always in the author's deft style."

—Joe P. Dunn, author of *"I Have Done the Work": The Times and Life of James Hutchison Kerr*

Eisenhower and Cambodia

EISENHOWER AND CAMBODIA

DIPLOMACY, COVERT ACTION,
AND THE ORIGINS OF
THE SECOND INDOCHINA WAR

WILLIAM J. RUST

UNIVERSITY PRESS OF KENTUCKY

Published by the University Press of Kentucky,
scholarly publisher for the Commonwealth,
serving Bellarmine University, Berea College, Centre College of Kentucky, Eastern
Kentucky University, The Filson Historical Society, Georgetown College,
Kentucky Historical Society, Kentucky State University, Morehead State
University, Murray State University, Northern Kentucky University, Transylvania
University, University of Kentucky, University of Louisville, and Western
Kentucky University.

Editorial and Sales Offices: The University Press of Kentucky
663 South Limestone Street, Lexington, Kentucky 40508-4008
www.kentuckypress.com

Library of Congress Cataloging-in-Publication Data

Names: Rust, William J., author.
Title: Eisenhower and Cambodia : diplomacy, covert action, and the origins of
    the Second Indochina War / William J. Rust.
Description: Lexington, Kentucky : University Press of Kentucky, 2016. |
    Series: Studies in conflict, diplomacy, and peace | Includes
    bibliographical references and index.
Identifiers: LCCN 2016006694| ISBN 9780813167428 (hardcover : alk. paper) |
    ISBN 9780813167442 (pdf) | ISBN 9780813167459 (epub)
Subjects: LCSH: United States—Foreign relations—Cambodia. |
    Cambodia—Foreign relations—United States. | United States—Foreign
    relations—1953–1961. | Eisenhower, Dwight D. (Dwight David),
    1890–1969—Influence. | Vietnam War, 1961–1975—Causes.
Classification: LCC E183.8.C15 R87 2016 | DDC 327.730596—dc23
LC record available at http://lccn.loc.gov/2016006694

Member of the Association of
American University Presses

Contents

Photographs follow page 168

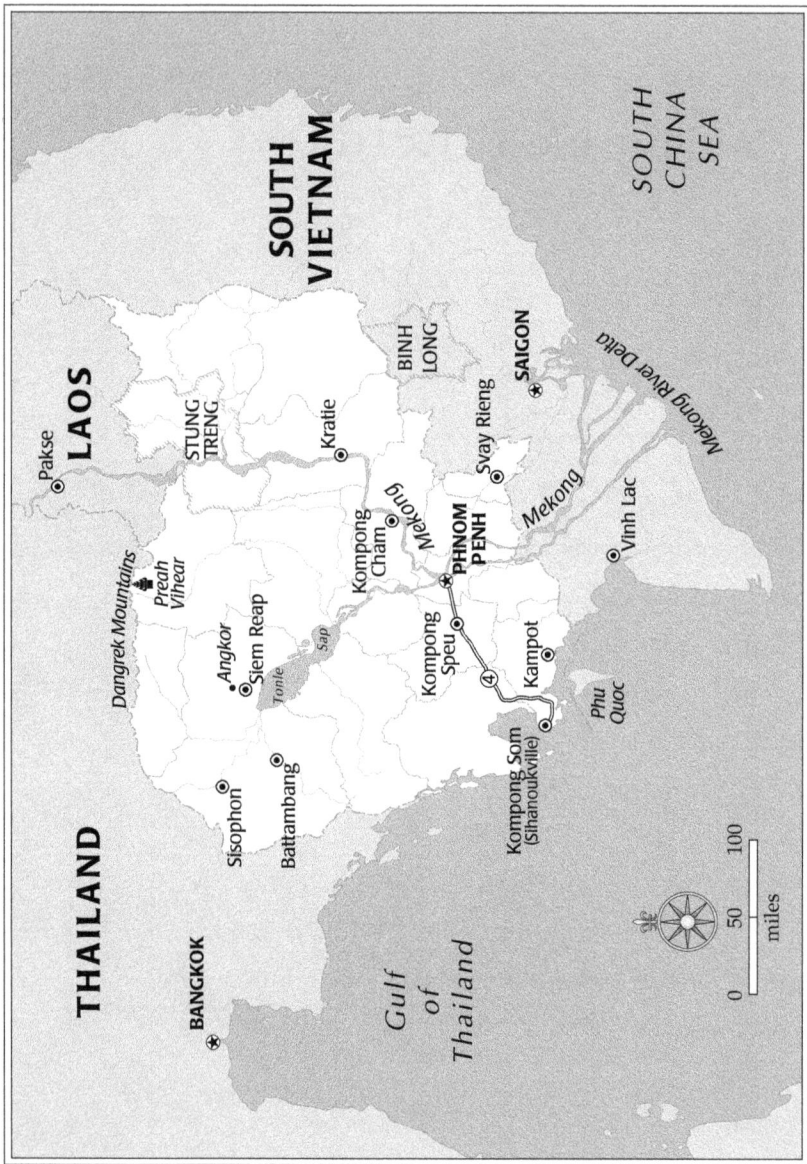

Cambodia and Bordering Countries, 1954–1975. (Map by Richard A. Gilbreath, University of Kentucky Cartography Lab)

Abbreviations

ARVN	Army of the Republic of Vietnam
CHICOM/ChiCom	Chinese Communist
CIA	Central Intelligence Agency
CIDG	Citizens Irregular Defense Groups
CINCPAC	Commander-in-Chief, Pacific
CIP	Commercial Import Program
DCI	director of Central Intelligence
DCM	deputy chief of mission
DRV	Democratic Republic of Vietnam
FARK	Forces Armées Royales Khmères
GVN	Government of (South) Vietnam
ICC	International Commission for Supervision and Control
KPRP	Khmer People's Revolutionary Party
MAAG	Military Assistance Advisory Group
MDA	Mutual Defense Assistance
NSC	National Security Council
OCB	Operations Coordinating Board
PRC	People's Republic of China
RKG	Royal Khmer Government
RTG	Royal Thai Government
SEATO	Southeast Asia Treaty Organization
SEPES	Service des Etudes Politiques et Sociales
UN	United Nations

Prologue

"Plausible Denial"

On November 20, 1963—three weeks after the assassination of South Vietnamese president Ngo Dinh Diem and his brother, Ngo Dinh Nhu, and only two days before his own death—President John F. Kennedy recorded a telephone conversation with Roger Hilsman, assistant secretary of state for far eastern affairs. The topic they discussed was the decision of Prince Norodom Sihanouk, the chief of state of Cambodia, to terminate all US aid to his country and to expel American military advisers and civilian officials from the kingdom. Hilsman, who described Sihanouk as "a highly emotional fellow," explained to Kennedy that there were two reasons for the prince's decision. The first was the propaganda and paramilitary activities of the Khmer Serei, an anti-Sihanouk movement operating out of Thailand and South Vietnam. "We have nothing to do with this," Hilsman declared.[1]

The second reason for Sihanouk's action, said Hilsman, was "this fear of what's happened to Diem and Nhu." A few days earlier, Philip D. Sprouse, the US ambassador in Phnom Penh, had put the matter more explicitly in a cable to the State Department. He referred to "Sihanouk's real fear of assassination and [the] attempted overthrow [of] his regime in [the] wake of [the] coup d'etat at Saigon and [the] death of Diem. Sihanouk [is] convinced of US complicity in [the] coup d'etat and of CIA [Central Intelligence Agency] backing [for] Khmer Serei activities."[2]

Hilsman told Kennedy, "There's a history, during the administration of President Eisenhower, where the agency did play footsie with opposition groups in there [Cambodia]." Kennedy, referring to a failed coup against Sihanouk by Brigadier General Dap Chhuon, asked: "Did they, was that a true story about the '59 or something?"

Hilsman replied: "Yes, sir, it is true."

"CIA did do it?" Kennedy asked.

"Sure," said Hilsman, "they supplied some money, and, uh, they were involved in a plot against Sihanouk back before this administration."

"As they did it in Indonesia. They did it in Laos. They did it Cambodia," said Kennedy, referring to plots in the late 1950s against President Sukarno, Prime Minister Souvanna Phouma, and Sihanouk, respectively.

"We just are paying for it all over Asia," said Hilsman. He added that during the Eisenhower administration the CIA "did things the State Department didn't know about." Hilsman assured Kennedy that he had the agency under "control."[3]

Kennedy's conversation with Hilsman is notable for both what was discussed and what was left unsaid. Their partisan and selective summary of US covert action in Southeast Asia blamed the Eisenhower administration for foreign policy difficulties but failed to mention the Kennedy administration's authorization of extensive CIA activities in Thailand, Laos, and Vietnam. Conspicuously absent from the telephone call was any reference to the US role in Diem's overthrow—even though Kennedy had privately admitted that his government "must bear a good deal of responsibility" for the coup.[4]

Hilsman's comments to Kennedy implied that the CIA had operated independently of policy control in the 1950s. This variation on the "rogue elephant" myth obscured a more complicated reality about the agency, a generally disciplined organization that was highly responsive to senior policymakers. It is true that in some countries, including Cambodia, the US ambassador was not fully informed of sensitive CIA operations. This did not mean, however, that the highest levels of government had not authorized them. "All CIA's power and authority derive directly from the president," writes Russell Jack Smith, who served in the agency from the 1940s to the 1970s, "and anyone who entertains seriously the notion that the CIA could assassinate a leader or topple a foreign government contrary to White House order or permission simply does not understand how power is disposed in Washington."[5]

Finally, there is Hilsman's unqualified declaration that the United States had "nothing to do with" the Khmer Serei, which was led by Sihanouk's longtime nemesis Son Ngoc Thanh. Hilsman, one of the administration's leading counterinsurgency authorities, was undoubtedly aware that US-sponsored irregulars in South Vietnam included Khmer Serei forces. Utterly loyal to the president, he almost certainly did not intend to mislead Kennedy about US involvement with the Khmer Serei. What seems a more likely explanation for his inaccurate comment to Kennedy was that Hilsman was following a principle of "plausible denial," the doctrine allowing the president to plausibly deny responsibility for or awareness of US intelligence operations. The chair of the so-called special group, a National Security Council (NSC) subcommittee that authorized and monitored covert operations and that served as a "circuit breaker" to insulate the Oval Office from CIA activities, "was usually responsible for determining which projects required Presidential consideration and for keeping him abreast of developments."[6]

Plots against Sihanouk, the US government playing "footsie" with Sihanouk's noncommunist opposition, and the doctrine of plausible denial are prominent themes in this book. A continuation of my research into the origins of the Second Indochina War, which are found not only in Vietnam but also in Laos and Cambodia, it examines the Eisenhower administration's inability to find common ground with a difficult leader who was, at least initially, pro-Western in his political orientation. The book pays particular attention to US relations with anticommunist Cambodian dissidents and with their patrons in South Vietnam and Thailand. As in Laos in 1958–1960, covert intervention in the internal political affairs of neutral Cambodia proved to be a counterproductive tactic for advancing the anticommunist goals of US policy.

During Dwight D. Eisenhower's presidency, Cambodia was an afterthought in US relations with the three states of Indochina, which was then a secondary theater of the cold war. Eisenhower entered office supporting a failing French effort to defeat communists in Vietnam, and he left it trying to prevent a communist victory in Laos. From 1953 to 1961, Cambodia avoided the kind of political-military crisis that required the sustained engagement of the president and that captured the attention of an anxious world. Yet when considered in the context of a still emerging understanding of covert operations in the cold war, the US experience in Cambodia in the 1950s deserves more attention in histories of the Indochinese wars and in assessments of Eisenhower's performance as president. In Cambodia, Laos, and elsewhere, Eisenhower's reliance on the CIA to help overthrow troublesome noncommunist leaders should be factored into judgments of his management of foreign affairs.

For much of Eisenhower's presidency, national security policy provided "explicit guidance for encouraging anti-Sihanouk groups and individuals."[7] In 1959, American relations with the prince were severely damaged by the exposure of CIA involvement with the Dap Chhuon plot and by the US failure to provide an explanation for agency operative Victor Masao Matsui's contacts with the rebels. Sihanouk emerged from the failed coup with enhanced power and prestige, forcing the Eisenhower administration to conclude that covert intervention in Cambodia's internal affairs had been "an obstacle to the pursuit of our objectives." Many years later William C. Trimble, the US ambassador to Cambodia from 1959 to 1962, summarized this conclusion more bluntly: "The Dap Chhuon operation was stupid, very stupid."[8]

In 1960, the NSC policy directive for Cambodia was formally amended "to eliminate language which might provide a basis for further abortive coup plots."[9] But the renewed attempt to establish an effective working relationship with Sihanouk was undermined by the unwillingness of the United States to take meaningful action to stop South Vietnamese and Thai support for the Khmer Serei. In the view of senior Eisenhower administration officials, withholding military aid or similar sanctions risked alienating staunch allies and jeopardizing the anticommunist struggle in Southeast Asia—all for the uncertain outcome of placating the troublesome Cambodian leader and halting his leftward drift. President Kennedy and his advisers inherited and shared this policy perspective.

From the Eisenhower administration's point of view, the basic problem with Sihanouk was his indifference to the global ideological struggle between the "communist bloc" and the "free world." In a speech to the Cambodian people in 1956, the prince declared: "We are resolved to remain neutral because we are ants. We do not want to participate in the conflict between two elephants." Many historians have concluded that the Eisenhower administration's view of neutrality was more complex than the sentiment famously expressed by Secretary of State John Foster Dulles in 1956: "[Neutrality] has increasingly become an obsolete conception, and, except under very exceptional circumstances, it is an immoral and shortsighted conception."[10]

Yet in Southeast Asia generally and in Cambodia particularly, the Eisenhower administration's Manichean impulses can be amply documented. According to a memorandum of conversation with British officials about the region, Dulles declared: "We must be more vigorous than we have been in combatting the idea of neutralism." He was "more than ever convinced that it will become difficult to prevent a Communist takeover of the neutral governments if they continue to adhere to their view that the world problem is merely a power struggle between two blocs which does not affect their countries. This kind of thinking fits right into the whole Communist conspiracy to take them over."[11]

Walter S. Robertson, assistant secretary of state for far eastern affairs from 1953 to 1959 and an influential voice in determining US policy in Asia, had the equally harsh view that neutrality, "if not supporting Communism, at least gave the impression of such support and assisted a regime which was dedicated to the suppression of individual liberties and the institution of a system of enslavement of the individual."[12]

Disapproval of Cambodia's policy of neutrality, however, does not fully account for the Eisenhower administration's toxic relationship with Sihanouk, whom most US officials viewed with contempt and condescension. Robert M. McClintock, the first resident American ambassador in Cambodia and author of the insulting nickname "Snooky," declared: "[Sihanouk's] instability of character, impetuous nature, oriental craftiness and cocky assurance that only he knows best what to do about all things at all times make him somewhat less than the Bismarck or the Gladstone of the Far East." McClintock's distaste for Sihanouk was shared by Robertson, who characterized Sihanouk as "an irresponsible person" and "not entirely rational." J. Graham Parsons, the US ambassador to Laos from 1956 to 1958 and Robertson's successor as assistant secretary of state, wrote in an unpublished memoir that he, too, "had taken an instant dislike" to the prince.[13]

What precisely did US officials find so irksome about Sihanouk? "He was shrill, wordy, vituperative, confrontational, and hysterical in tone," recalled Roy T. Haverkamp, a career Foreign Service officer who served in Cambodia in the early 1960s.[14] In December 1963, after the deaths of Diem, Kennedy, and Thai prime minister Sarit Thanarat, who had just succumbed to liver disease, Sihanouk outraged US officials by commenting on Cambodian radio:

> We can see that the power of our ancient kings is most efficacious: that is why, in only a month and a half—once every two weeks— the people who headed those countries which are enemies of our independent, neutral Cambodia have been destroyed, dead one after another, even while they were displeased with us, were mistreating us, and were constantly making us unhappy.
>
> Those who headed these three countries—some are truly wicked, others a little wicked or wicked enough—are gone to the other world. We had only three enemies, and the leaders of these three countries all died and went to hell, all three, in a period of a month and a half. They are meeting there in a conference of the Free World's SEATO [Southeast Asia Treaty Organization].[15]

A 160-page study of Sihanouk and his leadership, written in 1964 by CIA analyst John M. Taylor, concluded: "Should Sihanouk be overthrown, become incapacitated, or die, almost any successor would be more easy for the United States to deal with than the incumbent." That same year John S. Thomson, an analyst in the State Department's Bureau of Intelligence and Research, wrote: "Sihanouk is volatile, vain, egotistical and sensitive. He is given to flights of rage and frenzy of such proportions that observers have questioned his mental stability. Nonetheless, in all his fury he never has lost sight of what he considers to be Cambodia's national interests and, on the whole, he can cite a record of success in this field."[16]

Born in Phnom Penh on October 31, 1922, Norodom Sihanouk was a descendant of the rulers of the powerful Khmer Empire of the ninth to fifteenth centuries. In 1863, his great-grandfather, who ruled a kingdom greatly diminished by centuries of Thai and Vietnamese invasions, signed the agreement that made Cambodia a French protectorate. "By the beginning of the twentieth century," writes historian Kenton Clymer, "French protection became French control." During French colonial rule, according to a CIA analysis of Cambodian politics, "The monarch did not retain any real authority, but his presence symbolized the kind of paternalistic, autocratic government to which the Cambodians had long been accustomed."[17]

An only child, Sihanouk demonstrated an early talent for music and developed a lifelong passion for cinema. His parents, concerned about the amount of time he spent watching movies, enrolled him in the prestigious Lycée Chasseloup-Laubat in Saigon. Sihanouk received his political education in the Cambodian court, where French colonial authorities controlled the process of royal succession. When Sihanouk's grandfather, King Sisowath Monivong, died in April 1941, two logical candidates for the throne were Sihanouk's father and his maternal uncle, Prince Sisowath Monireth. The French, however, selected the eighteen-year-old Sihanouk to be the next king. According to a State Department biographical summary, "Sihanouk's youth, inexperience and taste for high living were counted on to ensure his continued docility to French control."[18]

Although submissive to the French, the young king enjoyed an exalted position within Cambodia. This "simple but frequently overlooked" point, his biographer Milton Osborne writes, had a significant influence on Sihanouk's later emotional volatility and hypersensitivity to criticism:

> Whatever restraints the French were able to exercise over Sihanouk during the early years of his reign, he was nevertheless the King of Cambodia and within the palace his word was law. Custom and practice might qualify his theoretically absolutist position, but in terms of the deference he was afforded and the efforts made to satisfy his whims Sihanouk enjoyed privilege and position far removed from the experience of any other person in the kingdom. His kingly status carried with it an assumption that he should not be gainsaid and that, at least in theory, he would know what was best for his country in all matters great and small.[19]

During World War II, Vichy French colonial officials in Cambodia subordinated their policy to the wishes of Japan, an ally of Germany and the conqueror of Southeast Asia. Near the end of the war in Europe, the Japanese grew suspicious of the continued reliability of the French in Indochina. On March 9, 1945, the Japanese seized French garrisons in Vietnam, Laos, and Cambodia and arrested colonial administrators. Four days later the Japanese allowed Sihanouk to proclaim Cambodian "independence." For reasons that are not entirely clear, he asked the Japanese to permit the return of exiled nationalist Son Ngoc Thanh. Historian David Chandler speculates, "Pressure on the king may have come from his father, a close friend of Thanh's before the war."[20]

Son Ngoc Thanh's reputation as a Cambodian nationalist was based on his prewar affiliation with the pro-independence newspaper *Nagaravatta* and with the Buddhist Institute, where he promoted his democratic ideas. After an anti-French demonstration in 1942, he fled to Thailand and then to Japan. He returned to Cambodia in May 1945 and, at the suggestion of the Japanese, was appointed foreign minister. His main goal, however, was political leadership, an ambition briefly realized when he became prime minister at the end of the war and doggedly pursued for the next twenty-five years. When the French returned to Indochina to reassert their colonial claims, Thanh was arrested, which only increased his stature as a nationalist among students, civil servants, and Buddhist bonzes. He was convicted of collaborating with the Japanese, but his twenty-six-year jail sentence was commuted to exile in France.

Sihanouk suffered no punishment for his own collaboration with Japan. And unlike Son Ngoc Thanh, he welcomed the return of French protection. Foreshadowing a foreign policy concern that preoccupied him for the next two and a half decades, the king told Admiral Georges Thierry d'Argenlieu, the governor-general of Indochina, that he feared Thailand and Vietnam's territorial "aspirations." The Cambodian government, according to a postwar US intelligence report, "prefers French control to being left at [the] mercy of possible Annamite [Vietnamese] encroachment." Sihanouk, the report added, "has yet to prove his capacity to rule."[21]

On January 7, 1946, Sihanouk signed a provisional agreement with the French that gave them control of foreign affairs, defense, and other matters. In remarks the following year, he rationalized the kingdom's limited autonomy: "No one is more desirous of complete independence than I, but we must look facts in the face. We are too poor to support or defend ourselves. We are dependent upon some major power to give us technicians and troops. If not France it would be some other great nation."[22]

Sihanouk's fear of Cambodia's historically hostile neighbors was well founded. For example, before World War II, Thai prime minister Phibun Songgram had advocated the recovery of Indochinese territory "lost to

France" in the late nineteenth and early twentieth centuries.[23] In January 1941, Thai troops, taking advantage of Germany's victory over French forces in Europe, crossed the border into northwestern Cambodia. After brief but sharp fighting, Thai forces occupied Battambang, Sisophon, and Siem Reap. Japan, acting as a "mediator," pressured France to cede the disputed territory to pro-Japanese Thailand. The United States and the United Kingdom considered the Thai acquisition illegal. After the war, US diplomatic pressure, combined with Thai eagerness for admission to the United Nations (UN), resulted in the reluctant return of the "lost" territory to French military authorities in Cambodia.[24]

The Thai threat to Sihanouk included government support for Cambodian rebels such as Phra Phiset Phanit (Poc Khun), who in December 1940 formed the first Khmer Issarak (Free Cambodia) group in Bangkok. Phra Phiset's group sought "to oust the French from Indochina and to restore Cambodian independence."[25] The Khmer Issarak movement soon splintered into multiple guerrilla bands with motivations ranging from rebellion to banditry. Early in the First Indochina War, the Vietnamese communists made contact with several Khmer Issarak groups. By the end of 1947, some of the guerrilla bands had "accepted the Communists' aid and sponsorship." From that point on, the French enemy order of battle included two groups of Cambodian rebels: noncommunist Khmer Issaraks "with many diverse tendencies" and the Khmer Viet Minh, who "were subordinate to the Indochin[ese] Communist Party."[26]

A domestic political threat to Sihanouk and Cambodia's French protectors was the newly established Democratic Party. After World War II, Cambodia's system of government changed from a nominal absolute monarchy to a constitutional monarchy with an elected legislature, prime minister, cabinet, and other democratic institutions. The Democratic Party, sympathetic to Son Ngoc Thanh's ideals, was the country's best-organized and most popular political group. Winning elections in 1946 and 1948, it was, in the words of historian Ben Kiernan, "the biggest force representing Khmer nationalism and modernism in this period."[27]

The Indochinese Communist Party, however, was developing ambitious plans for "a pro-Vietnamese Cambodian resistance government." Son Ngoc Minh, an ethnic Khmer born in southern Vietnam and the party's first Cambodian member, was appointed leader of several "Vietnamese-created Cambodian resistance organisations."[28] His revolutionary pseudonym invoked the prestige of both Son Ngoc Thanh and Ho Chi Minh. In April 1950, Son Ngoc Minh helped establish and became the leader of the Khmer Issarak Association, an organization whose name misleadingly implied unity among the diverse Issarak guerrilla bands. Son Ngoc Minh also led the newly established provisional People's Liberation Central Committee, a communist "proto-government."[29]

In 1950, when the First Indochina War was in its fourth year, the French National Assembly ratified agreements establishing Vietnam, Laos, and Cambodia as autonomous states within the French Union. Despite the nominal independence of the so-called Associated States, France retained considerable control over their military, economic, and judicial affairs. US State Department officials recommended that the United States recognize the Bao Dai government in Vietnam and the kingdoms of Laos and Cambodia, with the expectation of providing economic and military aid for the fight against the Viet Minh. For US officials, the choice seemed clear: "support the French in Indochina or face the extension of Communism over the remainder of the continental area of Southeast Asia and, possibly, farther westward." On February 3, 1950, President Harry S. Truman and the members of his cabinet unanimously agreed that "the only possible course" was recognizing Vietnam, Laos, and Cambodia. The president and his advisers, wrote Secretary of State Dean Acheson, "fully realized the hazards involved."[30]

Diplomats from the small US legation in Saigon delivered the official letter of recognition to Sihanouk on February 10. The king "appeared sincerely moved," reported Consul General George M. Abbot. During a discussion of Cambodia's status within the French Union, Sihanouk said that in the "long run" France had taken the "proper steps" toward his country's independence, but these steps were "too little and too late."[31] In a subsequent comment to US diplomats, Sihanouk "stated that he found himself in an unenviable position as regards [to] Cambodia's relations with France, as some extreme nationalists claimed that he was not doing enough to improve Cambodia's position, while he was blamed by the French and certain Francophiles for trying to go too far and too fast in establishing the real independence of Cambodia. Actually, he is trying to follow a moderate policy, between those two extremes."[32]

Like his commitment to independence, Sihanouk's dedication to democracy was limited. Vexed by squabbling politicians he considered irresponsible, he had dissolved the National Assembly in September 1949. In violation of the Constitution, elections for a new assembly were not held within sixty days of the dissolution of the old one. The reason for postponing the elections, according to French and Cambodian authorities, was "security"—that is, rebel intimidation of voters. Aware of the awkwardness of leading a constitutional monarchy that ignored the Constitution, Sihanouk was a "weak and inconsistent" advocate for elections, wrote Don V. Catlett, the US chargé d'affaires in Phnom Penh.[33] When elections for the National Assembly were finally held on September 11, 1951, the Democratic Party won approximately two-thirds of the seats.

The assembly approved a government led by Prime Minister Huy Kanthoul, a Democratic Party leader who had served in previous cabinets. Kanthoul pressed French officials for "true independence," which they were unwilling to consider until security conditions improved. An alarming symbol of the kingdom's insecurity was the assassination of French commissioner Jean de Raymond on October 29 by a Vietnamese servant who escaped and was "declared a national hero by the Viet Minh."[34] Coincidentally, on the same day as de Raymond's assassination, Son Ngoc Thanh returned to Cambodia from exile in France. An estimated one hundred thousand Cambodians cheered his motorcade from the airport into Phnom Penh, a display of admiration that angered Sihanouk.[35]

During his comfortable six years in exile, Son Ngoc Thanh had earned the confidence of French officials, who found his behavior "most correct." Before returning to Cambodia, he assured the French government that he had no intention of engaging in political activities and that he expected to join a "monastery for meditation." Yet soon after arriving in Phnom Penh, Thanh began publishing the nationalist newspaper *Khmers Awake*. French authorities shut down the paper, charging Thanh with "carrying on anti-French propaganda which is playing into the hands of the Viet Minh."[36]

Perhaps fearing arrest for disseminating "communist propaganda," Son Ngoc Thanh fled to northwestern Cambodia in March 1952. Protected by the noncommunist Khmer Issaraks, he issued a proclamation asking "all Cambodians to rally to him to fight for independence." French officials urged the Cambodian government to declare Thanh a rebel and an outlaw. Sihanouk initially resisted such a declaration, arguing that it would not be "practical politics" given Thanh's popularity. In a conversation with Donald R. Heath, the first US chief of mission for Vietnam, Laos, and Cambodia, the king said that he did not wish to "abuse" his own popularity and that Thanh and his associates "could do less damage as guerrillas than conspiring in Phnom Penh."[37]

On March 28, Khmer Issarak leader Phra Phiset Phanit told Robert Anderson, an assistant attaché in the US embassy in Bangkok, that Thanh's alliance with the Issaraks created an opportunity "to begin forming a government which would save Cambodia from the Viet-Minh and from French domination." Appealing for US weapons and equipment, Phra Phiset declared that with adequate arms the noncommunist Issarak bands "could defeat the Viet-Minh in Cambodia within three months." He defended this dubious assertion by predicting that many Cambodians serving with the Khmer communists would defect to the Issaraks "if they knew that French domination would be overthrown." He added that France "would voluntarily relinquish . . . control in Cambodia" when it "saw the 'might of his forces.'"[38]

In this and subsequent meetings with Phra Phiset, US officials reacted to his representations with considerable reserve. Although Phra Phiset was the brother-in-law of a leading Thai politician, he seemed an unimpressive figure. A CIA report from 1948 claimed that he was "stupid and unpopular and has no real influence." Perhaps most troubling to the Americans was his unwillingness to join forces with the Royal Cambodian Army in the anticommunist fight against the Viet Minh. Anderson, giving no encouragement to Phra Phiset, asked whether the communist leader Son Ngoc Minh was related to Son Ngoc Thanh. The Issarak replied that Minh "had been given his name by the Viet-Minh" to help rally support among the Cambodians.[39] The Americans were not entirely convinced, and the false rumor that Son Ngoc Minh was Thanh's younger brother lingered for years.

Although US officials initially refused to assist Son Ngoc Thanh, the CIA reported "strong indications that the Cambodian Government is abetting Thanh's activities as a means of pressuring the French for political concessions." The Cambodian army, according to the chief of the Sûreté in Indochina, was passing arms to Thanh's small but potentially dangerous forces.[40] Jean Letourneau, the French cabinet minister responsible for the Associated States, warned Sihanouk and Prime Minister Huy

Kanthoul that "France's contract to defend the country would be 'reconsidered'" if Cambodian officials continued to support Son Ngoc Thanh. Speaking to Donald Heath, who thought the situation in Cambodia was "becoming progressively worse," Letourneau criticized a system of government that allowed the "Democratic Party to dominate the King." Letourneau suggested as a remedy that Sihanouk "might dissolve the National Assembly and draft a new constitution 'more in accordance with political realities.'"[41]

The crisis in French-Cambodian relations deepened on May 26, 1952, when students and other demonstrators in Phnom Penh, Battambang, and Kompong Cham demanded complete independence. French officials charged that Son Ngoc Thanh had organized the protests, an allegation that Prime Minister Huy Kanthoul privately admitted was true. On May 30, Kanthoul spoke to Heath about the "dangerous stalemate" in Cambodia: there was popular agitation for greater independence, but the French refused to negotiate until the Cambodian government repressed all demonstrations.[42]

Heath, then fifty-eight, was generally sympathetic to the French point of view in Indochina, an attitude that C. D. Jackson, President Eisenhower's special assistant for psychological warfare, characterized as a susceptibility "to French neuroses." Heath's repeated declarations that the Associated States were independent prompted one State Department colleague to comment, "That is not true, and Ambassador Heath must know it is not true. It may be sound policy for us to act publicly as if it were true, but that is quite different from asserting it among ourselves under a confidential classification."[43]

In his meeting with Huy Kanthoul, Heath claimed that he himself "had no desire to plead the French cause" but then proceeded to argue their case: it was politically impossible for the French government to continue making large financial and military sacrifices in Indochina while simultaneously granting more autonomy to the Associated States. Expressing grave concern over the anti-French demonstrations, Heath declared that "unrepressed" student demonstrations would inevitably "lead to bloodshed[,] with disastrous results" for Kanthoul's government.[44]

On June 3, 1952, Sihanouk rebuked the Democratic Party in a speech to the Council of the Kingdom, the upper house of the Cambodian legislature. Criticizing the Kanthoul government for "antagonism towards the French," the king threatened to take charge if this policy continued. Twelve days later he dismissed the Democratic cabinet and assumed leadership of the government. The legislature deferred to the royal coup but did not endorse it. In a message to his people, Sihanouk promised to achieve "full independence" for Cambodia within three years.[45]

Sihanouk insisted to US diplomat Thomas J. Corcoran that the French had not been involved in the change of government. Corcoran, however, found the king's protests "excessive." On the night before the coup, the French military had dispatched tanks to Phnom Penh and posted machine guns on street corners. To US officials, it seemed "inconceivable that the King would have seized the initiative without securing French approval." Son Ngoc Thanh, who made another unsuccessful appeal to the US government "to act" on behalf of the Cambodian people, described the coup as a "manifestation of the French desire to perpetuate their domination of the Khmer."[46]

According to historian David Chandler, Sihanouk's royal coup inspired the first political writing by Saloth Sar, better known to history as Pol Pot. Then a student in Paris, where he became a member of the French Communist Party, Sar wrote an essay titled "Monarchy or Democracy?" for a student magazine. Using a pseudonym, he "accused Sihanouk of being an absolute monarch and defined monarchy as 'a doctrine which bestows power on a small group of men who do nothing to earn their living so that they can exploit the majority of the people at every level. Monarchy is an unjust doctrine, a malodorous running sore that just people must eliminate.'"[47]

After nearly two months of student strikes, isolated terrorist attacks, and political sniping by the Democratic Party, Sihanouk asked the National Assembly on January 9, 1953, to declare a national emergency that would suspend constitutionally protected civil rights. Svay So, the president of the assembly, said that the king's request "required careful study." So's own view was that the current situation did not warrant the suspension of free speech, habeas corpus, and other civil liberties. After four days of legislative inaction, Sihanouk dissolved both houses of Parliament, charging the Democratic Party with obstructing the government and following the orders of the outlaw Son Ngoc Thanh. Nine National Assembly deputies were arrested for "giving aid and comfort" to the rebel.[48]

During a radio broadcast announcing the dissolution of Parliament, Sihanouk discussed his decision to establish a new consultative assembly. Dismissed legislators who had "not betrayed the ideal of peace, of concord, of order and of unity of our People" were invited to apply for membership in the advisory body. The king selected the members of the council, which had no legislative power but could discuss the budget and vote on it. Joseph J. Montllor, the US chargé in Phnom Penh, declared that Sihanouk had "good reasons" for dissolving Parliament, but he "should have had the courage to rule on his own responsibility until such time as new elections could be held. Because of his great scruples in avoiding the label of 'dictator,' the King has taken a typical dictatorial measure: that of establishing a rubberstamp parliament."[49]

Sihanouk suddenly left Cambodia on February 9 for an extended vacation in Europe. Montllor reported to Washington that the king's holiday was the "object of much adverse comment locally." His vacation also raised questions about the need for declaring a national emergency. Montllor, then thirty-six, was a career Foreign Service officer who viewed French "schemes" somewhat less sympathetically than Heath. "The French aim is to encourage the destruction of the Democratic Party and replace it by a party less hostile to the French interests here," Montllor reported to the State Department. "So far it has been impossible to get popular appeal behind a party not using the anti-French theme."[50]

State Department officials were concerned by Sihanouk's behavior and his alienation of the small but disproportionately influential educated class, which produced the country's cabinet ministers, civil servants, and technicians. Robert E. Hoey, the department's officer in charge of Indochinese affairs, thought that the chances of improving the troubling situation in Cambodia had "been considerably lessened" by Sihanouk's recent actions.[51] Philip W. Bonsal, director of the Office of Philippine and Southeast Asian Affairs, informed the US missions in Saigon and Phnom Penh that Nong Kimny, the Cambodian ambassador to the United States, seemed "fairly pessimistic" about the situation: "He believes [the] French could ease [the] King's problems by taking [a] less overt role in Cambodia. What is your view?"[52]

In a joint reply to the State Department, Heath and Montllor observed that Sihanouk's problems with Parliament were "in some ways unfortunate" and that his methods of solving them were "perhaps not [the] best that could have been found." Nevertheless, the two diplomats were "not greatly concerned" by the possibility of adverse, near-term changes in Cambodia's military security or political stability. A less overt role for the French in Cambodia, however, was a "difficult and subtle" question. The main problem, according to Heath and Montllor, appeared to be French officials' tactless colonial mentality. Local French-language newspapers could also "possibly show more restraint" in their political commentary. A notable negative example was the editorial stance of *La Liberté*, which had "clamored" for the dissolution of Parliament weeks before Sihanouk acted. "French officials," the two diplomats wrote, "did not hide [their] complete satisfaction with [the] King's solution, thus evoking in some quarters [the] suspicion that [his] moves were French-inspired."[53]

The many years of suspicion and in some cases certainty that the king of Cambodia was a French puppet were coming to an end. He was about to embark on an international "crusade" for complete Cambodian independence. As some historians have noted, Sihanouk's conversion to the cause of full independence was somewhat dilatory and perhaps opportunistic. French resolve to continue the struggle in Indochina had been worn down by seven years of fighting with the Viet Minh and their Laotian and Cambodian partisans. Nevertheless, Sihanouk was on the verge of becoming a global figure whose idiosyncratic style of diplomacy confounded and enraged first the French and then the Americans.

1

"A Shrewd Move"
(1953–1954)

King Norodom Sihanouk's crusade for Cambodian independence began in March 1953, when he wrote to President Vincent Auriol of France appealing for greater Cambodian autonomy in economic, judicial, and military affairs. In two letters, with six explanatory annexes, Sihanouk declared that French policy was "leading to disaster in Cambodia." He criticized France for concentrating on the external threat posed by the Viet Minh at a time when the kingdom's two chief problems were native Khmer Issarak bands and the dwindling political support for the king's policy of "collaboration with the French." Son Ngoc Thanh, Sihanouk wrote, was gaining ground with Cambodian elites by portraying the king as "more French than the French themselves." Hyperbolically claiming that the monarchy was in danger, Sihanouk observed: "There is only one more step to take—and it has already by many of my countrymen in their minds—to see me as a traitor to my country, accepting the role of judas [*sic*] goat for France."[1]

Auriol and other French officials were unmoved by Sihanouk's request for greater Cambodian autonomy. In a meeting with the king in Paris, Auriol said that "France could not give any more concessions toward perfecting Cambodian independence at this time." Such concessions, said French officials, would undermine domestic political support for "the heavy French military effort and financial outlays in Indo-China." Jean Letourneau, who served as both the cabinet minister for relations with the Associated States and the high commissioner in Indochina, glibly remarked to Sihanouk that the king's prestige was so great that if he told his subjects "that Cambodia [is] in fact independent, the people would believe him." Sihanouk, who was revered by the vast majority of Cambodians, replied that "they had believed him to date," but public opinion "was getting dangerously out of hand due to the effective propaganda of the rebel Son Ngoc Thanh."[2]

After his unsuccessful appeal to the French, Sihanouk traveled to Canada, then the United States, which was then financing about 40 percent of France's war with the Viet Minh. Meeting with Vice President Richard M. Nixon at the Capitol and with Secretary of State John Foster Dulles at Blair House, Sihanouk warned that the situation in Cambodia was "potentially dangerous." His subjects were "bitterly suspicious" of the French, who should make further concessions to Cambodian independence. Nixon and Dulles were cordial, expressing understanding for the king's problems and advising him to continue his negotiations with the French. They did not, however, support his demands for greater Cambodian autonomy, arguing that any break in unity between his country and France would only benefit the Vietnamese communists. In his memoirs, Nixon wrote that he found Sihanouk intelligent but vain and flighty: "He appeared to me totally unrealistic about the problems his country faced."[3]

The comments from Dulles and Nixon reflected the US consensus emphasizing the power of communist ideology in international relations while paying scant attention to the history, people, and politics of individual countries, in particular those in Asia. In the 1950s and into the 1960s, American officials tended to reduce the complexity of relations within and among nations to a global zero-sum game in which countries were either lost to or won from an international communist conspiracy efficiently directed by the Kremlin. The failure to see the threats posed by the Soviet Union, the People's Republic of China (PRC), and the Democratic Republic of Vietnam (DRV) as related but distinct phenomena, each with its own dynamics, strengths, and limitations, led American officials to the dubious conclusion that Indochina was strategically significant to US national security.

Sihanouk was "obviously somewhat disappointed" with Nixon and Dulles's responses, according to Ambassador Heath, the king's escort during his Washington meetings. Royal councilor Leng Ngeth characterized Sihanouk's reaction in harsher terms: the king was "displeased" with the "cool reception" he received in the United States, and he "resented Vice President Nixon's views" that Cambodia's immediate concern should be the communist threat rather than independence. In a letter to French officials, Sihanouk wrote that Dulles and Nixon's comments "showed ignorance" of the situation in Cambodia, where the lack of independence "invites" communism by validating its anticolonial propaganda.[4]

Rebuffed in Paris and Washington, Sihanouk employed a negotiating tactic that became a hallmark of his statecraft: he dispensed with confidential diplomacy and went public with his campaign for greater Cambodian independence. An interview with the *New York Times* in April 1953 described him as declaring that "unless the French gave his people more independence 'within the next few months,' there was real danger that they would rebel against the present regime and become a part of the Communist-led Vietminh movement." The king observed that most Cambodian troops were under French command; that the country's judicial system did not apply to foreigners; and that France controlled the kingdom's imports, exports, and taxes. While calling the struggle against communism essential, Sihanouk said that he might not be able to rally his people against a Viet Minh invasion. "They do not want to die for the French and help them stay here," he said. What Sihanouk proposed was Cambodian independence within the French Union equivalent to the independence of India and Pakistan within the British Commonwealth.[5]

Commenting to Dulles on the interview, Ambassador Heath wrote: "Thanh's propaganda has been increasingly effective and has diminished the national support, almost veneration enjoyed by the King. This is probably the principal cause—plus inept French handling—of the anti-French outburst of the King in the interview he gave the *New York Times* [on] April 19th. Hitherto the King had been reasonable and appreciative of the necessity of French defense of Indochina."[6]

When his *New York Times* interview was published, Sihanouk correctly predicted that the French reaction would be "very bad."[7] Perhaps no French official was more disturbed by the king's remarks than Jean Risterucci, the high commissioner in Cambodia. The Cambodian government had protested Risterucci's appointment in 1952 because of his apparent favoritism toward the Vietnamese in their financial, boundary, and other disagreements with Cambodia and, according to Heath, because of his reputation as a "rather machiavellian [*sic*] type [of] colonial official."[8] Sihanouk had slighted the French diplomat by going over his head and making the case for Cambodian independence directly to senior officials in Paris.

After receiving a French translation of Sihanouk's interview in the *New York Times*, Risterucci met with the king's parents, Prince Norodom Suramarit and Princess Kossamak Nearireak, to denounce their son's remarks. Risterucci also revealed his knowledge of an even more upsetting document from New York—a coded telegram sent by Sihanouk to his parents ordering resolutions and motions of support from Cambodian government officials, students, and bonzes. Risterucci, claiming that he had obtained a copy of the cable from "a well-meaning Cambodian," described the telegram as "an invitation to open rebellion against the French." The king's parents disagreed with the diplomat's interpretation of the message, eventually persuading him that "the Palace [is] not planning a revolution but merely building up the King in the eyes of his subjects."[9]

Major General Paul Girot de Langlade, the French commander in Cambodia, was less sure of palace intentions. A forty-year veteran of the French army, de Langlade cabled General Raoul Salan, the commander of all French forces in Indochina: "Active preparations are underfoot to instigate open rebellion" in Cambodia. According to de Langlade's informants, "Cambodian army officers, dissidents Issaraks, government functionaries and Buddhist priests are being given orders to stand by for an uprising to take place within fifteen days unless [the] 'demands of [the] King are granted by the French.'"[10]

On April 27, General Salan shared this intelligence with Robert McClintock, the newly appointed US deputy chief of mission (DCM) in Saigon. Salan, preoccupied with the recent Viet Minh invasion of Laos, made two requests of McClintock: (1) ask Secretary Dulles to point out to Sihanouk the "extreme danger of [the] contemplated action" and (2) go to Phnom Penh to investigate the situation. McClintock reported the French allegations to the State Department, and Dulles immediately wrote to the king, who was in Tokyo. Although he did not mention General de Langlade's accusations, Dulles emphasized "the absolute necessity" of harmonious cooperation between Cambodia and France.[11]

McClintock traveled to Phnom Penh, where de Langlade assured him that his intelligence came from "highly placed persons." Convinced that the king had "run amok," de Langlade said, "The Cambodians [will] be in for a surprise if they [try] any funny business." If it appeared that "the King's Father and Mother had given the order for the uprising," he said, "they would have their heads chopped off in short order." De Langlade told chargé Joseph Montllor: "I will warn you so that you will not be there when the blow falls." Risterucci, whose view of the situation was less dire than de Langlade's, observed: "The Kingdom is now in the throes of a grave crisis and the King is behaving like a schoolboy."[12]

Robert D. Murphy, the US ambassador to Japan, personally delivered Dulles's message to Sihanouk on April 29. In an apparently "amiable mood," the king said that he was pleased to have the opportunity to explain his point of view. Without complete independence, he said, the Cambodian people had little motivation to fight the Viet Minh and the Khmer Issarak. Although the population was "generally loyal" to the throne, many people would "simply fold their hands" if armed resistance to the French broke out. The king said that it would be unwise for him to return to Cambodia "empty-handed." According to Murphy, Sihanouk hoped that the "United States would sympathetically support his position."[13]

That same day Sihanouk's representatives in Paris released a public statement warning of "the present danger that the Cambodians will revolt against the French authorities." Intended as a "clarification" of Sihanouk's comments to the *New York Times,* the statement reaffirmed that an independent Cambodia would remain within the French Union. It also argued that full autonomy would strengthen the Franco-Cambodian defense against the Viet Minh and attract "the support of nationalist anticommunist rebels."[14]

Georges Bidault, the French foreign affairs minister, criticized Sihanouk as "a weakling driven by fear"—afraid of both the Viet Minh and the Khmer Issarak. A former president and prime minister as well as an architect of French policy in Indochina, Bidault told C. Douglas Dillon, the American ambassador in Paris, that France was willing to change its judicial and economic relations with Cambodia but that ceding any military authority to Sihanouk would be "impossible." In his report to the State Department, Dillon wrote: "Bidault obviously has no respect for [the] King or for [the] Cambodian people. He says [the] country would long since have been partitioned by Siam and Vietnam if France had not intervened, and only the presence of France will keep [the] country independent."[15]

With French-Cambodian negotiations under way in Paris, Sihanouk returned to Phnom Penh on May 17, clearly satisfied by the results of his unconventional diplomacy. Addressing some fifteen thousand of his subjects, he described his "controversy" with France, summarized his conversations with Nixon and Dulles, and declared his willingness "to sacrifice his life" for Cambodia. Referring indirectly to his interview in the *New York Times* and to his talks with French and US officials, Sihanouk said: "The affair exploded and came to the attention of the entire world, resulting in [the] displeasure of my two great friends, as you know. One said that he was planning to give me what I wanted, but that I was too impatient, and that I have made insulting remarks which ridicule him before the world. The other said that I am young, that I am not experienced, and that this is the reason for my error."[16]

Sihanouk traveled to Battambang and Siem Reap Provinces on June 6, 1953, to accept the surrender of two leaders of small Khmer Issarak bands. According to the US legation in Phnom Penh, the rebels' public surrender was a propaganda ploy intended to prove the "success "of the king's crusade for independence. During this trip, however, Sihanouk learned of the "growing impatience of provincial political and military leaders for action, not words." US and French officials thought it likely that Sihanouk met with rebel leader Son Ngoc Thanh, who "may have told the King that he will not rally unless independence becomes a fact."[17]

Whether Sihanouk met with Thanh or not, he changed his plans to return to Phnom Penh and crossed over the border into Thailand with a few senior advisers. In a recorded statement broadcast on Phnom Penh radio on June 14, the king said that he had "personally observed [the] fervent desire [of] his people for immediate, full independence" and that the country's best interest required his travel abroad to "draw attention to [the] aspirations of Cambodians." Canceling further negotiations with French officials, Sihanouk vowed that he would not return to Cambodia until France agreed to "full and complete independence."[18]

The king's self-imposed exile was a complete surprise to French officials, who thought that their negotiations with Cambodia had been progressing normally. "[The] King may be not altogether sane," said Robert

Tézenas du Montcel, director general of the French Ministry for Indochina. "Certainly his behavior is not that of a sane person." But Edwin F. Stanton, the US ambassador in Bangkok, challenged the idea that Sihanouk's "rather theatrical gesture" was the "egocentric maneuver [of an] irresponsible youth." The king, Stanton wrote to the State Department, deserved credit for a "shrewd move" that brought "into sharp focus [the] problem of Indochina and [the] pressing need for remedial action" by the French.[19]

In Washington, the CIA observed that Sihanouk's abrupt move to Thailand had brought "relations between France and its Associated States much closer to a crisis."[20] The Western allies discussed the possibility of replacing Sihanouk with a less troublesome leader. Most Western officials, however, recognized that "any substitute monarch would be suspect in Indochina as a French puppet." Jean Letourneau's deputy in Saigon told Ambassador Heath "that in his opinion France will not seek to depose [the] King of Cambodia."[21]

The Thai government was "unquestionably extremely embarrassed" by Sihanouk's arrival, according to Ambassador Stanton.[22] Prime Minister Phibun Songgram, who resumed control of the government in 1947 through a coup d'état, the traditional Thai method for transferring political power, had been rattled by the Viet Minh invasion of neighboring Laos in April 1953 and by the implications of a French withdrawal from all of Indochina. Under pressure from the French to encourage Sihanouk's return to Cambodia, Phibun and his military associates neither welcomed him as a reigning monarch nor allowed him to engage in political activity. Sihanouk, undoubtedly insulted by his reception in Thailand, returned to Cambodia on June 20, residing first in Battambang then moving later that month to Siem Reap. A center of Cambodian nationalism and the site of the Angkor temple ruins, Siem Reap was a powerfully symbolic base of operations for Sihanouk's struggle with the French.

While in western Cambodia, Sihanouk met with Son Ngoc Thanh, according to Khmer Issarak leader Phra Phiset Phanit, then head of Thanh's supply unit in Thailand. "The King comes to Son Ngoc Thanh and not vice versa," Phra Phiset boasted to Albert D. Moscotti, an assistant attaché in the US embassy in Bangkok. Phra Phiset predicted that all of the Khmer Issarak leaders would rally to the king and that hostilities between Sihanouk and France were imminent. Once again Phra

Phiset's declarations did not inspire confidence among US officials. Bangkok embassy counselor Charles N. Spinks reported to Washington that Phra Phiset "exhibited the almost childlike faith in the ability of the 'real' nationalists to jettison their Communist partners once full independence [was] gained by the Associated States."[23]

On June 25, General de Langlade wrote to Brigadier General Guy Grout de Beaufort, a staff officer in the French Ministry of Defense, recommending "complete independence" for Cambodia. Concerned by official French interest in military moves against Cambodia, de Langlade had abandoned the bluster he exhibited to the Americans, warning his colleague: if Sihanouk called for a "revolt," the balance of forces would be against the French. "It is not possible to carry out a policy of armed force without having additional resources," he wrote. To "accept battle in Cambodia" would require "at least 15 battalions and the opening of a new front," a situation no one in Paris or Indochina desired. De Langlade also opposed a proposed sanction to withdraw all French troops from Cambodia, which would lead to "complete anarchy" and allow unimpeded Viet Minh infiltration from northern Vietnam into the south.[24]

But full independence for Cambodia, General de Langlade argued, would "guarantee peace" in the kingdom, support the fight against the Viet Minh, and allow France to maintain its "economic and cultural position" in the country. He wrote that Risterucci was in "complete agreement" with his analysis and recommendation. Apparently attempting to influence the new government of Prime Minister Joseph Laniel in France, de Langlade encouraged General de Beaufort to share his letter with "high French political personalities."[25]

Despite de Langlade and Risterucci's willingness to capitulate to Sihanouk's demands, an imminent military showdown between France and Cambodia seemed likely. The French military reinforced its presence in Phnom Penh with two battalions of North African troops, calling the buildup "a measure to safeguard French citizens and property."[26] Sihanouk, viewing the colonial infantry as a threat, ordered his army to occupy major government buildings. Ambassador Heath worried that "Viet-Minh agents provocateurs could with a few hand grenades start a holocaust." In Washington, Deputy Assistant Secretary of State U. Alexis Johnson warned Dulles, "The situation in Cambodia has reached a critical stage."[27]

The State Department instructed Ambassador Dillon to express US concerns about Cambodia to the Laniel government. In a top-secret telegram to the embassies in Paris and Saigon, dated July 1, 1953, department officials observed that an outbreak of fighting between Cambodian and French forces might "endanger [the] entire anti-Communist defense [of] Southeast Asia." The domestic political case for US assistance to France and the Associated States was based on the anticommunist purpose of that aid. A fight between the French and noncommunist Cambodians would be a purely colonial conflict, triggering an "extensive adverse reaction" in the US Congress and press. Among the department's suggestions for alleviating the tense atmosphere in Phnom Penh was the withdrawal of the North African troops, with the "prior evacuation [of] French inhabitants, if necessary." As for Sihanouk, department officials concluded that the situation might have gone beyond his power "to control or to reverse."[28]

The next day Dillon met with Laniel and his vice premier, Joseph Reynaud, who was in charge of Indochinese affairs. Acknowledging the seriousness of the situation in Cambodia, Reynaud said that the "French Government planned [to] issue [a] statement within 24 hours promising full and complete independence and sovereignty to all three Associated States." Acknowledging that the "wave of nationalism sweeping Asia could not be opposed," Reynaud "felt sure" that Vietnam and Laos would remain in the French Union. He was, however, uncertain about Cambodia, which was less dependent on French assistance. Reynaud said that Cambodia's leaders seemed "prepared for national suicide if necessary."[29]

On July 3, France delivered diplomatic notes to the governments of Vietnam, Laos, and Cambodia offering to "perfect" their independence through individual negotiations and agreements with each country. Although the State Department congratulated French officials on this "realistic and forward-looking" step, their declaration offered no specific concessions and was "vaguely worded," according to a CIA analysis for the NSC. The lack of precision in the French note reflected divisions within the Laniel government over the pace of granting autonomy to the Associated States. In Phnom Penh and Paris, Cambodian officials were dissatisfied with the offer, demanding "deeds, not promises," according to the CIA.[30]

In Washington, Cambodian ambassador to the United States Nong Kimny told the State Department that his government did not think the

French note of July 3 went far enough. An accomplished diplomat who was fluent in French and English, Kimny had established the Cambodian mission in Washington in 1951. Because of a wound he had received during World War II, he carried his right arm stiffly and shook hands with his left. His defining characteristic, however, was complete loyalty to the king. "If the French would issue a statement that Cambodia [is] independent," said Kimny, "the Cambodian Government would simultaneously issue a statement of adherence to the French Union."[31]

Kimny repeated his government's position in a meeting attended by Secretary of State Dulles and Foreign Minister Bidault, who had traveled to Washington to seek more US support for the war against the Viet Minh. Kimny, who acknowledged both the danger of communism and the French government's military and financial sacrifices, declared that the July 3 note did "not respond to the wishes of the Cambodian people." The minutes of the meeting suggest that Bidault made no direct response to Kimny's comments. The French foreign minister, however, had earlier asked the United States and the United Kingdom "to tell the King of Cambodia that the general interest would be served by his achieving independence within the French Union along the path indicated by the July 3rd Declaration of the French Government."[32]

The US government complied with Bidault's request. The State Department suggested that Ambassador Heath make an oral presentation to Sihanouk's government emphasizing the common interests of France and Cambodia in the war against the Viet Minh. The French note, according to the department's instructions, represented a "most important step" toward realizing the "legitimate aspirations" of Cambodia, Laos, and Vietnam. Heath should convey the US government's hope that Cambodia would not demand complete independence before agreeing to join the French Union, a condition the department characterized as an "insurmountable obstacle of a purely procedural nature."[33]

The cable to Heath also reflected another French concern: Sihanouk's stubbornness might be based in part on a belief that the United States would provide military and economic assistance to Cambodia if France withdrew its aid. On July 17, the State Department, responding to a specific request from Bidault, asked Heath to deliver the following message to the Cambodian government: "[The] present French contribution to [the] defense and development [of] Cambodia is not only vital; it is also irreplaceable, so far as [the State] Department [is] aware, from elsewhere in [the] free world." The awkwardness of Washington's position—supporting France's fight against the Viet Minh without opposing Sihanouk's quest for independence—was implicitly stated in the final paragraph of Heath's instructions, which acknowledged the "difficulty [of] making [the] above points sympathetically, tactfully and effectively in [the] present superheated Cambodian atmosphere."[34]

In Phnom Penh, French officials thought that Sihanouk had lost control of an increasingly dangerous situation. The murder of two Senegalese soldiers, stabbed by cyclo drivers, caused "panic" in the French community and created a fear of future "massacres." High Commissioner Risterucci did not believe that the Cambodian government had ordered the murders. But the deaths did indicate that Sihanouk's "hate campaign [was] beginning [to] filter [down] to [the] masses."[35]

General de Langlade insisted that Puth Chhay, a Khmer Issarak leader who reconciled with the king in May, had organized the cyclo drivers into "assassination squads." (The allegation was plausible. Puth Chhay was a gangster whose troops sold lottery tickets at the point of a gun.) The Cambodian government, however, claimed that the murders were the "result [of] bad behavior [by] African troops who insult[ed] lowly cyclo driver[s]."[36]

To avoid further incidents, de Langlade removed all Senegalese troops from Phnom Penh and issued strict orders to French troops to avoid clashes with the Cambodians. The general was also apprehensive about Sihanouk's recently announced "mobilization" plan to create regional and irregular forces. The king publicly stated that the plan would strengthen Cambodia's claim to independence by demonstrating the country's capacity for self-defense against the Viet Minh. To the consternation of both General de Langlade and Ambassador Heath, the newly recruited forces were "being told secretly [that] they are being mobilized against [the] French."[37]

The Laniel government, following Risterucci and de Langlade's recommendations, responded to Sihanouk's demands by agreeing "in principle" to the transfer of all economic, legal, and military powers to Cambodia. The only exception to complete Cambodian independence and sovereignty would be French control of military forces east of the Mekong

River, which were "indispensable" to defending southern Vietnam and the lines of communication into Laos. The French government pledged that operational control of these forces would revert to the Cambodian government "as soon as the improvement of the situation shall permit it."[38]

On July 25, Ambassador Heath traveled to Siem Reap, where he congratulated Sihanouk on his victory over the French. Heath commented to Sihanouk that the French "had gone much further in meeting his demands than I had thought possible." Sihanouk received Heath in "a very friendly manner," agreeing that the French response had been "very gratifying." There was, however, one problem. The French had bluntly stated that they would control certain Cambodian forces rather than asking for provisional command of them, something the king said he would have granted without question. Heath replied that he "felt certain this point could be amicably settled."[39]

In his summary of the meeting for the State Department, Heath wrote: "I believe the King is sufficiently intelligent and well disposed to France to realize the very great, not to say complete, capitulation of the French to his demands." The ambassador, however, was worried about Sihanouk's remoteness from French officials in Phnom Penh and the influence of royal advisers "whose good faith, honesty, and reasonableness are open to question."[40] In a subsequent report to Washington, Heath cabled: "I greatly fear that [the] King's entourage and his own fear of 'what will Son Ngoc Thanh say' will incline him to perpetuate this period of wary, distrustful, and unfriendly attitude toward [the] French."[41]

On August 28, Heath reported a new "sticking point" in the negotiations between Cambodia and France: a demand by Sihanouk for the return of five Cambodian battalions serving in the French regular army to the Forces Armées Royales Khmères (FARK).[42] General Henri Navarre, the new commander in chief of all French Union forces in Indochina, said that he depended on these battalions and could not release them at this time. In Paris, French officials were exasperated by this latest demand, which included continued French financing and maintenance of the units. CIA analysts observed: "The Cambodians are very sensitive to the French charge that they are incapable of defending themselves, and are likely to interpret French refusal to turn over Cambodian troops as a deliberate attempt to perpetuate Cambodian weaknesses. The current mobilization program in Cambodia is being undertaken with intense seriousness and strong popular support."[43]

Cambodia's relations with France and the United States, in Heath's words, took a "serious turn for the worse" when the royal government released an open letter prepared by Sihanouk and signed by Prime Minister Penn Nouth. An elder statesman with more than twenty years of experience in government, Penn Nouth was one of the king's most trusted advisers. A Canadian diplomat described him as "a devoted patriot and as wily as a fox. He is extremely powerful and few decisions are taken by the various ministers without his knowledge and approval."[44]

The open letter, dated September 10 and addressed to both the Khmer Issarak and the Viet Minh, declared that Cambodia's imminent independence removed any valid reason for internal resistance by the former or for external attack by the latter. To US officials, the most offensive passages of the document reflected Cambodian neutrality toward international communism and the fight in Vietnam: "Although we are not Communist, we have no reason to take sides against communism as long as it does not come to impose itself by force upon our people." To the Viet Minh, the Cambodian government stated: "It is not up to us to question your right to concern yourselves with Vietnam, we only ask you to leave our territory and allow us to live our lives freely. We do not wish in the least to interfere in [the] internal affairs [of] other countries so long as reciprocity of treatment is granted."[45]

The Quai d'Orsay viewed the statement as further evidence of Sihanouk and his ministers' "profound political inaptitude."[46] Maurice Dejean, the new commissioner general for Indochina, thought that France "would be justified in breaking off negotiations" with Cambodia. Ambassador Heath, after conferring with Dejean, sought authorization from the State Department to inform Penn Nouth that his "attitude of neutralism and of unconcern at [the] Communist menace is but an invitation by [the] Cambodian Government to lose that very independence which is its proclaimed desire to achieve." Heath also wanted to emphasize that the United States would not replace French military and economic aid if Penn Nouth's open letter reflected Cambodian policy.[47]

State Department officials, who replied that they were "seriously concerned" by the deteriorating situation in Cambodia, had been preoccupied with bolstering the French fight in Vietnam. To US officials, General Navarre appeared to have a plausible offensive plan for breaking the military stalemate. Moreover, the promise of independence to the Associated States made on July 3 seemed an important, if somewhat overdue, political contribution to defeating the Viet Minh. Concurring with Heath's proposed démarche to Penn Nouth, department officials admitted that they had not "had [a] chance [to] define our own position" toward Cambodia's insistent demands for complete and immediate independence. Instructing the ambassador to "avoid any final actions," the department suggested informing Nouth that "his statement has received wide unfavorable publicity" in the United States.[48]

Heath made his protest to Penn Nouth on September 14 at a previously scheduled lunch meeting in Phnom Penh with Senate majority leader William F. Knowland (R–CA), who was visiting East Asia on a fact-finding tour. Knowland's principal interest in the region was ensuring maximum US support for Generalissimo Chiang Kai-shek and his anticommunist military forces on Taiwan, which the senator had recently visited. President Eisenhower summarized the senator's views on international relations in a confidential letter to his friend General Alfred Gruenther, the supreme allied commander in Europe: "Knowland has no foreign policy except to develop high blood pressure whenever he mentions the words 'Red China.'"[49]

According to Ambassador Heath, Penn Nouth told him and Senator Knowland that he was "deeply injured" by US press descriptions of his message to the Viet Minh and the Khmer Issarak as an unauthorized peace bid in Indochina and as a declaration of Cambodian neutrality. His statement, said Nouth, was not an expression of Cambodian foreign policy but a message intended for local audiences. He described his open letter as "merely an invitation for [the] Viet Minh to get out [of Cambodia] and for [the] Issaraks to lay down their arms by October 1." If they did not, then the Cambodian government "would take action against them."[50]

Senator Knowland remarked that there were grounds for confusion in the American press. Penn Nouth's letter, the senator said, did state that "Cambodia had nothing against Communism as such." Knowland, describing himself as a staunch supporter of collective defense, declared that Cambodia's security depended largely on stopping communism before it reached the country's borders. He said that he was under the impression that Cambodia, Laos, and Vietnam cooperated militarily, under a unified command, "in defense against a common danger and enemy." If this were not the case, Knowland said, he would have to reconsider his views on support for Indochina and "report to [the] President and to [the] Senate on his findings."[51]

Knowland's threat was counterproductive. In a statement that presaged Sihanouk's truculent public diplomacy in the years ahead, Penn Nouth attacked France and the United States for their "unwarranted reaction" to his message to the Viet Minh and the Khmer Issarak. According to chargé Montllor, Penn Nouth reiterated Cambodia's refusal to fight the Viet Minh beyond the borders of the kingdom and resented the pressure "to consider Communists as anything but [a] mortal enemy." In a bitter reference to the recently signed armistice in Korea, he accused Cambodia's "allies of forcing little countries to fight communism to [the] death while these powers can sign armistices with Communists." Montllor reported to Washington, "Apparently Senator [Knowland]'s firm stand on [the] necessity for [an] unselfish common effort against [the] Communists had [the] effect to irritate further Penn Nouth and [the] King."[52]

Although Cambodia was hardly a regular stop for US members of congress, Senator Mike Mansfield (D–MT) coincidentally arrived in Phnom Penh ten days after Knowland's visit. Mansfield, a member of the Senate Committee on Foreign Relations, was touring Indochina "to obtain first-hand knowledge of the political, economic, military and psychological climate." One of the few US senators with expertise in Asian affairs, he had first visited China in 1922 as a private in the US Marine Corps and later studied and taught Far Eastern history at the University of Montana. According to Heath, Mansfield's meeting with the prime minister was "more relaxed" than Knowland's, but his message was similar: "Cambodia should join cause with all free nations in [the] common struggle against international communism."[53]

Penn Nouth argued that Cambodia "could do more in [the] common cause if it were given direct US military aid." Sihanouk had taken a similar line in his March correspondence to President Auriol, requesting permission to negotiate with the United States for "logistical, technical, and materiel means beyond those France is able to furnish." In principle, the US government was receptive to the idea of directly helping Cambodia defend itself against communist encroachment. In practice, such assistance would be a damaging violation of the agreement made in 1950 to channel economic and military assistance through the French. Senator Mansfield, according to Ambassador Heath, "dodged" the issue of direct US aid to Cambodia.[54]

In a subsequent meeting with French officials in Paris, Mansfield discussed his "unsatisfactory interview" with Penn Nouth and his "general pessimism" about the outlook for Cambodia. Concluding that US aid to France and the Associated States was "essential," Mansfield told the French that "General Navarre would be justified in taking whatever military steps were necessary to assure the security of his forces in Cambodia and the success of any military operations involving Cambodian territory." During a conversation with William M. Gibson, deputy director of the State Department's Office of Philippine and Southeast Asian Affairs, Mansfield said that a "'get tough' policy by France with regard to Cambodia would now be entirely justified."[55]

Ambassador Heath, reporting on the "confused and delicate situation," warned the State Department that the French might wash their "hands of Cambodia completely, withdrawing all residents from [the] kingdom and retaining control by force of arms" of those portions of the country essential to the defense of Vietnam and Laos. In Washington, the CIA concluded: "A complete withdrawal of French forces from Cambodia would strengthen the already great popularity of the king." Agency analysts noted: "Continuing pressure on Cambodia to accept French military control has served only to increase Cambodian intransigence."[56]

Two days before Sihanouk's October 1 deadline for the surrender of Khmer Issarak dissidents, the American embassy in Bangkok reported an appeal from Son Ngoc Thanh for US arms and financial aid. Thanh's emissary was Hang Thun Hak, a Cambodian intellectual who later became a cabinet minister after Lon Nol overthrew Sihanouk in 1970. Hak identified himself to Colonel George B. Vivian, the Bangkok embassy's assistant army attaché, as the secretary-general of the "Issarak Resistance Movement for Khmer National Independence." Vivian had met Hak several months earlier during a visit to Cambodia just across the Thai border, presumably on a mission to collect intelligence on the Viet Minh and the Khmer Issarak.[57]

A letter from Son Ngoc Thanh and comments by Hak explained that Thanh had not reconciled with the king because of Sihanouk's willingness to have Cambodia remain in the French Union. Hak framed Thanh's request for aid in terms likely to appeal to the Americans: anything less than complete independence provided an excuse for the Viet Minh to remain in Cambodia. "Thanh is now more worried by the presence of the Viet Minh than by the French," said Hak. The letter from Thanh, however, did not explicitly state such concerns. It merely expressed a naive belief that the Vietnamese communists would "automatically" leave Cambodia once the country achieved independence: "Otherwise they will be contradicting themselves, since they claim to have come into our country solely in order to liberate the country from the French colonial yoke."[58]

In his letter, Son Ngoc Thanh claimed that Cambodians had rallied to his movement because it was untainted by French colonialism or Vietnamese communism. Hang Thun Hak, likely aware of US concerns about Thanh's ultimate loyalties and his pursuit of opportunistic alliances with the Khmer communists, emphatically declared that his leader had no connection with Son Ngoc Minh. US officials were not entirely convinced. Colonial Vivian thought that Hak gave "the impression of being sincere in his anti-Communist expressions, and [was] unquestionably sincere in his anti-French attitude."[59]

Son Ngoc Thanh, whose armed followers most likely numbered only in the hundreds, asked the US mission in Bangkok for materiel sufficient to equip ten thousand men. His long, detailed list of weapons and supplies included recoilless rifles, mortars, carbines, clothing, medicine, and food. Colonel Vivian, according to an embassy report, "explained very carefully that the United States Government is supporting the Cambodian Government and is therefore not able to help groups which are fighting it." Hang Thun Hak appeared to accept this response "philosophically."[60]

Son Ngoc Thanh's reputation and his anti-French propaganda had helped motivate Sihanouk to launch his campaign for Cambodian independence. Yet as the king's struggle against the French intensified, Thanh's claim to leadership of Cambodia's noncommunist nationalists weakened. The conventional wisdom among French and US officials in Indochina was that Sihanouk's crusade would fail unless Thanh rallied to the king.

In Bangkok, however, First Secretary Gerald Warner observed: "Thanh's position is becoming increasingly difficult." With desertions from the Cambodian army to the rebels declining, the timing of Thanh's latest appeal to the United States seemed attributable to the looming deadline for dissidents to surrender.[61]

After months of contentious negotiations, French and Cambodian officials signed an agreement on October 17, 1953, that gave Sihanouk command of all military forces in the kingdom. With the king's assent, France retained operational command of military units east of the Mekong River. Sihanouk's negotiators accepted a French offer of the immediate transfer of two battalions of Cambodians from the French Union forces to FARK. A decision on three other battalions was deferred pending further discussions in Paris about long-range military relations between the two countries. General de Langlade told Joseph Montllor that the accord "was the best possible short of an open break with Cambodia, and the risk of bloodshed."[62]

Montllor reported to the State Department that the agreement had "greatly improved relations" between France and Cambodia. Nonetheless, bitter feelings remained. De Langlade, unable to hide his "contempt for Cambodia and its king," thought that the country was "on the road to suicide." Sihanouk was "cooked," the general believed, because the national movement toward a republican form of government would "bring about his abdication."[63]

High Commissioner Risterucci, more politically astute and more restrained in expression than de Langlade, thought that "a certain degree of anarchy" was likely in Cambodia "now that [the] issue of 'full independence' is a dead one." Although Sihanouk remained "the strongest power in Cambodia," Risterucci wondered whether the king would use his "strength to maintain political peace, or retreat to his palace and let the irresponsible political parties run the country." The French diplomat believed it would "not be long before army battalions will be identified as backing up this or that candidate in future elections."[64]

Sihanouk triumphantly returned to Phnom Penh on November 8—five months after his brief flight to Thailand and his self-imposed exile in Battambang and Siem Reap. Sihanouk told his subjects that "although all negotiations with France had not been completed, Cambodia had obtained all [the] attributes of internal sovereignty." The military-transfer ceremony the next day included a review of French Union and FARK forces as well as citizen volunteers who had responded to the king's mobilization plan. "The sight of these thousands and thousands of villagers and peasants, dressed in simple uniforms which each individual had personally paid for, was one which foreign observers would have believed impossible a short year ago," Montllor reported to the State Department. Sihanouk's mobilization plan, he wrote, "proved to be the great psychological stimulant that maintained the inhabitants' interest in the King's 'crusade for independence.'"[65]

During the transfer ceremony, High Commissioner Risterucci, General de Langlade, and Ambassador Heath joined Sihanouk on the reviewing stand. De Langlade formally turned over to Sihanouk all Cambodian troops and the military command of the country. "Speaking with obvious sincerity," according to Heath, de Langlade "paid tribute to [the] soldierly qualities of [the] Cambodian troops." The French general told Heath that "he would not have believed it possible for [the] King and his government to have persuaded Cambodian peasants to take military training. It is a tribute to [the] King's personal authority over [the] masses and [the] obedience of [the] latter."[66]

The ceremony's only discordant note was its exhausting duration. The parade of French and Cambodian forces, originally intended to last ninety minutes, dragged on for more than three hours under rainy skies. With thousands of Cambodian volunteers still waiting to march, the king instructed Penn Nouth to end the parade. The prime minister resented Sihanouk's criticism of his handling of the ceremony. Montllor viewed the contretemps between the king and Penn Nouth, which led to the prime minister's temporary resignation from government, as a symbol of the "great internal problems" Sihanouk faced in the "coming struggle for political ascendancy."[67]

On November 14, Sihanouk announced his intention to appoint a new government of national unity that would call for elections in the next few months. In remarks to the leaders of Cambodia's political parties, the king recalled his pledge in June 1952 to complete Cambodian independence within three years. In indirect but pointed criticism of the Democratic Party, he said that "none of the previous governments had succeeded in realizing such aspirations but had only provoked division and anarchy within the country." Commenting on the kingdom's security, Sihanouk declared that despite his success there were still threats from "the Communists of Son Ngoc Minh and the dissidents of Son Ngoc Thanh."[68]

Estimates of Cambodian security and rebel territorial control in 1953–1954 are inexact. In late 1953, according to David Chandler, "perhaps one subdistrict in six was under guerrilla control, and more than half the country, at night at least, was subject to pressure from Viet Minh or Issarak bands." Assessments of rebel military strength are similarly imprecise. Between 1953 and mid-1954, total Viet Minh–Khmer communist military strength in Cambodia ranged from 5,000 to 8,700 soldiers, according to French military intelligence. About half the troops were Vietnamese and half were Cambodian.[69] (Ben Kiernan, citing Vietnamese sources, estimates that Cambodians constituted two-thirds of the "Viet Minh" forces in the kingdom.[70]) Most of the Vietnamese and Khmer communist units operated in small bands that were capable of launching guerrilla operations and hit-and-run raids but were unable to inflict decisive defeats on the more than 30,000 Cambodian and French Union forces in the kingdom. Armed "non–Viet Minh" Khmer Issaraks, reduced by defections to Sihanouk, totaled no more than 1,300 men nationwide.[71]

The most significant military risk to the kingdom's security was an invasion by Viet Minh regulars, which occurred in April 1954, when two battalions of the 325th Division of the People's Army of Vietnam entered northeastern Cambodia. On April 21, Prime Minister Penn Nouth told US, UK, Japanese, and Thai diplomats in Phnom Penh that his country was on the "brink of disaster." General Nhiek Tioulong, the newly appointed defense minister, declared that the Viet Minh "could, by a concerted effort, take over Cambodia in a week." Nouth and Tioulong appealed to "friendly countries" for arms and other aid. "In an emotional ending that almost brought tears to his eyes," Montllor reported to Washington, "[the] Prime Minister asked whether [the] great powers that are leading [the] fight against Communism will stand by as a small nation that only wants to live in peace with [the] world is swallowed up by [the] Communist tide."[72]

Cambodian officials were not alone in their grim assessment of the kingdom's plight. A representative of Maurice Dejean, the French commissioner general in Indochina, met with Robert McClintock to express the "very deep concern" of the French at the rapidly deteriorating situation in Cambodia. According to McClintock's report to the State Department, the French "feel [the] King has lost control of [the] situation and at any time a coup d'etat may be expected which would place Son Nac [*sic*] Thanh and [the] Viet Minh in control of that kingdom."[73]

The crisis prompted General Navarre to share with McClintock his contemptuous view of the "Cambodian Army in particular and [the] Cambodian people in general." The French commander "described them as rabble unfit for independence." He added: "If it were not for a certain road which I need to maintain my lines of communications with Laos I should be tempted to see the whole wretched country go." McClintock disagreed with Navarre, observing that a communist coup d'état would have "disastrous consequences" for the Western position in Southeast Asia.[74]

On April 27, McClintock reported to Washington that the situation in Cambodia was still "serious" but "less grave" than Penn Nouth's "hysterical" assessment six days earlier. Under the leadership of General Tioulong, to whom Sihanouk had delegated full military authority, French Union and FARK battalions were deployed to Stung Treng and Kratie Provinces with the objective of holding a line east of the Mekong River. General Tioulong impressed French and American officials as an energetic and aggressive commander who "may be the man to inject spirit and badly needed confidence into Cambodian troops." To McClintock, Tioulong seemed "completely loyal to [the] King and is probably [an] effective block to [the] seizure of power by Son Ngoc Thanh or any other aspirant."[75]

The danger of Son Ngoc Thanh launching a coup d'état did not seem great to Pierre Gorce, the acting French high commissioner in Cambodia. Gorce admitted to the US legation in Phnom Penh that French intelligence had reported the possibility of a Thanh coup to authorities in Saigon. Gorce, however, believed that these "out of touch" officials, who included General de Langlade, then serving as a member of Navarre's staff, had "made a mountain out of a mole hill." Montllor reported to Washington his own estimate that Son Ngoc Thanh's "personal influence among students and intellectual groups (always his main source of strength) has greatly diminished in view of his continued aloofness during the trying days of Franco–Cambodian negotiations. His failure to express any concern over [the] Viet Minh invasion of Cambodia has likewise dented his claim as nationalist number one."[76]

2

"Not a Happy Omen" (1954)

On March 31, 1954, W. Park Armstrong, John Foster Dulles's special assistant for intelligence, informed the secretary of state of recent Viet Minh radio broadcasts that referred to the "Khmer Resistance Government," which claimed to represent all Cambodians. The broadcasts identified Son Ngoc Minh as the president of the government and Keo Moni as its foreign minister. As recently as February, Armstrong had written that "the Viet Minh arm in Cambodia was still referred to as the 'Cambodian Committee of National Liberation.'" Armstrong thought that this new name was a communist attempt to "manufacture" a resistance government to participate in the Geneva conference, scheduled to begin on April 26. The purpose of the international meeting, agreed to by the Soviet Union, United Kingdom, United States, and France, was to reach a political settlement in Korea and to discuss "the problem of restoring peace in Indochina."[1]

Although Western delegates in Geneva thought that Vietnam posed the most difficult military and political challenges, issues related to Cambodia and Laos threatened to paralyze the conference. During the first plenary discussion of Indochina, the head of the delegation from the DRV, Pham Van Dong, proposed inviting representatives of the Khmer and Lao "governments of resistance" to participate in the conference. Dong claimed that these governments had "liberated vast areas of their national territory" and represented "the great majority of the people" in Cambodia and Laos. Vyacheslav M. Molotov and Zhou Enlai, the leaders of the Soviet and Chinese delegations, respectively, supported the DRV proposal.[2]

Under Secretary of State Walter Bedell Smith, head of the US delegation, responded with a well-rehearsed rejection of "any idea of inviting these nonexistent so-called governments" to the conference. Smith, then fifty-eight, was nearing the end of a government career that included service as Eisenhower's chief of staff in World War II, US ambassador to the Soviet Union, and director of Central Intelligence (DCI). An effective administrator with a legendary temper aggravated by ulcers, Smith was a cold warrior prepared to intervene in Indochina with US air and naval forces. Yet like many senior army officers, he had been frustrated by the Korean War and was opposed to a limited *land* conflict in Asia. "American ground forces will go into Indo-China over [my] dead body," Smith told UK foreign minister Anthony Eden.[3]

Eden and French foreign minister Georges Bidault backed Smith's rejection of inviting representatives of the Khmer and Lao resistance movements to Geneva. Sam Sary, Sihanouk's "personal delegate" at Geneva, also appealed to the conference to dismiss the DRV proposal. The Khmer resistance government, he said, was "a body invented and created" by Vietnamese communists. Sary declared that inviting the Khmer resistance government to represent Cambodian interests would be equivalent to "suggesting that the Soviet Union should be represented by delegates from Poland or Czechoslovokia."[4]

In the days and weeks that followed, the DRV, PRC, and Soviet delegations insisted that the war in Indochina was a single fight between the forces of colonialism and the forces of liberation. The problems in Cambodia, Laos, and Vietnam were the same, differing "in degree, but not in fundamental character," said Pham Van Dong. Demanding that the conference consider the three states simultaneously, Dong sought to establish zones for regrouping resistance forces in Cambodia and Laos. He dismissed their national governments as former "servants of French colonialism" who had collaborated with the Japanese and who continued to serve the interests of French colonialists and "US interventionists."[5]

The Western delegates and the representatives of the Associated States, in contrast, argued that the military and political problems in Vietnam, Laos, and Cambodia were separate. On the one hand, the conflict in Vietnam was a civil war. The communist forces there were well organized and formidable and controlled a significant amount of territory. Resolving that conflict would be a complicated process, requiring a cease-fire, separation of the armed forces, prolonged negotiations, and supervision by a neutral international body. On the other hand, the anticommunists declared, Cambodia and Laos were simply victims of Viet Minh aggression. Reestablishing peace in these two countries merely required the withdrawal of Viet Minh forces. Because the indigenous resistance forces in Cambodia and Laos were weak and controlled little territory, creating zones for regrouping was out of the question.

The delegates at Geneva made virtually no progress toward an agreement on Cambodia and Laos until mid-June 1954, when the conference was on the verge of breaking up. On June 15, at a meeting of the PRC, DRV, and Soviet delegations, Zhou Enlai proposed that the communist states adjust their negotiating posture. A key concession to the West and the Associated States would be an acknowledgment that Viet Minh troops had fought in Cambodia and Laos, a fact the DRV had heretofore denied. "The advantage of making such a concession, Zhou contended, was that the DRV could later demand a compensation from France when the negotiations moved on to the agenda of the demarcation line in Vietnam."[6]

Molotov agreed with this approach, and Pham Van Dong acceded to it, though apparently with some reluctance. In a subsequent meeting with Bidault, Zhou said that the political differences between the Cambodian resistance forces and Sihanouk's government should be resolved through negotiations. In other words, regrouping zones would not be necessary in Cambodia. (In Laos, however, Zhou noted the relative strength of the Pathet Lao, the DRV-sponsored insurgents, and insisted on a regrouping zone for them in the region adjacent to northern Vietnam and China.) Zhou conveyed the same message to Eden, observing that the "Cambodia resistance forces were small." Eden told Winthrop W. Aldrich, the US ambassador in London, that Zhou was "apparently desirous" of resolving the problems in Cambodia and Laos.[7]

The concessions that communist delegates mentioned in their informal diplomatic conversations were not fully reflected in their written proposals to the conference. For example, on June 16 a Chinese proposal for ending hostilities in Cambodia and Laos made no mention of withdrawing Viet Minh troops from the two countries. Moreover, the political roles envisioned for the Khmer and Lao resistance movements were unclear.

A CIA report observed, "In addition to hinting that they would agree to reasonable military settlements in Laos and Cambodia, the Communists in the past week have encouraged the West to believe in the possibility of an acceptable political settlement in those two states. These hints, while possibly presaging a compromise, have [thus] far committed the Communists to nothing."[8]

On June 19, the conference delegates agreed that Viet Minh military commanders should immediately hold bilateral talks with their Cambodian and Lao counterparts to discuss a cease-fire in the two countries, beginning with the withdrawal of all foreign military forces. Sihanouk selected General Nhiek Tioulong to lead the Cambodian military mission in Geneva. In his brief tenure as defense minister and commander of the armed forces, Tioulong had improved the Royal Army's morale and effectiveness. Unfortunately for his future prospects as a military commander, he had also refused a direct order from Sihanouk to provide honors to General Navarre on his farewell visit to Cambodia. Tioulong explained to Herbert I. Goodman, Montllor's successor as chargé in Phnom Penh, that his "silent treatment" of Navarre was a response to a personal slight from the French commander, who had sent a sergeant to meet him.[9]

A State Department biography described Tioulong as "a staunch nationalist, but sufficiently realistic to believe that Cambodia's aspirations can best be met by participation in the French Union." The general told Goodman that he disagreed entirely with Sihanouk's "xenophobic" policies: "[The] King wants to tell the world to go hang at [a] time [the] country so badly needs assistance and allies." In a bitter mood, Tioulong said he "would not pull a coup d'état," a statement Goodman interpreted as "implying that he easily could."[10]

Sihanouk, angered by Tioulong's insubordination and independence, removed him from the Defense Ministry and banished him to Geneva (and then to Paris to serve as the Cambodian high commissioner). Included in Tioulong's military delegation in Geneva were three former Khmer Issarak chiefs—Dap Chhuon, Puth Chhay, and Norodom Chantaraingsey. According to Robert McClintock, Sihanouk ordered the noncommunist ralliers to Geneva to prove that all of the "native insurgents" supported the king.[11] The DRV, intending to make the exact opposite point, had brought two representatives of the Khmer Issarak Association to Geneva: Keo Moni and Mey Pho.

In Cambodia, government propaganda sought to undercut the claims of the Khmer Issarak Association, declaring that only "criminals and traitors to the nation" opposed Sihanouk. On July 6, the kingdom's official news service, Agence Khmere de Presse, issued a statement signed by four former Khmer Issarak leaders, including the three in Geneva. They declared that all "true Issaraks" had rallied to the king and that Cambodian independence had eliminated the movement's raison d'être. Although neither Son Ngoc Minh nor Son Ngoc Thanh was mentioned by name, the statement hailed Sihanouk as "the only Cambodian Chief of State." The US legation in Phnom Penh reported to Washington: "This declaration is directed toward all the remaining dissidents, but of course the major target is Son Ngoc Thanh."[12]

During the Geneva conference, Son Ngoc Thanh renewed his bid for US assistance and sought international recognition as a Cambodian leader. On June 7, 1954, Hang Thun Hak made another appeal on Thanh's behalf to the American embassy in Bangkok. Meeting with political officer George M. Widney, Hak said that he wanted to resume contact with the embassy; to inform the US government of "the political stand, aspirations and needs of the Issarak Movement"; and to request material assistance—"either open or secret." Widney explained that he had been informed of Hak's earlier approach to Colonel George B. Vivian and that Thanh's request for weapons and supplies had been communicated to the State Department "but without result." Because the United States supported Sihanouk's government, Widney explained, "it would not be possible for us to supply arms to a force that is opposed to the king."[13]

Responding to questions from Widney, Hang Thun Hak claimed that Son Ngoc Thanh had one thousand armed men, five thousand trained but unarmed men, and control of three provinces. US officials in Phnom Penh, however, estimated that Thanh's Khmer Issaraks numbered only about five hundred men, who served in four widely scattered bands, "the strongest of which totals fewer than two hundred men."[14] With the king still "tied to the French" and with the Viet Minh an "alien force," said Hak, the Issaraks believed that they were the only true nationalists in Cambodia. Referring to the Vietnamese as "the greater danger," Hak declared, "The Viet Minh are active now everywhere, trying to make a big show for the benefit of the Geneva Conference." Widney concluded the forty-minute conversation by assuring Hak that embassy officials were "always glad to receive and talk with him about Cambodian developments."[15]

Having failed to secure military assistance from the Americans, Thanh reportedly attempted "to make [a] deal with [the] Viet Minh." Unable to secure the support of Vietnamese communists, he sent a telegram to Molotov and Pham Van Dong in Geneva asking for their help. According to Goodman, Thanh claimed that he controlled "important areas of Cambodia." The US legation in Phnom Penh considered this assertion "ridiculous," observing that there was "some question as to whether he controls even his own band of fewer than one thousand men." Goodman characterized Thanh's unsuccessful appeal to the Soviet and DRV foreign ministers as the desperate move of a "still ambitious leader, once popular but now increasingly bypassed by events."[16]

Not every diplomat in Phnom Penh shared Goodman's dim view of Son Ngoc Thanh's popularity. George Littlejohn Cook, the British chargé in Cambodia, believed that Thanh might defeat Sihanouk in a hypothetical election. On July 8, Cook insisted on personally delivering this message to William J. Donovan, the US ambassador to Thailand, who was visiting Phnom Penh. An improbable diplomat, the seventy-one-year-old Donovan had been the director of the Office of Strategic Services, the World War II forerunner of the CIA. President Eisenhower selected him as ambassador to help build up Thailand as a "bastion if Indo-China fell" to the communists. Seeking to contain PRC influence in the region, Donovan led a mission that worked to develop Thailand "as the focal point of U.S. covert and psychological operations in Southeast Asia."[17]

During his visit to Cambodia in July 1954, Donovan joined McClintock and Goodman in meetings with Sihanouk and his senior ministers. Among the topics discussed was Cambodia's attitude toward the Southeast Asia collective-security organization the United States was organizing. The Cambodian officials indicated that in principle they "would go along" with such an arrangement, but basically they were "not greatly interested." To the chagrin of the Americans, the king and his ministers once again exhibited little concern over the communist threat beyond Cambodia's borders. According to a report to the State Department, the Cambodians said repeatedly, "Quarrels between the Vietnamese are of no interest to us, and the more they quarrel the better we like it."[18]

Cambodian leaders did, however, want direct US military assistance "as quickly as possible." Opposed to any Geneva settlement limiting the kingdom's capacity for self-defense, they made several requests for US weapons and military advisers. The Eisenhower administration, impressed by Cambodia's strong stand in Geneva, was willing to provide such assistance but remained obliged to channel US aid through the French. General Paul Ely, the commissioner general and commander of French forces in Indochina, declared "very sharply" to US officials that "he would not countenance [an] American training program in Cambodia at this time." In a despatch to Washington, Goodman explained that France "quite naturally" had no intention of allowing its influence in Indochina to "fade away." In Cambodia, which was "farther along the road to complete independence than Vietnam or Laos," the French seemed particularly determined to limit US influence.[19]

At Geneva, the PRC insisted that Cambodia's self-defense plans exclude US military assistance. In a meeting with Cambodian foreign minister Tep Phan on July 17, Zhou Enlai spoke with "great seriousness and emphasis" about the planned Southeast Asia Treaty Organization: "If Cambodia were to join such a pact or to permit foreign bases on her territory or to accept American military instructors, the consequences would be very serious and would aggravate the situation with unfortunate consequences for Cambodian independence and territorial integrity." Tep Phan, unintimidated by the threat, replied: "Cambodia must retain her freedom of action to [ensure] her own defense."[20]

That same day, in a meeting with Anthony Eden, Zhou emphasized his concern about "rumors" of the Associated States' participation in SEATO. If these countries were included in the alliance, said Zhou, "then peace would have no meaning other than preparation for new hostilities." According to minutes of the conversation prepared by the Chinese, Zhou said that "Laos and Cambodia must not have any foreign military bases and that the two countries must not enter into military alliances with foreign countries. Mr. Eden agreed with me at the time."[21]

The Geneva conference ended on July 21, 1954, with bilateral ceasefire agreements for each of the Associated States, a final declaration, and unilateral declarations by individual countries about aspects of the accords. The United States, which described itself as an "interested nation" that was not a "belligerent" in the conflict, merely noted the agreements but did not sign them. At the conference's final plenary session, Under Secretary Smith pledged that the United States "would not seek by force to overthrow the settlement" and that it would "view any renewal of the aggression in violation of the aforesaid agreements with grave concern."[22]

A discordant note during the final conference session—and a harbinger of future problems between Cambodia and South Vietnam—was a protest by the Cambodian delegation that Geneva cochair Eden had failed to note the kingdom's reservations about the Cambodian-Vietnamese border: the ancient Khmer Empire had once ruled southern Vietnam, and the current border between the two countries had been established by a "unilateral act of France." Eden replied: "Past controversies between Cambodia and Vietnam were not part of [the] task of [the] conference."[23]

Despite Eden's unwillingness to discuss Cambodian-Vietnamese border disagreements, the Geneva conference enhanced Sihanouk's reputation as a defender of his kingdom's independence. Of the three Associated States, only Cambodia emerged from the conference intact, without a regrouping zone for the country's communist-led forces. The agreement to end hostilities in Cambodia called for the withdrawal of Viet Minh troops and the demobilization of the Khmer resistance forces. The latter group, according to the accords, would be integrated into the national community without prejudice and would be allowed to participate in the general elections scheduled for 1955. Hard bargaining by Sihanouk's diplomats led to a declaration that barred (1) Cambodian participation in military alliances "not in conformity with the principles of the Charter of the United Nations"; (2) foreign bases on Cambodia territory as long as the country's "security is not threatened"; and (3) foreign military aid and instructors, "except for the purpose of the effective defence" of the kingdom.[24]

The Cambodian qualifications to communist demands prompted Under Secretary Smith to inform Dulles: "There are practically no restrictions on Cambodia's maintaining an adequate security arrangement." The CIA, however, warned that the Geneva accords were "filled with many ambiguities," and "both sides may raise objections when it comes time to put certain provisions into effect."[25]

Cambodia's diplomatic success at Geneva was attributable largely to the strength of US military power and the weakness of the Khmer resistance. The threat of US military intervention in Indochina, a possibility encouraged by ominous if generally vague warnings from Eisenhower administration officials, "caused nervousness in Beijing and Moscow and helped persuade the Viet Minh to accept concessions in the final agreement," according to historian Fredrik Logevall.[26] The communist delegations, which had successfully insisted on a regrouping zone for the Pathet Lao in northern Laos, were unwilling to take risks on behalf of the Khmer resistance. U. Alexis Johnson, a career Foreign Service officer and a member of the US delegation in Geneva, reported to the State Department: "It is quite evident that [Pham Van] Dong regards [the] Laotian resistance movement as [a] more valuable asset than [the] Cambodian resistance movement." The Geneva settlement, writes researcher Steve Heder, "was presented to Cambodian Communists as a shock *fait accompli*."[27]

The conclusion of the Geneva conference was the high point of US approval of Sihanouk and his government. Dulles admired the "spunk" of the Cambodians "in holding out for full freedom of action."[28] Ambassador Donald Heath, who had earlier found Sihanouk impetuous, unreasonable, and illogical, was extravagant in his praise for the king. Concluding that his "guidance and influence" were responsible for Cambodia's "remarkable unity of purpose" during the Geneva conference, Heath observed to the State Department that Sihanouk's leadership was "actively intellectual as well as spiritual and traditional."[29]

On the final day of the Geneva conference, President Eisenhower announced his intention to expand US diplomatic representation in Cambodia and Laos by appointing a resident ambassador in Phnom Penh and a minister in Vientiane. State Department officials had earlier recommended such appointments to emphasize "the 'separateness' of Cambodia and Laos from Vietnam." Dulles advised Eisenhower that expanding diplomatic relations in the two newly independent countries "would have a salutary effect if it were undertaken as a part of a coordinated plan to help those nations defend themselves against Communist aggression."[30]

The ambassador selected for Phnom Penh was Robert McClintock, the DCM in Saigon. Born in Seattle, McClintock had earned a bachelor's degree from Stanford University in 1931 and joined the Foreign Service the following year. He had served in Latin America, Europe, and the Middle East before arriving in Vietnam in March 1953. Among his

State Department colleagues, McClintock had a reputation for brilliance, humor, and arrogance. "He was one of the brightest people in the Foreign Service," recalled Marshall Green, a career diplomat who specialized in Asian affairs, "but he couldn't help parading his superior knowledge and intellect before others." McClintock had unwarranted confidence that Sihanouk was "susceptible to diplomatic handling." The king, who came to despise the American diplomat, later declared in his memoir: "No country could have been worse served by an ambassador than was the US by McClintock."[31]

Before assuming his duties in Phnom Penh, McClintock chaired a special Indochina working group established by the Operations Coordinating Board (OCB), the interagency body responsible for monitoring the execution of US national security policy. The mission of this working group was to help Cambodia, "Free Vietnam," and Laos "strengthen their position toward the Viet Minh" now that hostilities had ended.[32] In a memorandum to Walter Bedell Smith dated August 12, 1954, McClintock summarized conditions in Indochina and recommended policies for each state. In his discussion of Cambodia, McClintock dismissed both "the indigenous Viet Minh" and the noncommunist Khmer Issarak as potential threats to the king. He characterized Sihanouk as "a young man of undoubted intelligence and patriotic fervor despite the fact that he is emotional and inclined at times to advocate extreme courses of action." He described Son Ngoc Thanh as "a hero without much following and a prophet whose vision has already been achieved. His main motivation is personal ambition."[33]

McClintock recommended that to help Cambodia resist communist encroachment a US Military Assistance Advisory Group (MAAG) be established in Phnom Penh, which would provide weapons and training to the Royal Army. He also proposed direct budgetary support for the Cambodian armed forces and economic-development assistance managed by US officials in Phnom Penh. McClintock warned that the United States could "expect a decided resistance on the part of the French Government, and particularly on the part of the French military, to any program of direct U.S. aid to Cambodia." The French attitude was "probably more emotional than founded on any serious national interest," he declared. The United States should be "friendly but firm with the French."[34]

McClintock also suggested that Cambodia should be "a silent partner in the new Southeast Asia collective defense agreement"—that is, the kingdom should be protected by the pact but not be a member of the alliance.[35] Although State Department lawyers concluded that Cambodia could join SEATO, McClintock's recommendation reflected Washington's acceptance of a request from Anthony Eden: do not press for Cambodian membership in the alliance, which would violate "the implied 'neutralization' of the Associated States in the Geneva agreements." In a meeting with State Department officials, Sir Robert Scott, minister at the British embassy, explained: "Mr. Eden feels the entire Geneva settlement was based upon the presumption that Cambodia would not become a member of a collective security arrangement in that area." Scott added that the treaty could "still extend protection to Cambodia."[36]

On August 17, after months of discussion about Indochina among his senior advisers, President Eisenhower agreed to move forward with the establishment of SEATO and the provision of direct US military and economic aid to the Associated States. The next day the State Department instructed the ambassador to France, C. Douglas Dillon, to deliver a personal message from Dulles to Pierre Mendès-France, the French prime minister and minister of foreign affairs. Emphasizing French pledges "to accord full independence" to Vietnam, Laos, and Cambodia, Dulles informed Mendès-France that the United States planned to deal directly with these countries "in questions concerning economic or military aid." Moreover, the US government would consider requests from them "to undertake direct military training of their armed forces."[37]

As predicted, the French government objected to the change in relations between the United States and the Associated States. In Mendès-France's absence, Ambassador Dillon delivered a copy of Dulles's message to Alexandre Parodi, the acting head of the French Foreign Office. Dillon reported to the State Department that Parodi was "obviously distressed" by the "repeated references to 'independence'" and by US plans to provide direct aid to Vietnam, Laos, and Cambodia. Observing that French officials thought the United States had an "almost psychotic attachment to 'independence,'" Dillon wrote, "The French, rightly or wrongly, logically or illogically, believe it entirely compatible that they should grant full sovereignty to the Associated States while at the same time retaining the French Union relationship."[38]

In Washington, French ambassador Henri Bonnet relayed comments from his government to State Department officials. Among the French reactions to Dulles's message was agreement that the Geneva accords allowed Cambodia to request military advisers of any nationality. It seemed to the French, however, that sending a US military-training mission to Cambodia might appear to China as a "prelude to [the] installation [of] foreign bases." Bonnet said that the French government firmly believed the best interests of the free world be served by the US government advising "Cambodia to request instructors from France."[39]

France was not the only Western ally unhappy with US plans to establish a military-training mission in Cambodia. On August 24, Francis R. MacGinnis, a second secretary with the British embassy in Washington, told State Department officials that he had been instructed by the UK Foreign Office to convey the following message: the British government felt that sending US military advisers to Cambodia, an area of "unusual sensitivity" to China, would have "unfortunate consequences." The establishment of a US training mission, said MacGinnis, would inevitably lead to charges that "the spirit, if not the letter," of the Geneva accords had been violated. The British embassy made a follow-up démarche "strongly" opposing the creation of a MAAG in Cambodia: "The strengthening of the Cambodian Army is a French responsibility. Under the Geneva agreements, no other power can do this as freely as can the French."[40]

State Department officials were somewhat surprised by the British point of view. Assistant Secretary of State Walter S. Robertson speculated to Smith that Eden, in his private conversations with Molotov and Zhou Enlai in Geneva, had "committed the UK to influence the U.S. to refrain from instituting a training mission in Cambodia." (Robertson added that he was "unaware of any real or implied justification for such an assumption of British ability to influence us.") Robertson dismissed UK concerns about China's "sensitivity" to a MAAG in Cambodia: "I am pleased that they are sensitive to our plans. If we had some indication that they were satisfied[,] I would, to the contrary, consider that we were on the wrong track."[41]

At a time when virtually every US official was an ardent anticommunist, Robertson stood out for the intensity of his convictions. "Walter Robertson was a man who came to the conclusion that the only way you can treat with communis[ts] is to clobber them," recalled John M. Steeves, a career Foreign Service officer who admired Robertson, "and he was quite prepared to do that at any time and any place."⁴² Born in Virginia in 1893, Robertson was an investment banker and an Eisenhower Democrat with a deep interest in China. He had served in the American embassy in Chungking during and after World War II, becoming a passionate supporter of Chiang Kai-shek and an implacable foe of the Chinese communists. As Smith's deputy in Geneva, Robertson suspected the British of attempting "to promote a settlement at any price." For his part, Anthony Eden found Robertson's anticommunism "so emotional as to be impervious to argument or indeed to facts."⁴³

Despite British opposition, Robertson was convinced that the Eisenhower administration's decision to establish a MAAG in Cambodia was correct. The French defense arrangements, he argued, had been unsatisfactory to the Cambodians on both military and political grounds. Moreover, Cambodia had demonstrated the will to fight for its independence. Robertson recommended that the United States thank the British for their views and inform them of the US decision to negotiate with the Cambodian government on establishing a military-training mission. A failure to respond to Cambodia's request for military assistance, Robertson declared, would be "adverse to the general position of the Free World."⁴⁴

Robertson's superiors agreed. On September 29, Robertson informed Ambassador Nong Kimny that the United States planned to provide direct military aid to Cambodia. When the new US ambassador to Cambodia, Robert McClintock, presented his diplomatic credentials to Sihanouk three days later, he also delivered a brief letter from President Eisenhower. It read in part, "I desire Your Majesty to know that my Government will be pleased to consider ways in which our two countries can more effectively cooperate in the joint task of stemming the threats facing your territories and maintaining peace and prosperity in your Kingdom." According to McClintock, Prime Minister Penn Nouth was gratified by the letter and "highly pleased" by a White House announcement declaring that the United States would provide direct budget support for Cambodia's armed forces.⁴⁵

After months of attempting to negotiate favorable terms for his submission to the king, Son Ngoc Thanh surrendered unconditionally in the village of Kralanh in Siem Reap Province on September 30, 1954. Like most other dissidents covered by the Geneva agreement's amnesty provisions, Thanh and his followers, a total of approximately one thousand in three separate groups, registered with the government, received identity cards, and surrendered their weapons. In a meeting with Ambassador McClintock, Penn Nouth expressed regret that "Thanh's followers had surrendered with very few arms." The prime minister also said that Thanh was "as free to come and go as any other Cambodian citizen," an assertion McClintock characterized to the State Department as "probably eyewash." In a subsequent report to Washington, he wrote: "The King's immediate entourage hate and fear Son Ngoc Thanh."[46]

Son Ngoc Thanh's submission raised questions about the role he might play in Cambodian politics. Under the terms of the Geneva accords, he was free to participate in the general elections in 1955. McClintock, who was certain that the dissident would take part in the elections, reported mixed opinions about "the extent of Thanh's probable support." He had doubts about Thanh's popularity among Cambodians, with the exception of "three small but relatively important groups—the Buddhist hierarchy, the low-level bureaucracy, and idealistic students freshly returned from France."[47]

Unlike McClintock, British chargé George Littlejohn Cook thought that Thanh would be a formidable political force: "This man, who had been harmless while in armed rebellion against the increasingly popular king, will now be a man to reckon with in Cambodian politics—and a man furthermore dangerous to the political stability of this country." Acting French high commissioner Pierre Gorce also believed that Thanh had the potential to regain a "position of influence and leadership and again become [a] serious political opponent of [the] King."[48]

The Cambodian government took steps to limit the impact of Thanh's return to politics. A plan to hold the general elections in early 1955 seemed to Adrian B. Colquitt, first secretary in the US embassy in Phnom Penh, to be part of a "strategy of denying [Thanh the] time and opportunity to regain [a] position of political leadership." And a royal decree, extended for six months on September 10, 1954, proclaimed a state of national emergency, suspended constitutional guarantees of freedom of speech and association, and prohibited political campaigns. In Cambodia's heavily censored press, the government blocked publication of a statement by Son Ngoc Thanh claiming responsibility for the country's independence and promoting his views on democracy and social reform.[49]

Both the Cambodian general elections and Son Ngoc Thanh's role in them were topics of interest to the International Commission for Supervision and Control (ICC). Established in Geneva to monitor compliance with the accords, the ICC was a politically balanced group comprising anti-communist Canadians, communist Poles, and neutralist Indians. The Polish and Indian commissioners wanted the ICC to supervise the Cambodian elections. The Cambodian and US governments opposed such supervision, arguing that nothing in the Geneva agreement authorized the ICC to control elections.[50]

To Ambassador McClintock's distress, the Indian ICC delegates met with Son Ngoc Thanh in Siem Reap and were "greatly impressed" by him. McClintock reported to Washington that the delegates felt that Thanh would be an "ideal national leader." The ambassador added that Indian support would be "warmly appreciated by this unscrupulous opportunist" and would "certainly excite the mistrust and fear of [the] King." The Cambodian government subsequently told the ICC, "The Commission should neither correspond with nor contact in any way Son Ngoc Thanh." Because Thanh was no longer in dissidence, however, the ICC rejected the demand.[51]

Sihanouk and Son Ngoc Thanh met separately with Indian prime minister Jawaharlal Nehru, who made a serendipitous visit to Cambodia from October 30 to November 1. India, home to approximately one-sixth of the world's population and the preeminent democracy among the developing countries, had requested permission for Nehru's plane to overfly Cambodia en route to Vietnam. Sihanouk found out about the request and granted permission on the condition that Nehru visit Cambodia, too.[52] The king, disturbed that so few Asian countries recognized his country, wanted to show Nehru that Cambodia was independent of the French. The Indian prime minister accepted both the invitation and the fact that Cambodia was "more or less" independent.[53] After his visit, India sent a diplomatic representative to Phnom Penh and formally recognized Cambodia later in the year.

In a letter to Edwina Mountbatten, the last vicereine of India and a close friend, Nehru wrote that Sihanouk was active, popular, and "fairly clever." The king did not, however, seem "competent" to deal with Cambodia's postindependence social problems. Nehru did not believe that Sihanouk could "continue as an autocratic monarch for long." Sihanouk's only hope for political survival, Nehru commented, was an "alliance with the Democratic Party." In his fortnightly message to the heads of India's provincial governments, Nehru reported allegations that Sihanouk "was in the hands of [a] palace clique."[54]

One source for this accusation was undoubtedly Son Ngoc Thanh, who had made an urgent request for a meeting with Nehru. The Indian prime minister, having heard that Thanh was an able administrator with "a big following," received him in Siem Reap, a few miles from the ruins at Angkor. "Every stone in that ancient city," Nehru said, "reminded me powerfully of the glory of India's past, her culture, civilization, religion and the influence that she exerted on the countries all around her." He was also impressed with Thanh's "energy and intelligence," according to Ambassador Gopalaswami Parthasarathi, who chaired the ICC for Cambodia. Although Nehru agreed with Thanh on the need for free elections, he observed that "Cambodia confronted many difficulties," and he declared that "now was the time for all patriotic leaders to rally to [the] support of [the] King and his constituted government." Disappointed by this advice, Thanh protested that "he was loyal to [the] King and supported [the] Monarchy."[55]

After a briefing from Parthasarathi on the meeting with Thanh, Ambassador McClintock reported to the State Department: "Nehru's advice was sound and should have some effect. However, we are certain Son Ngoc Thanh will feel encouraged to participate in [the] forthcoming elections in hope that his special case has been recognized by an international body. [The] Indian Ambassador told me he thought Son Ngoc Thanh was [a] leader of much promise."[56]

On November 4, 1954, three days after his meeting with Nehru, Son Ngoc Thanh made another indirect appeal for US assistance. James H. W. Thompson, an American businessman in Thailand and a former Office of Strategic Services officer who maintained contact with Southeast Asian resistance leaders, informed the US embassy in Bangkok that an emissary of Thanh sought a clandestine meeting. The chargé, Howard Parsons, refused the invitation but said that Thanh's emissary could call on a junior diplomat. Herbert Goodman, a second secretary in the Phnom Penh embassy who was in Bangkok, was selected for the rendezvous. Goodman met with Phra Phiset Phanit and a man called "Virod," who introduced himself as Thanh's political counselor. Virod, whose name seemed to be an alias, said that Thanh "desired to make one last attempt to present his case to those foreign governments which are friendly to Cambodia."[57]

Thanh had submitted to the king, Virod explained, because the Geneva agreement had affirmed Cambodian independence, which was "more or less complete." (Cambodia still had financial, customs, and monetary ties with France and Vietnam that limited the kingdom's economic sovereignty.) Thanh was prepared to participate in Cambodian politics but "only under certain clearly defined conditions," said Virod. One of them was "absolutely free and unfettered" elections. The Cambodian government, Virod alleged, almost certainly had "no intention" of allowing Thanh to campaign freely. Thanh had intended to return to Phnom Penh shortly after his submission to the king. His "intelligence network," however, learned that local military and civilian officials had threatened severe punishment, including death, to villagers who organized welcoming demonstrations along his route to the capital. These warnings, said Virod, were "not a happy omen for Thanh's future safety."[58]

Virod, whom Goodman described as "a man of superior intelligence with a dedication bordering on fanaticism," stressed his belief that the king had not ordered these ominous warnings or was even aware of them. "His Majesty is surrounded by men who misinform him and take many steps without his knowledge," he said. "The King is an unstable man, still very young, who is easily influenced by the people around him." Despite this unflattering assessment of Sihanouk, Virod insisted that Thanh had no quarrel with the king and supported the monarchy. The problem, according to Virod, was that Cambodia's Constitution was "currently not being applied." Seeking to limit Sihanouk's role in the day-to-day governing of the country, he declared, "The King should remain, but he should simply be the King and nothing else."[59]

Son Ngoc Thanh, said Virod, wanted to reconcile with the king but was certain that Sihanouk's advisers had been blocking his requests for an audience. Because of the "transcendental importance" that Sihanouk understand "Thanh's orientation and the limited nature of his aspirations," his emissaries appealed to Goodman for US help in presenting their ideas to the king. Ambassador McClintock, commenting on the secret meeting to the State Department, was appalled by the idea of intervening on

Son Ngoc Thanh's behalf: "Nothing could shake the King more than a U.S. or British espousal of Thanh's cause." Sihanouk, McClintock wrote, viewed "a western-style constitutional democracy with an all-powerful parliament" as "a threat to his own personal power" and "an invitation to anarchy" in a country where a large percentage of the representatives in the National Assembly were illiterate.[60]

McClintock, who acknowledged that Son Ngoc Thanh might "one day play an important role" in Cambodian politics, characterized him as "a figure to be watched and constantly re-evaluated." Yet the ambassador was convinced that further secret meetings with Thanh or his emissaries risked exposure, damaging American relations with Sihanouk and US policy objectives. Therefore, McClintock wrote, the embassy in Phnom Penh would "have no more clandestine contacts with Son Ngoc Thanh during the period which lies immediately ahead."[61]

In its year-end report for 1954, the ICC in Cambodia proclaimed the successful achievement of key military provisions of the Geneva agreement, including the withdrawal of regular French and Viet Minh military units, the removal of mines and booby traps, and the release of most prisoners of war and civilian internees. A more difficult challenge was integrating the former Khmer resistance forces into the "national community," a process the commissioners described as "far from complete" and a problem of "first importance." Disturbed by reports of the arrest and detention of former resistance fighters, the ICC questioned the Cambodian government's commitment to integration without discrimination or reprisals.[62]

The ICC admitted that its operations had not been organized in time to monitor the unilateral demobilization of the Khmer resistance. Ambassador Parthasarathi had privately conceded that the commission had been unable to determine the size of the resistance forces, a number that "one side did not know and other side would not tell." The Cambodian government protested that only some of the Khmer resistance fighters had been demobilized and disarmed. Investigations by ICC teams, however, did "not bear out the Government's claims that large armed bands of former Resistants are at large in the country." Many Cambodian members of the resistance, particularly its leaders, had relocated to the DRV.[63]

Relations between the ICC and the Cambodian government were "correct but not exactly cordial," in the words of Canadian commissioner

Rudolphe Duder. Cambodian officials were "extremely suspicious" of Polish commissioner Wiktor Grosz, who had "gone out of his way to be critical of them and ostentatiously friendly to the Vietnamese and Khmer Resistants." In a report to Ottawa, Duder wrote: "The distrust of the Polish delegation is one of the stumbling blocks in the road of closer collaboration between the Government and the Commission."[64]

Another potential barrier to good relations between the ICC and the Cambodian government was the commission's role in the upcoming general elections. Sihanouk, resenting what he deemed intrusion into Cambodia's internal affairs, continued to oppose any ICC involvement in the elections. In a compromise advocated by Duder, the commission declared that it did "not contemplate supervising the elections." The ICC could not, however, "remain indifferent" to them and pledged to "keep a watchful eye" on the democratic liberties of all Cambodian citizens.[65]

In their year-end report for 1954, the commissioners mentioned their "frustration" in attempting to resolve outstanding problems in Cambodian compliance with the Geneva accords. This comment reflected ICC annoyance with the Cambodian government's "great administrative slowness" and with the small number of Cambodian officials who could make decisions. The commissioners privately suspected that Sihanouk and his advisers were consciously dragging their feet. In a report to the Canadian Department of External Affairs, Duder wrote that government officials' "apparent reluctance or inability" to meet with the ICC "may be due to Cambodian lethargy, but unfortunately strengthens [the] Polish recorded view that [the] government is deliberately obstructive."[66]

Charges of obstructionism were also leveled against the Polish delegates, whose procedural stalling was exhausting the patience of their Canadian and Indian colleagues. A message from the Canadian commissioner to the Department of External Affairs on November 12 complained that the Poles would "wrangle for hours over 1 word" in an ICC report. Another message to the department two weeks later characterized the Polish military adviser as "argumentative, intransigent, and rude."[67]

There were substantive disagreements between the Canadian and Polish ICC commissioners over such issues as the legitimacy of specific Cambodian allegations of Geneva violations. Yet a more pernicious influence on the harmonious operations of the commission, which aspired to unanimity in matters large and small, was a Polish attack on the integrity of Major General Sarda Nand Singh, the Indian delegation's military adviser. The Poles accused General Singh of issuing instructions to ICC investigation teams without approval from the other two delegations. Canadian commissioner Duder backed the indignant Singh in this festering dispute. In his final progress report for 1954, Duder observed—with diplomatic understatement—that the ICC meetings of the previous week had been "unsatisfactory and even unpleasant."[68]

3

"Time for Further Maneuvers" (1955)

In January 1955, Ambassador Gopalaswami Parthasarathi, the ICC chairman for Cambodia, worked on behalf of Son Ngoc Thanh to encourage a reconciliation with Sihanouk. This quixotic effort was rooted in Jawaharlal Nehru's belief that an alliance between the two enemies would lead to political and social stability in Cambodia. Indian assistance to Son Ngoc Thanh included drafting a letter to the king requesting an audience, an appeal Sihanouk summarily rejected. Son Ngoc Thanh had been engaged in "seditious activity," the king declared. Thanh's alleged promotion of a republic violated article one of the country's Constitution: "Cambodia is a monarchy."[1]

India's advocacy on Thanh's behalf created a dilemma for Sihanouk. On the one hand, the king viewed Son Ngoc Thanh as a threat. On the other hand, he sought to maintain friendly relations with India—an aspiration that restrained the Cambodian government "from taking direct repressive measures against Thanh." With Thanh's supporters reportedly making progress in village-level political organizing, Sihanouk decided that the general elections, scheduled for June, would be moved to April 17. "This decision," CIA analysts concluded, "reflects the king's determination to head off [Thanh's] budding political campaign."[2]

A more immediate attempt to reduce Son Ngoc Thanh's influence and to discourage Indian support for him was a national referendum to determine whether Sihanouk had fulfilled the pledge he made in 1952 to achieve national independence. Held on February 7, 1955, the referendum dispensed with secret ballots. Under the watchful eyes of local officials, voters selected a white card for a "yes" vote and a black one for "no." In the days preceding the election, the Cambodian government airdropped leaflets that provided voting instructions: "If you love the King—white; if you don't love the King—black."[3] According to the government, 99.8 percent of the more than 900,000 voters endorsed the king; the 31,952 military voters unanimously cast affirmative ballots; and the followers of Son Ngoc Thanh "used unfair means" to encourage negative votes. Nehru thought that "the whole procedure about this referendum was open to question." A CIA report concluded that the results reflected both "official pressure and the King's genuine popularity."[4]

The results of the referendum emboldened Sihanouk to propose politically advantageous changes in Cambodia's Constitution. Summoning Phnom Penh's diplomatic corps, the commissioners of the ICC, and his cabinet to the palace, Sihanouk said that he had received petitions with more than 190,000 signatures requesting the suppression or postponement of the April general elections. The "chief trouble," according to the king, was "the proliferation of political parties, whose contradictory propaganda puzzles the people." He charged the Democratic Party with deceiving the people through its espousal of Son Ngoc Thanh's "noxious ideas."[5]

To address Cambodia's governance problems, Sihanouk proposed a number of reforms to the Constitution, including a ban on the participation of political parties in elections, the indirect election of legislators by village mayors, a three-year residency requirement for candidates, and the appointment of ministers by the king. "The King must intervene directly into the executive function," said Sihanouk. "This conforms to the Cambodian spirit, where the people associate the government with the king." He told the assembled diplomats and officials that he intended to submit his proposals to the Cambodian people in a national referendum.[6]

At the end of the audience, Ambassador McClintock, then the dean of the diplomatic corps in Phnom Penh, thanked the king on behalf of his colleagues, fulsomely remarking that the "sovereign democracy of Cambodia was fitly represented by a democratic sovereign." In a telegram to the State Department, McClintock was less diplomatic, commenting on the "extraordinary spectacle" of a reigning monarch discussing internal political affairs with representatives of foreign countries. The king, McClintock wrote, "is evidently suffering a kind of political schizophrenia, torn between his desire for a theoretically pure democracy and his inner yearning to rule as a benevolent absolute monarch." CIA analysts provided a more hard-nosed assessment of Sihanouk's motives: "The Cambodian king is sensitive to any form of opposition, and his unilateral effort to change constitutional procedures shows he will go to almost any lengths to eliminate any real or fancied threat to his position."[7]

To ICC commissioners, some of Sihanouk's reforms appeared to violate the Geneva accords, which guaranteed citizen rights prescribed by the Cambodian Constitution. Particularly troubling was the proposed three-year residency requirement for legislative candidates, which would discriminate against former resistance fighters who had been living in the jungle. The Canadian government's "preliminary view" was that Sihanouk's reforms "would constitute a breach" of the Geneva agreement. The Canadian Department of External Affairs instructed ICC commissioner Rudolphe Duder "to make these views known to [the] King and to seek [the] support of American, British and French representatives" in Cambodia.[8]

The United Kingdom, as Geneva cochair, instructed its chargé in Phnom Penh, George Littlejohn Cook, to express concern over Cambodia's apparent intention to "renege" on its Geneva obligations. On February 26, Cook met with Prime Minister Leng Ngeth, an adviser to the king and leader of the caretaker government formed to oversee the elections. The British diplomat found Leng Ngeth unyielding on the need for constitutional reform. Royal councilor Sam Sary, who had drafted a proclamation for the reform referendum, insisted to Cook that changes in the Constitution were internal Cambodian affairs and that "outside powers had no warrant to interfere." According to McClintock, the "strength of [the] British representation apparently caused [the] King to think twice" about the referendum. On February 27, Leng Ngeth informed Cook "somewhat petulantly" that Sihanouk had changed his mind. He had decided not to issue a proclamation requiring popular acceptance or rejection of his proposed reforms to the Constitution.[9]

McClintock and his Western colleagues discussed ways the king might achieve his goals without violating the Geneva agreement. The best approach, the diplomats agreed, would be to make constitutional reform a key campaign issue in the general elections. Legislators elected on this platform could then amend the Constitution with a three-fourths majority vote in the National Assembly. McClintock also thought that Siha-nouk could "neatly finesse" objections to his reforms by exempting former resistance fighters from the residency requirement. "Since few politicians will care to proclaim their state of former rebellion," the ambassador wrote, "[the] practical effect would be that Khmer Issaraks would scarcely dare stand [for election] for fear of public opinion. At the same time, [the] legal charge of discrimination could not be levied against [the] King."[10]

The Western diplomats' pragmatic but largely irrelevant suggestions overlooked the impact of international pressure on Sihanouk to reverse his personal and public commitment. As with the French in 1953, Siha-nouk was about to engage in unconventional political maneuvers that the Americans deemed "utterly capricious and unrealistic."[11]

Secretary of State John Foster Dulles arrived in Cambodia on February 28, 1955. His seven-hour visit was part of a rapid tour of Indochina that followed the first meeting of the SEATO council in Bangkok and short visits to Rangoon and Vientiane. Dulles and other US officials described his audience with Sihanouk as "very general." The secretary briefly sum-marized the SEATO meeting and the military forces available to deter or defeat a communist attack against Cambodia. The king appeared satis-fied with the SEATO arrangements. Because Sihanouk had changed his mind about holding a constitutional-reform referendum, Dulles did not mention the topic.[12]

Congratulating Sihanouk on his leadership in securing Cambodian independence, Dulles noted his "pronounced democratic flair." Accord-ing to McClintock, the secretary's remark "brought forth [a] torrent of kingly comment on [the] nature of Cambodian 'democracy.'" Sihanouk denounced Cambodian politicians as "scum," declaring that his people preferred "to be ruled by a benign and patriarchal monarch." In an "eyes only" cable to President Eisenhower on March 1, Dulles wrote: "The King is vigorous and full of ideas. On the whole he is [a] healthy influence although some of his theories show immaturity."[13]

The local politics of Cambodia were of limited interest to Dulles, who was preoccupied with the danger of international communism. At the SEATO conference, he had described international communism as an "extremely formidable" force with a single "purpose—world domination." Dulles said: "I believe what goes on in different parts of Asia is all centrally planned, and it is quite probable what goes on in Asia is planned and coordinated with what goes on in Europe." The secretary conceived of SEATO as a broadly based approach to collective defense that would protect Cambodia, Laos, and South Vietnam from both overt invasion and internal subversion. Cambodia's role in the struggle against communism was to develop an army that could serve as a trip wire against external attack and maintain the country's internal security. The "big problem" in achieving this goal, Dulles wrote to Eisenhower, was resolving the long-standing dispute between France and the United States over military training.[14]

The French welcomed the idea of US financial support for the Cambodian army and had no objection to a small MAAG to monitor the use of US materiel, but they continued to resist the establishment of a US military-training mission. "It would not be completely in keeping with the spirit of the Geneva Accords," French ambassador Couve de Murville told Dulles. "It would raise political difficulties for France in Cambodia and elsewhere."[15]

US officials, particularly in the Pentagon, wanted a complete withdrawal of French military advisers, whose "inefficiency" and "interference" in training "would produce only negligible results." A memorandum to Dulles summarized the US viewpoint on military assistance to Cambodia: "There must be one doctrine and procedure accorded full and single responsibility from the Cambodians for modernizing their army in the shortest possible time. We believe this is a reasonable arrangement if the U.S. furnishes the bulk of money and equipment."[16]

During his brief visit to Phnom Penh, Dulles proposed a military-training compromise that President Eisenhower had approved despite objections by the Joint Chiefs of Staff: the MAAG chief would serve as the principal military adviser to the king, who was the commander in chief of the Cambodian armed forces. Sihanouk would also oversee a separate French military mission, which, in a concession to French prestige, would not be under the direct command of the MAAG chief. The French mission, however, would be obligated to adopt US standards of military training and doctrine. Dulles emphasized to Sihanouk's ministers that keeping or dismissing the French military advisers was a decision for the Cambodian government. Prime Minister Leng Ngeth, under pressure from both France and the United States, "expressed interest" in Dulles's formula but did not provide "unequivocal assent."[17]

In a cable to President Eisenhower, Dulles acknowledged that the compromise was "not satisfactory from a military standpoint." Although French officials in Indochina did not like the idea and the Cambodians had been noncommittal, Dulles declared that his compromise "provides a politically acceptable formula which might work." If not, he wrote, the plan could "be discarded in favor of something better. At least it would enable us to get going."[18]

At 1:00 p.m. on March 2, 1955, Cambodian national radio broadcast a prerecorded statement by King Sihanouk announcing his abdication. Thanking his countrymen for their loyalty, Sihanouk summarized his proposed constitutional reforms and lashed out at the politicians, intellectuals, and students who opposed them. Among the "traitorous" actions of his political enemies was promoting the idea to foreigners that the king "was sabotaging certain articles of the Geneva Agreements." Sihanouk said that the "systematic opposition" of the Democratic Party, Son Ngoc Thanh, and other adversaries had discouraged him from remaining on the throne. Although abdicating in favor of his parents, now King Suramarit and Queen Kossamak, Sihanouk pledged to find other ways of safeguarding Cambodians' interests: "I promise you that, even out of the Throne, all my moral, physical and intellectual efforts shall be to work for the well-being of the people, and I am willing to sacrifice my life for them."[19]

American embassy officials in Phnom Penh were "absolutely dumbstruck" by Sihanouk's abdication, according to William J. Cunningham, then an administrative assistant to McClintock. "We found out about it because one of the Embassy's Cambodian chauffeurs happened to be listening to the radio that afternoon," Cunningham recalled many years later. "He did not speak very good English and he did not speak French at all, so there was a great deal of hustling around the embassy that afternoon to try to find out exactly what it was that Sihanouk had said on the radio."[20]

With McClintock in the Philippines at a regional meeting of US ambassadors, embassy first secretary Adrian Colquitt met with royal adviser Khim Tit, who said that Sihanouk was "fed up with opposition to his proposed reforms." Khim Tit added that the "unsympathetic attitude" of Indian ICC delegates and their "friendly regard for Son Ngoc Thanh and [the] Democratic Party" contributed to Sihanouk's decision to quit the throne. "It is quite evident," Colquitt reported, "that [the] Indian delegation is deeply disturbed by [the] turn of events, as it is basically sympathetic to [the] Cambodian Government and feels it is simply doing its duty as it interprets the Geneva Agreement."[21]

McClintock, instructed to return to Cambodia immediately, believed he could "persuade [the] King [to] return to [the] throne." State Department officials had concluded that the interests of the United States and Cambodia required "more vigorous and alert leadership" than Sihanouk's fifty-nine-year-old diabetic father would likely provide.[22] After a day of meetings with Western, Indian, and Cambodian officials, McClintock reported that Sihanouk's reasons for abdicating were "complex and in some cases subtle." The ambassador agreed with the conclusion of his diplomatic colleagues that the British démarche over impending Geneva violations was the "last drop which made the cup run over." In his analysis of the king's motives and character, McClintock speculated that a decisive factor in Sihanouk's resignation was undoubtedly his "mystical desire for martyrdom." The ambassador declared that the king viewed himself as "a sort of royal Robin Hood" and Gautama Buddha: "Gautama, likewise a Prince, renounced [the] world for a cause, and [the] little King of Cambodia has done likewise."[23]

Sihanouk refused McClintock's request for an audience. Khim Tit told the ambassador that the former king, now Prince Norodom Sihanouk and, at his request, addressed directly as "monseigneur," "had decided to see no one." When McClintock, observing that the United States still had business to transact with the Cambodian government, asked who was responsible for affairs of state, the royal councilor replied that "power resided in [the] new King," an assertion McClintock did not believe. Only one day earlier Khim Tit had indicated that "real power" in Cambodia would "still remain in [the] hands of Sihanouk." The ambassador concluded that a triumvirate of royal advisers—Penn Nouth, Sam Sary, and Khim Tit—held power in Cambodia. They, in turn, were "henchman of [the] new Cambodian shogun, Norodom Sihanouk."[24]

Strengthening McClintock's conviction that Sihanouk remained in charge was the prince's performance at the opening of a new military command and staff school. The ceremony, held just four days after his abdication, was attended by the new king and queen and by the diplomatic corps. "Monseigneur was in fine fettle and handled all arrangements for

[the] ceremony practically single-handed," McClintock reported. "[The] only slip he made was to sit down before his father, the new King, managed to get to the throne." Sihanouk, who sat to the left of McClintock at the ceremony, told the ambassador "he had arranged" for the Cambodian government to promptly conclude its military-assistance negotiations with the United States. "Sihanouk [is] obviously vastly pleased with himself," McClintock wrote to his Washington colleagues, "and takes delight in seeing his old father go through the motions."[25]

On March 15, the Cambodian government announced the cancellation of the constitutional-reform referendum and the postponement of the general elections from April 17 until September 11. A government communiqué claimed that holding elections on the earlier date would be an affront to the hundreds of thousands of Cambodians who had recently expressed their hostility toward politicians "of the old pattern." The communiqué further stated that "a certain delay" in the elections was "indispensable" to public understanding of the government's decision to cancel the constitutional-reform referendum.[26]

"[The] [p]resent electoral situation [is] in [a] complete state of flux," McClintock cabled the State Department, and the postponement of the elections provided "time for further maneuvers [by] all parties." The ambassador noted that Sihanouk continued his bitter denunciation of political parties in general and of the Democratic Party in particular. To effectively "torpedo" Cambodia's politicians, McClintock wrote, the prince would "have to devise some means of carrying [his] campaign to the rice roots." The CIA reached a similar conclusion, noting that Sihanouk was now "free, like any loyal subject, to build a political organization to combat his arch-enemy Son Ngoc Thanh."[27]

Sihanouk was furious with the interference of India's ICC delegation in what he considered Cambodia's internal affairs. His anger, however, did not diminish his respect for Nehru or his gratitude for India's diplomatic recognition of Cambodia. Before his abdication, he had accepted an invitation from Nehru to visit India. Insisting that he was now merely a "distinguished Cambodian" traveling in an unofficial capacity, he began a weeklong goodwill trip to India on March 16. The visit was an inflection point in his and Cambodia's move toward neutrality in the cold war.

At a meeting with the prince, Nehru explained that the basis of

India's foreign policy was the "Panchsheel"—the five principles of peaceful coexistence. Articulated in an agreement between India and China concluded in 1954, the Panchsheel called for "respect among countries for the sovereignty and territorial integrity of each other and a policy of non-interference and non-aggression." According to the minutes of his meeting with Nehru, Sihanouk "expressed his approval and understanding of these principles." The prince also agreed with Nehru on "the dangers of foreign military alliances."[28]

Nehru mentioned his impression that France and the United States were engaged in a "tussle" over military training in Cambodia. Sihanouk confirmed this assessment, saying that the Cambodian government was "greatly embarrassed by this tussle and in fact found itself in great difficulties," presumably a reference to the pressure exerted by both France and the United States. Later in the conversation, the prince said that Cambodia faced a major problem: the government "found it impossible to balance its budget and to maintain its army and, therefore, it was forced to seek economic assistance which was being offered by the USA." Nehru replied that "economic assistance by itself was neither bad nor undesirable" as long as it did not jeopardize a country's sovereignty.[29]

On March 18, Nehru and Sihanouk issued a joint communiqué stating that the prince "expressed his appreciation of India's general approach to world problems." The two leaders agreed that "the best guarantee for peace in the world and for friendship between countries" was adherence to the five principles of peaceful coexistence. The communiqué also pledged that the Indian government would "give such assistance to Cambodia as lay in [its] power."[30]

After this meeting, in a letter to his sister Vijayalakshmi Pandit, a diplomat and the first female president of the UN General Assembly, Nehru described Sihanouk as "a bright young man with vague ideas about doing good for his people. Unfortunately, he has no good advisers and the few people, men and women, who surround him rather lead him astray. Then there is the continuing pressure of the United States. I think his visit to Delhi has had [a] good effect on him."[31]

Sihanouk made a triumphant return to Phnom Penh, where he was received at the airport with full military honors and a popular demonstration arranged by the Cambodian government. The prince said that he was "very satisfied" with his trip: the Indian people had been "very charmed by [the] sacrifices I've made to serve my country." American embassy officials thought it significant that both the government-controlled press and the opposition newspapers approved of Sihanouk's symbolic stand with "Indian neutralism in the face of the struggle between the Free World and the Communist Bloc."[32]

The possibility that Cambodia or any other country would adopt Nehru's neutralist foreign policy troubled US officials. Despite his stated policy of nonalignment in the cold war, Nehru criticized the West disproportionately, supported the admission of China into the United Nations, and opposed US collective-security arrangements. In a widely reported speech to India's Parliament, he charged that SEATO undermined peace and security in Southeast Asia and "the whole conception lying behind the Geneva Conference." Harold G. Josif, a US Foreign Service officer who worked in India and in the State Department's Office of South Asian Affairs in the 1950s, recalled: "Nehru was a moralizer and he would moralize against us. We were moralizers, too. So we rubbed each other's fur the wrong way."[33]

In April 1955, at the Asian–African Conference in Bandung, Indonesia, Prince Sihanouk publicly confirmed that Cambodia had joined "the community of neutral nations." Sponsored by five South Asian countries—Burma, Ceylon, India, Indonesia, and Pakistan—the conference "considered the position of Asia and Africa and discussed ways and means by which their peoples could achieve the fullest economic, cultural, and political cooperation."[34] This bland statement from the final conference communiqué, a consensus document accommodating the diverse views of twenty-nine countries, obscured Bandung's basic emphasis on nonalignment in the cold war.

US officials, who viewed the Bandung conference with hostility, had been apprehensive that the two communist participants, China and the DRV, would dominate it. The conference, warned Assistant Secretary of State Walter Robertson, "would provide Chou En-lai with an excellent forum to broadcast Communist ideology to a naive audience in the guise of anti-colonialism." More generally, the Eisenhower administration feared "the formation of an Asian–African bloc which could ultimately weaken relations between non-Communist Asia and the United States."[35] In the weeks before Bandung, State Department and CIA officials worked with friendly delegates—for example, Carlos P. Rómulo, the representative from the Philippines—to develop forceful anticommunist messages and resolutions.

Not every US official thought this approach was sufficient. At the NSC meeting on March 3, Vice President Nixon said: "The best strategy for the United States would be to attempt to ensure the failure of the Conference, rather than attempt to get such an ill-assorted group of nations to take a position favorable to the Western democracies." Although President Eisenhower shared his advisers' dim view of Bandung, he did not appear to take the conference too seriously. According to the minutes of the NSC meeting, "The President remarked facetiously that perhaps the best way for the U.S. to handle this matter was to give a few thousand dollars to each of the delegates. Indeed (again facetiously), the President added that he would approve of any methods up to but not including assassination of the hostile delegates."[36]

One of the first speeches at Bandung was delivered by Sihanouk, who acknowledged the risks of nonalignment: "Cambodia now finds herself on the separating line of two civilizations, of two races, of two political worlds . . . and as such she has the dangerous privilege of standing the test and the application of the principles of [peaceful coexistence]."[37] At a meeting of the conference's political committee, Sihanouk expressed his uncertainty about communist intentions more directly, according to George McT. Kahin, an expert on Southeast Asia who covered Bandung: "Most non-Communist countries, [Sihanouk] observed, even those who had given support to the principles of co-existence, in general mistrusted the Communist states. Therefore the viability of the concept of co-existence was up to the Communists; it was up to them to reassure the rest of the world of their peaceful intentions."[38]

Both China and the DRV pledged to adhere to the five principles of peaceful coexistence. Because some conference participants objected to the term *peaceful coexistence* as a communist expression, Zhou Enlai proposed substitute language from the United Nations charter: "Live together in peace." By all accounts a dignified, affable, and conciliatory presence at Bandung, Zhou expressed the hope that Cambodia and Laos would "become peace loving countries like India and Burma." He added: "We have no intention whatsoever to intercede or intervene in the internal affairs of these two neighboring states of ours."[39]

In a private meeting with Sihanouk, Zhou repeated both his commitment to the five principles and his usual warnings about the United

States. The prince wrote later in his memoirs that he found Zhou "open, friendly and very straightforward" and accepted an invitation to visit Beijing.[40] Sihanouk told Zhou that he would not allow the United States to establish military bases in Cambodia. It seems likely that the prince also said something similar to one of his public declarations at Bandung: "We are bound to the Western bloc by no commitment, by no treaty. We have accepted French and American aid, because they have been granted us without strings. . . . France and the United States of America offer us their instructors without asking for payment."[41]

Sihanouk's complimentary reference to France was an anomaly at a conference committed to "the abolition of colonialism." The final communiqué urged the French government to grant immediate independence to Algeria, Morocco, and Tunisia. "France came under fire from all sides," Commissioner General Paul Ely wrote to Foreign Minister Antoine Pinay. Ely found the attitude of Laos and South Vietnam "disappointing." Their delegations were "very aloof" from French observers at the conference. "Only Prince Sihanouk," wrote Ely, "took an honourable stance and spoke several times in our support."[42]

On his return trip to Cambodia, Sihanouk stopped in Singapore, where he was the guest of Malcolm MacDonald, the UK commissioner general in Southeast Asia since 1948. One British diplomat described MacDonald as "a kind of regional viceroy with ill-defined powers but considerable influence." The son of a Labour prime minister, he had developed a personal relationship with Sihanouk based in part on his own informality and what the State Department called his "lack of inhibitions." (To amuse the prince's seven-year-old daughter, he stood on his head and walked around on his hands.) While discussing Bandung with MacDonald, Sihanouk indicated that "Chou En-lai and Pham Van Dong had both given specific and emphatic assurances that they had no intention of interfering in the internal affairs of Cambodia." When MacDonald asked if Sihanouk "had any confidence in the sincerity of the Communist representatives," Sihanouk "laughed skeptically."[43]

By his declarations of neutrality in India and at the Bandung conference, Sihanouk had embarked on a hazardous geopolitical journey, navigating between the cold-war combatants with his own idiosyncratic brand of balance-of-power diplomacy. Working-level officials in the State Department theorized that Cambodia's "drift toward neutralism" was a consequence of the country's recent colonial domination by a Western power and its deep-rooted, historical fear of Chinese hegemony. Ambassador McClintock warned: "Any attempt to draw Cambodia into active co-operation with regional security arrangements is likely to be resisted at the present time." With more hope than prescience, McClintock predicted that the long-term combination of communist pressure and US selflessness would foster neutrality with a pro-Western "Swedish tinge."[44]

A more prophetic CIA analysis, however, concluded that Sihanouk's identification with India's neutrality "may ultimately damage Cambodia's relations with the West"—that is, with the United States.[45]

On May 16, 1955, Ambassador McClintock and Prime Minister Leng Ngeth signed a Mutual Defense Assistance (MDA) agreement to finance FARK, to provide it with weapons and other equipment, and to establish a MAAG in Cambodia. The accord was intentionally vague on the details of US military assistance, allowing the designated MAAG chief, Brigadier General George O. N. Lodoen, to make specific recommendations based on his on-the-spot assessment of Cambodia's needs. The agreement, which did not mention France, stated that US support could "possibly" include military training.[46] This tentative declaration hardly did justice to the scope of American ambitions. According to the State Department, financial support and military hardware were intended as a "lever" for "the introduction of adequate training programs and organizational reforms." Initial Pentagon plans called for a MAAG of more than 250 logistic and training personnel by the end of 1956.[47]

Because of the slow pace of news dissemination in Cambodia, opposition to the MDA emerged gradually. Hanoi Radio was one of the first media outlets to denounce it, and General Vo Nguyen Giap, commander in chief of the People's Army of Vietnam, subsequently protested to the ICC that the agreement "oversteps" Cambodia's self-defense requirements and "takes the character of a military alliance with the United States."[48] In Cambodia, a left-wing newspaper declared that Leng Ngeth's caretaker government had no right to conclude such a far-reaching agreement and that future governments "would not be bound by it." (Cambodian authorities promptly suspended publication of the newspaper and arrested the editor.) "No one has publicly commented favorably on [the] agreement," embassy officer Martin F. Herz informed the State Department.[49]

The Cambodian government, responding to what it called "lying propaganda," issued a communiqué on May 29 stating that the MDA did not violate the Geneva accords. The announcement explained that the United States would now provide aid directly to the kingdom rather than through the "anachronism" of a French intermediary: "There is no question of the granting of American military bases nor of a military alliance of any sort." The communiqué appeared to settle the question of whether the United States or France would train the Cambodian army by stating that no American military instructors would be sent to the kingdom. The government declaration also limited the number of MAAG personnel to thirty, who would be responsible for "the proper use" of US materiel delivered to the Royal Cambodian Army.[50]

Sihanouk, whom opposition politicians had linked to the MDA, issued a public statement defending the agreement while simultaneously dissociating from it. Claiming that he held "no power" and had "not a jot of responsibility" for the MDA, the prince denounced "the vile bad faith of those who accuse the Royal Government of having sold out the country by accepting American aid." He defended the MDA as entirely compatible with the neutrality he had proclaimed in New Delhi and Bandung. US military assistance, said Sihanouk, was "unconditional," and refusing it would require "very heavy financial contributions" from the Cambodian people: "Our compatriots may be certain that I would have publicly opposed the acceptance of that aid by our Government if it had involved the least quid-pro-quo."[51]

Although Sihanouk and Cambodian officials judged the MDA as consistent with their Geneva obligations, the Indian and Polish ICC commissioners disagreed, concluding that it did "contravene" the accords.[52] Their basic objection was that language in the MDA implied a Cambodian military alliance with the United States—for example, a footnote in the agreement referred to Cambodia's contribution to "the defensive strength of the free world." The Canadian commissioner, Rudolphe Duder, however, dissented from the majority opinion, arguing that his colleagues had taken passages of the MDA "out of context and judge[d] them in the light of political considerations extraneous to Geneva."[53]

The Indian government was "particularly disturbed" by the MDA. During a visit to Ottawa in June 1955, V. K. Krishna Menon, the Indian delegate to the United Nations, criticized Canadian officials for their "overly legalistic" approach to ICC deliberations. India, said Menon, "took more account of political realities."[54] In other words, although nothing in the Geneva accords required Cambodia to be neutral, Anthony Eden and Zhou Enlai had an unwritten agreement that the country would be. The political realities to which Menon referred also included a PRC warning to India that the MDA "would free [China] to rearm [the] Viet Minh."[55]

Krishna Menon, then fifty-nine, was a close associate of Nehru and a more abrasive advocate of Indian nonalignment. A State Department biography described Menon as "an able, fluent, and impassioned orator with a keen and nimble mind. . . . The viciousness of his criticism, combined with his saturnine figure, his cane and his shock of silver hair give the impression of an angry embittered prophet hurling the word of God at the human race." John Foster Dulles, reflecting many US officials' view, considered Menon "an unscrupulous maneuverer" and "strongly anti-American." William Clark Jr., a US ambassador to India, recalled, "We saw India as the embodiment of Krishna Menon, and the Indians saw the US as the embodiment of John Foster Dulles."[56]

During his visit to Washington in June 1955, Menon told Kenneth T. Young, the State Department's director of the Office of Philippine and Southeast Asian Affairs, that the United States had been operating "behind the backs" of other countries with an interest in Cambodia. The allegation was based on Dulles's stated interest in the possibility of an Indian military-training mission in Cambodia. In December 1954, Dulles had told Eden: "If India would be willing to effectively guarantee Laos and Cambodia against Communist domination, the U.S. would be glad to bow out of the picture." Eden enthusiastically embraced this notion, securing Dulles's permission to pursue the topic with Nehru. At the SEATO meeting in Bangkok in February 1955, Eden proposed to Dulles the establishment of an Indian military advisory mission in Cambodia as "a solution to the French–U.S. impasse over training."[57]

Dulles said that the idea was "intriguing" and discussed it with Prime Minister U Nu of Burma during a visit to Rangoon on February 26–27. Dulles asked Nu to "sound out" Nehru about his interest in providing military trainers to Cambodia. Nu agreed that "India could only be asked to do so if American or French military help was withdrawn from Cambodia." Within days of his conversation with Nu, Dulles had second thoughts about the wisdom of an Indian training mission, which posed many practical and political problems. In addition to almost certain opposition from France and the Pentagon, the US Congress would likely be unwilling to finance a Cambodian army trained by a country hostile to SEATO. Seeking to discourage British enthusiasm for Indian military advisers, Dulles informed Eden: "We greatly doubt the desirability of approaching the Cambodians on the subject at this time."[58]

Unaware of Dulles's reservations, U Nu spoke with Nehru and Zhou Enlai at the Bandung conference about Indian military assistance to Cambodia. Nehru said that his country might be prepared to help, "but there could be no question of India being able to spend large sums of money and certainly she could not undertake to cover the deficits of the Cambodian budget." If asked by Cambodia and other interested nations, Nehru said, India "might agree to send a team of about two hundred officers and men to train the Cambodian army." Zhou, who agreed to Nehru's offer, "did not want American or French military teams to be sent to Cambodia or Laos."[59]

Nehru persuaded his cabinet, "not without difficulty," according to Menon, to agree to provide Indian military advisers to Cambodia. Sihanouk, however, declined the offer, informing the Indian prime minister, "[The] French military mission is already there and no other country has thus far sent any military instructors to Cambodia." Accepting the prince's decision, Nehru and other Indian officials were therefore "astounded" to learn of the US military-assistance agreement with Cambodia. "Mr. Nehru," said Menon, "feels that the Americans let him down."[60]

In a conversation with U Nu on June 29, 1955, Dulles rationalized "the apparent misunderstandings" with the Indian government. The secretary insisted that the MDA "was in no way inconsistent with his suggestion" to explore the possibility of an Indian military-training mission in Cambodia. The US agreement, Dulles explained, was merely a legal requirement for providing military equipment to Cambodia. Moreover, he still thought it "desirable" for India to "undertake some responsibility for Cambodia and Laos." Taking advantage of the ongoing dispute with France over military training, Dulles said: "No agreement has been reached as to who should do the training of the Cambodian army."[61]

On June 16, 1955, Sihanouk released an "open letter" demanding that the Cambodian government refer the MDA to the ICC for an official finding. Well aware of the commissioners' ongoing review of the document, he nonetheless wrote that the ICC was competent to make a judgment about the agreement and that it should officially notify the Cambodian government if the MDA violated the Geneva accords. The prince repeated his belief that the agreement was unobjectionable, and he implied that the absence of a decision by the ICC contributed to the controversy over the MDA. Sihanouk, US embassy officials speculated, sought to seize the initiative by making it appear that the ICC was acting because of him.[62]

Ambassador McClintock, surprised by Sihanouk's latest maneuver, asked royal councilors Sam Sary and Khim Tit what the prince hoped to accomplish with his open letter. The "real purpose" of the statement, they said, was political: if the MDA controversy were not promptly resolved, the prince's opponents would take advantage of it in the September general elections. Sihanouk also felt that the ICC "should be made to fish or cut bait," as McClintock put it. The royal advisers assured McClintock that the Cambodian government had "no thought" of repudiating the MDA. If the ICC concluded that the agreement violated the Geneva accords, the government would submit the issue of US military assistance "to the will of the people," whose judgment would be "overriding."[63]

On June 19, the weekly US interagency summary from Phnom Penh reported that the ICC was continuing its "leisurely study" of the MDA.[64] The slow pace of decision making was attributable to the consultations each commissioner was conducting with his own government, to the ICC's bias for unanimous rather than majority decisions, and to the leadership style of Ambassador Parthasarathi, who believed "strongly in the healing influence of time," according to Commissioner Duder. Then thirty-two, Parthasarathi was an Oxford-educated journalist whose chairmanship of the ICC for Cambodia was the first of many significant diplomatic assignments for the Indian government. Reportedly a protégé of Krishna Menon and close to Nehru, he earned the respect of his diplomatic colleagues in Phnom Penh. Even the acerbic McClintock considered him "one of the most able and well-balanced young Indians I know."[65]

Although Parthasarathi agreed with Polish commissioner Zygfryd Wolniak that the MDA violated the Geneva accords, he seemed receptive to a fallback position: an ICC request to the Cambodian government for a formal statement explaining its understanding of the offending passages. US officials thought that Parthasarathi would probably view such a statement as a "reasonable compromise" between (1) publicly denouncing the MDA as a violation of Cambodia's Geneva commitments, which at the very least would damage India's relations with Sihanouk, and (2) approving the MDA, an alternative only the Canadians favored. "Urgent efforts," said Parthasarathi, "are being made to obtain a final decision from Nehru on what the Indian position should be."[66]

Nehru supported the "middle course" of a formal ICC request to the Cambodian government asking for an explanation of the MDA. Although opposed to the agreement, he feared that outright ICC opposition would be a futile gesture, undermining the commission's effectiveness and perhaps even leading to the collapse of the Geneva solution in Cambodia. In a meeting on June 24 with Prime Minister Jozef Cyrankiewicz of Poland, Nehru said that an ICC denunciation of the MDA "would not prevent Cambodia from going ahead with getting aid from the United States; so it would mean the Commission would cease to function and the Geneva Agreement would break down." Cyrankiewicz, who considered the MDA "another example of United States interference" in Indochina, found Nehru's "general idea" acceptable.[67]

Nehru proposed a similar compromise to Zhou Enlai, who had protested to the Indian government that the MDA was "destructive in nature and an open violation of Geneva." On the one hand, Nehru agreed with Zhou that the military-assistance agreement was "objectionable and goes against the spirit and to some extent even [the] letter of Geneva." On the other hand, he thought that Sihanouk had little interest in a military alliance with the United States. The prince, Nehru cabled Zhou, was "very anxious to have American money to cover his large deficits." ICC objections to certain provisions of the MDA—not a "total rejection" of the agreement—would be "a check on [the] Cambodian Government as well as [on] the US." If not, Nehru wrote, the commission reserved the right to take "stronger action."[68]

In Phnom Penh, the ICC finally expressed its views—and Nehru's— in a letter from Parthasarathi to Leng Ngeth on July 5. Steering a course between condemnation and approval of the MDA, Parthasarathi wrote that "doubts" had been raised about the "compatibility" of certain parts of the MDA with the Geneva accords. He summarized specific objections but also included statements by the Cambodian government addressing those objections. Parthasarathi requested confirmation that the Cambodian representations were correct. Leng Ngeth's affirmative response pledged that Cambodia would "scrupulously and always respect the terms of the Geneva Agreement." His reply effectively resolved the MDA matter as far as the ICC was concerned.[69]

The seventy-day season for legal political campaigning in Cambodia began on July 4, 1955. The principal competitors for ninety-one seats in the General Assembly were the Democratic Party and the Sangkum Reastr Niyum (People's Socialist Community), Sihanouk's party. Formally established in Siem Reap on April 6, the Sangkum did not initially have a socialist agenda, despite its name. Although claiming to be a popular movement that stood above political parties, it was created with a single objective: implementing Sihanouk's constitutional reforms.

A third political party, Krom Pracheachon (Citizens' Group), competed for thirty-five assembly seats. A front for the clandestine Khmer People's Revolutionary Party (KPRP), which had been established in 1951 when the Vietnamese dissolved the Indochinese Communist Party into three national communist parties, the Pracheachon described itself as a group of former members of the Khmer resistance. The Cambodian government initially rejected and then delayed the Pracheachon application to participate in the elections. Only ICC intervention and the threat of a Geneva challenge persuaded the government to allow the participation of Pracheachon candidates. "After a great deal of effort," the commissioners reported, "the matter was settled satisfactorily on the last day for receiving nominations."[70]

As the campaign got under way, the Democratic Party appeared to have a reasonable chance of winning enough assembly seats to stop the prince's reform agenda. According to one of Sihanouk's advisers, "opposition propaganda about [the] MDA agreement has materially worsened [the] electoral chances of [the] prince's movement." Sihanouk, who was "supreme counselor" of the Sangkum but not a candidate, was "far from optimistic" about the movement's prospects and "occasionally spoke as though he fully expected to be beaten," according to McClintock.[71]

To strengthen the likelihood of a Sangkum victory, the Cambodian government appointed Colonel Chhuon Mochulpich—better known by his nom de guerre "Dap Chhuon"—as the minister responsible for all police and security forces in the kingdom. Then forty-three, Chhuon was the governor of Siem Reap and commander of the military region comprising Siem Reap and Kompong Thom Provinces. A former Khmer Issarak leader who had rallied to the government in 1949, he was a tough-minded ascetic who suffered from tuberculosis. He disapproved of drinking, gambling, and prostitution, though his closest subordinates openly indulged in these vices. The warlord ruthlessly suppressed all opposition to Sihanouk in Siem Reap. "His preferred method of keeping order in his district is to hang a few trouble-makers from time to time," said French high commissioner Jean Risterucci in 1953. Ambassador McClintock, who thought Chhuon's fanatical devotion to the royal family bordered on the "lunatic fringe," noted that the political atmosphere during the election campaign "has been aptly described as one of 'terreur blanche,' or cold, intangible terror."[72]

Dap Chhuon kept his "blood enemy," Son Ngoc Thanh, bottled up in the Dangrek Mountains on the Thai border. According to US intelligence analysts, Thanh was "in hiding for fear of assassination by the ex-King." Like Sihanouk, Thanh was not a candidate in the elections, but both the Democratic and Pracheachon Parties invoked his name and cause. Earlier in 1955, left-wing radicals had taken over the leadership of the Democratic Party. (A liaison between the Democratic and Pracheachon Parties was an up-and-coming clandestine revolutionary named Saloth Sar.) "Hanoi radio is lauding both Democrats and Pracheachon as 'progressive and patriotic parties,'" embassy counselor G. McMurtrie Godley reported to the State Department. "Democrats refrain from attacking Communists, and Pracheachon candidates are attempting to draw on [the] prestige of Son Ngoc Thanh."[73]

Although committed to preventing the "loss" of Cambodia to international communism, US officials had virtually no understanding of the indigenous communist threat. Hypersensitive to the possibility of Soviet and Chinese subversion in Cambodia, the Americans had little capacity for penetrating the KPRP. The Intelligence Advisory Committee, a board made up of the chiefs of US military and civilian intelligence agencies, observed in 1955: "There exists practically no information concerning Communist activities, strength, or capabilities in Cambodia. While Communist strength in Cambodia is not believed to be significant at the present time, this is nevertheless an important deficiency."[74]

In the final weeks of the Cambodian political campaign, complaints about the government's electoral abuses increased sharply. Six opposition candidates and fifty-five campaign workers were jailed for violations of Cambodian laws prohibiting criticism of the royal family or slanderous attacks against the government. ICC commissioners met with Prime Minister Leng Ngeth and Prince Sihanouk to encourage "a wide measure of freedom" during the campaign. An implied threat was the possibility of a commission finding that the elections violated the Geneva accords. ICC intervention stopped further arrests for crimes of lèse-majesté. A Canadian report, however, indicated that Sihanouk and Leng Ngeth remained convinced that the Pracheachon and Democratic Parties "were out to subvert the regime."[75] According to McClintock, the ICC—in particular Parthasarathi—had "incurred the strongest displeasure of the government, the Court and Prince Sihanouk by its criticisms of the US–Cambodian military aid agreement, by its support of the Communist candidacies and by its apparent partisanship in the electoral campaign."[76]

The September 11 election was an overwhelming victory for Sihanouk: Sangkum candidates won 83 percent of the popular vote and all ninety-one seats in the National Assembly. A key factor in the Sangkum's success, McClintock concluded, was Sihanouk's energetic campaigning and his ability "to transform the elections into a plebiscite on the royal institution in general and [on] himself in particular."[77] Yet, as McClintock reported to Washington, Cambodia was "less united than [the] election results would indicate. [The] campaign has been, for this country, of unprecedented bitterness and violence, and although polling has been secret, [the] campaign has been less than free. Sihanouk would quite probably have won [the] elections even if there had been scrupulous fair play, but as it is[,] many people have voted for him because it was made amply clear that it was dangerous to do otherwise."[78]

The ICC unanimously certified that Cambodia had completed its electoral obligations under the Geneva accords. This certification, according to Martin Herz, "involved moral agonies at least for the Indian Chairman[,] who was well aware of the irregularities, pressure and outright terror that had preceded and accompanied [the elections]."[79] Arnold C. Smith, Duder's successor as the Canadian ICC representative, informed the Department of External Affairs that Parthasarathi had "become increasingly contemptuous of the Cambodian Government." Nonetheless, the Indian commissioner concluded that Sihanouk's "popularity was such that his party could have won" 65 percent of the votes in a free election. Commissioner Wolniak, Smith reported, went along with Parthasarathi. It was Smith's impression that the Pole had been instructed to "cultivate a cordial pattern of relations with India."[80]

Like Sihanouk, US officials thought that Parthasarathi and Wolniak had gone "out of their way to protect the interests of the Democratic and Communist candidates. Instead of awaiting receipt of election complaints, the Indians and Poles [have been] actively canvassing the country for evidence that electoral rights are being violated."[81] Yet when it came to certifying Sihanouk's electoral victory, Parthasarathi and Wolniak were unwilling to formally challenge the results and face a divisive dissent by Canadian commissioner Smith, not to mention the prince's hostility. As in Geneva, the Khmer communists' weakness contributed to their abandonment by an ideological ally. "Wolniak," Smith informed the Department of External Affairs, "shows no real solicitude for the protection of the [former Khmer resistance forces] and privately speaks with contempt of [the] Cambodian Communists."[82]

The day after the election, McClintock reported, Sihanouk spoke to foreign journalists, "apologizing" for his sweeping victory and implying that this rout somehow showed the fairness of the election. If the election had been "arranged" by the Sangkum, he observed, "it surely would have been smart to give a few seats to [the] opposition." Sihanouk announced that he would have no official position in the new government. He would, however, continue to lead the Sangkum. A Sangkum congress in late September would consider constitutional reforms and choose a prime minister. A subsequent congress would consider foreign policy and US military assistance. One of Sihanouk's advisers privately confided to US officials that the planned reexamination of the MDA was "merely an exercise to 'educate' the rank and file of the movement."[83]

Some of Sihanouk's closest associates sought the office of prime minister, but the grassroots representatives at the Sangkum congress resisted, declaring that "only Prince Sihanouk could fill that high office." Sihanouk, who had planned to rule through the Sangkum, seemed reluctant to become prime minister, initially accepting the position but then rejecting it. His hesitations reminded Ambassador McClintock of the behavior of the villainous Gloucester in *Richard III:* "Alas, why would you heap this care on me? I am unfit for state and majesty." After two days of quarreling among senior Cambodian officials and demonstrations by the prince's followers, Sihanouk agreed to serve as prime minister, but only for three months.[84]

McClintock, despite his reservations about Sihanouk's "erratic and unpredictable" personality, was pleased that responsibility for Cambodian government affairs "now lies where power has always been." In addition to serving as prime minister, Sihanouk was Cambodia's foreign minister, which meant that McClintock would likely have greater access to him. On October 14, the ambassador made his first official call on the new foreign minister, who was "exceedingly pleased" with a message of congratulations from John Foster Dulles. McClintock mentioned that the MAAG personnel ceiling of thirty-one officers and enlisted men limited the effectiveness of US military assistance to Cambodia. Sihanouk said that as far as he was concerned, the MAAG ceiling should be flexible. "Whether we increased it by 5, 10 or 15 was of no importance to him so long as the men were needed," reported McClintock.[85]

Sihanouk's flexibility on small increases in MAAG personnel did not resolve the larger question of who would train the Royal Army. The Joint Chiefs of Staff continued to press for a complete withdrawal of the "ineffective" and "unsatisfactory" French training mission and for the United States to assume "sole control over all training of [the] Cambodian armed forces." State Department officials, skeptical that Sihanouk would approve such a plan, asked McClintock to appraise the political feasibility of the chiefs' proposal and three alternatives to it: (1) continuation of the current French training program, (2) the introduction of Indian military advisers, and (3) Dulles's compromise of joint US–French training.[86]

McClintock agreed with the chiefs that French training was "ineffective" and that US training was "highly desirable." It would not, however, be possible to approach Sihanouk on this matter until the Sangkum ratified the MDA. "After this approval had been given," McClintock speculated, Sihanouk "might find it possible to edge his way" toward the West. The ambassador optimistically predicted that growing Cambodian familiarity with American weapons and MAAG administration would "automatically" lead to a government request for US training. Dismissing the State Department's three alternative proposals, McClintock replied that continuation of French training was a "jackass proposition"; that Indian advisers would be tainted by Nehru and Menon's "fixed and inveterate hatred" of SEATO; and that Dulles's compromise, disliked by the French, Cambodian, and US military, was not "presently a viable concept."[87]

Included in McClintock's response to the State Department was the notion of linking an approach to Sihanouk about US training with a study of his horoscope. The ambassador explained his thinking in a request to DCI Allen W. Dulles, the secretary of state's brother, for confidential horoscopes of the king, queen, and Sihanouk. Astrology reportedly informed many palace decisions—for example, royal astrologers were supposedly responsible for repeatedly postponing the coronation of Sihanouk's parents. As best as US embassy officials could determine, the astrology practiced in the palace was similar to that of Western countries. Characterizing his scheme as an "experiment in extrasensory politics," McClintock hypothesized:

> The horoscopes drawn up in the palace and the horoscopes which you may provide for us might show important similarities. It is my considered opinion that if such similarities exist, knowing them can be of great usefulness in advancing American policy interests in Cambodia. We should then be able to press ahead at times which the Cambodians are likely to consider propitious, and we should be able to anticipate more accurately the occasional surprise moves with which the Prince, in particular, likes to astound the world.[88]

McClintock concluded his request to Allen Dulles with the claim that the United States had "made progress" in Cambodia in 1955: "The next year should bring the harvest, provided the stars are propitious."[89] Although it is difficult to assess how seriously US officials took McClintock's musings on astrology, one can state with certainty that his optimistic prediction for the new year was wrong. In a policy paper written after his term as ambassador, McClintock himself referred to 1956 as the year when Cambodia's relations with the United States reached their "nadir."[90]

4

"Irresponsible and Mischievous Actions" (1956)

The US mission in Phnom Penh first learned of Sihanouk's planned visit to the Philippines in late November 1955, when the protocol office of the Cambodian Ministry of Foreign Affairs made a "casual inquiry" about the US embassy's ability to issue visas for the prince and his party. Apparently unsure whether Sihanouk had been invited by the Philippine government or "sounded out by intermediaries," US embassy officials thought that a trip to the capital of an "Asian SEATO member with laudable democratic accomplishments would be salutary in many ways and can be discreetly encouraged."[1] A confidential embassy biography of Sihanouk, requested by the Philippine government, described the prince as "a pro-western neutral" who may "eventually come to see the benefits to his country from collective security arrangements such as SEATO." Envisioned as an opportunity to influence Sihanouk, the goodwill visit to the Philippines turned out to be, in the words of Ambassador McClintock, a "fiasco" and a "disastrous experience."[2]

The trip began auspiciously. Arriving in Manila on January 31, 1956, Sihanouk was welcomed with full military honors, a twenty-one-gun salute, and a parade from the airport to downtown, where he was showered with ticker tape. In an address to a joint session of the Philippine Congress the prince said that he was "deeply touched" by the friendliness of the people and their representatives. Reviewing historical ties between the two countries, Sihanouk discussed Cambodian neutrality, which reflected a "mistrust [of] the quarrels of the great." Sihanouk attempted to assure his skeptical hosts that he was not naive about communism:

> The fact that we are neutral does not mean that we are simple-minded to the extent of being lured by the amiabilities of communist governments towards us. As in the past, we will not tolerate any interference in our affairs, nor threats, nor pressure on their part. Even at present, we remain very vigilant and keep our eyes wide open. The proof of it is that we have accepted American and French military aid and that we dare not reduce our army, which is at present forty thousand strong, in spite of our financial weakness. For we do not wish that communist powers (and also non-communist, for that matter) could threaten us with impunity.[3]

Sihanouk told the Philippine legislators that he was often asked, "If you do not sympathize with the communists, why are you friendly with Red leaders like Chou En-lai?" Explaining that he had met Zhou at Bandung, Sihanouk said that China's "policy towards my country has so far been friendly and correct." The prince declared that a small kingdom of five million people could not "rebuff the friendship of the leader of a people of 600 million." In a thinly veiled charge of Western hypocrisy, Sihanouk observed: "The powers who reproach me for not being hostile to Marxist governments do not fear to accredit to the latter diplomatic representatives or send their parliamentary or economic missions, and even conclude commercial treaties with them."[4]

Despite—or more likely because of—Sihanouk's strongly expressed commitment to neutrality, some Filipino officials and journalists "created a certain amount of unseemly pressure on him to establish some sort of military relations with the Philippines, or even to join SEATO," wrote William W. Walker, counselor of the US embassy in Manila. Disparaging the "clumsy efforts of Vice President [Carlos P.] Garcia and others to promote an interest in SEATO," Walker reported that some Filipinos were sympathetic to Sihanouk's views on neutrality: "In the give and take of ideas, the flow was the reverse of what we had hoped."[5]

The most egregious affront to Sihanouk's neutralism was a statement drafted for him that praised collective security, criticized communist aggression, and emphasized the value of American aid. Perceiving the prepared remarks as part of a "plot against Cambodian neutrality," the prince later said that his hosts "wanted me to proclaim myself as neutralist and anti-Communist, which is nonsense." According to Sihanouk's memoirs, a shadowy figure named François Baroukh, who had "passed several months in Phnom Penh," drafted the offending remarks. The prince claimed that Baroukh was "a CIA agent" who had posed as a businessman of Lebanese origin and who had asked for a ride to Manila on Sihanouk's plane. Members of the prince's party informed Sihanouk that "a secretary of the US embassy in Manila" dictated the proposed statement to Baroukh in the bar of the Manila Hotel.[6]

According to US embassy officials in Phnom Penh, Daniel François Baroukh was "a French citizen of Spanish Sephardic stock born in Jerusalem and at one time [a] resident of Manila." Described as "an international adventurer," Baroukh had "made [a] considerable investment of time, money and flattery of Sihanouk during recent months in hope of winning [a] mining concession." A Philippine government press release listing Sihanouk's six-person "official retinue" identified "Daniel Barourh [sic]" as a "personal guest of the Prince." In the US account of the incident, Baroukh was the intermediary for a statement written by Raul S. Manglapus, the Philippine under secretary of foreign affairs. Because President Ramón Magsaysay had been "embarrassed" by Sihanouk's attempt "to sell his neutrality policy to [the] Philippine Congress," Manglapus wrote remarks for the prince that promoted collective security and anticommunism.[7]

A British review of the incident contradicts the US account in one significant detail: Baroukh not only delivered the statement to Sihanouk but also drafted it. According to Granville Ramage, the British ambassador in Manila, Baroukh approached Manglapus, commenting that Sihanouk's speech would probably have a "bad effect," presumably on President Magsaysay. When Manglapus asked what should be done, Baroukh produced the draft statement for Sihanouk: "Manglapus altered it and it was sent to the Prince."[8]

Without more complete declassification of US government records, it is difficult to confidently confirm or deny Sihanouk's allegation that Baroukh was in any way affiliated with the CIA. It does, however, seem reasonable to speculate that the agency played a role in the self-defeating attempt to proselytize on behalf of anticommunism and SEATO. Before the prince's visit, US officials had viewed the trip as a "salutary" opportunity to "discreetly" promote collective security. Moreover, the CIA had helped US allies prepare statements for the Bandung conference that characterized communism as a form of colonialism. The continued classification of relevant CIA's documents precludes a detailed description of the agency's Bandung activities, but John Foster Dulles was sufficiently impressed with the aggressiveness of the anticommunist delegations to send "a note of appreciation" to his brother, the DCI. Allen Dulles replied that he would bring "the contents of your letter to the attention of the personnel involved and I know they will be highly pleased that they were able to make a contribution of value."[9]

The persistent anticommunism of his Philippine hosts was not the only topic that provoked the prince. At a private dinner at Malacañang Palace, President Magsaysay mentioned that US tractors and bulldozers were valuable to his rural development program. Sihanouk, who complained that Cambodia had no voice in its program of US aid, replied: "That is what we need in Cambodia, bulldozers and tractors, but we get only automobiles and refrigerators from the U.S." He added: "The manner is which American aid is distributed in Cambodia might more probably lead to Communism than away from it."[10]

Sihanouk's comments about American assistance were a critique of the Commercial Import Program (CIP). Also called the Commodity Import Program, the CIP was a form of US economic aid intended to finance the Cambodian armed forces and development projects without triggering inflation. Under the CIP, licensed Cambodian importers in effect bought US dollars with the local currency, the riel. The dollars paid for imported commodities, and the riels went into a "counterpart fund" that financed Cambodian government operations. In theory, the imported commodities would raise living standards and prevent inflation by "soaking up" the US-financed riels in the Cambodian economy. In practice, however, the CIP was susceptible to many forms of abuse—for example, the selling of consumer products at exorbitant prices on the black market and the submitting of invoices for phantom commodities. South Vietnam and Laos also experienced the ill effects of the CIP.

Sihanouk and his advisers, annoyed by the CIP's complexity, objected to three aspects of the program. One was the CIP's tendency to finance the importation of relatively expensive commodities that were beyond the financial reach of Cambodian peasants. A second objection was that counterpart funds were in riels rather than in stronger, more stable dollars. (At that time, when the dollar was still directly convertible to gold, US officials worried that dollars accumulating in foreign central banks could be redeemed at a rate that would destabilize the US economy.) Sihanouk's third problem with the CIP was joint US–Cambodian oversight of the counterpart funds, which he deemed an infringement of his country's sovereignty. US officials, however, had little sympathy for the prince's preferred approach to managing economic aid: "The Cambodians apparently want the U.S. to turn over dollar support to them, for them to use first and to account for later."[11]

Returning to Cambodia on February 6, Sihanouk spoke for forty-five minutes at the Phnom Penh airport, criticizing the Philippine and US governments. He complained about the "pressure to which he had been subjected to join SEATO" and unfavorably compared US aid to the Philippines with US assistance to Cambodia. "Of course, [the] United States gets more out of [its] cooperation with [the] Philippines than with Cambodia," he said. The US embassy in Phnom Penh reported to Washington that the prince's visit to the Philippines was "no success from [the] point of view [of] modifying Cambodian neutrality concepts[,] which were, if anything, reinforced by [the] psychological reaction of [the] vain and sensitive Cambodian leader."[12]

Perhaps a more troubling failure of the trip was noted by the US embassy in Manila: "American objectives of avoiding a Sihanouk visit to Peking do not seem to have been advanced." McClintock had learned about the Chinese invitation to the prince during a January visit to New Delhi, where he had a cordial meeting with Nehru devoted largely to Cambodia. Nehru said that Zhou Enlai had asked him whether a trip to Beijing "would be acceptable" to Sihanouk. When the India government passed this information to the prince, he replied that "he would be pleased to go if an official invitation were received." An invitiation was delivered to Sihanouk "through Indian channels."[13]

In Phnom Penh, US embassy officials heard from the Indian chargé, Ajai Kumar Mitra, that Sihanouk was soon leaving for China. Although the visit would strengthen the prince's reputation, embassy officers declared that "the trip must not be viewed as any veering toward Communism on Sihanouk's part." They also doubted that Cambodia's recognition of the PRC would result from the visit. The CIA, however, was not so sure: "In view of Sihanouk's unpredictable nature, it would not be surprising for him to agree to establish diplomatic relations with Communist China while visiting Peiping."[14]

The possibility of Cambodian recognition of China was particularly disturbing to Assistant Secretary of State Walter Robertson, whose defining personality traits were graciousness with colleagues and hostility toward communism. "He was absolutely committed to support for Chiang Kai-shek and to the conviction that the Chinese Communists were a source of evil," recalled Robert R. Bowie, then assistant secretary of state for policy planning. "He dedicated himself to whatever could be done to maintain the position and American support for Chiang and to oppose anything which in any way suggested or implied acceptance of Communist China."[15]

On February 10, 1956, Robertson met with Ambassador Nong Kimny, who came to the State Department to respond formally to US inquiries about Sihanouk's trip to China. According to the minutes of their meeting, Kimny said that "there was no question of Cambodian recognition of Communist China" and explained that "both the visit to Peking and the non-recognition of either side in China or Viet-Nam were in accord with the Cambodian policy of neutrality." Robertson, "speaking as a friend of Cambodia," said that he "sincerely regretted" Sihanouk's decision to embrace neutrality. Robertson "pointed out that such action, if not supporting Communism, at least gave the impression of such support and assisted a regime which was dedicated to the suppression of individual liberties and the institution of a system of enslavement of the individual."[16]

Robertson's comments on Cambodian neutrality reflected the views of John Foster Dulles, who had recently told UK officials, "We must be more vigorous than we have been in combatting the idea of neutralism." According to the minutes of a conversation about Southeast Asia with Foreign Secretary Selwyn Lloyd, Ambassador Roger M. Makins, and others, Dulles commented on how "these neutral governments do not seem to realize that the Communist intentions are so diabolical and so hostile to their freedom and independence" and on how he was "afraid that they would eventually succumb unless they could develop a crusading spirit against the evil forces of Communism." He thought it was "plain that the

Communist intention is to squeeze everything they can use out of each country one by one and then move on. This is characteristic of an expanding despotism which needs conquest in order to survive."[17]

In his meeting with Nong Kimny, Robertson asked why Cambodia couldn't be more like the Philippines or Thailand. He wondered aloud whether Nehru exercised excessive influence over Sihanouk. Kimny defended his country's neutrality. The Philippines, he said, had the geographic advantage of being "separated from Communist China by water," and Thailand had been receiving US aid longer than Cambodia. Referring to the Thais' long history of accommodation with larger powers while maintaining their independence, Kimny said that he "hoped Thailand lived up to the U.S. expectations of her."[18]

Kimny also denied that Cambodia was unduly influenced by India. He said that "Sihanouk made up his own mind." The ambassador, described by the State Department as "a man of considerable intelligence and ability," reminded Robertson that Cambodia was "now accepting U.S. military aid despite Nehru's displeasure." Expressing gratitude for that assistance, Kimny tried to reassure the American that "Cambodia recognizes the evil of Communism."[19]

Sihanouk arrived in China one week after the conclusion of his visit to the Philippines. Unlike the government leaders in Manila, Mao Zedong and Zhou Enlai praised Cambodia's foreign policy and the prince's statesmanship. "The Chinese told Sihanouk that neutrality was the best course for Cambodia and assured him that they would support Cambodia's independence and neutrality," according to historian Ang Cheng Guan. "Sihanouk assured the Chinese that Cambodia would remain neutral and would not resort to SEATO for protection. In return, China would restrain North Vietnam from interfering in Cambodia's domestic affairs."[20]

A joint communiqué, which affirmed both Cambodia's and China's commitment to the principles of peaceful coexistence, stated, "Contacts and relations between [the] two countries should be maintained and promote[d] continuously, especially economic and cultural relations." Zhou repeatedly told Sihanouk that China was "willing to give economic assistance to Cambodia with no strings attached." Although Cambodian neutrality precluded diplomatic recognition of the PRC until its dispute with Taiwan was resolved, the prince implied that his country would eventually recognize China: "In the political field, in the future we shall have more and more direct and frequent contacts."[21]

Upon his return to Cambodia, Sihanouk made an informal speech at the Phnom Penh airport. Stressing Cambodia's neutrality, he declared that "certain great powers" did not approve of his visit to China. He argued, however, that the trip had provided political balance for his earlier journey to the Philippines. "In order to have our sovereignty and independence respected and recognized by other countries," he said, "we must on our part respect and recognize [the] sovereignty and independence of those countries."[22]

Echoing his critical remarks about American aid when he had returned from the Philippines, Sihanouk made transparent references to US military assistance that were inaccurate or misleading. "Certain Anti-Communist nations," he said, "asked us to increase our forces in order to be able to fight against Communists." (In reality, the Pentagon had long advocated a smaller, less-expensive army than Cambodian officials wanted.) Sihanouk also expressed satisfaction that Cambodia had "refused any foreign command for our armed forces," a request the US government had never made.[23]

In a message to the Chinese minority in Cambodia, approximately 250,000 people, about half of whom lived in Phnom Penh, Sihanouk said that they should not jump to conclusions about his visit to the PRC: "Communism might be good for China but it has no place in Cambodia." He also denied that the Khmer communists had contributed to the kingdom's independence and declared that the "Viet Minh have no place in Cambodia." Restoring ideological balance to his rhetoric, Sihanouk denounced South Vietnam and Thailand for violating Cambodia's borders. Foreshadowing the most divisive long-term issue in Cambodia's relations with the United States, he said: "[South] Vietnam and Thailand have powerful friends and since those friends are so powerful they should tell those two countries to cease making trouble for Cambodia[,] which makes trouble for no one."[24]

US officials remained unimpressed by Sihanouk's repeated expressions of neutrality, and they resented the criticism of American military aid. Embassy officers in Phnom Penh, irritated that the Indian ambassador and Hanoi Radio endorsed Sino–Cambodian friendship, characterized the prince's visit to China as a "triumph for himself and for his hosts."

The "most charitable interpretation" of Cambodian policy, the embassy concluded, was "a shift from neutrality favorable to [the] West and critical of Communists to neutrality favorable to Communists and critical of [the] West."[25]

McClintock, who was disturbed by what he called Sihanouk's "canards" about US aid, chose an unlikely medium to communicate his unhappiness: the ambassador's traditionally anodyne public statement observing George Washington's birthday. The declaration in 1956, although making flattering comparisons between "America's founding father and Cambodia's hero of independence," included the comment, "George Washington did not spurn the assistance of friendly foreign powers." This sentence, the embassy reported to Washington, "met with an extremely unpleasant reception from Prince Sihanouk," who interpreted it as a personal rebuke and "contrary to diplomatic" practice.[26]

Senior State Department officials also disliked McClintock's comment. Robert D. Murphy, then deputy under secretary for political affairs, wrote a personal letter to the ambassador "to express the concern felt by a number of people in the Department." A venerable diplomat who had served as General Eisenhower's political adviser during the North African landings in 1942, Murphy wrote: "In retrospect, I imagine that you would agree that the sentence to which objection was taken was ill-advised and *de trop.*" While complimenting McClintock on "the great job" he was doing, Murphy also stated, "If I have learned anything about this business in which we are engaged, I think it is that public dispute between a diplomatic representative of a country and the officials of that country rarely produces profits."[27]

On the same day McClintock issued his controversial Washington's birthday statement, he reported that a recently imposed South Vietnamese embargo on trade with Cambodia was doing "nothing [to] improve [the] climate [of] opinion here." President Ngo Dinh Diem, who was consolidating his power in South Vietnam with US assistance, had abruptly prohibited river traffic along the Mekong from Saigon to Phnom Penh. Although the South Vietnamese government provided no explanation for the embargo, McClintock informed the State Department of British reports of Diem's concern that Cambodia might become a staging area for "various Vietnamese dissidents who would like to see his overthrow."[28]

From 1954 to 1956, noncommunist political-religious organizations in South Vietnam posed the most serious threat to Diem's rule. He defeated the military forces of the Cao Dai, Hoa Hao, and Binh Xuyen, but political opposition remained. In February 1956, when the Cao Dai pope Pham Cong Tac had fled to Phnom Penh, Canadian ICC commissioner Arnold C. Smith reported that the Cambodian government apparently had a "deliberate" policy of tolerating anti-Diem resistance and encouraging South Vietnamese dissidents to denounce the mistreatment of the Cambodian minority in Vietnam. "The Cambodian leaders," wrote Smith, "have thus been doing to South Vietnam exactly what they complain Thailand has been doing to Cambodia in connection with Son Ngoc Thanh."[29]

The South Vietnamese embargo infuriated Sihanouk, who viewed it as economic pressure sanctioned by the US government. On February 29, he criticized the United States during the investiture of a new Cambodian government by the National Assembly. Sihanouk, fulfilling the pledge he made in September 1955 to serve only three months as prime minister, had temporarily resigned before taking a vacation at his home on the French Riviera and traveling to the Philippines and China. Now resuming overt control of the government, the prince declared that the United States helped only those countries that accepted its supervision: "The Americans are dissatisfied because I have refused the proposals of the Philippines to adhere to SEATO and because I have declared that American aid is used for enriching those who are already rich. . . . If the Americans want to cut off their aid to Cambodia, we on our part are resolved to remain faithful to our neutrality."[30]

McClintock urged the State Department to authorize a "formal" communication to Sihanouk setting the record straight on US aid. The ambassador's Washington superiors, however, disagreed. A "limited distribution" cable informed him: "[The] Department is concerned that difficulties between yourself and Sihanouk if continued may become public with consequent damage [to] our relations with Cambodia." Washington officials conceded that Sihanouk's public statements "perhaps call for corrective action of some kind." They hoped, however, that McClintock could improve his "personal relationship" with Sihanouk through "informal consultations" with the prince and his advisers.[31]

There are striking similarities between McClintock's poor relationship with Sihanouk and Ambassador J. Graham Parsons's policy and personal differences with Prince Souvanna Phouma, the neutralist prime minister of Laos. Souvanna, a more conventional statesman than Sihanouk, also sought to keep his country out of cold-war battles and felt a practical need to reach some sort of understanding with China. And like Sihanouk, Souvanna shared his country's historical animosity toward Vietnam and Thailand. A key difference between the two princes was that Souvanna favored a coalition government to control his country's communists, whereas Sihanouk preferred outright suppression.

McClintock and Parsons, both experienced diplomats and ambitious first-time ambassadors, were optimistic about achieving US objectives in these small, newly independent countries. Much to the ambassadors' annoyance and anger, neither Souvanna nor Sihanouk could be persuaded to harmonize their countries' policies with US anticommunism. There was, however, one difference between the two diplomats. Parsons—despite his reciprocated dislike of Souvanna—could not quite match McClintock's condescension toward a foreign leader. McClintock often referred to "Snooky" and to his father as "the little king," a disparaging reference to their height and to a character in the eponymous comic strip. "He made fun of Sihanouk, and Sihanouk knew it," recalled John Gunther Dean, a career Foreign Service officer who first met the Cambodian leader in 1953 and who served with McClintock in Indochina. "This was poor psychology. Sihanouk also had an ego, and he did not appreciate any gesture or remark which did not give him his due as Chief of State of an ancient kingdom."[32]

A temporary pause in the deteriorating relations between Cambodia and the United States began with a "long and extremely cordial conversation" between Sihanouk and McClintock on March 8, 1956. Apparently anxious about the possibility of the US government ending all aid to Cambodia, the prince expressed "deep appreciation" for American assistance and hoped that "recent misunderstandings" about it could be swiftly dispelled. For his part, McClintock stressed that the CIP operated in the same fashion in Cambodia as it did in other countries. Sihanouk said that "so long as Cambodia was treated on [the] same footing as other nations [receiving] United States assistance he could have no complaint."[33]

Contributing to the meeting's friendly atmosphere was McClintock's revelation that Son Ngoc Thanh had recently approached the American embassy in Bangkok with an appeal for assistance. The State Department, said McClintock, had instructed the embassy to reject Thanh's entreaty. In his report of the meeting with the prince, McClintock wrote that Sihanouk was gratified by the "Department's attitude on Son Ngoc Thanh." A few days later Phnom Penh Radio broadcast the news of Thanh's "treasonable proposition" to the Americans and praised the "exemplary correctness" of the United States for rejecting that appeal and for bringing it to the attention of the Cambodian government.[34]

Although McClintock undoubtedly withheld many details from Sihanouk, an emissary of Son Ngoc Thanh had indeed delivered a letter to the US embassy in Bangkok on March 2. The message was addressed to John Foster Dulles, who was scheduled to arrive in Bangkok later that month. Signed by Thanh, it attacked Sihanouk and asked for US "intervention" to protect the Cambodian people. Attached to the letter was a nine-page memorandum that denounced Sihanouk's domestic and foreign policies. Neutrality, for example, was criticized as "an impractical policy for Cambodia in view of its insecure exposed position and the pro-U.S. policies of its immediate neighbors." Robert N. Magill, chief of the political section in the Bangkok embassy, noted an emphasis in the memorandum that likely reduced its appeal to the US government: its author appeared preoccupied with traditional Cambodian unease about "Vietnamese expansionism" rather than concerned about the threat posed by communism.[35]

Son Ngoc Thanh had made a similar appeal to Nehru criticizing Sihanouk and his policies. Tailoring this message to its recipient, Thanh declared: "Cambodia represented Indian civilization in Indo-China and there was a serious risk of Cambodia and her civilization being submerged by the Annamite [Vietnamese] tide." Nehru, whose views of Thanh and Sihanouk had changed since he first met them in 1953, did not reply to the letter. Unwilling to offer further encouragement to the dissident, Nehru concluded that Son Ngoc Thanh's criticism of Sihanouk was "very much exaggerated." Gratified by the prince's commitment to neutrality, Nehru thought that Sihanouk had "grown in stature" since his visit to New Delhi in 1955. (The Indian prime minister still found the prince's concept of democracy "odd" but observed that there was "nothing to be done about it by us.")[36]

Rebuffed by the United States and India, Son Ngoc Thanh still received support from Thailand. His principal patron was Phao Sriyanon, director general of the Thai national police and one of the three top officers in the military junta that ruled the country. The Thai police, a formidable paramilitary force that received weapons and training from the CIA, was responsible for frontier and internal security. "I consider Phao probably [the] most powerful individual in Thailand," wrote US ambassador to Thailand John E. Peurifoy in August 1955. Peurifoy characterized Phao as "highly intelligent, tremendously energetic, but willful, lacking balance and maturity in both domestic and international politics. His active cooperation has been of very great value to [the] US and should be maintained."[37]

American embassy officials in Bangkok euphemistically characterized Phao's preferred foreign policy tactics as "blunt." In a conversation between Phao and Foreign Service officer Rolland H. Bushner, Phao said that the United States "should permit Thailand to cause difficulties in Burma and Cambodia so that they would be forced to give up their neutralist stand. For example, Sihanouk should be punished or 'removed from the face of the earth.'"[38]

Phao's association with Son Ngoc Thanh dated back to at least May 1952, when he arranged a meeting with the dissident in Bangkok. At that time, Thanh was reportedly living in Surin Province near the Cambodian border "with the knowledge and consent of the Thai police." Charles N. Spinks, counselor at the US embassy, speculated on reasons why General Phao would cultivate the dissident: "A Cambodia ruled by Son Ngoc Thanh friendly to Phao might represent a valuable buffer for Thailand, should Vietnam fall to the Communists." The US intelligence community subsequently concluded: "It is probable that Thai officials, uncertain of future political developments in Cambodia, wish to maintain contact with all Cambodian groups that could possibly gain power."[39]

General Phao's interference in the political affairs of Thailand's neighbors was not restricted to Cambodia. He also supported the conspiratorial activities of Prince Phetsarath, a Lao exile in Thailand whose circumstances were in some ways comparable to Son Ngoc Thanh's. A former leader of the Lao Issara, a short-lived Lao independence movement formed at the end of World War II, Phetsarath was a noncommunist nationalist who intrigued against the royal family and government of Laos. In a meeting with Ambassador Peurifoy in December 1954, Phao admitted that "the Thai Government had given assistance to Phetsarath and had expended 1 million baht (approximately 50 thousand dollars)" to support an abortive coup earlier that year.[40]

Phetsarath eventually reconciled with Lao leaders, but Son Ngoc Thanh continued to receive support from General Phao to plot against Sihanouk. Phao's assistance to Cambodian dissidents was an open secret. "The evil genius of Thailand, General Phao," James E. Cable of the UK Foreign Office wrote in 1956, "is all the time dabbling in covert intrigues against the rulers of Cambodia." Sihanouk, too, was "fully aware" of Phao's aid to Son Ngoc Thanh, according to McClintock. This knowledge, combined with Phao's reputation as an "American stooge," fed the rumor that the United States was "encouraging difficulties for Cambodia via Thailand."[41]

Yet in March 1956 McClintock's exposure of Son Ngoc Thanh's unsuccessful appeal to the Bangkok embassy apparently diminished Sihanouk's suspicions about possible US collusion with Thailand. In a cable to the State Department, McClintock wrote that Sihanouk "seemed convinced [the] United States is genuine in its refusal to back that dissident Cambodian leader."[42]

On March 9, McClintock informed Washington that Sihanouk's "pendulum approach to international relations has now begun to swing more in our direction." The ambassador warned, however, that the US government should not interpret this change in attitude "to mean that he has any intention of joining a Western bloc."[43] Perhaps acting under instructions from Washington, McClintock asked Sihanouk on March 14 for his "observations on SEATO." The ambassador began the conversation by quoting a comment from the prince's press conference in Beijing: "SEATO has taught us we would be automatically protected. We reject such protection[,] which can only bring us dishonor."[44]

Sihanouk confirmed that he had made such a statement. "Cambodia," he said, "had been [a] protectorate of [the] French[,] and it rankled deeply [to] be considered [an] involuntary protectorate of even [an] international organization." He added: "If we get into trouble, we know where our friends are and we will turn to [the] US for help, but we do not want [to] be protected without our request by SEATO." The prince, referring to the Thai occupation of Battambang and Siem Reap Provinces during World War II, said that Cambodians had another reason to fear the alliance: Thailand might use communist infiltration as the pretext and SEATO as the "instrument to annex Cambodia."[45]

McClintock argued in response that the SEATO agreement and the protocol extending protection to the kingdom made it "very clear that no action could be taken on Cambodian territory without [the] consent [of the] Cambodian Government." Unpersuaded, Sihanouk observed that "he had a variety of means [to] protect [the] monarchy from Communist attacks," including the friendship of Zhou Enlai and his pledge to restrain Hanoi. Displaying his personal antipathy toward domestic communism, the prince said that he had "no doubt whatever that [the] monarchy in Cambodia would not last [a] minute if Communists took over this country."[46]

Sihanouk claimed that his "problem" was Cambodia's "ignorant and emotional" public, much of which was suspicious of outside influence and aid. During the elections in September 1955, he said, the Democratic and Pracheachon Parties had campaigned against his decision to accept US military assistance. If he had publicly taken stands that were "unpopular" with his Western friends, it was only to "convince his people that he was not a tool of anyone." His voice rising to a "higher tremolo," as McClintock put it, Sihanouk declared, "I am fully aware of [the] dangers [of communism,] but you must let me choose my own means in meeting them."[47]

One day earlier in Bangkok, John Foster Dulles and Walter Robertson had a very different conversation with Prime Minister Phibun Songgram of Thailand about Cambodia and neutrality. Leader of an intermittently stable military oligarchy comprising some three hundred officers, Phibun and his two "strong men"—army commander Sarit Thanarat and national police director Phao—maintained an uneasy balance of power. General Phao characterized the ruling triumvirate as a "vicious circle with Phibun in fear of Sarit, Sarit in fear of Phao and he, Phao, in fear of Phibun."[48]

While discussing neighboring states with Dulles, Phibun said that Thailand had "good" relations with Laos, Malaya, Burma, and South Vietnam. Cambodia, however, was another matter. He pointed out "the rather erratic behavior and unstable character of Prince Sihanouk, particularly his statements regarding neutralism and friendship with Communist China." As an example of the difficulty of achieving "sound" Thai relations with Cambodia, Phibun cited the two countries' dispute over the ownership of an ancient temple on their border.[49]

According to the minutes of his meeting with Phibun, Dulles never specifically mentioned Cambodia. He did, however, speak at length about his

> conviction that in order to fight the evil forces of international Communism, it is necessary to have a strong, vigorous and active spirit of anti-Communism. Such a strong spirit is necessary as an "inoculation" to provide the "fighting corpuscles" necessary to resist the attacks of the Communists. He further emphasized his belief that a policy of indifference or of aloofness to the problem of the spreading of the Communist evil is not [a] sufficiently strong inoculation to protect the body politic from this Communist attack. He said that while the neutralists might be correct, that in the remote and far-distant future—in 100 years or so— the Communists might cease to be predatory, it would be too late for those who had been indolent or indifferent for they would have been consumed meanwhile.[50]

Sihanouk, aware of US hostility to Cambodian neutrality (but not of Dulles's comments to Phibun), "went out of his way to say nice things about the United States and its ambassador" at a press conference on March 18. According to the US embassy in Phnom Penh, the prince referred to McClintock as "*mon ami.*" The prince's public pleasantries were likely intended as political balance to the news that Zhou Enlai had been invited to visit Cambodia. Sihanouk said that diplomatic missions would not be exchanged because "our two countries do not have [the] same political regime and we therefore cannot exchange political ideas." In response to a reporter's question, the prince said that his statement to the National Assembly—that the United States "gives aid only to countries that accept its control"—was mistranslated. "Americans," he said, "do not prevent us from being neutral."[51]

The brief improvement in US–Cambodian relations came to an end soon after the publication of the March 19, 1956, issue of *Time* magazine. An article entitled "Cambodia: Honorable Comrade" began with an irreverent summary of Sihanouk's reign as king before 1953: "For 14 years

Norodom Sihanouk was King of Cambodia and a frolicsome young monarch was he. He played the sax and composed jazz, kept a stable of race horses and a troupe of dancing girls, produced and acted in his own movies, collected concubines and fast cars." Turning to his political career, the article disapproved of the influence of "Uncle Nehru," Sihanouk's visit to "Red China," and the prince's retreat from "a brave pro-Western anti-Communist policy." The sentence that Sihanouk found most offensive was a quote from an unnamed Frenchman: "When he was King, we used to say le Roi est fou [the King is mad]."[52]

Because of the slow distribution of American publications overseas, the initial howls of outrage came from US officials offended by the article's description of the prince's political behavior. Admiral Felix B. Stump, commander of US forces in the Pacific, asked his subordinate, Brigadier General George Lodoen, the MAAG commander in Cambodia, whether the *Time* article was a "true representation of Sihanouk's position toward US aid and . . . a factual report of his actions[.] If so, I consider this antagonistic attitude will threaten damage to [the] entire US assistance program, particularly [in] Southeast Asia." Lodoen replied that the story was "essentially accurate from [a] factual standpoint but [was] decidedly slanted by judicious quotes out of context [from the] verbose Sihanouk." Characterizing Cambodia as "still politically solid, solidly anti-Communist, and [a] potential strong spot in SEA [Southeast Asia]," Lodoen opposed "any precipitate action because of [a] few ill-considered words and actions on [the] part [of the] Prince."[53]

Sihanouk took precipitate action on March 24, when he unexpectedly submitted his resignation as prime minister. "[The] present difficulties of the kingdom, which are caused by certain countries, have their root in foreign policy," he said. In other words, the United States, displeased with Sihanouk's policy of neutrality, had some role in Cambodia's problems with Thailand and South Vietnam. The prince asked the king to accept his resignation because his continued service as prime minister "prevents adjustment of [the] difficulties in question." In a radio address, Sihanouk denounced American press criticism, specifically mentioning *Time* magazine's characterization of him as "mad."[54]

In his analysis of Sihanouk's resignation, McClintock declared that the prince was "repeating another cycle in his tempestuous governance of Cambodia but this time in [a] descending spiral." Discussing various palace intrigues and power struggles among Sihanouk's advisers, McClintock observed, "Forces are coming to light which may eventually challenge Sihanouk's formerly supreme dominance [of] this Kingdom."[55]

One of these forces was Dap Chhuon, the ostensibly loyal military commander of Siem Reap Province and the embodiment of the "*terreur blanche*" in the elections of 1955. McClintock reported that Sihanouk, immediately after his resignation as prime minister, traveled to Siem Reap, where Dap Chhuon told him "in no uncertain terms that he considered his falling out with the United States to be a blunder." The communists, Dap Chhuon declared, were "Cambodia's only potential enemies." Sihanouk, unaccustomed to such blunt talk, immediately left Siem Reap and traveled to the beach town of Kep on the opposite side of the country.[56]

In addition to criticizing Sihanouk to his face, Dap Chhuon wrote a "confidential" letter to McClintock, informing him that he was "awaiting a favorable opportunity to frustrate the policy" of the Cambodian government and to "declare a diplomatic rupture with Communist countries."[57] In a paper drafted after his term as ambassador, McClintock wrote that Dap Chhuon "had been outspoken in private criticism to the American Ambassador of Prince Sihanouk's policies and had expressed a determination to resort to forceful measures rather than to see Cambodia communized." Alluding to the overthrow of the Stuart monarchy in Britain in the seventeenth century, McClintock quoted an unnamed French military commander who predicted that Dap Chhuon "would some day become the Cromwell of Cambodia."[58]

Dap Chhuon's letter to McClintock was the impetus for US deliberations about the possibility of "Sihanouk's removal."[59] In a retrospective discussion of the prince's "irresponsible and mischievous actions in 1956," McClintock wrote, "An examination was quietly made to possible alternatives to Sihanouk. Those closest to the scene were forced to the regretful conclusion that although the absence of Sihanouk from control of Cambodian policy might be heartily desired, there were in fact no adequate alternates to his rule."[60]

The continued classification of sixty-year-old documents prevents a detailed parsing of the US government's "quiet" examination of alternative leaders or potential methods of removing Sihanouk from power. What is known, however, is that on April 4, 1956, the CIA prepared a top-secret briefing on Cambodia for the NSC. The first three topics were

Sihanouk's resignation, Dap Chhuon's letter, and other "oppositionists" who had recently disagreed "more or less publicly with the Prince." The conclusion of the CIA briefing: "The removal of Sihanouk from Cambodia's politics in the near future, far from improving things, would probably bring in a government lacking popular support."[61]

5

"Change from the Top" (1956)

On April 6, 1956, Prince Sihanouk made an incendiary anti-American speech in Kampot, a quiet provincial capital in southern Cambodia. Widely disseminated within the kingdom, the speech covered the full range of Sihanouk's grievances against the United States: pressure on Cambodia to abandon its neutrality, economic assistance that undermined the country's sovereignty, and a hostile press that portrayed him as a "dictator" and "madman." Acknowledging the importance of American aid to Cambodia, Sihanouk declared that he had resigned as prime minister to appease the US government. "My retreat is a moral victory for the Americans," he said. "I hope it will be sufficient for them. In any case the Americans[,] who have so often promised to defend the liberty of small countries[,] have now shown their true face. It is not noble."[1]

US embassy officials in Phnom Penh characterized Sihanouk's speech as a "fantasy" and a "tantrum." His overwrought state, they reported to Washington, was at least in part attributable to the South Vietnamese trade embargo and the threat of a Thai economic blockade. At Kampot, Sihanouk said: "We must relax [the] stranglehold of our neighbors on our economy." He also compared himself favorably to the "real dictator Diem, who is [an] American puppet, oppressor of his people and divider of his country."[2] His comments reflected not only hostility toward the South Vietnamese president but also the widespread Cambodian belief that the US government could force Diem to lift the embargo if it so desired.

In a démarche to Nong Kimny, the newly appointed Cambodian

foreign minister, McClintock protested Sihanouk's speech: "[It] went beyond all bounds in falsely describing [the] situation and injuriously distorting [the] real facts before [the] Cambodian people and [the] world." McClintock was outraged by Sihanouk's allegation that the United States had unilaterally insisted on providing economic aid in counterpart riels rather than dollars. The American diplomat pointedly reminded Kimny that Kimny himself was among the Cambodian officials who had agreed to this practice and who had reported Sihanouk's concurrence with it. Kimny's "only defense of the indefensible," according to McClintock, "was to murmur that probably the translation of what the prince had said was wrong."[3]

US officials were also disturbed by India's role in stoking Sihanouk's anti-Americanism. In the weeks preceding the prince's speech at Kampot, US embassy officers suspected that Indian chargé Ajai Kumar Mitra had "been going around claiming first-hand knowledge [that] Americans are behind [the] current friction between Cambodia and [its] neighboring states."[4] McClintock, who neither liked nor trusted the Indian diplomat, referred to him as "a fly in every ointment." After the Kampot speech, Assistant Secretary of State Walter Robertson informed Secretary John Foster Dulles of "good evidence" that Mitra had "been exceedingly active in spreading anti-American and anti-SEATO rumors, which found a receptive audience in the neurotic Crown Prince Sihanouk, ever playing the martyr, and in neutralist India."[5]

This view of Mitra and the prince was not exclusive to US officials. According to reports from Canadian ICC commissioner Arnold Smith, the Indian chargé shared the "blame with Sihanouk" in promoting the idea that the United States was "'putting pressure' on Cambodia to align itself with the West." John C. Cloake of the UK Foreign Office thought Mitra was a "sinister influence."[6]

Mitra's rumormongering apparently influenced the beliefs of Prime Minister Jawaharlal Nehru, who publicly stated that his "sympathies" were with Sihanouk's resistance to the pressure from South Vietnam and Thailand. Nehru wrote privately to Marshal Josip Broz Tito, president of Yugoslavia, "I have little doubt that the United States encouraged this pressure, probably because they did not like Cambodia's independent policy of nonalignment and the visit of its Prime Minister to Peking."[7]

The Indian press amplified Nehru's views in articles denouncing the

United States and praising Cambodia for foiling American efforts to "convert [the] region into [a] vast military base." In Cambodia, the government news service Agence Khmere de Presse—the only source of foreign news for the Cambodian-language press—disseminated the Indian news stories. When US embassy officials in Phnom Penh asked Mitra about the reports, he replied that he was responding to a request from Sihanouk for clippings from Indian newspapers. Mitra explained that he "could not help [it] if [the] Prince had chosen for publication those which speak of US pressure." In a meeting with McClintock, the Indian diplomat defended himself by saying that he was not alone in reporting American "pressure on Cambodia to change its neutrality policies."[8]

McClintock sought an audience with Prince Sihanouk, who replied by letter that he would likely remain in the provinces and did not see the possibility of a meeting in the near future. Aware of US concerns about his Kampot speech, Sihanouk offered to respond in writing to any questions that McClintock might have. "I obviously assume entire responsibility for what I have said and written," the prince wrote, "but I am obliged [to] draw your attention to [the] fact that I am no longer an official personage belonging to [the] group directing Cambodia."[9]

On April 16, McClintock met with the king and queen. As on a similar occasion two weeks earlier, Queen Kossamak did all of the talking for the royal couple. Then fifty-two, she was politically influential with King Suramarit and their son. American embassy officials considered her "one of the smartest women of Cambodia." Based on his meetings with the royal couple, McClintock reported to Washington: "The queen showed herself to be thoroughly briefed on the details of the recent difficulties, capable of making decisions on the spot and incidentally completely dominating her husband."[10]

The American ambassador reported that the queen agreed with him that "something must be done to inform [the] Cambodian people of [the] true facts" about US aid. McClintock proposed a royal communiqué that included the statement: "The American Ambassador remarked to Their Majesties that the United States Government has never criticized the Cambodian policy of neutrality and has never asked for military bases on Cambodian soil. The Ambassador likewise assured Their Majesties that United States aid to Cambodia entails no condition whatever that might alienate the independence and neutrality of Cambodia."[11]

The queen, Prime Minister Khim Tit, and Foreign Minister Nong Kimny accepted the proposed text of the communiqué with minor changes. The Cambodians deleted any reference to Prince Sihanouk and added language attributing the "recent misunderstandings" to inaccurate press reports. Sihanouk, who reviewed the communiqué after McClintock's royal audience, wanted to remove a reference to SEATO from the text. Otherwise it might be "necessary for him once more to explain his position." McClintock, presumably appalled by the thought of further explication by Sihanouk, told Nong Kimny that he "would be very happy to accede to [the] Prince's desire."[12]

The royal communiqué was issued on April 18. Whatever contribution it might have made to better Cambodian understanding of American aid was almost immediately negated by another official document—a letter from John Foster Dulles to Nong Kimny—and Sihanouk's reaction to it. Even before the prince's resignation as prime minister and his speech at Kampot, Dulles had expressed frustration with US–Cambodian relations. At a meeting of American ambassadors to Asian countries in March, he had said: "I am not sure that it would be an unmitigated evil if something happened to cut off our economic aid to Cambodia. I think that is one of the places where it seems to be producing the least returns."[13]

After Sihanouk's Kampot speech, McClintock proposed and Robertson endorsed "a high-level public statement" intended to preempt further "anti-American attacks." State Department officials optimistically reasoned that a letter from Dulles restating America's commitment to Cambodian independence and its respect for the kingdom's neutrality would "give Sihanouk a face-saving method of resuming normal and comparatively calm relations with the U.S. by permitting him to state his acceptance of our bona fides."[14]

Cambodian officials, however, found nothing calming in the opening two paragraphs of Dulles's letter:

> I am disturbed to learn that recent statements from various quarters have given increasing publicity to allegations that the United States has been attempting to coerce Cambodia into the SEATO alliance under the penalty of withholding economic aid, and that the United States has obliged the independent and friendly

nations of Viet-Nam and Thailand to impose measures of economic warfare upon Cambodia for the same alleged end.

I regret that these allegations have been made since they are utterly false and could harm the friendly relations existing between our two countries.[15]

On April 19, Khim Tit and Nong Kimny told McClintock that the US embassy's intention of publishing the secretary's letter in Cambodia might create "new difficulties." Dulles's comments, they said, could be perceived as the United States "placing the Cambodian Government on notice." Moreover, McClintock summarized, the reference "to SEATO and to alleged pressure on Cambodia's neighbors might inflame [the] situation." Both Khim Tit and Nong Kimny wondered why such a letter had been sent since the "same ground had been covered in [the] Cambodian communiqué."[16]

McClintock defended the secretary's "dignified and friendly" letter as "reinforcing" the royal communiqué. In his report to the State Department, McClintock wrote:

I said [that] since [the] beginning of this year we had been going through nightmares in our relations with Cambodia, generated by false assertions and deliberate misconceptions. Throughout this period we had maintained with great patience an attitude of friendship and [a] desire to help Cambodia which, to any other onlooker, might seem miraculous. I wondered if in [the] future we should have [an] unending series of crises resulting from Cambodian sensitivity. I said there were other nations in [the] world which had not been born with their heart on [the] outside and which did not bleed so easily.[17]

McClintock asked Khim Tit and Nong Kimny who they were afraid of—the Cambodian people or Sihanouk? "Both," they replied.

The next day Nong Kimny told McClintock that he and the royal family had "done much soul searching." Because US officials in Washington had released the text of the secretary's letter, there was no point in asking the embassy to refrain from publishing it. In fact, local distribution of the statement would be preferable to "street rumors" about the communication. Responding to a question from McClintock, Nong Kimny said that Sihanouk had read Dulles's letter and that he interpreted the "first and second paragraphs as being directed against him personally." The prince, however, had promised that he would not refer to the secretary's statement in his speech to the Sangkum congress on April 21. Nong Kimny, McClintock reported, was "afraid [the] Prince may brood as is his custom and fly off [the] handle" after the congress.[18]

True to his word, Sihanouk made a restrained speech to the Sangkum congress. (McClintock characterized these gatherings as a way "to give a democratic appearance to [Sihanouk's] de facto dictatorship.") The prince spoke of "detente" with the United States and Thailand and the "prospect of detente" with South Vietnam. The principal theme of the congress was the importance of balancing relations with the East and the West. "We are resolved to remain neutral because we are ants," Sihanouk said. "We do not want to participate in the conflict between two elephants."[19]

Three days after giving the speech to the congress, as Nong Kimny feared, Sihanouk publicly responded to Dulles's letter with an intemperate seven-page statement. The prince wrote that he felt compelled to "clarify [the] situation" because the secretary's letter implied that he was the source of the allegations Dulles called "completely false." Sihanouk took issue with Dulles's declaration that "the United States at no time had made any official public observation" on Cambodia's policy of neutrality. Characterizing this phrasing as "very careful," Sihanouk observed, "Private American advice, semi-official criticisms have been abundant and [the] American press has distinguished itself in that respect." Once again mentioning the quote in *Time* calling him "mad," he indignantly referred to the following sentence in a *New York Times* article reporting his wariness about US aid: "[Sihanouk] concluded that the hospitality the Filipinos had heaped upon him was part of a United States plot to woo his country into the Southeast Asia Collective Defense Treaty system." In his statement, the prince commented: "For of course, my imagination is supposed to be too active. I am supposed to be suffering from persecution mania."[20]

As evidence of a Manila "plot" against Cambodian neutrality, Sihanouk cited Philippine news stories and made his first public reference to Daniel Baroukh and Baroukh's role in drafting the offensive anticommunist remarks. Prefiguring his memoirs' more detailed allegations of CIA skullduggery in Manila, Sihanouk charged that an "unknown person who was not of Philippine nationality" practically dictated the proposed speech to Baroukh. In an annex to his statement, Sihanouk included a copy of the handwritten remarks.[21]

Baroukh arrived at the American embassy in Phnom Penh on April 25 in a state of "understandable perturbation" for being singled out by Sihanouk, according to McClintock. Baroukh claimed that the Indian diplomat Mitra had visited him and advised him to leave town immediately. To McClintock, the reason for such advice seemed "obvious": Mitra knew that Philippine under secretary Raul Manglapus had dictated the speech to Baroukh and feared that Baroukh might publicly contradict Sihanouk's account of the incident.[22] (McClintock's "obvious" explanation for Mitra's warning to Baroukh seems convoluted and not entirely persuasive. How, for example, did Mitra know that Manglapus had allegedly dictated the speech to Baroukh?) McClintock subsequently reported Baroukh's willingness to issue a press statement accepting sole responsibility for drafting the speech he gave to the prince. According to McClintock, Mariano Ezpeleta, the Philippine chargé in Phnom Penh, was "keen" for this idea, which would "get Manglapus off [the] hook." Nong Kimny, however, observed that a statement from Baroukh "would merely stir-up matters more."[23]

Sihanouk, apparently concerned that his response to Dulles's letter might offend Philippine public opinion, issued a clarifying comment on April 26. Its main point was that he was not accusing the Philippine government of pressuring him to do anything. To "defend himself," however, the prince had been obliged to mention the Philippines in his statement. Expressing sincere friendship for that country, Sihanouk indirectly blamed the United States for "the pro-Western pressure [that] was exerted against him at Manila." In a cable to Washington, McClintock reported: "Sihanouk wants it believed that anything improper that happened during his Philippine visit last February was [the] fault not of [the] Philippines but of [the] United States."[24]

McClintock, who saw no value in responding to Sihanouk, hoped that the Philippine government would "not be provoked into replying" to the prince.[25] President Magsaysay, however, instructed Ezpeleta to deliver a note to Cambodian officials that reportedly called Sihanouk's comments "false and ridiculous." At a press conference on April 27, the prince said that he was deeply pained by the "injurious" communication from Magsaysay. He reiterated that he had never made any accusations against the Philippine government. The persuasive power of the prince's disclaimer was weakened considerably by his "off the record" comment that Magsaysay had indeed pressured him in Manila.[26]

Although few Cambodian officials knew what Magsaysay wrote to Sihanouk, the prince's pique was sufficient to spark more than two weeks of protests and demonstrations. The president of the National Assembly reproached the Philippine government for using language that was "unjustified, undiplomatic, and uncalled for, particularly since 'Sihanouk is [a] full-blooded prince.'" In Phnom Penh and the provinces, demonstrators pledged their devotion and loyalty to Sihanouk. An ironic feature of the government-organized protests was the ubiquity of statements of friendship for the Philippines. McClintock, observing that the prince had never intended to attack Magsaysay, wrote to the State Department, "Very few people are really angry at the Philippines."[27]

Cambodia's spat with the Philippines overshadowed a more deeply felt international dispute—the South Vietnamese trade embargo and the Cambodian "counterblockade." As the more dependent trading partner, Cambodia suffered disproportionately from the restrictions on exports and imports. With active mediation by US diplomats in Saigon and Phnom Penh, South Vietnam and Cambodia simultaneously announced the reestablishment of normal commercial relations on May 17. As part of the accord, the Cambodian and South Vietnamese governments agreed to an exchange of diplomatic representatives.[28] The South Vietnamese representative was Ngo Trong Hieu, an operative for the innocuous sounding Service des Etudes Politiques et Sociales (SEPES), the Diem regime's intelligence service.

Despite his personal and policy differences with Sihanouk, Ambassador McClintock had a better understanding of the dynamics of Cambodian neutrality than most US officials. In May 1956, he took exception to a colleague's cable about the problem of "pro-communist neutralism" in Asia. The analysis was written by Max W. Bishop, then the US ambassador to Thailand and a career Foreign Service officer "who saw Reds everywhere," according to Norbert L. Anschutz, his DCM in Bangkok. In retirement, Bishop appeared to confirm Anschutz's assessment when he recalled that the State Department's "two particular problems" in the mid-1950s were "homosexuals and Communists."[29]

In his telegram discussing neutralism, Bishop parroted Dulles's observation about the importance of a "'massive inoculation' of militant anti-communist spirit" in Asia. McClintock, unwilling to question the treatment's usefulness in Thailand, commented that "such inoculation would not achieve [the] desired results in Cambodia." Critical of Bishop for labeling all neutralism in Asia as "pro-communist," McClintock expressed his belief that this "appellation" did not apply to Cambodia. Writing from experience, he warned that Western opposition to Cambodian neutrality would be "counter-productive" and would likely "drive [the] country closer to [the] Communists."[30]

In a separate despatch to Washington, McClintock wrote a more detailed analysis of Cambodian neutrality, which he characterized as "primarily an expression of the country's intense nationalism." Politicians on the left and right unanimously endorsed Sihanouk's policy of neutrality. Moreover, it was widely believed that taking sides in the cold war meant surrendering sovereignty. From the Cambodian perspective, there was an Eastern bloc and a Western bloc, each with its own submissive satellites. A cautionary example for Cambodians was Thailand, whose membership in SEATO reflected "subservience to" rather than "alignment with" the United States. Such beliefs led "most newspaper-reading Cambodians" to conclude that the United States controlled the actions of both Thailand and South Vietnam.[31]

Cambodia, McClintock wrote, sought to protect its independence "by judiciously balancing Eastern and Western influence." In practice, this meant that Sihanouk sought military aid from the United States and economic assistance from China. His willingness to accept Chinese aid did not indicate any greater sympathy for communism. It did, however, reflect "a distinct lessening of fear of the Communist countries." McClintock thought that Sihanouk was naive for ignoring the subversive potential of a Chinese economic aid mission in the country. He also criticized Cambodia's "moral neutrality[,] which involves the danger of closing one's eyes to the evils of Communism."[32]

McClintock made his assessment of Cambodian neutrality at a time when US aid to India, Egypt, and other nonaligned nations was a controversial topic internationally and domestically. Some foreign governments questioned whether it was more economically advantageous to be a neutral in the cold war than an ally of the United States. An OCB report on South Asia, for example, stated, "The view that neutralism has 'paid off' for India and Afghanistan has been growing in Pakistan and has led to widespread questioning of Pakistan's policy of cooperation with the West and exclusive dependence on the U.S. for outside aid." Many Americans shared the view held by *US News & World Report* founder David Lawrence, who opposed economic assistance to countries that remained neutral "in the struggle between slavery and freedom and between morality and immorality."[33]

The Eisenhower administration attempted to explain its thinking about foreign aid to neutral nations in two public pronouncements. The first was a statement by the president at a press conference on June 6, 1956. Discussing the benefits of providing economic assistance—which he characterized as "waging peace"—Eisenhower said,

> If you are waging peace, you can't be too particular sometimes about the special attitudes that different countries take. We were a young country once, and our whole policy for the first 150 years was, we were neutral. We constantly asserted we were neutral in the wars of the world and wars of Europe and its antagonisms.
>
> Now, today there are certain nations that say they are neutral. This doesn't necessarily mean what it is so often interpreted to mean, neutral as between right and wrong or decency and indecency.
>
> They are using the term "neutral" with respect to attachment to military alliances. And may I point out that I cannot see that that is always to the disadvantage of such a country as ours.[34]

Eisenhower further observed that foreign aid was "a very intricate subject" and that a press conference provided insufficient time to discuss it adequately. He pointed out that the secretary of state would be delivering a speech three days hence "to try to bring all of these details out, etch them clearly in simple form for us so that we can all understand exactly what it is we are trying to do in waging the peace." Contributing to the stereotype of a president who was disengaged, inarticulate, and overly dependent on Dulles, Eisenhower said that the secretary's talk would be "a definite attempt to bring this thing down to its realities, to its specifics, so we can all understand it. He is doing it not only with my approval but really with my great support and urgent hope."[35]

Shortly after Eisenhower's press conference, the White House issued a statement "supplementing" the president's comments. The statement emphasized the president's commitment to "collective security" and to the forty-two countries with which the United States had mutual-defense treaties. Declaring that such arrangements were "the modern and enlightened way of obtaining security," the White House statement reframed Eisenhower's remarks about neutrality: "The President does believe that there are special conditions which justify political neutrality but that no nation has the right to be indifferent to the fate of another, or, as he put it[,] to be 'neutral as between right and wrong or decency or indecency.'"[36]

The reason for the quick White House revision of the president's comments was undoubtedly the embarrassing fact that they bore little relation to Dulles's planned speech, which he delivered at Iowa State College on June 9. In his remarks, Dulles discussed in detail military assistance to US allies. Collective-defense treaties, he declared, "abolish, as between the parties, the principle of neutrality, which pretends that a nation can best gain safety for itself by being indifferent to the fate of others. This has increasingly become an obsolete conception, and, except under very exceptional circumstances, it is an immoral and shortsighted conception."[37]

The differing emphases in Eisenhower's comments and Dulles's speech confused many, including US allies in Europe and Asia. Vice President Nixon, scheduled to participate in the tenth anniversary celebration of Philippine independence, added visits to South Vietnam, Thailand, Pakistan, Taiwan, and Turkey to reassure these allies of the US commitment to collective security and anticommunism. In a highly publicized speech in Manila, Nixon denounced the "brand of neutralism that makes no moral distinction between the Communist world and the free world. With this viewpoint, we have no sympathy."[38]

Although neither Dulles nor Nixon directly criticized India, Nehru responded to their comments about neutralism and morality. At a press conference in London, he said that "dividing the world into good and evil nations" was an unwise approach to international relations. "No country is totally good and no country is totally evil, just as no individual is totally good or totally evil." Equating alignment with either the United States or the Soviet Union as "regimentation," Nehru said, "I object to the communist regimentation of individuals or countries. I object equally to the non-communist regimentation of individuals or countries."[39]

Sihanouk did not publicly reply to the statements by Dulles and Nixon. Privately, however, he apparently seethed. Nixon's remarks at Manila—the site of the "plot against Cambodian neutrality" six months earlier—particularly angered him. According to Nong Kimny, Nixon's comments about neutrality "undid all" of the foreign minister's efforts "to bring about closer relations between the United States and Cambodia."[40]

Sihanouk's neutrality, though widely supported by Cambodian politicians, disturbed some leaders of the kingdom's armed forces. The US army attaché in Phnom Penh, Lieutenant Colonel William A. Lucas, reported that "a Cambodian army clique" was plotting to install General Nhiek Tioulong as an anticommunist "dictator." A former defense minister whose insubordinate comments had offended Sihanouk, Tioulong had been banished to Tokyo, where he served as the Cambodian ambassador. One of his alleged co-conspirators was Dap Chhuon, who had "recently reiterated to Ambassador McClintock his determination to 'take action' if Sihanouk persisted in being a 'Communist dupe.'" Also reportedly implicated in the plot was the army chief of staff, Colonel Lon Nol.[41]

Ambassador McClintock heard rumors of similar conspiracies from Thai and Indian diplomats in Phnom Penh. A key feature of all the plots was that the leadership of the Cambodian military would "prevail upon the palace to oust (or at least rusticate) the Prince." The queen was reportedly "vexed" with the "constant gadding about" of Sihanouk, who in June 1956 began an extended tour of Europe that included stops in Prague, Warsaw, and Moscow. McClintock doubted that the king and queen were either willing or able to consign their son "to an honorable foreign post" or otherwise remove him from power. The ambassador did, however, conclude that FARK might be a "source of healthy restraint on Prince Sihanouk."[42]

This was a notion that intrigued officials in Washington. A joint State–Defense Department telegram to McClintock requested a "more detailed and up-to-date evaluation [of the] effectiveness [of the] Cambodian Armed Forces and its possible influence on [the] Cambodian internal political scene." The cable asked for further elaboration of McClintock's

statement "concerning possible army restraint on or ousting of Sihanouk." A specific request to the ambassador was an "evaluation of needed
US action to ensure [the] armed forces remain basically friendly" to the
United States even if there were an "outright break" with Cambodia's
neutralist politicians. The cable concluded: "[In] view [of the] sensitive
nature [of the] material discussed [in] this message [we] urge utmost dis-
cretion in handling."[43]

Much of McClintock's "limit distribution" reply was a discussion of
the Cambodian army's military effectiveness. An "anachronism" by US
standards, the Cambodian army was nevertheless the "only disciplined
body of armed men in Cambodia." Its main deficiencies were in training, planning, and logistics. Discussing the army's loyalties, McClintock
declared that it was reliably anticommunist. "Rank and file as in most
armies owe immediate allegiance to NCO's [sic] and local superior officers," he wrote. "Allegiance to Prince Sihanouk or [the] King is imminent
but not immediate. Rank and file, under firm leadership, would shoot
first and ask questions afterwards."[44] In other words, well-disciplined
units could be counted on to execute a coup d'état planned by their leaders. Unfortunately, parts of the ambassador's reply, which presumably discussed the more "sensitive" political issues raised by Washington, remain
classified.

McClintock shared some of his thinking about the Cambodian military's role in restraining or ousting Sihanouk in a top-secret letter to Daniel V. Anderson, counselor of the US embassy in Saigon: "We have been
extremely careful to warn Washington that any attempt to bring forward
Dap Chhuon as [an] antagonist against Sihanouk must be handled with
extreme caution, and I made a specific request to CIA that they stay out
of this business unless they receive prior clearance from me." McClintock
also wrote that he and other mission officials had given Colonel Edward
G. Lansdale "our tentative appraisal of Dap Chhuon as a possible leader
in the event Sihanouk has to be got rid of."[45]

A military intelligence operative assigned to the agency, Lansdale had
been "a ranking CIA representative" in the Philippines (1950–1953) and
the chief of station of the Saigon Military Mission in Vietnam (1954–
1956). As leader of the Saigon Military Mission, a small agency group
separate from the CIA station in Vietnam, Lansdale reported directly
to DCI Allen Dulles. According to CIA operations officer and historian

Thomas L. Ahern Jr., Dulles regarded Lansdale as "the Agency's preeminent authority on Vietnam." In July 1955, President Eisenhower awarded Lansdale the National Security Medal for his work in helping defeat the Huk rebellion in the Philippines. The following year he received the Distinguished Service Medal for "outstanding service in Vietnam."[46]

Lansdale visited Cambodia in June 1956 and then discussed the kingdom's operational environment with Allen Dulles on July 12. Dulles, commenting on the CIA's limited capacity for intelligence gathering and other operations in Cambodia, said: "We haven't many assets, and it isn't going to be very easy to build them, is it?" Agreeing with him, Lansdale thought that "at least half" of the CIA's initial efforts in Cambodia would have to be based in Thailand and South Vietnam.[47]

Although Lansdale had no "definite thoughts" on a comprehensive CIA program for Cambodia, he suggested economic and political activities "to counter Sihanouk's organization," the Sangkum. He recommended beginning in the two provinces "around the old ruins of Angkor Wat." One of these provinces, Siem Reap, was under the military control of Dap Chhuon. Lansdale also thought there were opportunities to create problems for the Chinese economic mission in Phnom Penh: "I don't see much harm if a group of natives would overturn a car or something and burn it up and the attendant publicity for some reason or other."

"It would be a very good thing," Dulles replied.

"I think that's very much in our province," said Lansdale, "and something that we might bring out ways and means of achieving."[48]

Dulles's operational ambitions in Cambodia—and those of the Eisenhower administration—went far beyond small-scale dirty tricks in Phnom Penh. At an NSC meeting earlier that same day, Vice President Nixon had expressed concern over Sihanouk's visit to the Soviet Union. Nixon asked the DCI "what were we going to do with regard to Cambodia," and Dulles replied that "a small group had been set up to meet and consider the problem, and presumably this group would make recommendations for action."[49]

The Pentagon representative on this committee was General Graves B. Erskine, director of the Office of Special Operations, the Defense Department's focal point for psychological warfare and other clandestine activities. The CIA member of the group was most likely Alfred C. Ulmer Jr., chief of the agency's Far East Division. During his meeting with Lansdale, Dulles telephoned Under Secretary of State Herbert C. Hoover Jr., who served on the interagency committee that approved and monitored covert operations: "Herb, in light of the discussion this morning [at the NSC meeting]," said Dulles, "I'm anxious to get going on this little committee for 'C.'"[50]

After nearly three months of travel in Europe, Sihanouk returned to Phnom Penh on August 20. In his remarks at the airport, he spoke at length about the enthusiastic reception he had received in the Soviet Union and Poland. Both countries, said the prince, would be sending economic missions to Cambodia to study ways of providing "unconditional aid." He also discussed the communiqués he had signed with the Soviet Union, Poland, and Czechoslovakia, which affirmed their commitment to the principles of peaceful coexistence and recognized Cambodian independence. Acknowledging Ambassador McClintock's presence in the audience, Sihanouk said that Cambodia was "deeply grateful for American aid." McClintock, unimpressed by the prince's self-satisfied account of his "triumphal procession" through communist capitals, reported to the State Department: "Little Jack Horner [has] come home."[51]

McClintock's Washington colleagues were "extremely concerned" by the communiqués Sihanouk had signed with communist countries and by the "seemingly closer relationships" he sought to establish with them. "We have not yet fully made up our minds whether some of the recent statements in which he has joined have been due to his desire to be a pleasant guest, is being fooled by his hosts, or is reflecting his genuine convictions," wrote Eric Kocher, deputy director of the State Department's Office of Southeast Asian Affairs. "No matter what the reason, however, the joint statements are still disturbing."[52]

Members of Congress were also alarmed by Sihanouk's travels and communiqués. Clement J. Zablocki (D–WI), who chaired the Far East Subcommittee of the House Foreign Affairs Committee, summoned Assistant Secretary of State Walter Robertson to Capital Hill to explain why the United States should continue to provide aid to Cambodia. Robertson argued that military and economic assistance to Cambodia served US interests: as long as there was the possibility of preventing the kingdom from becoming communist, the United States should continue to provide aid to Cambodia. "I pointed out that some of the things Nehru does and says are not at all pleasant but we are continuing to give aid to India, not Mr. Nehru," Robertson wrote to McClintock. "Likewise, Cambodia is bigger than Sihanouk."[53]

Robertson's dialogue with the Zablocki committee mirrored a disagreement between the State Department and the Pentagon over foreign aid to neutral nations. During a discussion of US policy in Southeast Asia at the NSC meeting of August 30, the Department of Defense sought a declaration that the US government would "give preferential treatment in the fields of economic and military assistance to countries which participated with the United States in collective security arrangements." John Foster Dulles, who generally agreed with this principle, objected to a "fixed rule or statement of policy that would actually prevent the United States from providing military assistance to neutral countries like Burma if it proved to be in our strategic interest to do so."[54]

In the debate that followed, the Pentagon's most tenacious advocate was Admiral Arthur W. Radford, chairman of the Joint Chiefs of Staff. He insisted that military assistance should be provided only to US allies: "We would never be able to retain our allies in Southeast Asia if our allies felt that other countries were in a position to obtain U.S. assistance without ever joining any kind of an alliance with the United States." Dulles replied, "We had better begin getting rid of our allies if having such allies [is] going to prevent us from doing what is in the best interests of the United States." Offering a pragmatic example, Dulles said that he would rather see the US ally Thailand lost to communism than the more populous neutral India. President Eisenhower resolved the dispute by agreeing to a Dulles-proposed compromise that gave allies "preferential treatment" in foreign aid but allowed exceptions to this principle when US "strategic interests" were involved.[55]

A few days after the NSC meeting on August 30, President Eisenhower approved NSC 5612/1, a statement of policy that declared, "The national independence of the mainland Southeast Asian states is important to the security interests of the United States. If such independence is to be preserved, U.S. policies must seek to build sufficient strength in the area at least to identify aggression, suppress subversion, prevent Communist political and economic domination, and assist the non-Communist governments to consolidate their domestic positions." The policy guidance for Thailand included utilizing its "central location in Southeast Asia as a point from which to create discontent and internal difficulties within nearby Communist-dominated areas and thwart Communist subversive efforts in neighboring free countries."[56]

When presenting the policy statement to the NSC, National Security Adviser Dillon Anderson commented that US efforts to strengthen Cambodia's alignment with its anticommunist neighbors and "the West have not of late met with much success, and have, in fact, lost ground." NSC 5612/1—specifically numbered paragraph 39—provided far-reaching guidance for redressing the situation: "In order to maintain Cambodia's independence and to reverse the drift toward pro-communist neutrality, encourage individuals and groups in Cambodia who oppose dealing with the Communist bloc and who would serve to broaden the political power base in Cambodia."[57]

Although not mentioned by name, Dap Chhuon was undoubtedly one of the anticommunist "individuals" whom US officials had in mind. Precisely how they would "encourage" him and other anticommunist opponents of Sihanouk was left unsaid. One of the regional courses of action in NSC 5612/1, however, provided at least part of the answer: "Implement as appropriate covert operations designed to assist in the achievement of U.S. objectives in Southeast Asia."[58]

During an unprecedented global tour by a director of Central Intelligence, Allen Dulles met with Sihanouk in Phnom Penh on September 21, 1956. Accompanied by Ambassador McClintock, Dulles found the prince "supremely confident of the correctness" of his neutrality policy and "over-confident of his ability of dealing with Communist subversive tactics." In a cable to his brother, the DCI concluded: "I see no early prospect either of arguing or cudgeling him out of his position and no likelihood of affecting a change in government." Dulles also reported that South Vietnamese president Ngo Dinh Diem was "outspoken in his hostility toward the present Cambodian regime. He is more optimistic than I that a change can be effected."[59]

With Sihanouk "the focus of virtually all power in Cambodia," the DCI thought it vital "to increase and improve our relations and our access to him." Noting that the prince was "aloof from American representatives other than on official occasions," Dulles recommended the appointment of a senior US official in Phnom Penh who "should be skilled in French and have a flair for music and other cultural interests of Sihanouk." He wrote that the prince was "unwilling to accept anything like direct criticism, but can be flattered by attention to his personal tastes and interests."[60] The DCI was apparently suggesting the appointment of someone such as Lansdale, whose empathetic approach to political manipulation had been effective with Philippine president Magsaysay and less so with Diem.

For Allen Dulles and other US officials, a hopeful development in Cambodia was a new government that included two anticommunists in key cabinet positions. Although Sihanouk returned as premier, he selected Dap Chhuon and Prince Sisowath Monireth to lead the Ministries of Interior and Defense, respectively. The appointment of Dap Chhuon as the nation's top police official reflected government concern over the subversive potential of the Chinese and other communist aid missions in Cambodia. Monireth, a former major in the French Foreign Legion and the Cambodian army's inspector general, was responsible not only for overseeing the armed forces but also for rooting out government corruption.[61]

Charges and countercharges of graft among Cambodian officials had been the primary cause of the previous government's resignation. (Prime Minister Khim Tit had also unwisely supported Thai diplomat Prince Wan for the presidency of the United Nations General Assembly, an act Sihanouk considered "unneutral" because of Thailand's membership in SEATO.) According to McClintock, rival factions within the Sangkum and the National Assembly were "somewhat distressed by reports of graft but really enraged because so much graft was going to so few people." In an unusual public statement of royal concern about corruption, King Norodom Suramarit "called for radical measures to 'cut out dishonest practices' and 'extirpate sinister corruption and diversion of public funds, to give tranquility to [the] people.'"[62]

Prince Monireth, assured by Sihanouk of his authority to pursue government "big shots," aggressively investigated official corruption. Within the Ministry of Defense, he found a "quasi-catastrophic" abuse of basic financial controls. Colonel Lon Nol, for example, admitted that "it had never entered his mind" to account for the funds for which he was responsible. According to a subsequent CIA biographical sketch, Lon Nol was popular with military officers "perhaps more because of their appreciation for his personal interest in their financial welfare than because of their respect for his military ability."[63]

Monireth sought sweeping powers to prosecute corruption, which neither Sihanouk nor the cabinet nor the National Assembly was willing to grant. US embassy officials observed that Sihanouk was "honestly concerned with fighting corruption but handicapped by the fact that most of the top echelon of the administration, including important elements of the Court entourage and of his own Sangkum, are implicated in corruption affairs. Corruption is deeply rooted in the Cambodian body politic."[64]

Monireth threatened to publicly accuse the government of not wanting a "real clean-up" of corruption. Although the king and queen managed to silence him, the bitter disagreement prompted Sihanouk once again to resign as prime minister. In a long radio address broadcast on October 15, the prince cited "overwork" as the principal reason for his resignation. He also referred to budgetary difficulties and to "insulting anonymous letters" that blamed him for corruption and accused him of being "power-hungry" and "power-mad." Despite resigning as prime minister, Sihanouk retained firm control of Cambodia's internal and external affairs. A US embassy report commented, "[The] power of state remains in his hands whether he [is] active or on vacation or [in] retirement, in office or out of office, on [the] throne or [a] commoner."[65]

Sihanouk's latest resignation coincided with the end of Robert McClintock's term as ambassador in mid-October. At a farewell dinner hosted by Sihanouk, the two antagonists exchanged pro forma expressions of friendship and good feelings. The Cambodian government and people were "losing a friend," said Sihanouk, and the ambassador's imminent departure was a source of "lively regret." Discussing Cambodia's foreign policy, the prince said: "We only hope that everyone, big or little, West or East, may respect our independence, our neutrality, our sovereignty." McClintock replied that he would be leaving "part of his heart" in Cambodia. In his remarks about US assistance to the kingdom, the ambassador declared that "the United States recognized that being a completely free country, Cambodia should choose its own foreign policy and if that foreign policy was one of strict neutrality that was purely the affair of Cambodia."[66]

Despite his rhetorical commitment to Cambodian sovereignty, McClintock and most other US officials found Sihanouk's neutrality insufficiently "strict"—in other words, insufficiently pro-Western. In a valedictory letter to Kenneth Young, the State Department's director of

Southeast Asian affairs, McClintock commented on NSC 5612/1, expressing his belief in the "possibility of saving the country in our own interest."
He hoped that the US government would not prematurely "throw in the
sponge" and end military and economic aid to the kingdom:

> Cambodia possess healthy forces of resistance to Communism
> that can well come to the fore, with appropriate encouragement,
> if the present neutralist trend is carried too far in the Commu-
> nist direction. We must not overlook the possibility of a change
> coming from the top, whether it be by a palace revolution, a coup
> d'état with palace acquiescence or simply a break-up of the gov-
> ernment under circumstances which might bring about an impor-
> tant change in orientation.
>
> Furthermore, I interpret paragraph 39 of NSC 5612/1 to mean
> that we need not only think in terms of change from the top
> but can also quietly work for a broadening of the political power
> base in a democratic sense, which can also pay important politi-
> cal dividends.[67]

6

"Many Unpleasant and Difficult Things" (1957–1958)

Carl W. Strom, Robert McClintock's successor as US ambassador to Cambodia, arrived in Phnom Penh on November 26, 1956. Then fifty-six, Strom was a midwesterner whose academic credentials included a PhD in mathematics from the University of Illinois. After teaching math at Luther College in Decorah, Iowa, he joined the Foreign Service in 1935, spending much of his career as an administrative officer. Immediately before his appointment as ambassador to Cambodia, he served as DCM in Seoul. He was a precise diplomat whose poor French proved to be a handicap in his dealings with Sihanouk. This was not, however, an immediate problem because Sihanouk avoided an audience with the new American ambassador for more than two months.

Strom's courtesy calls in Phnom Penh included a visit with Dap Chhuon, whose title had recently been raised to "minister of state" for internal security. Before arriving in Cambodia, Strom had been briefed by State Department officials on Chhuon's treasonous correspondence with McClintock.[1] In his initial meeting with Chhuon, Strom received mixed messages about Chhuon's loyalties. On the one hand, Chhuon urged the ambassador to be patient in judging Sihanouk. On the other hand, he criticized the prince for his "blindness" in dealing with communists and for his inability to get along with Thailand and South Vietnam. Chhuon also requested US assistance in establishing confidential relations with South Vietnamese officials.[2]

Ambassador Strom dodged this diplomatically inappropriate request, asking Chhuon if he knew Ngo Trong Hieu, the South Vietnamese representative in Phnom Penh. According to Strom, Chhuon said that he could not deal "overtly with Hieu," who was being watched by the Cambodian police. The chief of the national police, a nominal subordinate of Chhuon who reported directly to Sihanouk, had arrested one of Hieu's agents for engaging in anticommunist "political activity." The prince was reportedly "most annoyed" with Hieu and "considering his expulsion." Chhuon told Strom that he kept in touch with Hieu through a female intermediary.[3]

Hieu acknowledged his clandestine relationship with Dap Chhuon to G. McMurtrie Godley, the US DCM in Phnom Penh. The South Vietnamese operative, however, apparently feared entrapment by Chhuon, declaring that the Cambodian "was playing me for a sucker."[4] In a meeting with embassy political officer Martin Herz, Hieu observed that Ngo Dinh Diem was "losing ground" among the estimated three hundred thousand Vietnamese in Cambodia. Claiming to have a network of agents working in the kingdom's rubber plantations, the SEPES representative said: "The Communists are becoming bolder all the time, and the Cambodian Government either does not care or deliberately favors them." According to Herz, Hieu thought "that it would work a 'spectacular change in the atmosphere' if a few of the Communist or pro-Communist leaders among the Vietnamese minority here were assassinated."[5]

Another scheme Hieu mentioned to Herz was to provide Sihanouk with a list of Viet Minh agents in Cambodia and inform him of reports that "attempts"—presumably assassination attempts—"would be made upon the leading men on the list." Hieu would tell Sihanouk that he was supplying this information to give the Cambodian government the opportunity "to protect those people." He would then add that perhaps a "better solution" was to order these undesirables out of Cambodia altogether. "In any event," Herz reported, "Hieu would finally tell Sihanouk, having warned the Prince he hoped he would not be responsible for any harm that might befall the persons in question."[6]

Hieu, described by Strom as "not very subtle," received no US encouragement for these schemes.[7] US officials in Phnom Penh and Washington did, however, share his concern over increasing communist influence among the Vietnamese in Cambodia. Hieu's concluding statement to

Herz implied that South Vietnam would be intervening in Cambodia's affairs: "Hieu remarked that he would not and could not stand by indefinitely, with his pants conveniently let down to his ankles, while the Cambodians and the Communists were bestowing kicks on his posterior. The time would come when he would have to fight back. Perhaps the time is not yet."[8]

Strom had his first private meeting with Sihanouk at 10:00 a.m. on February 1, 1957. Prime Minister San Yun, "a mere instrument" of the prince, according to Herz, greeted the ambassador at the palace and then left Strom and Sihanouk alone. Their conversation, touching on such topics as the US aid program, the Cambodian army, and the approaching visit of the San Francisco Ballet, was punctuated by awkward silences and moments when the ambassador caught only a few words of what Sihanouk was saying in French. In his summary of the meeting for the State Department, Strom wrote that the usually loquacious prince was "reserved and diffident. I sat back on the divan, turned toward him, while he perched himself on the edge and sat in a rather expectant attitude as if he was wondering throughout what I was going to say next."[9]

To help improve US relations with Sihanouk, Strom proposed that the State Department extend an invitation to the prince to visit the United States. Recommending a stay of at least four weeks, the ambassador envisioned Sihanouk touring automobile factories in Detroit, conducting one of his own musical compositions with a symphony orchestra, and observing life in a typical small or midsize town. Strom's hope was that the prince would return to Cambodia with "useful knowledge about America that would benefit us for a long time." In making this suggestion to Assistant Secretary of State Walter Robertson, Strom observed: "I am quite aware that the idea of a visit by Sihanouk will not give rise to rejoicing in the halls of the Department, but there are many unpleasant and difficult things that have to be done in our national interests."[10]

Robertson was not persuaded by Strom's appeal, noting that the State Department was "having trouble in fitting in visits from Magsaysay and Diem," two allies with impeccable anticommunist credentials. This was not the first time that Washington had rebuffed a recommendation from Phnom Penh to invite Sihanouk to the United States. In August 1956, when the prince was touring Europe and visiting communist capitals, the department had rejected a similar proposal from Ambassador McClintock:

> We believe he [Sihanouk] would consider [an] invitation submitted directly on his return from iron curtain success as proof he could insult [the] US and still receive as [a] reward [an] invitation [to] visit this country. Also unless there is [a] change in Sihanouk's public statements and attitudes [a] visit might do more harm than good since US officials could not be expected [to] flatter [the] Prince or congratulate him on his policies or actions. Given [the] Prince's constitutional inability [to] accept differences [of] opinion some unfortunate exchange might take place.[11]

A recurring irritant to Sihanouk's relations with the United States was commentary from *Time* magazine, which Cambodian officials viewed as an accurate reflection of US policy. A brief article in the issue dated February 11, 1957, mocked not only Sihanouk's "Nehru-type" neutralism but also Buddhist monks "cruising [in] Tampa-blue four-hole Buicks" to gilded pagodas.[12] In Phnom Penh, the semiofficial weekly *Réalités Cambodgiennes* used the *Time* story as a news peg for a front-page editorial criticizing Americans as "too rigid and uncompromising in their foreign operations, too disdainful of local problems, too ignorant of [the] Asian mentality, too anxious to push [a] materialistic system which [was] not appreciated by old Asian civilizations, and too intransigent in their anti-communism."[13]

Time's reporting from Cambodia in the 1950s—written by a variety of correspondents and rewritten by editors in New York—reflected the ideological convictions of the magazine's editor in chief, Henry Luce. The son of a missionary in China and author of the essay "The American Century," published in 1941, Luce was an ardent anticommunist and a passionate advocate for Chiang Kai-Shek. Chiang's defeat by Mao Zedong "was the greatest disappointment of Luce's life," according to his biographer Alan Brinkley. In a memorandum to his editors, Luce observed that US leadership "is in decline, neutralism and appeasement are growing among our allies, communism is gaining among the masses, and the Kremlin is coming daily closer to . . . the domination of the world."[14]

Ambassador Nong Kimny formally denounced the *Time* article of

February 11 to the State Department, charging that it was "insulting" to the Cambodian monarchy, the Buddhist religion, and Prince Sihanouk. On March 5, Walter Robertson handed Kimny a diplomatic note "expressly" dissociating the US government from the views expressed in *Time*. Robertson reminded the ambassador that the press in the United States was "completely free to attack governments, both domestic and foreign," and reassured him that the *Time* story "did not reflect the views of the United States Government just as he felt that recent articles in the Cambodian press containing vitriolic attacks against the United States did not really represent the attitude of the Cambodian Government towards the United States." According to the minutes of the meeting, Kimny nodded his head in agreement.[15]

Despite Robertson's soothing words to Nong Kimny, officials in Washington continued to view political and foreign policy developments in Cambodia with alarm. An OCB progress report on NSC 5612/1 stated, "The United States was unable to influence Cambodia in the direction of development of a stable government, nor was it able to restrain it from becoming more involved with the communist bloc. Sihanouk, the most powerful political leader, is reluctant both to assume and maintain the responsibilities of high office and to delegate authority. Such an attitude makes it almost impossible to carry out the ordinary functions of government and prejudices the accomplishment of U.S. objectives."[16]

Although unmentioned in the OCB progress report, the NSC policy guidance to encourage anticommunist opposition to Sihanouk—what McClintock had called "change from the top"—remained in force. An unsigned document in the files of the State Department's Office of Southeast Asian Affairs, dated April 2, 1957, analyzed the question of "a possible alternative to the leadership of Prince Norodom Sihanouk." Noting the unfavorable trend in Cambodia's foreign policy, the paper concluded that "an attempt to induce changes in the pattern of leadership would be unduly risky" unless three questions could be answered affirmatively: (1) Were there sufficiently powerful individuals or groups who could "carry out a successful move to reduce or eliminate Prince Sihanouk's domination of Cambodian political life?" (2) Could such individuals or groups provide popular leadership and effective administration? (3) Would an "alternative government" be more likely to resist communist pressure?[17]

The paper observed that Dap Chhuon "might be willing to lead or

share in an effort to remove the Prince from his position or power." Yet
the one-time Issarak and his slovenly former guerrillas in Siem Reap—
described by the US Army attaché as "one of the poorest units of the
FARK"—were disdained by the regular army, reducing the likelihood of
disgruntled military leaders joining forces with Chhuon. It also seemed
"doubtful" to Washington officials that the king and queen "would consent to a change in leadership which involved discrediting Sihanouk." The
bottom line of the State Department analysis echoed the conclusions the
US government had come to in 1956: there was no obvious alternative to
Sihanouk, and any attempt to remove him from power would be opposed
by the throne and other elements of Cambodian society.[18]

On the morning of May 2, 1957, eighteen volunteers from the 1st Battalion of the 38th Regiment of the Army of the Republic of Vietnam
(ARVN) crossed the Cambodian border into Svay Rieng Province.
Patrolling for "rebels," the South Vietnamese troops entered two villages
approximately two and a half kilometers inside of Cambodian territory.
When some of the villagers ran, the soldiers fired on them. The ARVN
troops also looted property. Cambodian civilians, with help from local
Royal Army forces, killed one of the raiders and captured seven. One of
the South Vietnamese prisoners was an officer, Lieutenant Huyn Tan Tai,
who later said that people in his country did "not run on seeing troops
approaching villages."[19]

The Cambodian government reported the ARVN incursion to the
ICC and requested an investigation to verify the facts of the raid. Without prejudging any aspect of the incident, including the identity of the
attackers, the Indian, Polish, and Canadian commissioners agreed to send
an ICC military team to Svay Rieng Province for a preliminary investigation. After a day of interviews with villagers and prisoners, the team submitted a unanimous report documenting the basic facts of an incursion
by regular South Vietnamese forces. But the Canadian representative of
the investigating military team, Colonel H. J. Lake, noted that his participation in the investigation did not change his delegation's long-standing
conviction that monitoring border violations by South Vietnam exceeded
the ICC's authority and jurisdiction.[20]

For more than a year, Canadian officials had maintained that Cambodia had fulfilled its Geneva obligations and that the ICC in Cambo-

dia should be dissolved as soon as possible. Narrowly interpreting the ICC's authority to supervise and control border incidents, the Canadians argued that the goal of the Geneva cease-fire agreement for Cambodia was bringing about peace between the opposing forces of the Cambodian government and the DRV. Noting that the only two signatories of the Cambodian cease-fire were military representatives of these governments, the Canadians concluded: "The Commission is competent to deal with frontier violations only when it is the Democratic Republic of Vietnam forces which violate the border." The Canadians further observed that Cambodia, a sovereign nation and a new member of the United Nations, had recourse to traditional diplomatic means of dealing with border problems with South Vietnam or Thailand. To insert the ICC between Cambodia and its neighbors, said L. H. LaVigne, the acting Canadian commissioner, "would be quite inappropriate as well as legally beyond its jurisdiction."[21]

The governments of India and Poland disagreed with the Canadian arguments. In their more expansive view of ICC authority, both the Geneva accords and the security of Cambodia, Laos, and Vietnam must be considered as a whole. Until there was a satisfactory settlement in Vietnam, the commissions in Cambodia and Laos should continue to operate. Finding the ICC "competent" to deal with the Svay Rieng incursion, Major General Chand N. Das, the chairman of the ICC for Cambodia, said that all of the signatories of the final declaration of the Geneva conference had agreed "to respect the territorial integrity of the States of Cambodia, Laos and Vietnam. The intrusion into Cambodian territory by foreign armed forces is definitely a violation of the integrity of Cambodia's frontiers and is, therefore, a violation of the Geneva Agreement. It is mandatory on the Commission that it should see that Cambodia's frontiers are respected."[22]

With the Canadian delegate dissenting, the ICC for Cambodia determined that it had the authority to deal with the Svay Rieng border incident. Canada also objected to a Polish proposal to send the report by the ICC military team to the ICC in Vietnam "with a request to take the matter up with the South Vietnamese government." Under the terms of the Geneva agreement, the lack of unanimity in this case called for the submission of majority and minority reports to the conference cochairs. In their majority report on the incident, the Indian and Polish commissioners sought "instructions" from the United Kingdom and the Soviet Union. But because of cold-war politics, the ICC in Cambodia received no reply. Reports to the Geneva cochairs, "whether unanimous or otherwise, seldom had any effect," recalled Paul Bridle, a Canadian diplomat and ICC commissioner in Laos. "The Co-Chairmen represented all the other members of the Geneva conference but, in fact, were also guardians of Communist and Western interests, respectively."[23]

Sihanouk, who had earlier considered ICC activities to be an infringement of Cambodian sovereignty, now wanted the commission to remain in the kingdom to serve as "a witness in case of eventual aggression" by his neighbors. In 1956, the Cambodian government had informed the ICC of eighteen border incidents involving South Vietnamese personnel. That number doubled the following year. President Ngo Dinh Diem of South Vietnam, however, had a different view of the border problem. He objected to the sanctuary that Cambodian territory provided opponents of his government. During his visit to the United States in May 1957, Diem told John Foster Dulles that the Viet Minh were organizing commando units in the region where the borders of Cambodia, Laos, and Vietnam formed a triangle. "It appear[s]," said Diem, "that Prince Sihanouk of Cambodia [is] unable to put a stop to such activities on the Cambodian side of the frontier."[24]

Diem's effectiveness in repressing communists inside South Vietnam "forc[ed] them to rebuild their bases in eastern Cambodia," according to researchers Thomas Engelbert and Christopher Goscha. To protect its leadership, the clandestine Cochin China Party Committee, the predecessor organization of the Central Office for South Vietnam (better known by its acronym COSVN), moved its headquarters in early 1957 to Phnom Penh, where it remained undisturbed until 1959. The committee's main activities in South Vietnam were political agitation and targeted assassinations aimed at destabilizing Diem's government. According to the CIA, South Vietnamese leaders believed "anti-Diem Vietnamese in Phnom Penh" were responsible for the assassination attempt against him in February 1957. In a later study of communism in Cambodia, agency analysts commented on Sihanouk's and Diem's harboring of each other's enemies: "In retrospect, Diem's embrace of Son Ngoc Thanh seems a mere peccadillo."[25]

The Cambodian communists were relatively quiescent in this period.

Tou Samouth and Sieu Heng, leaders of KPRP's urban and rural networks, respectively, returned to Cambodia from the DRV in the mid-1950s. In Phnom Penh, Saloth Sar became a schoolteacher who did clandestine party work for his mentor, Tou Samouth. "It is hard to say what this political work entailed, how important Saloth Sar was, or where he fit into the Communist chain of command," writes historian David Chandler. "His name never came up in Sihanouk's speeches or in the government press in connection with the Pracheachon. Although widely known as a progressive, Sar apparently was never questioned by the police, and the U.S. Embassy had no biographical information on him, as it did for hundreds of supposedly Communist figures. Unlike militants in other countries, he never spent a night in jail."[26]

On May 11, 1957—more than three months after his awkward initial tête-à-tête with Sihanouk—Ambassador Strom had his second personal audience with the prince. This time Strom was accompanied by DCM G. McMurtrie Godley, the MAAG chief and his deputy, and the top two officials from the US economic aid mission. With the help of a fifty-two-page illustrated brochure, Strom and his colleagues briefed Sihanouk, royal counselor Penn Nouth, and Defense Minister Sak Suthsakhan on US military and economic assistance to Cambodia. In a letter sent to Walter Robertson before the presentation was given, Strom described the briefing as "a major effort to remove misconceptions concerning our activities."[27]

In the short run, at least, it appeared that Strom had achieved his objective. Sihanouk, who had resumed overt leadership of the government in April, thanked the US officials for their "excellent and informative presentation" and expressed his "heartfelt appreciation for the generous and effective American aid." The prince's own effort to remove misconceptions included an explanation of Cambodian neutrality and a declaration that the kingdom "will not participate in the world-wide conflict nor join any bloc." In a typically indirect reference to South Vietnam and Thailand, he added: "Presently, Cambodia is menaced not by a bloc but by neighbors who are unquestionably anti-Communist. It is perfectly all right for them to follow an anti-Communist line but they should not be anti-neighborly in their foreign policy."[28]

Defending the monarchy and its commitment to democracy, Siha-

nouk stated that communism was incompatible with the kingdom's political institutions. He dismissed Cambodian communists as Viet Minh
"employees" who lacked "faith, self respect or honor." The prince told
the Americans that a more serious menace to the throne was "republican-
ism," an idea spread by "outlaws" and leaders of the Democratic Party.
Mentioning former prime minister Huy Kanthoul and other party leaders by name, Sihanouk said that such men were "dangerous," "against the
King," and inadvertently "playing the communist game."[29]

Despite Sihanouk's fears, the Democratic Party was a moribund
political institution with no plans to participate in the general elections
scheduled for 1959. Its leaders, however, continued to meet regularly. Secretary-General Norodom Phurissara and Huy Kanthoul told US embassy
officials that the party's "main line of action" was to try "to exert some
beneficial influence on Sihanouk and the Sangkum." Left unsaid was the
means of exerting such influence. Phurissara and Kanthoul declared that
"the most serious" problem in Cambodia was the parlous state of the kingdom's economy: "Without corruption Cambodia would have a balanced
budget and plenty of money for extensive economic development."[30]

Sihanouk's management of the economy, arguably an opportunistic concern of Democratic Party leaders, "completely disgusted" Cambodia's business community, as Strom put it.[31] Business leaders were also
disturbed by the prince's inconstant approach to governing and by his
refusal to delegate authority. Ung Tin Pak, president of the Chamber of
Commerce and one of Cambodia's wealthiest men, spoke to DCM Godley about "the incredible breakdown of administration in the country, its
lamentable lack of discipline and the impotence of local, provincial and
even national authorities." Pak and his father-in-law, Tan Pa, a wealthy
Chinese business leader, had concluded that Dap Chhuon was the "only
man to lead the country out of its present administrative morass." Pak
added that he and Tan Pa "had made these views known around Phnom
Penh."[32]

This information contributed to Godley's reassessment of Dap
Chhuon as a potential alternative to Sihanouk. Heretofore, Godley and
other US officials had viewed Dap Chhuon as a solitary force incapable of
effectively leading Cambodia. Recent conversations with diplomats and
Cambodian officials, however, convinced the DCM that Dap Chhuon
could successfully head a government or be "pushed as the strong man by

a group that believed Prince Sihanouk should retire from active political life." A French embassy official told Godley that royal councilor Sam Sary "felt a radical change had to occur and that Dap Chhuon was the one man who could effect such a change." Sam Sary had earlier made "treasonous statements" to Godley, declaring that "sound people must stop our Prince" if his policy of neutrality threatened Cambodian security.[33]

"Mac" Godley, then thirty-nine, was a career diplomat who had graduated from Yale and served in the Marine Corps. Unlike Strom, he was fluent in French, mixing easily with Cambodia's elites, including Sihanouk's opposition. Godley observed to Strom that for the first time Dap Chhuon was "supported by a group of intelligent, knowledgeable men with power and money who are willing to place their country's future in his hands." The DCM's bottom line: "I am convinced that if the Queen so wished, he [Dap Chhuon] could easily take control of the country legally or by force and lead it in a fashion satisfactory to US objectives here." Strom, concurring with this estimate, reported to the State Department on May 29, 1957, "Anti-Sihanouk elements [are] turning to Dap Chhuon as their leader. Do not believe [a] violent change will take place within [the] next few days."[34]

With cabinet members openly criticizing Sihanouk, the prince submitted his resignation as prime minister to King Suramarit seven times between May 8 and June 14, 1957. None of the resignations were accepted. The king, queen, and royal councilor Penn Nouth may have realized that quitting "after less than two months in office would do no good at all for Sihanouk's prestige," speculated Robert S. Barrett, a political officer in the US embassy. Another possible reason for refusing the prince's resignation was the risk of "Dap Chhuon becoming premier and then proving hard to dislodge." Indirectly referring to Chhuon, Sihanouk commented to his cabinet that a "certain person" mentioned as a potential prime minister lacked the "capabilities necessary for [the] position."[35]

The king finally accepted Sihanouk's resignation on June 21. Poor health was the stated reason for relinquishing his governing responsibilities, an explanation US officials were inclined to credit, at least partially. "Obviously approaching obesity," the embassy reported to Washington, "[Sihanouk's] breathlessness and fatigue [are] increasingly striking." Uncertain about who would succeed him as prime minister, Strom informed the State Department that Dap Chhuon did not appear to be a candidate: "Some observers opine he is sitting this one out and continuing [to] build his political fences."[36]

Another disparaging article in *Time* in June contributed to Sihanouk's emotional distress. In a story about the crisis in Cambodian governance and administration, the magazine described the prince as "lonely," "unhappy," and "soft." *Time*'s portrait of weak leadership included a derisive characterization of Sam Sary's long-planned decision to observe the 2,500th anniversary of the death of Buddha by temporarily retiring to a monastery: "Sad Sam Sary crawled up to Sihanouk on his hands and knees and asked to be relieved of his economic responsibilities. Distressed to see his friend in this state, Sihanouk acceded to the request. Sam Sary sadly crawled away, had his head and eyebrows shaved, and betook himself to a Buddhist monastery. Sihanouk was so upset himself that he burst into tears."[37]

An immediate consequence of the article was Sihanouk's cancellation of his planned attendance at a dinner honoring him, hosted by Ambassador Strom. In a letter to Kenneth Young, Strom complained about the damaging impact of the magazine's insulting commentary: "If *Time*'s reporting was factual or fair I would not have a thing to say. But it is exasperating to have seven months of patient work with the Prince very largely destroyed by *Time*'s lack of responsibility. I do not object to their opposing our policy with respect to Cambodia if they think it is wrong, but I don't think it is decent to hit below the belt as they have done in their last two articles. Sam Sary's religious devotion should not be the object of sneering comments no matter what *Time* may be trying to accomplish by its reporting."[38]

Although the depth of Sam Sary's religious convictions would soon come into question, US diplomats considered him "one of Cambodia's most able officials." (The State Department also described him as "opportunistic, ambitious, rather ruthless against his political enemies, and not entirely honest.")[39] Then forty years old and one of Sihanouk's five closest advisers, Sam Sary had visited the United States in 1956 as a grantee of the Foreign Leader Program. Sponsored by the State Department, the program sought to promote better understanding of the United States by inviting prominent foreign individuals to design a program of study, typically lasting a few months. Commenting on the embassy's "close relations" with Sary, Strom wrote to Robertson that the Foreign Leader grant had "really paid off. As a result of visiting us he knows what we are doing and why."[40]

To Strom's relief, Sihanouk changed his mind about attending the dinner in his honor on June 28. Described by the embassy as an "affable" guest, the prince once again thanked the United States for its assistance to the Cambodian government and people.[41] Some two weeks later, however, Sihanouk was back on the attack, denouncing the United States in a speech before the semiannual Sangkum national congress. Alleging that the US government provided financial support to the Democratic Party, Sihanouk declared, according to Strom's report, "The Americans are not pleased with me because I follow a program of neutrality which doesn't make them happy, it is contrary to their policy. They want to overthrow me, and they have given this task of eliminating me to the Democrats."[42]

Ambassador Strom was horrified by Sihanouk's "incredible outburst," which was broadcast over national radio. "I can only explain his remarks in terms of [his] extreme volatility and unpredictability, and lingering rancor over the June 10 TIME article," Strom reported to the State Department. "Until [the] appearance [of] that article, his public attitude toward me and all Embassy officers was most cordial and pleasant."[43] The ambassador's emphasis on the difficulties created by *Time*'s commentary and by Sihanouk's hypersensitivity ignored his own and McClintock's diplomatic deficiencies and the Eisenhower administration's hostility toward the prince's concept of neutrality. Strom's reporting also suggested a limited appreciation of the disturbing impact on Sihanouk of US officials freely associating with his political opposition.

With the prince retiring to a Buddhist monastery for two weeks, Strom and Godley met with Penn Nouth on July 24. The royal councilor had recently offered to be helpful if a difficult situation arose, and Strom was eager to avoid a "bitter and acrimonious incident."[44] Providing Nouth with a transcript of Sihanouk's remarks, Strom said that the prince's speech had "greatly disturbed" him and "caused a certain amount of consternation in the Department of State in Washington." Categorically rejecting the accusations of providing money to the Democrats and seeking to overthrow the prince, Strom said that he would eventually have to make a formal denial. Before taking such a step, however, he "felt in need of advice from someone who possessed wisdom and foresight and whom he could approach on a friendly and personal basis, completely unofficially."[45]

Strom's flattery had little impact on Penn Nouth, who remained a loyal retainer and a tough negotiator. Nouth appeared puzzled by the transcript in Khmer and questioned its accuracy. When Strom offered to provide him with a tape recording of the speech, Nouth said that he would have to get an official version of Sihanouk's remarks from the Ministry of Information. After further discussion, Nouth said that he could not comment on the speech until he had spoken with the prince. According to Strom's report of the meeting, Nouth referred to Sihanouk's "extreme nervous tension" since the publication of the *Time* article and a critical story in the *Observer* (London): "He implied that Sihanouk had been acting somewhat irresponsibly ever since these articles appeared."[46]

In response to Strom's démarche, Sihanouk released a statement "clarifying" his remarks at the Sangkum conference. He denied ever accusing the United States of giving money to the Democrats and did not mention the allegation that the United States wanted to overthrow him. This statement had "obvious defects," Strom wrote to the State Department, and he considered Sihanouk "a spoiled and willful brat." Nonetheless, the ambassador recommended that the United States drop the matter. The incident had attracted minimal attention locally and no coverage in the United States. Moreover, Sim Var, the new prime minister, had expressed regret over the speech and hoped the prince's clarification would satisfy the US government. Then fifty-one, Sim Var was an elder statesman in Cambodian politics. An ardent nationalist and Sihanouk loyalist, he was an independent-minded official who supported Cambodian neutrality but "consistently warned against excessive friendliness with the Communist bloc."[47]

Sihanouk, who returned from his religious retreat in a belligerent mood, challenged the Democrats to a debate on national issues. Reluctant to participate, Democratic leaders requested that their audience with the prince be private. Sihanouk accepted this condition but then reneged on his commitment, broadcasting the debate live from the palace on national radio. The so-called confrontation was a one-sided farce, with the cowed Democrats meekly professing their loyalty to Sihanouk. Adding injury to insult, soldiers beat up four of the debaters on their way out of the palace. Over the next three days, the Cambodian military assaulted some forty civilians for their alleged affiliation with the Democrats. This violence—which the US embassy characterized as "moderate" but "extreme for Cambodia"—led to the "virtual disappearance" of the Democratic Party. "The elimination of the only non-Communist alternative to the Sangkum," wrote Strom, "can only result in the eventual driving of all opposition elements into an absolute opposition to the regime."[48]

Sihanouk left Phnom Penh for France on August 20, 1957. To US embassy officials, he seemed in a "despondent" mood and a "tortured" state of mind, an assessment informed by reports from his French physician. The Americans found public confirmation of their diagnosis in a *Réalités Cambodgiennes* article expressing the belief that the prince's trip would help him recover the "serenity which [is] often impossible [to] maintain in [the] present political climate."[49] Sihanouk, traveling through Saigon to board the SS *Vietnam,* declined an invitation to meet with Diem, who had arranged to receive him with appropriate honors. Speaking to Elbridge Durbrow, the US ambassador to South Vietnam, "Diem reiterated his low opinion of Sihanouk."[50]

Shortly after Sihanouk's departure, the Cambodian government "launched violent press attacks against South Vietnam."[51] *La Dépêche du Cambodge,* a newspaper published by Sim Var, described the buildup of South Vietnamese military forces near the Cambodian border. Tim Dong, the kingdom's secretary of state for information, went on national radio quoting communist press accusations that South Vietnam was "doing [the] dirty work of SEATO imperialist[s] and preparing for [a] military incursion [into] Cambodia to destroy [its] neutral policy."[52]

On October 11, the *Times of Vietnam,* a pro-Diem daily published by a former employee of the US Information Service, responded with an article that was critical of Sihanouk. Prime Minister Sim Var went before the National Assembly to denounce the "unfortunate" timing of the story—Cambodia and South Vietnam were about to discuss "mutual problems." He asked the South Vietnamese government "to show that it could not have encouraged such an insult to Sihanouk." US embassy officials in Phnom Penh concluded that the likelihood of Cambodian–South Vietnamese talks were "dim in view [of the] present exacerbated feelings and [the] fact President Diem does not seem to take Cambodian willingness [to] negotiate very seriously."[53]

Sihanouk, whose period of rest and recuperation was expected to last only two months, extended his stay in France. On October 24, he participated in the ceremonial opening of a government-sponsored Cambodian student center in Paris. A small but important constituency exposed to republican and communist political ideas, the students in France were disturbed by the lack of white-collar jobs in the kingdom and by "the venality of Cambodian officials and the corruption in official life," according to the CIA. In his speech, Sihanouk stressed "the duty of the Cambodian elite to respect the Cambodian ethos, religion, and monarchy."[54] In two subsequent addresses to Cambodian students, he acknowledged their unhappiness, defended the Sangkum, and attacked the Democratic Party and communism. Appealing for national unity, the prince emphasized that "Cambodian political life cannot be conducted according to the experience of other countries, above all not that of France."[55]

After his speeches in Paris, Sihanouk "apparently devoted himself to own amusement," according to US embassy officials in Phnom Penh. King Suramarit seemed to be "disgusted by [Sihanouk's] failure [to] return or even disclose [his] whereabouts."[56] On December 13, the prince finally arrived in Cambodia, noticeably trimmer but without the usual advance announcement or welcoming ceremonies. After three days of public silence, he spoke on national radio, declaring that he did not want to lead the government. If he were prime minister, said Sihanouk, his political enemies would soon create insurmountable obstacles to effective governing. Praising Sim Var's performance as prime minister and encouraging the inclusion of "young intellectuals" in government, Sihanouk concluded his speech with a "solemn appeal" for his opponents to join the Sangkum. "Former opposition leaders," Strom informed the State Department, "[are] reportedly convinced this appeal [is] really serious and that [the] Prince will dissolve parties by force unless they in effect dissolve themselves."[57]

In his quest for national unity, Sihanouk denounced Cambodian communists on four separate occasions at the Sangkum national congress of January 4–6, 1958. After the congress, he told Ambassador Strom that propaganda by communists in Cambodia "had gone beyond the permissible limit." Pointing to the publication of "particularly objectionable brochures and pamphlets," the prince noted that "the Communists had adopted the technique of the repeated lie, which inevitably some Cambodians would believe." On January 10, an estimated five thousand Cambodians participated in a government-organized anticommunist demonstration. Petitions supported the throne and opposed the "Khmer Viet Minh, the trouble makers who weaken neutrality and sabotage the policy carried out by Sihanouk."[58]

The prince's aspirations for Cambodian unity were undermined by a bitter fight between Sim Var's cabinet and the deputies of the National Assembly. While Sihanouk was in France, the cabinet had angered the legislators by limiting their opportunities for graft. The National Assembly responded by launching investigations into alleged cabinet improprieties. Sihanouk, criticizing the deputies' irresponsibility, resolved the dispute by having his father dissolve the National Assembly on January 8. This drastic step, which included a constitutional obligation to hold elections for a new assembly within two months, benefited the prince politically. "By moving up the date of the elections normally scheduled for 1959," US embassy officials reported to Washington, "the opposition and the Communists in particular are deprived of the opportunity for a year's further preparation for the campaign." To ensure the nomination of "good" legislators, Sihanouk announced that "he would take full responsibility for the selection of Sangkum candidates."[59]

Sihanouk's anticommunist pronouncements at the Sangkum congress attracted the attention of the US press. A widely circulated Associated Press report declared that he "had turned against the Communists he previously had patronized." On January 20, 1958, in an article titled "Late Wisdom," *Time* magazine called the prince's remarks "his most forthright anti-Communist speech to date." Disturbed by the implication that Cambodia was now siding with the West in the cold war, Sihanouk responded in *Réalités Cambodgiennes*. In an article promoted by the Cambodian government as a major policy statement, he denied any deviation from strict neutrality and said that he would "never be 'wise' in [the] sense TIME wants."[60]

Sihanouk was less restrained in his response to an editorial in the *Times* of London on March 5. Headlined "Living on Aid," the editorial noted the ten changes in the Cambodian government since the elections in 1955 and attributed this instability to the prince's "mercurial temperament." Commenting on the diverse sources of economic assistance to Cambodia, the *Times* concluded that there was an "obvious need" for a government capable of administering foreign aid in an efficient and honest manner. Sihanouk responded to the editorial by lashing out at "the arrogance shown by the Anglo-Saxons in their treatment of neutrals and small countries." Henry Norman Brain, the UK ambassador to Cambodia, wrote to the Foreign Office: "This is the first time that the Prince has publicly attacked British policy in this way and it is hard to believe that we would have been so bitterly pilloried but for the appearance of 'The Times' article."[61]

In a letter to the king dated March 22, Sihanouk implied that newspapers in the United States, Great Britain, and Thailand were conspiring to undermine the Sangkum and "make a criminal of me." Evidence of a "premeditated accord," the prince wrote, was the three countries' common foreign policy and their membership in SEATO. These states were showing "their anger at seeing that they, who are giants, are incapable of making me, an ant compared to them, change my policy of neutrality." Sihanouk appealed to the king for government help in finding "a means of wiping out the affront that these nations have given us, contrary to the principles of international law."[62]

While waging a war of words against his real and imagined enemies, Sihanouk energetically campaigned for his handpicked Sangkum candidates, virtually all of whom ran unopposed. At each campaign stop, the prince would speak to villagers and distribute cloth coupons that were redeemable at government cooperatives. Responding to effective door-to-door campaigning by the handful of Pracheachon candidates—no Democrats ran for assembly seats—the Cambodian government unleashed the secret police to harass and intimidate the opposition. To no one's surprise, Sihanouk's candidates captured every National Assembly seat in the elections, held on March 23, 1958. US embassy officials reported that the results were a "tribute" to Sihanouk's personal drawing power and to effective organizing by the Sangkum and local authorities. The embassy also acknowledged that "largely psychological" pressure by the police had a "definite role" in the campaign.[63]

Sihanouk's overwhelming electoral triumph provided him with little peace or satisfaction. He was particularly disturbed by a Thai newspaper article quoting charges by Son Ngoc Thanh that Sihanouk "was responsible for the growth of Communism in Cambodia." The day after the elections, the prince made an emotional speech on national radio devoted almost exclusively to denouncing Son Ngoc Thanh. Describing himself as "bitter and sad," Sihanouk said that as a king and prince he had "met with only hatred and opposition." He concluded his remarks by declaring, "Fellow countrymen, my responsibility is finished. I have saved my country from a political storm and I would like to hear you tell me when I can put an end to my political life."[64]

Ending Sihanouk's political life remained Son Ngoc Thanh's enduring goal. In 1957, Thanh had formed the Khmer Serei. A successor organization to the noncommunist Khmer Issarak bands, the Khmer Serei comprised armed dissidents who received covert support from Thailand and South Vietnam. Thai army commander Sarit Thanarat, who overthrew Phibun Songgram and Phao Sriyanon that same year, retained the previous regime's interest in intriguing against Sihanouk. In 1965, the *National Intelligence Survey*, the comprehensive CIA-produced source of basic intelligence on individual countries, summarized early Thai support for the Khmer Serei: "Reports indicate that approximately 1,000 rebels were located along the Thai–Cambodian border and were receiving assistance from Bangkok. These elements reportedly received training and equipment from Thai Army and police units in early 1958. They had been integrated into the local economy and engaged in farming, cattle raising, and other pursuits. Liaison with the rebels was handled directly by the office of the Prime Minister and was closely monitored by former Prime Minister Sarit Thanarat."[65]

South Vietnam's military, logistic, and financial support for the Khmer Serei was even "more extensive than Thailand's," according to the *National Intelligence Survey*. Thanh, well aware of the military weakness of his rebel band, believed "in the importance of psychological warfare in order to erode Cambodian confidence in Sihanouk." In 1957, the South Vietnamese government gave the rebels a civilian truck mounted with a radio transmitter to broadcast propaganda into Cambodia. The Diem regime also "began training *Khmer Serei* rebels in 1957 at a secret base in Binh Long Province." Other paramilitary-training centers in South Vietnam were subsequently established. In a memorandum to President Lyndon B. Johnson, dated June 14, 1966, NSC staffer James C. Thomson Jr. explained the basic operating principles of the Khmer Serei: "The GVN [Government of South Vietnam] trains Cambodians and ships them to Thailand[,] where they are then put into action on the Cambodia border in order to broadcast anti-Sihanouk appeals and to foment frontier incidents."[66]

Details about CIA support for the Khmer Serei in the 1950s are hard to pin down with precision. Relevant CIA operational files remain classified, and declassified "finished" intelligence reports for the national security bureaucracy excluded discussions of US covert operations for reasons of security and plausible deniability. "One of the theological bug-a-boos of American intelligence was the so-called American factor, which was supposed to be off limits in our commentaries," recalled Thomas L. Hughes, a former director of intelligence and research at the State Department. "In a curiously antiseptic view, US intelligence analysts were not supposed to consider or refer to the covert American role in situations they were analyzing."[67]

Despite the limited documentary record of clandestine American assistance to Son Ngoc Thanh and the Khmer Serei, statements by former officials confirm that the United States provided such support. "It is indisputable that the Agency did in fact give covert support to Sihanouk's long arch-rival, Son Ngoc Thanh, and his Khmer Serei rebels in the late 1950s," wrote James Thomson in the early 1970s.[68] In 1977, William E. Colby, whose positions at the CIA included chief of station in Saigon, head of far eastern operations, and DCI, told British writer William Shawcross that "the US was working with Son Ngoc Thanh."[69] (Another statement by Colby—this time to a Senate committee investigating US intelligence activities—provided insight into the attitude of many US officials toward Sihanouk: "There was a suggestion [from an 'expert'] that it would be possible to put some kind of a drug or something in a book to be given to—which, if it could be gotten to Prince Sihanouk would have given him some serious disease.")[70]

There is a Holmesian dog-that-did-not-bark aspect to the declassified history of US contacts with Son Ngoc Thanh. At the National Archives, the State Department's declassified records include many appeals by Son Ngoc Thanh to the United States for assistance. These unsuccessful requests come to an abrupt halt in 1956. The absence of declassified approaches by Thanh to the US government during the rest of the 1950s suggests one of two possibilities. First, Son Ngoc Thanh, discouraged by negative US responses, simply stopped seeking American help in toppling Sihanouk. This seems an unlikely course of action for someone the CIA characterized as "tenacious and persevering."[71] The second, more likely possibility, is that communications with Son Ngoc Thanh after 1956 were handled by the CIA through covert channels and remain classified.

There is another, more fundamental reason for concluding that the CIA began to assist Son Ngoc Thanh and the Khmer Serei sometime after 1956: doing so was consistent with US policy. On April 2, 1958, Eisenhower reaffirmed American support for Sihanouk's opposition by approving NSC 5809. Superseding NSC 5612/1, the new directive for mainland Southeast Asia repeated verbatim the earlier policy guidance for Cambodia: "In order to maintain Cambodia's independence and to reverse the drift toward pro-communist neutrality, encourage individuals and groups in Cambodia who oppose dealing with the Communist bloc and who would serve to broaden the political power base in Cambodia." The regional courses of actions outlined in NSC 5809 also repeated the authorization for "covert operations designed to assist in the achievement of U.S. objectives in Southeast Asia."[72]

On April 4, 1958, two South Vietnamese security officers who had entered Cambodia bearing diplomatic passports kidnapped an anti-Diem dissident in Phnom Penh. The dissident escaped in Svay Rieng Province, and the Cambodian police arrested the two kidnappers. Seeking their release, Ngo Trong Hieu, the South Vietnamese representative in Phnom Penh, approached the Cambodian Foreign Ministry with a proposition: the Diem government would free fifty-seven Cambodian peasants who had been arrested in March on the South Vietnamese side of the border in exchange for the release of the two kidnappers. The arrest of peasants, who had allegedly stolen cattle and included fifteen women and four children, was disturbing enough to the Cambodian government. The Vietnamese attempt to hold women and children as hostages "greatly exacerbated" the incident, Strom wrote to the American embassy in Saigon. The Cambodian government was "now seriously considering terminating the Vietnamese representation" there.[73]

The arrest of the peasants and "the general problem of Cambodian–Vietnamese relations" prompted Strom to schedule a meeting with US diplomats and intelligence officials in Saigon. Because a broken foot prevented him from traveling, Strom sent Edmund H. Kellogg, Godley's successor as DCM. A graduate of Princeton and Harvard Law School,

Kellogg was an intelligence officer during World War II who disseminated the highly classified German Ultra intercepts to Allied commanders. After the war, according to Strom, Kellogg's work was "divided between intelligence matters and UN affairs," presumably on behalf of the CIA. He was "integrated" into the Foreign Service in 1954, initially serving as an inspector of US missions overseas. His first field assignment for the State Department was as DCM in Phnom Penh. In March 1958, Kellogg distinguished himself by arranging the defection of a second secretary from the Soviet embassy in Phnom Penh, an operation Strom praised for its absence of US "fingerprints."[74]

Kellogg's meeting with US officials in Saigon on May 20 produced hard feelings on both sides. "He could not find a flicker of interest in the subject of Cambodian relations in the top command," wrote Strom. Ambassador Elbridge Durbrow, who was on home leave at that time, reported that "his boys"—DCM Howard Elting Jr., political counselor Thomas D. Bowie, and CIA chief of station Nicholas Natsios—thought Kellogg had "an obsession with the problem of RKG [Royal Khmer Government]–GVN relations almost to the exclusion of other issues." The US officials in Saigon were disturbed to learn that Kellogg, in Durbrow's words, "was devoting little time to analyzing or reporting on communist activities and strategy in Cambodia. The only villain in the piece seemed to be Viet Nam. It was difficult, if not impossible in these conversations, not only to distinguish between Kellogg's personal reactions and Cambodian reactions, but even to get him to listen to what our people had to say."[75]

Kellogg's request to Natsios for assistance in adding a Vietnamese to the CIA station in Phnom Penh was rejected out of hand. The idea of hiring a Vietnamese to spy on his countrymen was a "preposterous [idea]—at least as presented," wrote Durbrow.[76] Strom later insisted that there must have been some sort of misunderstanding between Kellogg and Natsios. The Phnom Penh mission had two Chinese Americans on staff who provided useful reports on the Chinese minority in Cambodia. When CIA chief of station Roger Goiran arrived in Phnom Penh in early 1958, Strom told him, "I should like to have access to non-Communist Vietnamese elements similar to that which we already had to non-Communist Chinese groups." Acknowledging the small number of Americans of Vietnamese descent, Strom hoped to find a US "missionary's son who could speak Vietnamese and who could do this job for us."[77]

To some US officials, the misunderstandings between the American missions in Phnom Penh and Saigon appeared to be a case of "localitis"— a diplomatic malady in which envoys indiscriminately advocate the interests of the countries hosting them. For Durbrow and his colleagues, helping Diem suppress the Vietnamese communists was the overriding objective. To them, any "obsession" with the problems Diem created for the neutralist Sihanouk indicated "a serious lack of balance and perspective."[78] To Strom, however, it seemed that Diem's provocations would have the undesirable effect of pushing the prince closer to China. In a letter to Eric Kocher, then director of the State Department's Office of Southeast Asian Affairs, Strom wrote, "Cambodia's minimum demands against South Vietnam must be satisfied before long if we are to avoid real trouble in this part of the world."[79]

7

"Numerous Reports of Plots" (1958)

On June 18, 1958, an estimated fifteen hundred ARVN troops surrounded Ban Pak Nay, a Cambodian village in the hilly, jungle-covered border area of Stung Treng Province. The soldiers, reportedly two battalions from the ARVN 181st Regiment, may have been looking for ninety political prisoners who had escaped from their South Vietnamese captors and crossed into Cambodian territory seeking asylum. During the operation, ARVN soldiers erected a new boundary marker, ringed with barbed wire, some eighteen hundred meters inside Cambodian territory. A subsequent inspection of the enclosed area by an ICC military team revealed hidden antipersonnel mines.[1]

After hearing fragmentary initial reports of the Stung Treng incident, Cambodian officials appealed to the ICC to investigate. The commission delayed dispatching a military team because of Canada's minority view that investigations of border incidents involving South Vietnam exceeded the ICC's mandate. Canadian commissioner Eric H. Gilmour, using obstructionist tactics that the West associated with the Poles, not only requested more time to study Cambodia's brief diplomatic notes but also objected to ICC consideration of verbally transmitted government information. Major General Ghanshyam Singh, chairman of the ICC for Cambodia, said that he was "astonished" that the Canadian commissioner sought to exclude verbal comments from the prime minister of Cambodia.[2]

Perhaps influenced by the ICC's procedural torpor, the Cambodian government issued an alarmist proclamation on June 25, denouncing the "invasion" and alleging that South Vietnamese forces "were actively organizing themselves with a view to an attack in depth." The proclamation included a specific request to the United States to stop South Vietnam's "aggressive annexationist activities." Outgoing prime minister Sim Var, who had just been censured by the National Assembly for his handling of economic affairs, told the press that Cambodia would turn to "other friendly powers" if the United States did not restrain South Vietnam. On June 27, Sihanouk asked the United States to participate in a multinational commission to verify the accuracy of the Cambodian claims.[3]

The Diem government denied any South Vietnamese violation of Cambodian territory. US military officials, however, thought it probable that ARVN units had entered Cambodia. The State Department sought to downplay the seriousness of the border incident, but the Cambodian government was determined to substantiate its complaint against South Vietnam. During a meeting with Canadian diplomat Norman Robertson on June 30, Assistant Secretary of State Walter Robertson observed that the Cambodian reaction to the Stung Treng incident was "somewhat psychopathic." In an indirect reference to the Cambodian appeal for US intervention in the dispute, he declared, "We are not going to get in the middle of this one."[4]

The State Department informed Ambassador Carl Strom that a direct US role in mediating Cambodia's disagreement with South Vietnam would be "unwise." One reason for this hands-off attitude was a lack of clarity about the Cambodian government's motive for requesting US intervention. Washington officials were concerned that Prince Sihanouk might be more interested in discrediting an anticommunist ally of the United States than in settling differences through good-faith negotiations. Another reason for avoiding a formal US role in the dispute was that only Cambodia had requested American "good offices." In 1956, when US diplomats had helped resolve the Cambodian–South Vietnamese trade embargoes, both countries had requested American mediation. The State Department instructed Strom to point out to Cambodian officials that South Vietnam "is independent and takes action over which the US has no influence."[5]

The absence of US influence with South Vietnam was not a credible argument with Sihanouk, who said, "We are bitterly disappointed our appeals have been unheeded."[6] Voted full powers by Parliament to deal with the Stung Treng incident, the prince announced that he would personally visit Saigon and Bangkok to seek settlements with President Ngo Dinh Diem and Prime Minister Sarit Thanarat. Sihanouk said that Cambodia would try to reduce its international isolation through more "active" neutrality and visits to India, China, and other countries. On July 3, Ambassador Strom delivered a diplomatic note to the Cambodian Foreign Ministry welcoming Sihanouk's "wise initiative" to visit Saigon and Bangkok. The note also communicated the embassy's disingenuous assumption that requests for US intervention in the dispute with South Vietnam had been "superseded by events."[7]

Offensive articles in the South Vietnamese press quickly derailed Sihanouk's planned trip to Saigon. On July 3, the French-language paper *La Gazette de Saigon* attacked the prince in the story "A Ninny's Policy." On July 4, an editorial in the *Times of Vietnam* that described Sihanouk as spoiled, emotional, erratic, and foolish declared, "Though we value friendship with [the] Cambodian people we do not think negotiations with Sihanouk at present serve any purpose."[8] Ambassador to South Vietnam Elbridge Durbrow speculated that Ngo Dinh Nhu, Diem's conspiratorial younger brother and political councilor, was behind the editorial in the *Times of Vietnam.* The ambassador later reported to Washington that Nhu had approved the insulting Gazette article without informing the South Vietnamese president.[9]

Sihanouk, in addition to canceling his visit to Saigon, responded to the South Vietnamese articles by blaming them on the United States and denouncing American indifference to the Stung Treng incident. In a speech on July 5, he said,

> While [the Cambodian government] has asked [the] US to go to verify facts on the spot, [the] US contents itself to say, of what use? The incident is closed[,] as has been established. The free world insults us and we are to blame but it refuses to verify our charges. How can they say we are guilty if they refuse to check? The US considered my meeting with Diem a good idea but sensing that this meeting might bear fruit and that new violations might not recur they pushed the (Vietnamese) newspapers and the members of the government to oppose the meeting.[10]

Perhaps most disturbing to US policymakers was Sihanouk's thinly veiled threat to seek closer relations with the PRC: "For our tranquility we ought to choose a great ally who is not too far from us and who is ready to aid us. I do not mean that we want an ally as in the time of the protectorate. I do not think we ought to go as far as that. Our peaceful means have not yet been exhausted. On the other hand we should not hesitate to find [a] flesh-and-bones ally to prepare ourselves against every eventuality."[11]

To Ambassador Strom, it seemed that Cambodia was at a "crossroads." He thought that Sihanouk still viewed Western countries as "Cambodia's true friends" and that closer ties to the "Communist bloc would be basically distasteful to him." Strom, increasingly out of step with US officials in Washington and Saigon, reminded the State Department of his recommendations to "intervene in [a] strong and unequivocal fashion with [the] GVN to require them to settle their difficulties with Cambodia." Unpersuaded by the department's claim that the United States could not tell the South Vietnamese government "what to do," he wrote that the absence of "firm action" by the United States had allowed Diem to pursue a Cambodian policy that was "exactly contrary" to Western interests. Strom urged Washington "to insist" that Diem negotiate with Cambodia in good faith.[12]

Ambassador Durbrow, asked by the State Department to comment on Strom's analysis, disagreed, observing that Cambodia did "not appear to be at [a] crossroads but rather somewhat past that point along [a] road to the left." A career Foreign Service officer whose three tours of duty in Moscow had made him "a 100-percent containment man," Durbrow noted that Sihanouk had extended diplomatic recognition to the Soviet Union, had allowed China to open an economic mission in Phnom Penh, and had accepted aid from both communist countries. He considered the prince an "opportunist" and thought that his talk about closer relations with "a great ally" was either a "smokescreen" or "crude blackmail." Acknowledging unhelpful actions by South Vietnamese officials, Durbrow thought that Sihanouk "deliberately elected to exacerbate Cambodian–Vietnamese relations and that [the] time has clearly come for us to call his bluff."[13]

Durbrow had already urged Diem to make some gesture that would improve South Vietnam's relations with Cambodia. The appeal fell on deaf ears. It was "impossible to reason with [Sihanouk]," said Diem. One could "not count on Sihanouk to keep his word." Diem, optimistic about the prospects for a political upheaval in Cambodia, told Durbrow that the "Cambodian people [are] getting fed up [with] Sihanouk's changing attitudes and actions." Within six months to a year, the South Vietnamese president predicted, the politicians and intellectuals would "get rid of him." When asked who might take control of the government, Diem "spoke highly" of Yem Sambaur, a former prime minister who had served in Cambodian cabinets between 1953 and 1956. Within the royal family, Diem praised Sihanouk's uncle, Prince Monireth, describing him as "an intelligent sensible man who also is fed up."[14]

One potential plotter mentioned by Diem was Sam Sary, who was reportedly "issuing derogatory pamphlets to foreigners exposing Sihanouk's machinations."[15] Sary had returned to Phnom Penh on June 24, 1958, after serving as the Cambodian ambassador to the United Kingdom for only five months. He was recalled from London after two UK newspapers reported that he and his wife had beaten a young Cambodian woman who was a live-in governess as well as Sary's mistress. Sam Rainsy, Sary's son and nine years old at the time, later wrote that his "long-suffering mother" was the sole assailant. His father, however, accepted responsibility for the beating, commenting that such "punishment is common in my country."[16]

Upon his return to Phnom Penh, Sam Sary immediately became embroiled in an ugly public dispute with Sim Var and other longtime political rivals, who accused him not only of "disgracing the nation" but also of disobeying government orders. Sary responded in kind, calling his attackers desperate ministers who were trying "by all means to hang onto power and [were] now busy discrediting all friends of democracy." Phnom Penh's atmosphere of intrigue can be inferred from Sam Sary's comment to Ambassador Strom that "he could not be away from the royal palace more than a few minutes without his absence attracting undue attention."[17]

Sary made this statement on July 7—the same day he informed Strom that Prince Sihanouk had decided against resuming his role as prime minister. The reason for this decision, said Sary, was Sihanouk's realization that the Saigon press attacks had "made it clear he would be unable [to] arrive at a settlement with the Vietnamese." Sary further revealed that the king had asked him to form a government. This request, said Sary, put him in a difficult position. On the one hand, he did not want to disappoint the king. On the other hand, his previous experience in government suggested that he would have "frequent collisions with Sihanouk" and a short tenure as prime minister, perhaps "no more than two or three days." Sam Sary asked Strom "to advise him as a friend" whether it would be worthwhile to form a government with such unpromising prospects.[18]

In light of subsequent events, it is reasonable to wonder whether Sam Sary was discreetly angling for a sign of US support for some action that might reduce Sihanouk's political power. If so, he received no encouragement from Strom. According to his report of the meeting, the ambassador told Sary that "he was one of the few people around who had his feet on the ground." What Strom did not say was his belief that Sary could not attract broad political support. Wishing Sary luck if he formed a government, Strom wrote to Washington expressing certainty "that a Sam Sary government would be in trouble from the day of its formation and that the whole proposal represents a rather forlorn hope as far as we are concerned."[19]

During a meeting with Sihanouk the next day, Strom heard nothing that confirmed Sam Sary's dubious story about a royal request to form a government. In fact, the ambassador received the impression that the prince was "still definitely in [the] driver's seat."[20] Strom had sought the audience with Sihanouk to discuss his anti-American speech of July 5. The ambassador "denied categorically" that the United States had sabotaged the prince's planned trip to Saigon. Sihanouk replied that Diem's representative in Cambodia, Ngo Trong Hieu, had told him the "Americans were responsible" for the South Vietnamese press attacks.[21]

When Strom referred to the prince's comment about Cambodia's need for "an ally not too far distant," Sihanouk said that he needed support to counter South Vietnam and Thailand's "nibbling away at the border." Strom then mentioned the persistent rumor that Cambodia was looking toward China as a new ally. Sihanouk replied that Cambodia's policy of "pure neutrality" had not been working well, but there had been no decision to abandon it or to "look for another ally." According to Strom, Sihanouk "resolute[ly] avoided mentioning China." Royal councilor Penn Nouth, however, declared that "Cambodia had asked all well-disposed nations to help them and no one has responded except Red China."[22]

After the meeting, Strom discussed his conversation with Sihanouk with the diplomatic representatives of France, the United Kingdom, and Australia. He appealed for their help in warning the prince of the danger of pursuing closer relations with China. According to a Canadian official, Strom also sought the diplomats' assistance in convincing "the Vietnamese that they are misguided in their present belief that Sihanouk is about to fall and it is in our interests that this should happen."[23] In a cable to the State Department on July 10, Strom wrote:

> It is my view and that of my western colleagues in Phnom Penh that Diem is in general badly informed on [the] political situation in Cambodia, probably in large part as a result of the slanted reporting by Ngo Trong Hieu, who is believed here to have twisted his reports to suit Diem's known attitude toward Sihanouk. Even granted all Diem's reasons for dissatisfaction with Sihanouk, I strongly doubt [the] wisdom from [the] GVN and western points of view of encouraging any moves to replace him. [The] overthrow of Sihanouk, assuming this [is] possible, would inevitably be followed by [a] period of chaos as new forces emerged.[24]

When informed by a "high-ranking" Cambodian source that Sihanouk would "definitely" seek closer relations with China and perhaps even a military-assistance agreement, Ambassador Strom blamed Diem for the "present crisis in Cambodian affairs." In another cable to the State Department on July 10, Strom declared that the United States must "eliminate [the] dichotomy in US and Vietnamese policy vis-à-vis Cambodia" and "reestablish Cambodian confidence in US good faith." His most recent instructions from the department, urging Sihanouk to travel to Saigon and to ignore South Vietnamese press attacks, "do practically nothing to serve this end." The situation, Strom wrote, required "something of a more positive or dramatic nature if I am to accomplish anything." He suggested a visit to the region by Assistant Secretary Robertson to resolve the differences in US and South Vietnamese policy. The announcement of such a trip would demonstrate US interest in Cambodia's problems with South Vietnam and "satisfy Sihanouk for [the] time being."[25]

Strom's appeal received little sympathy from the State Department. With Robertson on leave, J. Graham Parsons, who had been appointed deputy assistant secretary earlier in the year, replied on his boss's behalf.

Well aware of Robertson's low opinion of Sihanouk and neutralism, Parsons thought that the proposed visit to the region was "out of [the] question." (This judgment may also have been influenced by Robertson's health problems, which included an ulcer and migraine headaches.) "It [is] difficult [to] know how to remove [the] 'dichotomy' in U.S. and Viet-Nam policy towards Cambodia," Parsons declared to Strom. "We cannot require Diem to do what we wish."[26]

If Sihanouk wanted to sign a military treaty with China because the United States failed "to impose on Viet-Nam what he wants," Parsons did "not see what we can do to stop [him]." Parsons also implicitly rejected Strom's judgment that Diem was responsible for the crisis, observing that both Cambodia and South Vietnam shared a "measure of fault." In Parsons's view, the US government would "support any orderly approach to [a] settlement but there is nothing of [a] dramatic nature which we can ask you to tell Sihanouk."[27]

An orderly, negotiated settlement with Cambodia was not Diem's preferred option for resolving his differences with Sihanouk. At a meeting with Durbrow on July 16, Diem told Durbrow "pointedly for [the] first time [that] he felt Sihanouk should be induced to relinquish power and leave [the] country." Referring to the bloody overthrow of the monarchy in Iraq three days earlier, Diem said with a smile that "no one should of course try to assassinate Sihanouk." Durbrow, who had continued to urge Diem to establish good relations with Cambodia, said there was no evidence of Sihanouk losing his popularity with the people. "It would be most dangerous and very risky for anybody to try to maneuver to eliminate Sihanouk," said the ambassador. Diem replied: "While Sihanouk [is] undoubtedly popular with [the] easy-going Cambodian peasants, there are many thinking people who fear he is driving [the] country to ruin."[28]

Diem repeated this theme at a meeting with Durbrow two days later. This time Diem specifically mentioned the "Cambodian national hero," Son Ngoc Thanh, who was "now in Thailand" and a "potential leader" of the opposition. Durbrow emphasized that the US government "had no information confirming" Cambodian opposition to the prince and that "efforts to overthrow Sihanouk would only play into [the] Communists' hands." Diem replied that a "careful reading" of the situation would reveal that "many thinking people are worried [that] Sihanouk's ambitions, sensational publicity stunts, and war scares will bring [the] country to ruin and therefore [they] are seriously thinking of getting rid of him." Diem's insistent claim of growing opposition to Sihanouk, Durbrow warned the State Department, might indicate that Diem was "actively trying [to] operate in this field."[29]

On Saturday, July 19, 1958, Sihanouk informed Pierre Gorce, the French ambassador to Cambodia, that he had agreed to extend full diplomatic recognition to the PRC, including an exchange of ambassadors. The prince, Gorce informed Strom, said that he had been under "continuous pressure" from China for closer relations over the past two years. During that period, the West had failed to support Cambodia in resisting the "aggressive attitude [of the] Vietnamese and Thais." Gorce told Strom that a public announcement of Sihanouk's decision would be made within a few days.[30]

To confirm this and other reports of Cambodia's recognition of China, the State Department instructed Strom to seek an immediate appointment with Sihanouk. If the prince did not deny these reports, Strom should express "concern" over an action that would harm the interests of the United States and Cambodia's neighbors and that would likely preclude an early settlement of Sihanouk's problems with Diem: "Viet-Nam has had to fight for its life against Communists to [the] north and Diem[,] who has faced great odds in [the] past[,] could hardly be expected to come to terms with Cambodia just after [the] latter's recognition [of] its mortal enemy."[31]

Strom replied that he would carry out his instructions but reported that Sihanouk was out of town and would be unavailable for a few days. Repeating his unsuccessful appeal for a more active US role in reducing tension between Cambodia and South Vietnam, Strom wrote: "It would immeasurably increase [the] effectiveness [of] my representations if I could give [Sihanouk] assurance of some specific assistance in obtaining [a] settlement." The ambassador, again identifying Diem as the "principal reason" for the discord between the two countries, declared that South Vietnam's policy conflict with the United States was "intolerable and must be resolved whether Cambodia recognizes Red China or not." And despite the department's obvious reluctance to intervene in the dispute, Strom proposed that the United States "should now offer our good offices toward [a] general settlement [of] Cambodian–Vietnamese problems."[32]

Ambassador Durbrow, who received a copy of Strom's appeal to the State Department, opposed giving Sihanouk "some definite assurance" of US involvement in the resolution of his problems with Diem. Durbrow explained that he had "hammered for some time to bring about a meeting" between South Vietnamese and Cambodian officials. His arm twisting had produced "some, however slight, assurances" that Nhu would travel to Phnom Penh "with instructions to adopt [a] friendly, constructive, conciliatory line." (The ambassador warned, however, that there was no guarantee "Nhu will act along [the] conciliatory lines we have pressed for.") What Durbrow objected to was telling Sihanouk that the United States had "put very heavy pressure on Diem to meet the RKG halfway or better." Such a revelation, Durbrow argued, would only encourage further "blackmail" by Sihanouk.[33]

On July 22, the State Department sent a cable to Strom that disagreed with his assessment of the situation and refused his request for a direct US role in settling the problems between Cambodia and South Vietnam. Drafted by Parsons and approved by Robertson, the telegram began by claiming that Diem was responding to "persuasion and pressure" from Durbrow. The department cited the encouraging example of Nhu's planned visit to Phnom Penh. "Thus," the message reasoned, "[the] conflict of US and GVN policy vis-à-vis Cambodia may be less than Sihanouk thinks."[34]

This statement to Strom, a tranquilizing comment aimed at minimizing the difficulties between Cambodia and South Vietnam, was disingenuous at best. Only one day earlier the CIA had reported to senior policymakers that "South Vietnam would undoubtedly support any scheme aimed at removing Sihanouk from power."[35] (Of course, in the highly unlikely event that the State Department intended to remind Strom that encouraging noncommunist opposition remained a desirable objective, there was indeed little conflict between the policy of the United States and the policy of South Vietnam.)

The department's telegram of July 22 further observed that an offer of US "good offices" required assurances that both parties were reliable and sought a reasonable settlement: "We are not convinced Sihanouk desires [a] solution on terms short of his own and [it] does appear he is seeking [to] use [the] weight of [the] US to achieve this kind of solution." The cable pointedly asked Strom, "Do you believe Sihanouk [is] stable and reliable?

There is great reluctance here to put [the] US in [a] position where we would repeatedly be exposed to possible blackmail and double-cross."[36]

Beyond suggesting the possibility of mediation by small neutral states, the department had no proposals for settling the problems between Cambodia and South Vietnam. If Strom desired, the message continued, Washington could "consider" issuing a public statement of US concern for the current status of Cambodian-Vietnamese relations. Having raised this possibility, the department then immediately dismissed it without explanation: "We seriously doubt [the] wisdom of such [a] statement and do not believe you should propose it to Sihanouk."[37]

During the drafting and clearing of this message to Strom, Washington officials learned that Sihanouk had publicly announced Cambodia's recognition of China. The initial impulse within the State Department was to cancel Strom's planned meeting with the prince because it appeared that "nothing can be gained by providing Sihanouk [with an] opportunity [to] expound [on] RKG recognition [of] Red China at [a] meeting you requested in [an] effort [to] prevent such action."[38] Nonetheless, Strom did meet with Sihanouk on July 24 to inform him of the department's concern over developments in Cambodia and to tell him about his recall to Washington to discuss US policy going forward. Strom reported that despite his warnings about the threat posed by the PRC, Sihanouk declared that "no Cambodian would ever believe [the] Chinese were more dangerous than [the] Vietnamese."[39]

There was at least one Cambodian who disagreed with Sihanouk's statement: Dap Chhuon. Recently promoted to brigadier general, Chhuon sent word to Ambassador Strom on July 25 that he was "deeply distressed" by Sihanouk's recognition of China. Using his brother, Slat Peau, as an intermediary, Chhuon said that "he had spent his life fighting Communism and was still opposed" to it. In a statement similar to his conspiratorial communications with Ambassador McClintock in 1956, the warlord proclaimed his loyalty to the monarchy and the prince but stressed that he was a "patriot above all and loved his country more than either." Slat Peau, who had received an education grant from the US Information Service to attend the University of Southern California in 1957, told Strom that his brother wanted to meet with the ambassador the next time Strom was in Siem Reap.[40]

Such a meeting was not immediately possible because of Strom's trip to Washington. While passing through Saigon, "Strom appeared to be under some strain," according to Australian minister Frederick J. Blakeney. In a memorandum to the Department of External Affairs, Blakeney wrote that Strom "gave the impression that he was expecting his visit to Washington to be a most unpleasant one for him. Durbrow thinks that Strom's continuing harping on Vietnamese iniquities (in Cambodian eyes) as being the root cause of the whole trouble will find little sympathy in Washington and is calculated rather to make Strom's relations with the State Department more difficult."[41]

Strom's relations with the State Department could hardly have been enhanced by an extraordinary letter from Durbrow to Parsons denigrating the US mission in Phnom Penh. Dated July 25, 1958, the letter expressed concern about DCM Kellogg's fitness to serve as chargé d'affaires during Strom's absence from Phnom Penh. Kellogg's principal shortcoming, according to Durbrow, was an obsessive, biased view of Cambodian–South Vietnamese relations. Durbrow had also "heard" that the DCM had been "crude and brusque" to a South Vietnamese official at a dinner party. "Kellogg acts quite differently with RKG officials—he believes everything they say," wrote Durbrow.[42]

Although Kellogg was the primary target of his attack, Durbrow criticized the entire mission in Cambodia and, by extension, Strom's leadership of it: "You will have noticed a number of Phnom Penh's telegrams which reflected the same obsession" with Cambodian–South Vietnamese relations. Moreover, erroneous reports from Phnom Penh conveyed to Diem by Durbrow might have led the South Vietnamese president to conclude that "our intelligence on Cambodia is not too good." Simultaneously criticizing the reporting from Cambodia and questioning the policy of encouraging Diem to negotiate with Sihanouk, Durbrow wrote: "Frankly I wonder whether any of us have a clear enough picture of what's really going on over there to permit us to take decisions and continue to bring pressure on the Vietnamese to 'bury the hatchet.'"[43]

Durbrow, who acknowledged that his letter "breaks all the rules, i.e., don't meddle in personnel matters outside your own pond," appeared to anticipate, if not encourage, an early end to Strom's term as ambassador: "If Carl is going to be away for some time, or if for any reason he might decide under the chain of circumstances he should not return permanently to Phnom Penh, I believe serious consideration should be given to sending an experienced senior officer as Chargé to make sure that Kellogg does not make matters worse, pending the arrival of a new chief of mission."[44]

Parsons asked Ambassador Strom to comment on Durbrow's letter. Strom complied: "I think it is unnecessary for me to say that it is most distasteful to me to write anything of this kind." Reviewing Kellogg's "extensive background in responsible positions," Strom defended his DCM as "a loyal and competent member" of his staff. The ambassador had never found an occasion when Kellogg's behavior with foreigners was "improper or discourteous." During Strom's previous absences from Phnom Penh, Kellogg had performed the role of chargé "in a highly satisfactory manner." Commenting on Durbrow's "principal complaint," Kellogg's alleged obsession with Cambodian–South Vietnamese relations, Strom wrote that his DCM had found an "atmosphere of indifference" to the subject in Saigon: "Kellogg was completely disgusted and may have well shown it."[45]

During the first week of August, Ambassador Strom, MAAG commander Brigadier General Edwin S. Hartshorn, and Alvin Roseman, chief of the economic aid mission in Phnom Penh, met with officials in Washington to consider the US response to Cambodia's recognition of China. At the State Department, there was agreement that the United States should not "punish" Cambodia by ending military and economic assistance. (Gradual reductions based on across-the-board cuts in US foreign aid would, however, go forward as planned.) Terminating US assistance, said Walter Robertson, "would mean abandoning Cambodia to the Communists." He added: "Sihanouk would not live forever."[46] Robertson's observation about the prince's mortality may have merely been an expression of US "frustration" with the situation, as historian Kenton Clymer suggests.[47] Given the context of the conversation, however, it seems reasonable to wonder if the comment had a more ominous meaning. At the very least, the statement appears odd when referring to a reasonably healthy thirty-five-year-old.

During a discussion of US "assets" in Cambodia, Robertson asked about the Royal Army's awareness of the communist threat. General Hartshorn replied that overall "there was no real recognition of the danger." Strom and Hartshorn agreed that the Cambodian army was "loyal to the throne and to Sihanouk and would follow wherever Sihanouk led." Listing US assets in the kingdom, Strom and Roseman ranked Dap Chhuon as number one.[48] A new group of young anticommunist government officials and anticommunist business leaders was also deemed valuable to American interests. Strom, however, disagreed strongly with Diem's belief that there was "serious opposition to Sihanouk within Cambodia."[49]

The absence of serious opposition to Sihanouk did not mean there was an absence of plotting against him. On August 12, the director of the Office of Southeast Asia Affairs, Eric Kocher, forwarded to Robertson three CIA reports containing "information about a possible coup in Cambodia." The "most interesting report," according to Kocher, discussed "a purported request by Dap Chhuon for covert Thai assistance in overthrowing Sihanouk." Prime Minister Thanom Kittikachorn, who led the government as Sarit's front man, reportedly "approved the idea of extending such assistance." The other two CIA reports also mentioned Dap Chhuon, whose following was limited largely to the three thousand troops under his command. "We are doubtful that a serious coup effort is being planned," wrote Kocher, "but we are watching the situation closely."[50]

Ambassador Strom concluded upon his return to Phnom Penh—where, despite Durbrow's personnel suggestions, Kellogg had continued to serve as chargé—that Dap Chhuon's contacts with the Thai government were "more in the nature of feelers" rather than an indication of immediate action. Strom reported that Dap Chhuon "is insisting on heavy material support from the Thais. He is also telling the Thais that before he could move he would have to have the support of a larger portion of the Cambodian Army than he now has." CIA reports indicated that Dap Chhuon "was far from certain what course he should follow." State Department officials, who retained their doubts about the seriousness of the plotting, provided Robertson with a list of other Cambodians "mentioned as possible leaders of a coup." The others included army chief of staff Lon Nol, who owed his "position to Sihanouk and the Royal Family"; Sam Sary, who had "little known popular support"; and Son Ngoc Thanh, who received "aid from both the Thai and Vietnamese" but whose following among the Cambodian elites had largely "disappeared."[51]

Thai officials' motives for conspiring with Cambodian rebels included both anticommunist and irredentist impulses. Many Cambodians thought Thailand was using Son Ngoc Thanh as leverage in settling the bitter disagreement over ownership of an ancient temple Cambodia claimed and Thailand controlled. Called Preah Vihear by the Cambodians and Khao Phra Wihan by the Thai, the more than seven-hundred-year-old ruin was a small-scale version of Angkor Wat built on the top of a cliff some fifteen hundred feet above the Cambodian plain. Because the temple was located in territory that had alternately been Cambodian or Thai depending on the historical era, the dispute over ownership aroused nationalistic fervor in both countries. Preah Vihear, the US embassy in Phnom Penh observed, was a "perpetual issue for demagogy[,] and no statement" from Cambodia or Thailand could go unanswered by the other side.[52]

On September 4, 1958, three weeks of Cambodian-Thai negotiations on border, customs, and other issues broke down completely over Preah Vihear. Cambodian officials, who considered their claim to the temple to be legally sound, threatened to take the dispute to the International Court of Justice in The Hague. Thai officials, however, preferred to try the case in the court of public opinion. In Bangkok, a demonstration on September 7—"inspired, if not directly staged, by Interior Minister Prapat [Charusathian]," according to the CIA—turned into a riot in which more than one hundred civilians and police officers were injured. Eric Kocher described General Prapat, a Sarit confidant who succeeded Phao Sriyanon as leader of the Thai national police, as "a gangster at heart." In the days before the anti-Cambodian riot, Prapat exploited Thai nationalist sentiment with several demagogic public statements and "strongly hinted to the press that orderly demonstrations in support of the Thai Government's position would be welcomed."[53]

Nine days after the temple riot, Thailand's deputy foreign minister Visutr Arthayukti told U. Alexis Johnson, the US ambassador in Bangkok, that the Thai government had word from the South Vietnamese that a "coup to overthrow Sihanouk would shortly take place." When asked if the Diem regime was encouraging the coup, Visutr said that he did not know, but "Nhu had asked to come to Bangkok and was expected shortly." According to Johnson, Visutr implied that Nhu wanted to discuss a "coordinated effort with Thailand to overthrow Sihanouk." Questioned further by the US ambassador, Visutr said that "he did not know who might lead such a coup or furnish [an] alternative to Sihanouk."[54]

According to Johnson's report to the State Department, he told Visutr

that "Diem had long thought Sihanouk's position was weakening but neither our representatives in Phnom Penh nor [the] British, French, [and]
Australians felt that Sihanouk's position was in danger." Johnson assured
the Thai diplomat that the United States was "not encouraging" Sihanouk's overthrow. During a meeting with Prime Minister Sarit on September 18, Johnson tried to "discourage consideration" of Thai support
for a coup but did not think he made "much progress."[55]

The report of Johnson's conversation with Visutr triggered a series of
cables from Ambassador Strom, who advised the State Department that
the possibility of a coup in Cambodia was "minimal." Although acknowledging disaffection and dissatisfaction among intellectuals and bureau-
crats, Strom wrote that these elites had not "united to create an effective
opposition" and that their discontent with Sihanouk had not spread to
"the police or the military with the exception of Dap Chhuon." Strom
added that he was unaware of any changes in Dap Chhuon's "attitude of
watchful waiting," the message Chhuon had conveyed to the ambassador
after Cambodia's recognition of China.[56]

In another telegram to the department, Strom shifted his analysis
from Cambodia's internal affairs to its relations with South Vietnam.
Returning to a familiar line of reasoning, Strom cited Visutr's conversation with Johnson as an additional indication of the "opposing" US and
South Vietnamese policies on Cambodia. A recent article in the *Times
of Vietnam,* which characterized Sihanouk as a royal "usurper" who still
feared his uncle, Prince Monireth, was "particularly damaging" to the
US objective of achieving a Cambodian–South Vietnamese "rapprochement." It was, wrote Strom, "imperative" for the United States to heal this
"breach" that "endangers our whole position" in Southeast Asia. Chal-
lenging an assumption underlying US policy in Cambodia—that is, a
successful coup would serve US interests—Strom declared, "Although
Sihanouk is highly unsatisfactory from our point of view his elimination
will lead to complete chaos from which [the] Communists [are] in [a]
good position to profit."[57]

In a third telegram to the State Department, Strom discussed briefly
the "numerous reports of plots against Cambodia and against Sihanouk
personally" and their implications for US relations with the prince. Referring to Visutr's comments to Johnson and to intelligence from Bangkok
and Saigon, Strom wrote: "It must be assumed some or all of these reports

have reached Sihanouk." The ambassador advised the department to "be prepared to counter [the] idea [that] Americans may have been involved in any of these plots."[58]

State Department officials disagreed with fundamental aspects of Strom's analysis. In their view, the Diem government had taken steps to reduce tensions with Cambodia—for example, offering to remove the mined border marker constructed during the Stung Treng incident. The Cambodian government, however, had reportedly failed to give its consent to the removal or even reply to the South Vietnamese offer. It seemed likely to the department that Diem was justified in believing that Sihanouk did not want the removal of such a valuable propaganda symbol. The "tentative conclusion" in Washington was that Sihanouk "evinces no desire [to] reach [a] settlement at present, and [the] onus for continuation of the dispute falls chiefly on Cambodia."[59]

The State Department did agree with Strom that the United States and South Vietnam had differing assessments of "the possibility for eliminating Sihanouk from [the] political scene." The United States had conveyed to Diem and Nhu its pessimistic estimate of a coup's chances without much impact on South Vietnam's plotting. Department officials, therefore, "doubt[ed] the advisability [of a] further direct approach to either of them at this time on this score. We believe it [is] preferable [that the] next effort for dampening any [coup] plans [of the] Vietnamese may have [to] be made indirectly through [the] Thai."[60]

In a telegram to Bangkok dated September 23, the State Department instructed Johnson to approach Visutr "to discourage [Thai] consideration of a coup." Johnson could stress that the United States "in no way condones Sihanouk or his actions but sees danger in [a] coup possibility." Department officials, who did not share Strom's fear that Sihanouk's removal would lead to political chaos, stated their own concern bluntly: "If [a] coup should be attempted by [the] Vietnamese and/or Thai and as [it] appears highly likely it should fail, [the] US and SEATO would receive [the] brunt [of] adverse repercussions in Cambodia and elsewhere."[61]

Johnson was not optimistic about his ability to influence Thai officials. In his reply to the department, he noted that speculation about a coup "has now hit the press." An article in the *Bangkok Post*, quoting "usually reliable officials sources," reported that the Thai government "is going to wait until [a] new government [is] set up in Cambodia before reopening negotiations on [the] border dispute. There is [a] feeling that conditions in Cambodia are such that [a] new government may come into being soon."[62]

Prince Sihanouk traveled to the United States in September 1958 to lead the Cambodian delegation at the thirteenth session of the UN General Assembly. Before the trip, the Cambodian government informed the State Department of Sihanouk's desire to visit Washington and to "see President Eisenhower if only for a short meeting." Ambassador Nong Kimny told Deputy Assistant Secretary Parsons that the prince wanted to give the president a statue from the ruins at Angkor. Talks with President Eisenhower and Secretary Dulles, said Kimny, would also be a good opportunity for Sihanouk "to explain directly the sincerity of his policy of neutrality" and for US officials "to dispel the idea" that the Diem government "could with impunity create trouble with Cambodia because of Viet-Nam's close relationship with the U.S."[63]

Because Dulles was traveling, Parsons could not reply immediately to Sihanouk's request. For three consecutive years, the State Department or President Eisenhower or both had denied embassy proposals for an official state visit by Sihanouk. The most recent rejection had been made on February 24, 1958, when Eisenhower told Dulles that visits by the prince and two other heads of state should be "deferred" because of an already crowded schedule of official visitors that year.[64] As an interim response to Kimny, Parsons observed that the US government "wanted to be sure the visit will advance American–Cambodian friendship rather than harm it." Referring to Sihanouk's recent visit to China, where he spoke with Mao Zedong for six hours and spent an entire day with Zhou Enlai, Parsons said: "We are worried that, if Sihanouk is not received on the same grand scale as in Communist China, he may feel we are less friendly or trying to penalize him for recognition of Communist China." Kimny assured Parsons that he would explain to Sihanouk that his trip to Washington was not an official state visit and that he "should not expect the same kind of reception."[65]

Sihanouk's trip to the United Nations and his subsequent visit to Washington occurred during the Taiwan Straits crisis of 1958, a military confrontation between the PRC, Taiwan, and their allies over control of offshore islands. As the crisis threatened to escalate into nuclear war, Sihanouk offered to serve as mediator between China and the United States. In a meeting with Walter Robertson on September 15, Nong Kimny explained what the prince had in mind: Sihanouk could receive "a list of United States desiderata," the feasibility of which he would assess based on his recent conversations in Beijing. "If necessary," said Kimny, Sihanouk would "be willing to fly to Peking to present [the US] point of view." Kimny emphasized that the prince's proposal "was being made in all humility and that there would be no offense taken if the offer was rejected."[66]

Sihanouk undoubtedly believed that both his relations with the United States and China and his commitment to neutrality in the cold war made him a uniquely qualified mediator of the Taiwan Straits crisis. There also can be little doubt that Robertson was appalled by the proposal from Sihanouk. The prince, considered unstable by Robertson and other US officials, had not only recognized China but also advocated its admission into the UN—a policy no one in the State Department opposed more tenaciously than the assistant secretary of state for far eastern affairs. According to the minutes of their meeting, Robertson diplomatically thanked Kimny for Sihanouk's offer and said that he would promptly inform Secretary Dulles of it. Robertson also spoke "at some length" about the US view of "Red China, which was unable to fulfill the only qualification for membership in the United Nations, namely that a country should be peace-loving."[67]

The next day Robertson spoke with Sihanouk at the prince's suite at the Waldorf Astoria. The notes of the conversation show neither a direct rejection of the prince's offer of mediation nor the slightest interest in his proposal. The notes do indicate that Robertson delivered another lecture on the international misdeeds of China, characterizing it as an "an outlaw state." US officials may have expected Sihanouk to inform the Chinese of Robertson's comments about the Taiwan Straits crisis. If so, the message was simple: (1) the United States would not be intimidated by communist threats, and (2) a renunciation of the use of force by China "would help reduce the tension in the Taiwan Straits."[68]

Robertson's denunciation of the PRC had little impact on Sihanouk. During his address to the UN General Assembly on September 23, the prince supported China's admission into the United Nations. Sihanouk argued that China's absence from the UN was detrimental to the aims and purposes of this world body and that China's admission would impose obligations on it in its relations with other member states. To settle the crisis in the Taiwan Straits, Sihanouk declared that the Nationalist Chinese "must withdraw peacefully" from the offshore islands and that the PRC must "solemnly renounce" the use of force in acquiring Taiwan. The US embassy in Phnom Penh found Sihanouk's UN remarks "moderate" and "reasoned."[69]

Prince Sihanouk met with President Eisenhower in the Oval Office for twelve minutes on September 30, 1958. Much of the visit was devoted to a ceremonial exchange of gifts. Sihanouk gave the president a twelfth-century stone statue of Buddha from Angkor. Eisenhower reciprocated with a Steuben crystal bowl engraved with the presidential seal. After the meeting, the president hosted a White House luncheon with Sihanouk as the guest of honor. The two leaders chatted amiably about the prince's planned tour of the United States.[70]

The brevity and ceremonial character of Sihanouk's meeting with the president reflected both the suddenness of the prince's request for a visit and the low priority of Cambodia in US foreign affairs. Between July and November 1958 alone, the Eisenhower administration was engaged in cold-war crises in Lebanon, the Taiwan Straits, and Berlin. Even among the former states of Indochina, Cambodia received less high-level attention than South Vietnam and Laos, both of which faced more serious communist threats. One measure of limited presidential interest in Cambodia is the single mention of Sihanouk in Eisenhower's two-volume presidential memoir.

During his visit to Washington in 1958, the prince met with John Foster Dulles at the State Department. Robertson, perhaps alluding to his own conversation with Sihanouk in New York, had warned the secretary of state that Cambodia's recognition of China and the attendant risks of communist subversion were "extremely sensitive" topics with the prince: "He has manifested considerable irritation at what he considers the US-shaking-the-finger-at-the-small-boy approach on these subjects."[71] Dulles, heeding this warning, pitched his anticommunist rhetoric in a lower-than-usual key. According to the minutes of his meeting with Sihanouk on September 30, Dulles

> said he would not be frank if he did not say that we have some concern over the motives and ambitions of the Chinese Communists in Southeast Asia. We believe they as Communists desire

to bring all governments everywhere under the control of the Communist party. The Communist creed of peace, order, and maximum productivity is aimed at bringing everything into conformity and having it run by the Communist party. The Communists thus take a mechanistic view of the world. We, on the other hand, do not believe that human beings can be brought into that kind of mechanistic order. As human beings differ from each other, a world program of trying to make them act and think alike is not possible.[72]

Sihanouk said that he agreed with Dulles's views on communist rule and declared that Cambodian neutrality served US interests. "Uniting the whole Cambodian nation behind the monarchy," said Sihanouk, "is the best defense against Communism. If another policy were followed, there would be serious division within the country." The prince added that "the best proof that neutrality has prevented Communist success in Cambodia is the results of the general elections in [my] country." Referring to the Sangkum's overwhelming margins of victory in 1955 and 1958— rather than to his government's dubious electoral practices—Sihanouk "doubted that better results could be obtained in other countries under free elections."[73]

The prince's visit to Washington did little to increase understanding between Cambodia and the United States. Although US officials repeatedly said that they respected Cambodian neutrality, Walter Robertson bristled—as Dulles and Nixon had in 1956—at the moral equivalence implied by Sihanouk's foreign policy. "We have no objection to [the] policy [of] neutrality or non-commitment," Robertson told the prince, "but we do object to neutralism, a concept that there are two power blocs in [the] world and little for other nations to choose between them." Robertson also rejected Sihanouk's request for US "good offices in inducing Viet-Nam to agree to negotiations" on the border-marker dispute and other problems. Noting Cambodia's neutrality, Robertson expressed the hope that Sihanouk understood "why we have to be neutral at times in disputes between our friends."[74]

The main temple at Angkor Wat in Siem Reap Province, Cambodia. (Foreign Operations Administration/National Archives and Records Administration)

Assistant Secretary of State Walter S. Robertson, King Norodom Sihanouk, and Vice President Richard M. Nixon on the steps of the US Capitol, 1953. (Oliver Pfeiffer/National Archives and Records Administration)

Nong Kimny, Cambodian ambassador to the United States, with John F. Simmons, chief of protocol for the State Department, 1951. (Joe O'Donnell/National Archives and Records Administration)

US Army attaché Lieutenant Colonel Robert D. Burhans, Ambassador Robert M. McClintock, Secretary of State John Foster Dulles, and an unidentified Cambodian officer reviewing troops at the airport in Phnom Penh, 1955. (US Information Agency/National Archives and Records Administration)

McClintock and Dulles on the balcony of the American embassy in Phnom Penh, 1955. (US Information Agency/National Archives and Records Administration)

The coronation of King Suramarit and Queen Kossamak, 1956. (US Information Service/National Archives and Records Administration)

Carl W. Strom, US ambassador
to Cambodia, 1956–1959.
(Robert McNeill/National
Archives and Records
Administration)

Sihanouk exchanging gifts with President Dwight D. Eisenhower in the Oval Office,
1958. (National Park Service/Dwight D. Eisenhower Library)

Ngo Dinh Diem, president of South Vietnam, addressing the nation, 1955. (US Information Agency/National Archives and Records Administration)

Field Marshall Sarit Thanarat, Thailand's leader, 1957–1963. (John Dominis/Time Life Pictures/Getty Images)

Sihanouk leading a pilgrimage to the Preah Vihear temple on the Thai-Cambodian border, 1963. (Horst Faas/Associated Press)

Dissidents Sam Sary (left) and
Son Ngoc Thanh (below).
(*National Intelligence Survey,
Cambodia,* 1965/National
Archives and Records
Administration)

Ambassador William C. Trimble at the ceremony to present his diplomatic credentials to King Suramarit, 1959. (Princeton University Library)

Elbridge Durbrow, US ambassador to South Vietnam, 1957–1961. (Whit Keith Jr./National Archives and Records Administration)

U. Alexis Johnson, US ambassador to Thailand, 1958–1961. (US Department of State/National Archives and Records Administration)

Construction of the Khmer–American Friendship Highway. (US Operations Mission, Cambodia/National Archives and Records Administration)

Sol H. Brown, a US public-works official who advised the Cambodian government on dredging operations. (US Operations Mission, Cambodia/National Archives and Records Administration)

Allen W. Dulles, director of Central Intelligence, and President Eisenhower at the ceremony to lay the cornerstone for the new CIA headquarters in Langley, Virginia, 1959. (Abbie Rowe/Dwight D. Eisenhower Library)

Major General Lon Nol, Cambodia's defense minister and armed forces chief, visiting Secretary of Defense Thomas S. Gates Jr. at the Pentagon, 1960. (US Department of Defense/National Archives and Records Administration)

Philip D. Sprouse, US ambassador to Cambodia, 1962–1964. (Robert McNeill/National Archives and Records Administration)

UN ambassador Adlai Stevenson, Sihanouk, and President John F. Kennedy meeting in New York, 1961. (Cecil W. Stoughton/John F. Kennedy Library)

8

"A Shady Matter"
(1958–1959)

In a letter to Assistant Secretary Walter Robertson dated October 20, 1958, Ambassador Carl Strom wrote that he would seek to promote better relations between Cambodia and South Vietnam while adhering to the US policy of neutrality in disagreements between the two countries. Yet any possibility of successfully encouraging "Sihanouk from the sidelines," Strom warned, would require Ngo Dinh Diem to "accept the fact that for the foreseeable future Sihanouk is here to stay and that he must be treated with a certain minimum amount of respect. Obviously, if Sihanouk should become convinced that the Diem regime was in any way working against him personally, all the Cambodian suspicions of the Vietnamese would come into full play and we would have little ability to influence the Cambodians."[1]

Because Diem's behavior affected US relations with Sihanouk, Strom was "much concerned by evidence that the Vietnamese delude themselves that it may be possible and useful to work for the overthrow of Sihanouk. There is almost conclusive evidence that they have been working actively to this end." Strom cited a September conversation between councilor Ngo Dinh Nhu and US ambassador to South Vietnam Elbridge Durbrow as probably "the most important evidence" of plotting by South Vietnam. Noting "several reports of plans for a coup," Strom reminded Robertson that the South Vietnamese government "had considered a coup to overthrow Sihanouk at the height of the Stung Treng crisis and abandoned its plans because of lack of U.S. support."[2]

Other "strong indications" of Diem's unhelpful attitude were the personal press attacks against Sihanouk in the *Times of Vietnam*. "Although the Government [of South Vietnam] may disavow responsibility for the *Times of Vietnam*," Strom wrote, "no realistic person would be so naïve as to put any stock in their disclaimers." The ambassador concluded his summary of South Vietnamese coup plots, press attacks, and bad faith by observing that "these activities have already gravely damaged our position in this country and will cause even greater harm if they continue."[3]

Strom ended his letter on an optimistic note. There currently seemed to be "a considerable *détente* in Vietnamese–Cambodian relations," and recent reports from Durbrow indicated Diem's willingness to resolve the border-marker dispute: "If Diem and Sihanouk can both realize that no matter how unpalatable it may be, they are going to live as neighbors for a long time, some progress may be possible."[4]

Robertson's reply did not address any of Strom's long-standing complaints about Diem. The most likely explanation for this evasion was that Robertson neither agreed with the ambassador nor wished to argue with him further. Emphasizing areas of agreement with Strom, Robertson wrote that the department shared the ambassador's view that Sihanouk was "the real power in Cambodia," that there was "no prospect of successful removal of him from the scene," and that there had "been a considerable relaxation of tension between Viet-Nam and Cambodia."[5]

Whatever optimism Ambassador Strom might have felt about Vietnamese–Cambodian relations was badly shaken by a new report that the Diem regime "will attempt to overthrow Sihanouk by [the] end of November." The plot included a group "led by Sam Sary" and an armored unit in Phnom Penh. The source for this information was Ngo Dinh Nhu, who controlled SEPES, South Vietnam's intelligence service. In a cable to the State Department, Strom disagreed "emphatically with [the] idea it would be desirable even from [the] GVN point of view to eliminate Sihanouk, particularly by end of November." The ambassador saw no evidence of a "cohesive group opposed to Sihanouk" or of the military force to execute a coup: "If Nhu is, nevertheless, considering action along [the] lines [of the] report, he should be promptly disabused."[6]

Ambassador Durbrow's initial reaction to Nhu's plotting was less categorical. In a conversation with Nhu on November 13, Durbrow said that "we"—presumably a reference to the US mission in Saigon—"had been thinking about the matter quite seriously." Nhu, acknowledging that a lack of Cambodian military support precluded "a coup d'état per se," provided Durbrow with a convoluted analysis of Cambodia's internal politics that led to the possibility of Prince Monireth assuming power. "If Monireth should become Prime Minister," said Nhu, "it is in the interests of Viet-Nam, the United States, and other free countries to do all they can to keep him in power."[7]

Durbrow voiced skepticism about Nhu's information and questioned whether any effort to unseat Sihanouk would be successful. "While there may be certain anti-Sihanouk elements in Cambodia," said Durbrow, "we [have] had no information indicating that they are strong, cohesive, or effective in any way." An unsuccessful coup "would only enhance [Sihanouk's] prestige," the ambassador said. "It might even drive him further into the arms of the Chinese Communists." Durbrow declared that any move against the prince "would not have U.S. backing." Nhu, disagreeing with Durbrow's analysis, reminded the diplomat of pessimistic US estimates of Diem's staying power in the mid-1950s. "We were wrong then," Durbrow cabled the State Department, "and he [Nhu] is convinced we are wrong now."[8]

Although Durbrow made it clear to Nhu that the United States would not support an attempt to overthrow Sihanouk, John Foster Dulles may have diluted the strength of this message during a conversation with Vu Van Mau, South Vietnam's foreign minister, on November 11. Discussing the communist threat to South Vietnam, Mau mentioned the "unsatisfactory situation in Cambodia." Dulles, obviously referring to Sihanouk, commented that Cambodia's foreign policy "[is] somewhat erratic due in part to various unstable individuals." Expressing admiration for Diem, Dulles said that the United States shared South Vietnam's concerns about Cambodia, where "there [is] not adequate awareness of the danger of Communist infiltration."[9]

In a conversation with Walter Robertson, Vu Van Mau declared that Sihanouk's foreign policy was "harmful to [the] free world." Acknowledging pessimistic US estimates of successfully "replacing" the prince, Mau said: "Vietnamese intelligence indicates [that] internal opposition to Sihanouk [is] growing."[10]

On November 24, 1958, the Cambodian ambassador in Bangkok informed the Thai Foreign Ministry that his government was "temporar-

ily suspending" relations with Thailand. The stated reason for the diplomatic break—"strained relations" between the two countries and Thai
press attacks—made little sense to US officials. There had been no recent
Cambodian-Thai incidents, and suspending diplomatic relations because
of objectionable news stories seemed a "drastic rejoinder completely out of
proportion to [the] provocation." Cambodian ambassador to the United
States Nong Kimny told Walter Robertson that severing relations with
Thailand was "a regrettable measure" but "the only means by which a
weak country such as Cambodia [can] protest the abuse heaped upon it
by a more powerful country."[11]

Thailand responded to Sihanouk's diplomatic affront by recalling its
ambassador in Phnom Penh and closing the border with Cambodia. One
unintended consequence of Sihanouk's action was unification of the Thai
leadership, which had been unsettled by Sarit Thanarat's military move in
October 1958 to consolidate his power. In November, Ambassador Johnson had informed the State Department of "increasing reports [of] dissatisfaction among senior members [of the] military group extending even
to plots to assassinate Sarit." The insulting withdrawal of the Cambodian
diplomatic mission, Johnson wrote a month later, reduced factionalism
in the ruling group and "directly served to strengthen Sarit's position."[12]

Among the Thai leadership, "military extremists" favored an "air raid
on Cambodia," a proposal that Ambassador Strom and presumably every
other US official found "alarming." More moderate Thai officials, Strom
commented to the State Department, must recognize that an air attack
would be a "major disaster for [the] western cause and for [the] US in particular since American equipment would be used." He added: "I am quite
confident that no government established in Cambodia as [a] result [of]
Thai or other outside intervention would be able to govern [the] country."[13]

In Saigon, Diem told Ambassador Durbrow that Cambodia's suspension of relations with Thailand was further evidence of Sihanouk's
political unreliability: "He will take harmful precipitous action without
thinking of [the] consequences." In a conversation with Leland J. Bar-
rows, director of the US economic aid mission in Saigon, Diem said that
Sihanouk was "primarily interested in causing trouble with his neighbors
and should be eliminated."[14]

The most significant consequence of Cambodia's diplomatic break
with Thailand was an intensification of anti-Sihanouk activities, both

inside and outside the kingdom. Thai officials "apparently became more actively interested in the dissident Cambodians," according to a later CIA account of the plotting, and were more receptive "to long-standing proposals from Diem for a joint effort to remove Sihanouk." The "impetus" for action by Cambodian dissidents and their Vietnamese and Thai backers was Sam Sary's defection to South Vietnam in December 1958: "Sary brought news of [Dap] Chhuon's plans to Saigon."[15]

The plans called for Dap Chhuon's three battalions to "seal off" his headquarters in Siem Reap: "With his troops in place, he would then declare the large area of western Cambodia an autonomous province and mobilize supporters there. Meanwhile, the Thai and South Vietnamese would make threatening gestures along the border, perhaps infiltrating some rebels under Sam Sary. Chhuon hoped that Sihanouk, realizing that the Cambodian people were disaffected and lacking support from his own armed forces, would come to terms and agree to the installation of a pro-Western regime. If Sihanouk was not reasonable, Chhuon planned a guerrilla war."[16]

During the first week of January 1959, Ngo Trong Hieu, the SEPES representative in Phnom Penh, traveled to Bangkok, where he discussed the plot with Sam Sary and Thai officials, including General Prapat Charusathian, who had inspired the anti-Cambodian demonstrations in September. In a conversation with someone whose name has been redacted by the CIA, Prapat said that "the Thais had determined to support an anti-Sihanouk coup, but conceded that its success involved cooperation by Cambodian army chief of staff Lon Nol." Prapat also claimed "that he was in 'full control' of the coup plotting."[17]

The conspirators' order of battle included the forces of Son Ngoc Thanh, who was now working closely with Sam Sary and who controlled some twelve hundred Khmer Serei on the Thai side of the border. On January 6, Thanh told a group of Cambodian dissidents in Bangkok that he had an "armed and trained force on [the] Cambodian–South Vietnam border and another in Phnom Penh ready to move against Sihanouk." He added that the "proposed action had [the] support [of] SEATO and the RTG [Royal Thai Government]."[18]

At almost the same moment that Cambodian, Vietnamese, and Thai conspirators were in Bangkok planning their coup, Sihanouk learned about aspects of the plot from the Chinese, Soviet, and French embassies in Phnom Penh. "It appears likely," CIA analyst John Taylor concluded in the mid-1960s, "that all three governments derived their information from the same source: insecure SEPES messages from Saigon to Bangkok." The United States also intercepted these messages but, unlike the Chinese, Soviets, and French, did not inform Sihanouk of the plotting.[19]

The intelligence Sihanouk received was incomplete, however. The prince learned about Sam Sary and Son Ngoc Thanh's participation in the plot but not about Dap Chhuon's. In fact, Sihanouk ordered Dap Chhuon to capture the rebels. In a speech at Kampot on January 10, Sihanouk made his first public comments about the conspiracy, indirectly accusing Thailand of a "two-pronged plan" to overthrow the government—"one inside Cambodia, and the other outside." He rhetorically asked, "Who knows what giant" is encouraging internal and external opposition to the regime?[20]

In a message to the State Department dated January 12, Ambassador Strom commented on the public exposure of the "Sam Sary" coup, opining that "this plot had at best [a] very slight chance [of] success. Soviet and ChiCom [Chinese Communist] revelations reduced that to zero." Despite assurances from Prime Minister Sarit that "Thailand will withdraw support from Sam Sary," Strom urged the State Department to "take every step [to] convince both [the] RTG and GVN of [the] utter folly [of] continuing [to] support [the] plot." Criticizing the poor security of Thai and South Vietnamese communications, Strom appeared relatively untroubled by Sihanouk's "thinly-veiled accusation [that] we are at least silent partners in the RTG–GVN Sam Sary Plot." He recommended that the United States "ignore" the prince's comment "if no more reference is made to it."[21]

When Strom made this recommendation to the State Department, he was aware that the Chinese and Soviets had told Sihanouk about the plot by Sam Sary and his Thai and South Vietnamese backers. He did not know, however, that French ambassador Pierre Gorce had also informed Sihanouk of the conspiracy. To the prince, the conspicuous absence of an American warning raised the disturbing possibility that the United States was behind the plot. US officials later concluded that Gorce's talk with Sihanouk but silence with Strom was a French attempt to retain "their inside position" in Cambodia. Laurin B. Askew, the State Department's officer in charge of Cambodian affairs, observed a few weeks later with diplomatic understatement: "This French bias in favor of themselves may have caused the US serious damage."[22]

On or around January 13 the Quai d'Orsay informed Cecil B. Lyon, DCM of the American embassy in Paris, of Gorce's warning to Sihanouk. Perhaps intending to soften the impact of an unwelcome revelation, French officials noted that Gorce had told the prince to be wary of Chinese allegations of US involvement in the plot.[23] The French, however, did suspect the United States of complicity in the planned coup. Frederick Blakeney, the Australian minister in Saigon, reported to Canberra, "The French here claim to be convinced that Americans are involved in the alleged plot. The French Ambassador [in] Phnom Penh is apparently making no secret of [the] same (besides claiming Sihanouk's earlier rupture with Thailand now appears justified)."[24]

Charles Lucet, minister of the French embassy in Washington, called on State Department officials on January 15. He said that he wished to discuss "a shady matter (ténébreuse affaire)"—that is, reports that "Viet-Nam and Thailand were plotting to set up a new regime in Cambodia under Son Ngoc Thanh and Sam Sary." Lucet asked Deputy Assistant Secretary J. Graham Parsons "if there were anything to this rumor" of US sponsorship of Thai and Vietnamese plotting. Parsons flatly denied that the United States was "involved in anything of the sort." When asked if "the Thai and the Vietnamese were plotting on their own," Parsons disingenuously responded that US officials "could not believe there was anything under way with the approval of Sarit and Diem." He added that "if they were plotting they would be less amateurish."[25]

In Phnom Penh, Pierre Mathivet, counselor of the French embassy, called on his counterpart at the US embassy, Edmund Kellogg, "with the plea to avoid involvement at all costs" in the Sam Sary plot. Francis Stuart, the Australian minister in Phnom Penh, wrote to Canberra: "Kellogg behaved as though he knew CIA had been engaged in something of the sort. The U.K. Chargé d'Affaires had a similar interview with Kellogg and got the same impression."[26]

French officials suspected that the plotting was the handiwork of their bête noire in Vietnam in the mid-1950s: Colonel Edward G. Lansdale. According to sources the US government deemed reliable, Ambassador Gorce opined, at least to other French nationals, that Lansdale was "one of the U.S. agents involved" in the Sam Sary plot. One of those French nationals was likely Charles Meyer, a Sihanouk adviser who said that Lansdale, operating from Bangkok, "was the key to the whole story."[27] Lansdale later denied to the MAAG commander in South Vietnam any involvement in plotting against Sihanouk.[28] The intelligence operative did have a conversation with Ambassador McClintock in June 1956 in which he discussed Dap Chhuon "as a possible leader in the event Sihanouk has to be got rid of."[29] There is, however, no currently available documentary evidence indicating that Lansdale was in Southeast Asia between 1957 and January 30, 1959, when he arrived in Manila and subsequently traveled through the region as a representative of the so-called Draper committee reviewing US military-assistance programs.

The Australian minister to Cambodia, Francis Stuart, reported that Ambassador Strom, "realizing how widespread the rumors of American complicity had now become," denied them to Gorce and other Western diplomats. Yet Strom still resisted denying the allegations of a plot to Cambodian officials, "arguing that this would indicate a guilty conscience."[30] This attitude changed when the Cambodian police intensified its surveillance of the homes of US diplomats and called in servants and friends of embassy officials for questioning. The State Department instructed Strom to express US concern over the behavior of the police and "to assert in the strongest possible terms that the U.S. is not meddling, directly or indirectly, in Cambodian affairs."[31]

Unfortunately for Strom, neither Sihanouk nor Foreign Minister Son Sann would see him. What the prince did do was publicly accuse the United States of failing to inform him of the Sam Sary plot. In an interview in *Réalités Cambodgiennes,* he said: "Although our American friends have intelligence services which are very active and enjoy great resources and are assured of every facility by our neighbors to the east and west, they have not thought it necessary to inform us." Sihanouk also indirectly alleged that the United States was supporting Son Ngoc Thanh, who, Sihanouk said, had been "regrouping his forces on the frontier, armed with material from the Thais (and from a great western power)."[32]

Although Sihanouk did not explicitly charge the United States with participating in the Sam Sary plot, Strom informed the State Department that the *Réalités Cambodgiennes* interview was "tantamount to accusing [the] US of being directly involved." The ambassador finally arranged to see Sihanouk on January 26. Denying US involvement in the conspiracy,

Strom said that the United States "had no knowledge of [a] plot apart from rumors similar [to] those often heard during the last two years." He reported to Washington that Sihanouk appeared to be reassured by his comments but "probably still believes or at least suspects [the] US may have been in on [the] plot."[33]

Despite the exposure of plotting by Sam Sary and Son Ngoc Thanh, Dap Chhuon moved forward with his plan to declare an autonomous region in western Cambodia, to demand the installation of a pro-Western regime, and to threaten guerrilla warfare. The operation was "fraught with all sorts of dangerous possibilities," according to Richard P. Peters, the acting political adviser to Admiral Harry D. Felt, commander of US forces in the Pacific. On February 3, Peters wrote to Marshall Green, the State Department's regional planning adviser for the Far East, "I am particularly disturbed that Dap Chhuon's plan, which apparently he is determined to carry out beginning February 8 to 10, gives Sihanouk, or the throne in his absence, time to react after Chhuon's hand is shown. Obviously one of the possible reactions is a call for CHICOM assistance."[34]

Green and his Washington colleagues appeared less concerned about the possibility of Chinese intervention than about widely circulated military intelligence summaries suggesting US involvement with Dap Chhuon's plot: "The [intelligence report] on Cambodia, distributed to armed forces personnel all over the Pacific, seems to us to be worded so as to predict a coup attempt, while the 'CIA Comment' reveals such awareness of detail that it would not be at all impossible for officers unaware of what is actually going on to impute false connections with the U.S."[35]

US knowledge of the details of Dap Chhuon's plan was attributable in part to the intelligence activities of Victor Masao Matsui, who worked for the CIA in Phnom Penh. Then thirty-five, Matsui was a Japanese American who ostensibly served in the embassy's political section. Raised in Southern California, he was one of the more than one hundred thousand US citizens and permanent resident aliens of Japanese ancestry who were interned in "war relocation centers" when the United States entered World War II. He joined the US Army in 1945, translating captured Japanese documents and interrogating prisoners of war for the Military Intelligence Service. After an honorable discharge in 1952, Matsui began his work for the CIA. Arriving in Phnom Penh in 1957, the intelligence operative achieved a measure of local notoriety after Dap Chhuon's coup failed in late February 1959. According to James R. Lilley, a CIA case officer in Phnom Penh in the early 1960s, Matsui's "name became the word for 'spy' in Cambodian."[36]

Matsui's principal contact among the plotters was Slat Peau, Dap Chhuon's brother, who had served as a messenger to Ambassador Strom after Cambodia's recognition of China. A deputy in the National Assembly, Slat Peau had been part of the Cambodian delegation at the UN General Assembly in 1958. Sihanouk later alleged that during this trip to the United States "agents of Mr. Allen Dulles" recruited Slat Peau.[37] In February 1959, SEPES operative Ngo Trong Hieu provided Slat Peau and Dap Chhuon with mobile broadcasting equipment, two Vietnamese radio operators, and 595 pounds of gold bars. Hieu also reportedly "carried [a] personal message from Diem to Dap Chhuon to [the] effect there was [a] tacit understanding [the US government] would support Dap Chhuon when [the] coup [was] launched."[38]

On February 16, Ambassador Strom sent an eyes-only cable to Walter Robertson, urging that the United States "must insist in a most categorical manner that [the] GVN break off all relations with [the] Dap Chhuon conspiracy." Repeating now familiar arguments about achieving a "modus vivendi" among Cambodia, Thailand, and South Vietnam, Strom warned:

> There is [a] very real danger of revelations day by day which may cause an explosion. Discovery of [the] Sam Sary plot by [the] Soviets, Chinese, French and ourselves is adequate testimony to [the] looseness of Vietnamese security. As far as Vietnam's involvement with Dap Chhuon is concerned, there must be many people who know about [the] shipment of [a] mobile broadcasting station from Saigon to Siem Reap for use by Dap Chhuon in making his intended announcement to [the] Cambodian people. Chances are that a considerable number also know about the shipment of the box of bars of gold to Dap Chhuon.[39]

In a telegram to Strom two days later, Robertson replied that the United States would not intervene further with South Vietnam: "I believe that US representations already made at various levels will discourage

[the] GVN for the moment and induce further caution." He wrote that another appeal to the South Vietnamese government "might easily antagonize Diem to [the] detriment [of] US interests." Although the United States had successfully induced the strong-willed Chiang Kai-shek of Taiwan and Syngman Rhee of South Korea to adopt policies they found distasteful, Robertson declared, "Thailand and Viet-Nam are not amenable to US policy dictates, particularly on matters close to home which they feel themselves better qualified to judge than [the] US. [The] Vietnamese in particular hold [the] view that Sihanouk [is] drifting rapidly toward [the] Communist bloc, that US efforts to stem [the] trend [have been] unsuccessful, and that [the] prompt removal [of the] Sihanouk regime [is the] only hope [to] avert [the] Communist satellization [of] Cambodia."[40]

It is difficult to resist the conclusion that Robertson and Dulles shared this view. Earlier that same day, Robertson had spoken to Ambassador Nong Kimny about remarks that Sihanouk had made in Jakarta to the Indonesian Press Service. In an interview on February 14, the prince had accused SEATO of "gross and open interference in Cambodia" and had named Ngo Trong Hieu as the "head of foreign subversion." Sihanouk had further claimed that there was "not a single Chinese agent in Cambodia" and had congratulated himself and his people for "having chosen to be friends of China." Robertson rejected the accusation against SEATO, telling Kimny that the United States had "exerted every possible influence and effort to bring about amicable relations between Cambodia and neighboring Thailand and Viet-Nam." Moreover, he said that Sihanouk's attack on SEATO and Cambodia's "Free World neighbors" and his "lavish praise" of China did not appear to conform "to the concept of neutrality expressed by Sihanouk to the President and the Secretary, and the statements disturb us very much."[41]

Kimny replied that he had not read the remarks mentioned by Robertson but would communicate the US views to the Cambodian government. The ambassador then turned to a topic that "he had hoped he would not have to raise." Prince Sihanouk and other Cambodians, he said, "were disturbed and puzzled by the apparent discrepancy between the official statements made by the President and the Secretary and the actions of certain young American officials in Cambodia." Without naming the individuals, Kimny said that he "knew that these officers were indulging in activities which were not in keeping with the spirit of mutual friendship between Cambodia and the U.S." In a transparent reference to the CIA, Kimny said that the Americans he had in mind were civilians who "had gone too far in the direction of seeking contacts with opposition elements, had gone to the point of sympathizing with the opposition, and even as far as to deal with Communist sympathizers."[42]

Robertson, pressing Ambassador Kimny for particulars, said that he "could not conceive of any U.S. officer indulging in activities, particularly with Communists, against the interests of Cambodia." He added that "Cambodia had no better friend than Ambassador Strom," who "would not tolerate improper activities by any member of his staff." Robertson blamed communists for "falsely implicating the U.S. in coup plots," saying that they "will continue to spread lies and attempt to attribute to the U.S. their own base characteristics."[43]

Dap Chhuon made his move on February 20, 1959, sending a letter to the king that declared his "dissidence" against the Sihanouk regime. The CIA reported that the letter was "probably concerned with Chhuon's terms for calling off a planned general uprising, which include Sihanouk's withdrawal from politics and the reorientation of Cambodia's policies toward a firmly anti-Communist position."[44] Apparently hoping that his fierce reputation would encourage negotiations, Dap Chhuon was surprised two days later when a convoy of some seventy armored cars and trucks arrived in Siem Reap to arrest him for treason. His rebellion collapsed without a shot being fired, and he fled into the jungle with some of his followers. "Although the convoy was under the nominal command of Lon Nol," the CIA commented several years later, "the uncharacteristic efficiency of the operation suggests that French military officers were involved." Ambassador Gorce, who was ostensibly visiting the ruins at Angkor, was in "Siem Reap when Lon Nol arrived to apprehend Dap Chhuon."[45]

On February 23, the Cambodian government released a communiqué reporting that unnamed "foreign and national" intelligence sources had revealed the plot. The announcement pointedly accused the South Vietnamese government of "inciting and supporting Dap Chhuon." Lon Nol's forces had captured two Vietnamese in Dap Chhuon's villa and discovered "much money," a "radio set of a different type from that used in Cambodia," and "documentary proof of treason and foreign involvement."[46]

The Royal Army also captured Slat Peau. At his trial for treason later that year, Slat Peau testified, "Victor Matsui gave me [a] radio sending–receiving set [on] February 12, 1959." Unlike the transmitter provided by Ngo Trong Hieu, which was intended for Dap Chhuon's announcements to the Cambodian people, the radio set supplied by Matsui allowed Dap Chhuon to communicate with the "American Embassy Phnom Penh," Hieu, Son Ngoc Thanh, and Sam Sary.[47]

Slat Peau's testimony, likely coerced and perhaps unreliable, nonetheless raises questions about the precise role of the US government in the Dap Chhuon plot: Passive reporting? Opportunistic acquiescence? Direct sponsorship? In a memorandum written some two months after the failed coup, Walter Robertson declared, "We maintained intermittent confidential contact with Dap Chhuon, but refused his request for help and emphatically urged him not to undertake illegal action against Sihanouk."[48] William Colby, then the new deputy chief of station in Saigon, wrote in his memoirs that the CIA sought to dissuade Vietnamese and Thai plotters from a coup that "we felt was unlikely to succeed and would only exacerbate the problems of dealing with Sihanouk. But to be certain that we would know what was happening among the coup-makers, CIA had recruited an agent on the Cambodian general's staff, and had given him a radio with which to keep us informed. And we were indeed informed."[49]

There is evidence, however, that Robertson and Colby understated US involvement in the Dap Chhuon plot. The claims that the CIA merely reported on the dissident's activities and that the US government tried to stop the coup appear to be a cover story for a more complicated reality. William Trimble, Strom's successor and the American official responsible for damage control after the Dap Chhuon debacle, recalled that the CIA played an active role in the conspiracy. In an oral history interview conducted more than thirty years after the attempted coup, Trimble said, "The CIA Station Chief in Phnom Penh [Roger Goiran] had been instructed to establish contact with Dap Chhuon, the strongly anti-commie Governor and military commander in the northern Province of Siem Reap, and to provide him through a South Vietnam intermediary with a sum in gold."[50]

Trimble's recollection is consistent with Roger Hilsman's recorded comment to President Kennedy in November 1963 that the CIA "supplied some money" to the plotters.[51] Hilsman, a former director of the State Department's Bureau of Intelligence and Research, was assistant secretary of state for far eastern affairs when he made this observation to Kennedy. Like his previous assignment at the bureau, his position as assistant secretary of state offered abundant insights into CIA operations in Southeast Asia. For example, Hilsman was the State Department official who authorized CIA-sponsored paramilitary operations from South Vietnam into Laos.[52]

The recollections of CIA case officer James Lilley, who later served as the American ambassador to the PRC, also indicate an active US role in the Dap Chhuon conspiracy. "This was set up by a Japanese-American guy attached to our Station there," said Lilley, observing the official ban on naming CIA personnel whose employment has not been acknowledged by the agency. "This was the so-called 'Dap Chhuon' plot centered in Siem Reap. The Cambodian authorities exposed the operation. In this operation we were working with the South Vietnamese."[53]

What might have persuaded officials in Washington to approve such an operation? In his monograph for the CIA, John Taylor commented on international perceptions of the likelihood of Dap Chhuon's coup succeeding: "The only Western power which assumed from the first that the plot would fail was France."[54] In other words, it appears that at some point the US government thought Dap Chhuon's plot could succeed. Evidence that Washington perceived strength in the conspiracy is a statement in a CIA briefing for the NSC after Dap Chhuon's coup was crushed: "Although [the] plotters had considerable assets in [the] aggregate, they never coalesced."[55]

If the president and his senior advisers decided that the CIA should provide covert assistance to Dap Chhuon through the South Vietnamese, Ambassador Strom might not have been informed of this aspect of the operation. In Laos, for example, the State Department approved CIA intrigues against Prime Minister Phoui Sananikone in late 1959 without informing Ambassador Horace H. Smith.[56] To be sure, the documentary record is quite clear that Ambassador Strom was aware of South Vietnam's delivery of gold and mobile radio equipment to Dap Chhuon. Yet Strom's knowledge of a possible CIA role in providing that support is unclear. Trimble, overstating Strom's ignorance of the plotting, recalled years later the aftermath of the failed coup:

The gold was found as well as incriminating evidence that it had come through Vietnam and the name of the CIA contact. And all that had been done without the knowledge of my predecessor. He knew nothing about it until he was called into the Foreign Office and given hell, and shortly removed.

As soon as I heard about this, I went over to see Alan Dulles and said, "Look, I'm not going to have any more of that! If I go there, I want to know exactly what your people are doing. If not, I'm not going to take the post. I'm not going to have someone doing things surreptitiously while I'm chief of mission." He gave me his word, and it stopped.[57]

A more contemporaneous account of this criticism of the CIA is found in a letter from Trimble to William R. Tyler, his successor as counselor at the US embassy in Bonn. On October 8, 1959, one week after Slat Peau's trial for treason publicly revealed Victor Matsui's involvement in the Dap Chhuon plot, Trimble made a veiled reference to the agency: "The techniques of some of our brethren were not especially skillful and, while I put a stop to all this even before I left Washington, the damage had already been done and we are now suffering the consequences."[58]

The conflicting claims about the degree of US involvement in the Dap Chhuon conspiracy could be resolved by more enlightened declassification of fifty-five-year-old government documents. Until then, there is a theory that accommodates the differing accounts from Robertson and Colby, on the one hand, and from Trimble, Hilsman, and Lilley, on the other. At some point in early 1959, senior officials in Washington agreed to provide deniable covert assistance—gold bars, mobile radio equipment, and other support—to South Vietnam and Dap Chhuon. Acutely aware of the disastrous implications of a failed coup, the State Department instructed Durbrow on February 2, 1959, to "*be prepared* [to] approach President Diem on short notice" if, in the ambassador's "opinion," South Vietnam's "activities [were] endangering [the] situation [in] Cambodia." Durbrow should then emphasize to Diem, "[The] US cannot see [the] chance for [a] successful coup [in] Cambodia under present conditions."[59]

In other words, in early February Durbrow was given discretionary authority to intervene with Diem and attempt to pull the plug on an unpromising attempt by Dap Chhuon to overthrow Sihanouk. According to Strom, however, Durbrow did not exercise this authority until February 14—after the delivery of the gold and communications gear and after "Diem was irremediably committed."[60] A last-minute US effort to abort Dap Chhuon's coup would be consistent both with the accounts given by Robertson and Colby stressing efforts to discourage the move against Sihanouk and with the statements by Trimble, Hilsman, and Lilley describing covert US assistance to the conspiracy.

On February 23, 1959, with Dap Chhuon in the bush and Sihanouk clearly aware of South Vietnamese participation in the plot, the State Department aptly characterized the situation in Cambodia as "extremely delicate." In a telegram to the US ambassadors in Saigon, Phnom Penh, and Bangkok, department officials expressed concern that the Cambodian communiqué accusing South Vietnam of "inciting and supporting Dap Chhuon" might trigger a "strong reaction" from Diem. One fear in Washington was that Diem—already incensed by the prince's interview in Indonesia—might say or do something to "push Sihanouk further toward [the] Communists and seriously prejudice salvaging [the] free world position [in] Cambodia."[61]

Allaying Sihanouk's suspicions about American involvement in plots against him posed a particularly tricky challenge for the US government. Durbrow, who became more sympathetic to Strom's point of view after the failed Dap Chhuon coup, suggested telling the prince that the United States would "not countenance any action by [the] GVN aimed at overthrowing [the] Sihanouk regime." This recommendation, the State Department commented, had "advantages as well as serious dangers." On the one hand, such a declaration might reassure Sihanouk that the United States was not involved in the coup attempt and that the Americans were prepared "to pressure our allies to stop any such attempts [that] they may be planning." On the other hand, the proposed statement "would indicate to Sihanouk [that the] US had been and still is aware of GVN plots[,] thereby confirming his suspicions [of] US and GVN involvement."[62]

A more fundamental problem with Durbrow's suggestion—one that lasted into the 1960s—was US unwillingness to take meaningful action on behalf of the "irresponsible" and "unreliable" Sihanouk against a "staunch ally and anti-Communist" in South Vietnam. The United

States could not "stop all GVN action against Sihanouk over [an] indefinite period of time unless we are prepared to use sanctions such as aid reduction to force Diem [to] accept our position [in] this matter," the State Department informed the three ambassadors. "This of course would again weaken [the] GVN and lay [the] ground work for increased Communist influence in South Viet-Nam, a situation which we certainly are unable to countenance."[63]

US officials had feared that Sihanouk would respond to a coup attempt by appealing to China for military assistance. Instead, he wrote a letter to President Eisenhower on February 23 asking for "the speedy intervention of the friendly government of the US of America with our Thai and South Vietnamese neighbors." Cambodia, Sihanouk wrote, was "the object of grave threats of aggression on the part of neighbors both larger and more powerful." Referring indirectly to the Dap Chhuon plot, Sihanouk charged South Vietnam and Thailand with attempting to establish "a puppet government ready to align itself to their policy and to give its consent to various concessions."[64]

Sihanouk acknowledged the argument that the United States did not "wish to inject itself" into the sovereign affairs of South Vietnam and Thailand. He pointed out, however, that the strength of these two countries was attributable to US military assistance. The prince opined that the United States was "twice entitled to make its voice heard" in Saigon and Bangkok: first, to support the UN doctrine of "respect for the sovereignty and the integrity of its member states" and, second, to prevent US military assistance from being improperly "used to support territorial and political ambitions or policies against non-Communist neighbors."[65]

Sihanouk sought to convince Eisenhower that he was not a dictator who had imposed neutrality on Cambodia. He offered to resign with his government, to dissolve the National Assembly, and to hold new elections in which all parties, including those of Sam Sary and Son Ngoc Thanh, would be allowed to participate. Such an election could be supervised by the United Nations and include observers from Thailand and South Vietnam. If the election results were "hostile to the Sangkum," Sihanouk pledged "to withdraw from politics." Expressing confidence in and respect for President Eisenhower, Sihanouk wrote, "Only the intervention of the United States of America can save the free Khmer democracy from an unjust and unmerited subversion, entirely artificial and mounted from without, as elections organized under the most severe international control would clearly demonstrate."[66]

Although the United States generally treated correspondence between heads of government as strictly confidential, the prince provided copies of his letter to the British, French, and Australian mission chiefs in Phnom Penh. Without any advance consultation with US officials, Ambassador Gorce gave a copy of Sihanouk's letter to Roger Lalouette, the French ambassador in Saigon, who promptly informed Diem of its substance.[67] Like Gorce's revelation of the Sam Sary plot to Sihanouk, this unilateral communication undermined a chief of state's confidence in the United States and aggravated US–French relations.

Sihanouk wanted a quick response to his appeal to Eisenhower. When forwarding the letter to Ambassador Strom, Foreign Minister Son Sann asked him to transmit it to Washington by cable and to provide a reply with the "least possible delay." Son Sann also conveyed a quixotic request from the prince that his "letter be read to the US Congress." Strom asked the State Department "most earnestly for a very prompt reply, if only an interim reply, to avoid the possibility of Sihanouk turning elsewhere through fear and desperation before hearing from us."[68]

On February 28, Strom delivered President Eisenhower's initial response to Sihanouk. It indicated that the prince's appeal was receiving Eisenhower's "earnest attention" and that a substantive reply would be sent "very soon." Acting under instructions from the State Department, Strom emphasized that "a definitive reply would require several more days." Sihanouk responded that "he was quite prepared to wait." In a report to Washington about the meeting, Strom acknowledged the awkwardness of his position: "In several conversations during [the] last six weeks I have had to insist I have never had any information about recent plots excepting widely circulated rumors and published newspaper accounts." Strom had assumed the Chinese ambassador was the source for much of Sihanouk's knowledge about Dap Chhuon's attempted coup but was unaware that the French ambassador had once again provided advance warning to Sihanouk. With Strom declaring to the prince how "profoundly shocked" he was by Dap Chhuon's actions, it is small wonder that this meeting was "tense at the beginning."[69]

Assuring the prince of US efforts to promote amicable relations among Southeast Asian countries, Strom told Sihanouk that he "must not lose sight of his responsibility for [the] maintenance [of] peace and friendly relations in [the] area." Sihanouk interrupted the ambassador, denying any regional responsibility and declaring that his "responsibility" was "toward Cambodia." When Strom expressed satisfaction with Sihanouk's "denial" of his statements in Indonesia in a recent interview in *Réalités Cambodgiennes,* the prince disagreed with the ambassador's characterization of his comments, calling them a "correction" rather than a "denial."[70]

Sihanouk, presumably seeking to improve the diplomatic environment for his appeal to President Eisenhower, had stated in *Réalités* that he had "never criticized SEATO as such since I believe all countries [are] entitled [to] associate with others [for defensive purposes.]" The prince also revised his comments about the absence of Chinese agents in Cambodia: "It [is] hard to uncover Chinese subversion, which [is] extremely discreet and impalpable, when I must spend my time combating overt subversion which is sponsored by two countries, one of which is [a] member of SEATO, the other aligned with [the] policy [of] this organism."[71]

Strom concluded his thirty-minute meeting with Sihanouk by expressing the hope that Cambodia's problems with South Vietnam could be resolved and that the prince would pursue a solution to them through diplomatic rather than public channels. Sihanouk appeared to understand the US desire for discreet diplomacy but made no commitments. "I think [the] Department will appreciate," Strom cabled Washington, "that it is not quite reasonable to expect Sihanouk to be enthusiastic about regional relations at present."[72]

Sihanouk did take one step that US embassy officials thought would improve Cambodian-Vietnamese relations: his government asked South Vietnam to recall its representative Ngo Trong Hieu, who left Phnom Penh permanently on March 1. "[The] two nations can probably never be genuinely friendly," DCM Kellogg wrote to the State Department, "but Hieu's deportment and activities here had antagonized most RKG officials and added [a] personal element and [a] new dimension to their traditional dislike and fear of [the] Vietnamese."[73]

Dap Chhuon was shot and killed on March 3, 1959. The circumstances surrounding his death are unclear. According to an announcement by the Cambodian government, he was fifty kilometers from Siem Reap, heading toward the Thai border, when local militia mortally wounded him. On the return trip to Siem Reap, before dying, he reportedly made "important declarations." Sihanouk later told Cambodian students in Paris that Dap Chhuon "named in particular all the countries incriminated in the business but I won't give their names, hoping they will mend their ways and try to leave us alone; actually I have had no choice but to act like this, for we would otherwise have found ourselves face to face with 'the giant.'"[74]

A brief account of Dap Chhuon's death by the CIA differed in certain details from the Cambodian government's report. The agency's version made no reference to a confession by the rebel: "[Dap Chhuon] was shot to death by army personnel who were led to his hiding place in Siem Reap Province by his aide, who was an army officer." In his history of Cambodia, David Chandler, citing Cambodian and French sources, writes that Dap Chhuon was captured in Siem Reap Province: "Shot in the foot, he was taken on a litter to the main road, where he was assassinated, probably on Lon Nol's orders, without making a detailed confession."[75]

The source for the allegation that Lon Nol ordered the killing of Dap Chhuon is Sihanouk's memoir. The prince claimed that he wanted Dap Chhuon captured alive "in order to unravel the whole plot." But Lon Nol, in Sihanouk's telling, sought to silence the rebel, who "would have implicated Lon Nol" in the conspiracy. According to Sihanouk biographer Milton Osborne, this after-the-fact allegation had "more to do with the prince's fury over Lon Nol's part in the coup that toppled Sihanouk in 1970 than with the events of 1959."[76]

Whether operating under orders from Sihanouk or silencing witnesses to his own treasonous behavior, Lon Nol demonstrated unusual zeal in hunting down Dap Chhuon's associates. "The French had been surprised by the effectiveness of Lon Nol's operation in cleaning up Dap Chhuon," according to Pierre Mathivet, counselor of the French embassy in Phnom Penh. "The operation had been carried out far more ruthlessly than the French had expected and Lon Nol had caused the disappearance of a number of people in the Dap Chhuon entourage with a dispatch which had not been anticipated."[77]

Ambassador Strom, who had been scheduled to conclude his term as ambassador on February 26, extended his stay in Phnom Penh for ten days to cope with the immediate diplomatic fallout from the failed coup. On the day Dap Chhuon was killed, Strom reported to the State Depart-

ment that he was at a "disadvantage" in conversations about the conspiracy with Cambodian officials. They inevitably asked, "Did you know
about plot?" and "If you did, why didn't you tell us?" The department-
approved line—the United States was unaware of the planned coup and
did not repeat rumors—was not an "advantageous position from which to
talk." Strom also wrote that he faced skepticism about the stated inability
of the United States to control Diem: "In view of [the] complete dependence of Vietnam on [the] US, it has been impossible [to] convince Sihanouk and other prominent Cambodians that we were not behind certain
aggressive and menacing actions of [the] GVN during [the] last year and
[a] half. Sihanouk and his associates are convinced that if we wanted to,
we could keep Vietnam in line."[78]

Strom was convinced of this, too. In a telegram to Washington, he
listed all of the major South Vietnamese depredations that had occurred
during his tenure as ambassador, including the border incidents in Svay
Rieng and Stung Treng Provinces, the bungled political kidnapping in
Phnom Penh, the imprisonment of Cambodian peasants, and, of course,
the failed Dap Chhuon coup. Urging a US "showdown" with Diem,
Strom wrote: "Sihanouk is not a Communist and I am convinced he will
not willingly allow his country [to] come under Communist control. I am
equally certain that more incidents like those above will drive him irre-
trievably into [the] Communists' arms."[79]

When Strom left Phnom Penh, US relations with Cambodia were at
an all-time low. More than any other incident, the failed coup by Dap
Chhuon convinced Sihanouk that the United States was implacably hostile to Cambodian neutrality and to him personally. "The long-term
repercussions of this affair cannot be exaggerated," comments Osborne
in his biography of Sihanouk. "Sihanouk's deep suspicion of the United
States shaped his foreign policy thinking for the following decade and led
him to give a ready ear to those Cambodians and foreigners who wished
to denigrate the United States."[80]

9

"Stupid Moves" (1959–1960)

It took four weeks to produce President Eisenhower's seven-hundred-word reply to Sihanouk's appeal in late February 1959 for US intervention with South Vietnam and Thailand. Early in the drafting process, the State Department instructed ambassadors Elbridge Durbrow and U. Alexis Johnson to obtain conciliatory statements from their host governments. The diplomats should explain that the United States wanted to document its consultation with South Vietnam and Thailand and to include their declarations in the president's response to Sihanouk. Department officials hoped that the statements from Saigon and Bangkok would express respect for Cambodian independence and neutrality and show a willingness to cooperate in strengthening friendly relations with the kingdom: "[The] value of [the] statements would be seriously diminished by [the] inclusion [of] contentious reservations or remarks." Durbrow and Johnson were advised to provide assurances that Eisenhower's letter would not "indicate acceptance of Cambodian charges against Thailand and Viet-Nam."[1]

The initial reactions from the two ambassadors were equivocal, at best. On March 6, Johnson cabled that it would be "difficult" for him to ask for another statement from Thai officials, who had already denied furnishing arms to Cambodian dissidents. He also pointed out that the "strength" of the Thai statement would depend on the degree to which the letter to Sihanouk addressed Thailand's "legitimate concerns" about Cambodia's foreign policy.[2]

In Saigon, Durbrow foresaw difficulty in obtaining a conciliatory

191

statement from Ngo Dinh Diem: "I fear in his present mood (he has been extremely cool bordering on anger toward me during last three interviews) it might be difficult, if not impossible, [to] obtain [a] favorable statement. With Dap Chhuon's death, which ends all hope for [the] change Diem desired, he [is] probably in [an] angrier mood today and even less amenable to suggestion." In a subsequent telegram, Durbrow noted an improvement in Diem's temper but was discouraged to report that "recent events have failed to budge him an inch from his well-known position that 'you cannot do business with Sihanouk.'"[3]

On March 7, Durbrow handed Diem a seemingly innocuous two-sentence draft statement: "The Government of Viet-Nam recognizes that internal disorder and instability in any free nation, including Cambodia, prejudices [the] interests of the free world and serves only the interests of international communism. The Government of Viet-Nam respects the independence and integrity of the Royal Khmer Government, and is prepared to cooperate with it in strengthening friendly relations on a basis of mutual respect and good will."[4]

Upon reflection—and after a conversation with his brother Ngo Dinh Nhu—Diem found both the form and the substance of the proposed statement unsatisfactory. He thought it "rather extraordinary" that the president of the United States would make a declaration on behalf of South Vietnam. The communists, he argued, could use the US consultations with South Vietnam and Thailand as proof that the two countries were American "satellites." In Diem's view, the statement falsely implied that South Vietnam had the military ability to threaten the independence of Cambodia, that Sihanouk was "really afraid of Viet-Nam," and that Cambodia was "incapable of doing harm to Viet-Nam."[5]

An aide-mémoire signed by Foreign Minister Vu Van Mau argued that South Vietnam was weak, "menaced both internally and externally," and faced a wide range of social and economic problems. "Prince Sihanouk knows this full well. That is why for four years he has not ceased to alternate abuse, slander and ridicule against Viet-Nam and its leaders." Diem was particularly bothered by Sihanouk's habit of forgoing traditional diplomacy in favor of appeals to public opinion. Until Diem knew more about the US reply to Sihanouk and consulted with Thai officials, he did not want the American response to the prince to "contain any statement" from South Vietnam.[6]

As diplomatic discussions about President Eisenhower's draft letter dragged on, Cambodian–South Vietnamese relations grew increasingly bitter. On March 21, *Réalités Cambodgiennes* printed a copy of a handwritten "conspiratorial letter" from SEPES representative Ngo Trong Hieu to Dap Chhuon. If South Vietnam did not at least repudiate Hieu for "acting without official sanction," the weekly warned, "more embarrassing documents" would be published. According to the CIA, Cambodia was "incensed at Vietnam's flat denial of any wrongdoing in the face of 'irrefutable' evidence that it has been involved in plotting against Premier Sihanouk."[7]

Cambodian attitudes toward the United States were hardly better. According to French ambassador Pierre Gorce, Sihanouk alleged that "the radio set found in [Dap] Chhuon's house was delivered by [Victor] Matsui, Second Secretary, American Embassy."[8] The widespread suspicion of US collusion with South Vietnam provoked hostile comments by Cambodian officials. A US embassy source reported that anti-Americanism within the palace was "extreme." On March 23, chargé Edmund Kellogg informed the State Department that Foreign Minister "Son Sann and other responsible Cambodians recently made statements indicating they [are] now convinced [that the] US backed [the] plots. [The] Embassy believes [the] lack [of a] public denial on [the] part [of the] US despite public charges against us has been taken as evidence [of] our complicity. Also certain top officials [have] undoubtedly [been] influenced by [the] long delay in answering [the] Prince's letter."[9]

Sihanouk, who had not spoken publicly about his letter to President Eisenhower, began making veiled accusations of US involvement in the plotting. In speeches in Battambang and Siem Reap during the last week of March, the prince suggested that the United States had provided financial support to the conspirators. A report from the US mission in Phnom Penh on April 3 stated, "[The] belief [the] US [was] involved in plots has hardened during [the] past two weeks among [the] upper levels [of] government."[10]

Eisenhower's reply to Sihanouk's letter was finally ready for the president's approval on March 27. Christian A. Herter, the acting secretary of state during Dulles's leave of absence for advanced cancer, attributed the delay to consultations with Thai and South Vietnamese officials. The statements the latter did approve were unexceptional declarations acknowledging Cambodian sovereignty, independence, and freedom to abstain from collective-security arrangements. The president's letter to the prince stated his belief that resolving the "underlying problems" between Cambodia and its neighbors depended primarily "on the actions and attitudes of the countries directly concerned." Because of his "vital interest" in promoting "amicable relations among all free nations," Eisenhower was "glad to request the Department of State to consult the Governments of Thailand and of the Republic of Viet-Nam in the context of our friendly relations with these countries." The president declared that he could not "appropriately comment" on Sihanouk's proposal for internationally supervised elections because it appeared "to involve a purely internal Cambodian matter."[11]

Because the State Department assumed that the prince would make Eisenhower's correspondence public, a private, "less exploitable" oral message was prepared. Intended to reinforce the written response, the oral message had a tougher tone. For example, the president was "disturbed" by the implication in Sihanouk's letter that the United States condoned the improper use of its military aid to Thailand and South Vietnam. Expressing Eisenhower's concern over the misunderstandings between Cambodia and its neighbors, the oral message included the news that Deputy Assistant Secretary of State J. Graham Parsons would be traveling to Southeast Asia and would seek to encourage "greater confidence and trust" among the leaders of Thailand, South Vietnam, and Cambodia: "The President would be gravely disappointed should his intentions in this regard be misinterpreted. In particular, he trusts it will be clearly understood that actions taken in this instance by the United States to help Cambodia and its neighbors improve friendly relations do not constitute an assumption of responsibility on the part of the United States for these relations or for the actions of any of the three countries concerned."[12]

Assistant Secretary of State Walter Robertson, who had overseen the preparation of Eisenhower's letter and the oral response to the prince, thought that the text of the written message was "a positive response to Prince Sihanouk's appeal to the President since it demonstrates that we have discussed the problem of regional relations in Southeast Asia with the Thai and Vietnamese and it incorporates reassuring and conciliatory statements by the two neighboring governments. At the same time, it avoids implying that we accept Sihanouk's charges against the Thai and Vietnamese at face value and should not carry the implication that we are prepared to exert pressure on our friends in Thailand and Viet-Nam."[13]

Cambodian officials did not share Robertson's enthusiasm for the president's letter. To be sure, Son Sann was relieved to receive a reply before the prince left Cambodia for France to rest and recover from various maladies. Otherwise, Sihanouk might have published his letter to Eisenhower without consulting the Americans. In a meeting with Kellogg on April 2, Son Sann said that Sihanouk "had only [a] short time [to] study" the president's letter but appeared "disappointed" by it. Speaking for himself—and undoubtedly for Sihanouk, too—Son Sann said that he was "disappointed" by Eisenhower's apparent confidence in the "alleged good faith" of Thailand and South Vietnam.[14]

Son Sann, who served as acting prime minister in Sihanouk's absence, was also the governor of Cambodia's national bank. Educated in Paris, he had served in postwar Cambodian governments, most often as the minister of finance or economic affairs. He had been a Democratic Party leader but had retired from politics in 1952, when Sihanouk dismissed the cabinet. Convinced that Sihanouk was the only person capable of achieving Cambodian independence, Son Sann urged his former party colleagues to support the king. A frequent representative at international conferences, he had been a member of the Cambodian delegation at Geneva in 1954. According to a State Department biographical sketch prepared for the conference, "Son Sann's great prestige stems from his ability, his energy, and what the French term an intransigent and narrow nationalism but which American diplomatic observers have described as a sound regard for Cambodian interests."[15]

During his meeting with Kellogg on April 2, Son Sann said that he was "dismayed" by President Eisenhower's reaction to Sihanouk's offer to hold supervised elections. Son Sann "could not see why [the] United States [was] so sensitive re Cambodian internal affairs in connection with [the] proposed elections, but had interfered in connection with plots." In response to this comment, Kellogg sought the basis for the allegation of American "intervention" in Cambodian affairs. Son Sann mentioned US "contacts with Dap Chhuon" and other conspiratorial actions. He emphasized that the "United States must have known of [the] plots and had not disclosed them to the government." Son Sann commented that "flat statements of denial would do no good in view of [the] hard information in [the] possession of [the] RKG of [the] involvement of 'Americans.'" Kellogg reported to Washington, "My efforts to pin him down for [the] particulars of his 'evidence' of United States participation always fail."[16]

The previous evening an unnamed US official had a similarly frustrating conversation with Jean Barré, the French editor of *Réalités Cambodgiennes* and an adviser to Sihanouk. An anti-American leftist, Barré had earned professional praise from his ideological opposite, Colonel Edward Lansdale, who once called him "a very clever psychological warfare man. One of the best."[17] Barré told the anonymous embassy officer that initially he had neither believed nor wished to believe that the United States was "involved [in the] Dap Chhuon–Sam Sary plots." He had, however, seen "hard evidence" that "certain Americans" had supported the conspiracy. When asked to reveal this evidence, Barré refused but later "rhetorically" suggested checking "into whether arms were not transported from Bangkok to Son Ngoc Thanh bands by official American vehicles."[18]

The newly arrived American ambassador to Cambodia, William Trimble, faced similar accusations of conspiratorial behavior and a generally hostile attitude toward the United States: "I found the situation deplorable when I arrived in Phnom Penh: bitter attacks on the United States in the press, accusing us of all sorts of things; resentment against individual Americans; slashed tires, breaking of windows, American vehicles stoned and so on. It was pretty bad and the morale of the Embassy staff was just about as low as it could be, largely because of the Dap Chhuon affair."[19]

Born in Baltimore in 1907, Trimble was a graduate of Princeton University and a career diplomat who had served in Latin America, Europe, and Washington, DC. He was, however, a self-described "neophyte" in Asian affairs before his assignment in Cambodia. Although fully qualified for an appointment as a US chief of mission, he was not the department's first choice to succeed Carl Strom. The "non-availability of various candidates" had hindered the selection of a new ambassador in Phnom Penh, Walter Robertson wrote when proposing Trimble for the position. "One otherwise particularly well-qualified candidate was so lacking in French that his appointment seemed inadvisable." Trimble spoke better French

than Strom and was less arrogant than McClintock. Whether this dignified, soft-spoken diplomat established a closer rapport with Sihanouk
than his predecessors is questionable. As late as July 1960, more than a
year into his appointment, Trimble admitted to Nong Kimny that "he did
not know how he stood personally with the Prince."[20]

During his introductory meeting with Son Sann, Trimble "tried to
dispel rumors of U.S. involvement in coups against Sihanouk," according to a State Department summary of their conversation. But "Son Sann
remained skeptical and asked why the United States did not inform Cambodia of the plotting. Trimble responded it was not U.S. policy to circu-
late rumors. Son Sann insinuated that three Americans met in Bangkok
with Cambodian coup plotters, a charge that Trimble denied."[21]

At a regional meeting of US ambassadors held in Baguio, Philippines,
Trimble discussed the "not very convincing" American replies to plotting allegations with Ambassadors Durbrow and Johnson as well as with
Parsons, the designated successor to Robertson as assistant secretary of
state for far eastern affairs. (Robertson's poor health, which prevented
him from traveling to the Philippines, forced his resignation later in the
year.) A fatal weakness in the plausibility of the US denial of conspiring
against Sihanouk was Slat Peau, who had been captured by Lon Nol's
forces and who had undoubtedly revealed his relationship with CIA operative Victor Matsui. To strengthen the credibility of US representations
to the Cambodian government, the officials meeting in Baguio made a
unanimous recommendation to the State Department: Parsons, who was
scheduled to travel to Phnom Penh and other Southeast Asian capitals,
should "be authorized [to] tell Son Sann [the] nature [of] Matsui's contact
with Slat Peau and that we had urged Dap Chhuon not [to] act against
[the] RKG."[22]

In a reply to Parsons, approved by Robertson, the State Department
rejected the diplomats' recommendation. The belated admission of Matsui's contact with Dap Chhuon, officials in Washington reasoned, would
confirm that the US government had been "less than frank and forthcoming" about Thai and South Vietnamese intentions and about American
awareness of the plots: "[The] Department also believes it [is] undesirable [to] refer to contacts with Dap Chhuon after [the] latter decided [to]
oppose Sihanouk regime, since [the] RKG could validly challenge [the]
propriety of such contacts. [This] admission would probably raise further

questions on [the] extent of US involvement with dissident elements and [the] means by which contacts [were] maintained."[23]

On April 22, the same day the department replied to Parsons, Ambassador Nong Kimny delivered to Robertson a letter from Siha-nouk addressed to President Eisenhower. Writing from Paris, Sihanouk expanded on his initial correspondence of February 23 and commented on Eisenhower's letter. Cordial and respectful, the prince wrote: "Khmer rebels who have taken refuge in the neighboring countries and who may at any time attack our people thanks to the support they have received and the weapons distributed to them, claim openly—but wrongly, I am sure—that your great country is backing them in their struggle against our Monarchy and our Government." Sihanouk added: "Perhaps, Mr. President, in your great wisdom you will find the means to make such a claim impossible or more difficult."[24]

Eisenhower's reply unequivocally denied any US involvement in plot-ting against Sihanouk: "I wish to assure you most emphatically that the Government of the United States is in no way supporting any efforts to overthrow the Monarchy or the duly constituted Government of Cam-bodia. Any claims to the contrary, whatever the source, are without the slightest foundation."[25]

Among the international leaders skeptical of US innocence in plot-ting against Sihanouk was UN secretary-general Dag Hammarskjöld. His personal representative, the Swedish diplomat Baron Johan Beck-Friis, had helped broker the reestablishment of diplomatic relations between Cambodia and Thailand in February 1959. Hammarskjöld himself trav-eled to Cambodia as part of a mission to promote better relations among Southeast Asian nations. According to American officials at the UN, "The Secretary General may well be convinced of US complicity in the Cambo-dian plots on the basis of French misapprehensions or purposeful falsifica-tions expressed to him."[26]

During a meeting with Acting Secretary Herter on April 23, Ham-marskjöld did not voice any direct suspicions about US involvement in coup plotting. Yet when mentioning the large number of foreign "agents" in Cambodia, Hammarskjöld did refer to *The Quiet American* (1955), Graham Greene's novel about a US spy who meddles dangerously in Viet-namese affairs. Eric Kocher, director of the Office of Southeast Asian Affairs, subsequently reported to Walter Robertson that Hammarskjöld "has quoted Cambodian Foreign Minister Son Sann to the effect that the US must have known of the plots and should have informed the Cambodian Government."[27]

During the last week of April, Parsons made visits to Saigon and Phnom Penh that contributed little to better relations between South Vietnam and Cambodia. In a meeting with Diem, Parsons declared "firmly [that] Sihanouk [is the] full master [of the] situation [in] Cambodia and will remain so [for the] foreseeable future." It was, therefore, in the interests of South Vietnam and the free world to reach equitable agreements with him on outstanding issues. Diem, however, ignored Parsons's arguments, stressing that the border region with Cambodia was "both a refuge and a breeding ground" for South Vietnam's communist enemies—a threat Sihanouk viewed with indifference "or worse." In a cable to the State Department, Parsons wrote: "No Vietnamese whom I saw showed any responsiveness to Durbrow's and my reiterated suggestions that they continue [to] seek [a] basis for negotiation [with Cambodia]." Noting undisguised South Vietnamese contempt for Cambodians, Parsons warned, "I fear there persists a restless desire to get rid of Sihanouk."[28]

In Phnom Penh, Parsons received a warm official welcome. Son Sann hosted a formal dinner with a performance by the Royal Ballet, and his public speeches were "very friendly in tone," according to the US embassy. Privately, Parsons found Son Sann "just as emotional as Sihanouk" about Vietnamese interference in Cambodian affairs, and he "documents his case exhaustively and impressively." Son Sann told Parsons that US military equipment supplied to South Vietnam had been diverted to Dap Chhuon. The Cambodian minister also charged that "US funds, channeled through [Nationalist Chinese] sources [in] Bangkok, subsidized [the] Thai press attack [against] Cambodia and provoked riots." Parsons informed Washington that his "well worn denials and arguments" had not allayed Son Sann's suspicions about US involvement in the plotting.[29]

Parsons concluded, based on his talks in Saigon and Phnom Penh, that the "psychopathic" attitudes of South Vietnamese and Cambodian leaders made an "immediate or overall settlement" between the two countries unlikely. Their relations, he reported, were "more thoroughly poisoned with emotion and suspicion than I had comprehended." Sounding much like Ambassador Strom, Parsons wrote that plotting by South Vietnam had jeopardized the fight against communism in Southeast Asia. He recommended that the United States issue a warning to Diem: American aid to his country would be reduced "unless Vietnam ceases interference in [the] internal affairs of [its] neighbor."[30]

The State Department, however, opposed cutting "aid to Viet-Nam for purposes of political pressure." Such a reduction would undermine "over-riding U.S. interests"—that is, the maintenance of South Vietnam as "a strong anti-Communist bastion in Southeast Asia." In a memorandum to Walter Robertson, Eric Kocher wrote:

> We doubt that Diem could ever come to understand how the U.S. could threaten or reduce aid to Viet-Nam (or a close ally) in an effort to compel it to take a definite course of action toward neutralist Cambodia when the U.S., after deliberate consideration, decided against threatening or reducing aid to Cambodia following its recognition of Communist China—an act not only contrary to the most fundamental U.S. policy in the Far East but the one which has led Viet-Nam to engage in maneuvers against Sihanouk.[31]

This estimate of Diem's reaction to the threat of US aid reductions may have been correct. Kocher's analysis did not, however, propose any new strategy for ending South Vietnam's destructive interference in Cambodia's internal affairs. Unwilling to pressure Diem, the State Department provided "guidance" to the embassies in Saigon and Phnom Penh that merely restated the obvious: the "amelioration" of Cambodian–South Vietnamese relations was an "essential precondition" to reversing the leftist trend in Sihanouk's neutrality. "Cessation of [South Vietnamese] support for Cambodian dissidents obviously must be sought on [a] priority basis." And Sihanouk, who was "understandably sensitive" to such support, was "unlikely [to] move closer to [the] Free World much less make concessions to [South Vietnam] while [the] latter [is] supporting [his] opposition."[32]

Parsons interpreted the "excessive courtesies" he received in Phnom Penh as possible evidence of Cambodia's willingness "to let bygones be bygones" and to start "a new phase" in its relations with the United States.[33] Yet the apparent progress in US–Cambodian relations suffered an immediate setback. On May 4, the American embassy learned that the Ministry of Information had produced posters showing a "giant," Sihanouk's traditional characterization of the United States, holding three snarling dogs on a leash. The dogs were labeled "Dap Chhuon," "Sam Sary," and "Son Ngoc Thanh." Ambassador Trimble protested to Son Sann, who claimed that the posters had been printed "a long time ago" and that he had issued orders to remove them from public spaces. In his report to the State Department, Trimble observed: "This is [a] weird country and in [the] very short time I have been here [I] believe anything can happen."[34]

What happened over the next few days was that the offensive poster remained on display at the Ministry of Information, Sangkum headquarters, and other public buildings. Trimble criticized Son Sann for failing to remove the posters. Son Sann, who had earlier complained to the ambassador about continuing Vietnamese training of Khmer Serei units, "replied heatedly, 'Why don't you in turn exercise pressure to stop rebel activities?'" Trimble responded with "equal heat" that the United States "had nothing to do with [the] rebels."[35]

Tempers cooled in a subsequent meeting between the two officials. Son Sann said that he had personally removed a poster in front of the Ministry of Foreign Affairs and had instructed the Ministry of Information to "obliterate" all others. He also made the improbable claim that the poster was not aimed at the United States but at Thailand, where Cambodian dissidents had printed a pamphlet depicting Sihanouk as a dog on a leash held by Chinese communists. Trimble, raising a long-standing US complaint, cited the "giant" poster as evidence that the Ministry of Information and other sources of news in Cambodia were hardly neutral. Influential newspapers, he said, increasingly relied on handouts from communist news agencies. Son Sann acknowledged the communist influence on the press and the Ministry of Information—a first for any Cambodian foreign minister, according to Trimble. Son Sann assured the ambassador that the palace was "less unfriendly" toward the United States than it had been: although suspicions of US complicity in the plotting remained, the court's attitude was "improving."[36]

The same could not be said about Cambodian attitudes toward South Vietnam. Trimble reported Son Sann's denunciation of the Diem government's "perfidy" and its "continued official support [for] Cambodian

202 EISENHOWER AND CAMBODIA

dissidents." Recent Khmer Serei broadcasts from South Vietnam had blamed Sihanouk's "dictatorial regime" for Cambodia's political and economic problems. The radio propaganda also alleged that a female Viet Minh agent had seduced Cambodia's minister of information, Tim Dong. Son Sann told Trimble that Phnom Penh and Saigon faced a common communist enemy but that Cambodia currently viewed South Vietnam as its "principal foe."[37]

From Saigon, Ambassador Durbrow reported that Vietnamese attitudes toward Cambodia were "still very poisoned." Diem, who considered Sihanouk a "liar," was "genuinely perturbed" by Vietnamese rebels operating in the border region of Cambodia. US and French intelligence tended to confirm that Vietnamese communists had "established headquarters in Cambodia for guerrilla activities against [South Vietnam]." Despite the crushing defeat suffered by Dap Chhuon, Diem and Nhu insisted that Sihanouk was losing his popularity among the Cambodia masses. To support this claim, Nhu cited Cambodians' "keen interest" in the propaganda pamphlets distributed by the Khmer Serei. When Durbrow asked where these tracts were printed, Nhu replied, "Thailand."[38]

Although South Vietnam was the leading sponsor of Cambodian dissidents, Thailand continued to shelter and support them. Immediately after the collapse of the Dap Chhuon coup, an emissary representing Sam Sary appeared at the US embassy in Bangkok to make an appointment for the rebel to meet with Ambassador Johnson. The emissary, unidentified by the embassy, brought a personal letter from Sam Sary to Johnson denouncing Sihanouk's attitude toward the United States and his friendship with China. The letter complained of American pressure on the Thai government to prevent assistance to the Cambodian resistance. Another document handed over to the embassy was a "delegation of powers," signed by Son Ngoc Thanh, authorizing Sam Sary to represent the Cambodian resistance in Bangkok. An unnamed embassy officer initially gave a "non-committal" answer to Sam Sary's request for an appointment with Johnson.[39]

When Sam Sary's emissary returned to the embassy the next day, the documents were returned "unopened" with the message that Ambassador Johnson recalled their collaboration in 1954 in Geneva and hoped to renew their friendship in the future. "At this time," however, it was "better not [to] meet Sam Sary." The emissary's request that an embassy officer meet with Sam Sary was also denied. Johnson reported to the State Department that he informed Thai general Prapat Charusathian of the approach by Sam Sary's representative. Because of Prapat's close relations with the Cambodian dissidents, Johnson thought it "highly likely" that he would learn about the "démarche." Prapat, Johnson speculated, may have even "suggested it to Sam Sary."[40]

The May 16, 1959, edition of *Current Intelligence Bulletin,* a top-secret CIA intelligence summary prepared daily and circulated to the president and top national security officials, reported: "Thai and South Vietnamese officials are to meet secretly in Vietnam this month at Saigon's initiative to plan future covert operations against the Sihanouk regime." General Prapat, according to the agency, "approved the general aims of the conference and appointed an emissary." The meeting apparently took place. A State Department memorandum dated March 15, 1960, and titled "Thai and Vietnamese Support of Cambodian Dissidents" referred to "a secret meeting in mid-1959 between Thai and Vietnamese officials concerned with the anti-Sihanouk Cambodian dissident movement."[41]

Because of Sihanouk's two-month respite in France, Ambassador Trimble did not have his initial meeting with him until June 9, 1959, three months after his arrival in Phnom Penh. Compared with his lively exchanges with Son Sann, Trimble's initial conversation with the prince was long on ceremonial pleasantries and short on diplomatic substance. Sihanouk was "very friendly," expressing his admiration for President Eisenhower and his gratitude for US aid. He spoke of his "cordial relations" with Ambassador Strom and wished Trimble "every success" in his new post. When the ambassador said that such success would require Sihanouk's "confidence and support," the prince replied that Trimble would have them.[42]

During this meeting, Trimble listened to a lengthy exposition of Cambodia's socioeconomic problems and to a predictable defense of the kingdom's policy of neutrality. The ambassador hand delivered two lengthy analyses of communist propaganda in the Cambodian press, which the prince said he would read. Because Sihanouk did not refer to Cambodian relations with South Vietnam or to the Khmer Serei, Trimble did not make department-authorized statements on these subjects. He reported to Washington that he would "save them for [a] more appropriate occasion."[43]

Despite his gracious behavior with Trimble, Sihanouk was privately "singularly ill-disposed and cynical" toward the Americans, according to Australian minister Francis Stuart. Referring to a four-hour anti-American speech that the prince had made to students in Paris—subsequently serialized and broadcast in Cambodia—Stuart reported to Canberra: "Sihanouk continues to taunt the United States in his public utterances to an extent that might have seemed injudicious to any other political leader as dependent as Sihanouk is on American financial support."[44]

Trimble complained to the Cambodian government about the prince's broadcasts, which referred to "ogres and giants," the diversion of US arms from South Vietnam to Cambodian dissidents, and the "guilty conscience" implied by American protests over the leashed-dogs poster. Nong Kimny, who had recently returned to Cambodia for home leave, agreed with the ambassador that Sihanouk's remarks were "most unfortunate." Making excuses for the prince's speech—he had just recovered his health and was addressing "communist influenced students"—Nong Kimny claimed that US–Cambodian relations were "progressing most favorably." Trimble apparently accepted this assessment at face value. In a subsequent report to the State Department, he cited Sihanouk's appearance at the embassy's Independence Day celebration as evidence that US–Cambodian relations were on a "definite up-swing."[45]

Although unwarranted official optimism in political and military affairs was characteristic of the US experience in Indochina, it is difficult to understand Trimble's and other US diplomats' eagerness to interpret episodic and short-lived improvements in US–Cambodian relations as meaningful trends. Sihanouk was, of course, capable of intermittently observing basic diplomatic courtesies with a country that provided Cambodia with substantial financial and military support and that served as an ideological counterpoise in his concept of neutrality. He was not, however, likely to forgive or forget US involvement with plots aimed at overthrowing him. Like the leashed-dogs poster, the broadcast of Sihanouk's speech in Paris seems a more accurate reflection of the prince's view of the United States than a polite appearance at an American embassy function.

US–Cambodian relations were so troubled that even the most benign American aid could be counterproductive. With much fanfare and mutual expressions of good will, US and Cambodian officials inaugurated the 136-mile Khmer–American Friendship Highway on July 23, 1959. Linking Phnom Penh with the new, French-built port at Sihanoukville

(Kompong Som), the road was a major US construction project, initially proposed five years earlier. The highway was particularly important to Sihanouk, who was eager to reduce Cambodia's dependence on the port of Saigon. Construction of the highway, however, had been plagued by "seemingly interminable delays of contract procedures and official red-tape" in Washington.[46] Such delays fostered Cambodian suspicions that the United States was dragging its feet for political reasons.

The completion of the Khmer–American Friendship Highway did contribute to better relations between the United States and Cambodia, but only in the short run. Less than two months after the highway's inauguration, Cambodian officials noted weather damage to the road, which the US embassy initially attributed to the "normal settling process."[47] Yet in December 1960 Trimble warned Parsons "of a potentially bad black-eye to our aid program here arising out of deficiencies in the construction of the Friendship Highway." In a more emphatic letter to the department five months later, Trimble wrote: "It seems incredible, but is nonetheless true, that the highway which we completed only two years ago at a cost of upwards of $34,000,000 is literally falling apart for nearly a third of its length."[48]

As with the initial construction of the road, delays in repairing the highway dragged on for years. The problems with the Friendship Highway remained sufficiently troubling that Sihanouk mentioned them in his film *Shadow over Angkor* (1968). "The road was constructed by our great friends in a deplorable way," says a character in the movie. "Khmers have had to spend millions of riel for repairing it."[49]

On August 3–5, 1959, Prince Sihanouk and senior Cambodian officials visited Saigon for private talks with President Diem and his top ministers. Their conversations about frontier security, trade, and other issues were cordial, and the absence of "excessive demands" from Sihanouk and "rigidly negative" replies from Diem suggested "the possible beginning of a new era of better relations," according to the State Department. The CIA, however, concluded that a "lasting rapport" between the two countries seemed "improbable, given Sihanouk's fatalistic belief in inevitable Communist victory in the East–West struggle—a view which conflicts directly with Diem's aggressively anti-Communist position."[50]

Any temporary improvements in Cambodian–South Vietnamese

relations were destroyed when a plastic explosive was delivered to the royal palace in Phnom Penh on August 31. Wrapped in a package addressed to the queen, the bomb killed protocol director Prince Norodom Vakrivan and at least two servants. Based on an examination of the handwriting on the card accompanying the package, Sihanouk concluded that Sam Sary was responsible for the outrage. The assassination attempt, the prince told Trimble, was obviously the work of a "mad man." If Sam Sary was in Vietnam, as Cambodian intelligence indicated, then Sihanouk wanted the Diem regime to "turn him over to" the Cambodian government. On September 3, Sihanouk made a speech in Prey Veng alleging that the "bomb was produced with foreign assistance since [the] traitors Sam Sary and Son Ngoc Thanh [are] incapable [of] fabricating such [a] device without [the] aid [of] foreign powers."[51]

There were many rumors about who was responsible for the palace bombing but little irrefutable evidence. The leftist Cambodian-language press alleged that "foreign imperialists"—a term generally associated with the United States—were the perpetrators. Trimble protested the accusation to Acting Foreign Minister Nhiek Tioulong, who replied that no government official believed the United States was "in any way connected with the bombing."[52] Pierre Mathivet, the French chargé in Phnom Penh, told Trimble that "while Sihanouk had been suspicious of US involvement in the Sam Sary plots and, particularly in the Dap Chhuon affair, the Prince and the Court [are] convinced that the Americans [have] nothing whatsoever to do with the recent bombing attempt."[53]

On September 19, Trimble reported to the State Department that the US mission in Phnom Penh was unaware of any "concrete evidence [that] Sam Sary actually [was] responsible [for the] bomb attempt." The ambassador was also not "convinced" that South Vietnam was "still backing Sam Sary." Trimble did, however, recommend that United States point out to Diem the desirability of closing down or jamming Khmer Serei radio broadcasts and "inhibiting Sam Sary's activities by protective custody of himself and other dissident leaders." Although unable to identify the people responsible for the palace assassination attempt, Trimble suggested that US "overt and covert propaganda effort might concentrate on pinning [the] blame for [the] bombing on [the] Communists."[54]

Many years after the Vietnam War, communist spy Ba Quoc, who infiltrated SEPES and its successor South Vietnamese intelligence organizations, alleged that Ngo Dinh Nhu had ordered the palace assassination attempt. The commander of the operation, according to Ba Quoc, was the deputy director of SEPES, Hoang Ngoc Diep.[55] There are a number of factual errors in Ba Quoc's account of the incident, but his fundamental allegation matches the conclusion that most Western historians have come to: the Diem government was responsible for the palace bombing.

On September 21, 1959, Trimble met with Durbrow in Saigon, where they agreed on steps to prevent further deterioration in Cambodian–South Vietnamese relations. The diplomatic maneuvers proposed by the ambassadors included an appeal to Diem to join the United States "in overcoming Sihanouk['s] growing belief [that] Sam Sary, with possible GVN connivance, carried out [the] palace bombing." In a cable to the State Department, Durbrow acknowledged the US failure to stop South Vietnam from "such stupid moves as [the] Dap Chhuon plot" and the difficulty of persuading the Ngo brothers to end their intrigues against Sihanouk. Durbrow firmly believed that "'clever' Nhu has convinced Diem they can go ahead with their stupidities no matter what we say because we 'need' Vietnam and would not dare take any drastic step to hurt them."[56]

Rather than recommending the threat of reduced aid to South Vietnam—a course of action already rejected by the State Department—Durbrow suggested that the US government try to manipulate Diem's "sensitivities to outside criticism." Diem had been "very shocked and hurt" not only by a recent series of articles in the Scripps–Howard newspapers criticizing his regime's corruption and authoritarianism but also by congressional interest in the stories' allegations. Durbrow and members of his country team traveled to Washington and effectively rebutted the charges before a Senate committee. Diem was reportedly relieved that the ambassador and his colleagues had "saved the day."[57]

Durbrow proposed to the State Department that it exploit reports that the Cambodian government was considering submitting to the UN a well-documented "white paper" on South Vietnamese plotting. The ambassador wanted to inform Diem that such a paper would "immeasurably hurt" South Vietnam's reputation in the free world because only communists would gain from the "exposé." To convince Sihanouk that his suspicions about South Vietnam were unfounded, Durbrow would recommend that Diem eliminate the clandestine Khmer Serei radio broadcasts, offer to help the Cambodian government find the perpetrators of the palace bombing, and state that antigovernment activity by Cambodian dissidents would not be allowed in South Vietnam. If Sam Sary were in Vietnam, he should be arrested and deported.[58]

Durbrow, who received the State Department instructions he sought, made a "firm démarche" to Diem on September 25. Diem, however, displayed little sensitivity to the risk of international criticism. He denied South Vietnamese involvement in anti-Cambodian activities and requested details about alleged Khmer Serei activities in his country. After the meeting, Durbrow wrote to Washington that without authorization "to pass on to Diem some precise details" about South Vietnamese support for the Khmer Serei, "I am afraid Nhu will induce Diem to take no action."[59]

That same day in Phnom Penh, Sihanouk told Ambassador Trimble that Cambodian–South Vietnamese relations had "deteriorated." The prince's grievances included recent violations of the Cambodian border by ARVN troops, increased infiltration of Khmer Serei forces from South Vietnam, and anti-Sihanouk radio broadcasts transmitted from South Vietnamese territory. Sihanouk also claimed to have "good reason" for believing that the Diem regime was implicated in the palace bombing. Sihanouk was "polite and friendly," according to Trimble's report to the State Department, but "much more preoccupied than on previous occasions I have talked with him." The ambassador added: "I received [the] impression from his general attitude and remarks that he may well be working himself up to [an] outburst such as he has done in the past."[60]

On September 30, 1959, a special military court, established after the palace bombing, tried, convicted, and sentenced eighteen of Dap Chhuon's followers for plotting against Sihanouk earlier in the year. Sixteen conspirators were sentenced to death; two received life sentences. Son Ngoc Thanh and Sam Sary received death sentences in absentia. The next day the leftist newspaper La Dépêche du Cambodge published verbatim excerpts from the trial. Most disturbing to US officials was the publication of testimony by Slat Peau. Discussing his relationship with American "embassy" employee Victor Matsui, Slat Peau revealed that he had initially met him in Washington, DC, and that the American subsequently provided a radio for communicating with other plotters and the US embassy. The public release of Slat Peau's testimony, Trimble concluded, had "undoubtedly [been] done with [the] foreknowledge [of] Sihanouk."[61]

In a "no distribution" cable to Parsons, Trimble criticized the State Department for its earlier refusal to inform the Cambodian government about the "nature [of] Matsui's contact with Slat Peau" and about the US attempt to discourage Dap Chhuon from acting. Had the department taken this step, Trimble observed, the current situation "might well have been avoided." To repair the diplomatic "damage in so far as possible," Trimble urged Parsons to discuss Matsui's activities with Ambassador Nong Kimny or Foreign Minister Son Sann, who was in New York for the fourteenth session of the UN General Assembly. "Otherwise," Trimble warned, "[I] believe we [are] in for another period [of] distrust and suspicion, with [the] consequent possibility [of a] new move to the left."[62]

In response to press inquiries about the trial and Slat Peau's testimony, Trimble proposed taking the following line: As part of their official duties, US embassy officers naturally came into contact with Slat Peau. Moreover, it was "possible" that Slat Peau had met Matsui in the United States. The embassy could not, however, verify this detail because Matsui had completed his two-year assignment and had moved on to another diplomatic post. "[The] allegation [that] Matsui gave Slat Peau [a] radio [is] unfounded," Trimble planned to say, and the reference to a communications network linking the embassy and the conspirators was "false." Trimble also sought permission from the department to issue a statement denying "any involvement whatsoever in any plot against the RKG."[63]

The State Department, however, did not want Trimble to volunteer any public comment about Slat Peau's testimony. The very brief US wire service reports of the trial mentioned only the conspirators' sentences. It was felt that a statement by the embassy would likely bring unwanted attention to Matsui's activities. The department suggested an informal meeting with the Cambodian Foreign Ministry to deny Slat Peau's allegations. Either the ambassador or a lower-ranking embassy officer should say that "sensational" press accounts implicating foreign governments threatened to undermine the progress in Cambodia's relations with its neighbors, progress "brought about in large measure by [the] highly effective and praiseworthy statesmanship of Sihanouk."[64]

An unnamed embassy officer did meet with the secretary-general of the Foreign Ministry, who said that he "had been expecting some approach from the United States." He added that the representative of South Vietnam had already protested the *Dépêche* article, which had been reprinted and broadcast by the official Agence Khmere de Presse. The secretary-general called the *Dépêche* story "regrettable," saying without any trace of irony that it was Sihanouk's policy to "let bygones be bygones." The Cambodian diplomat claimed to be "at a loss to explain how [the] Minister of Information had allowed [the] matter to get out of control."[65]

To top Washington officials, the Foreign Ministry's low-key reaction to the *Dépêche* article indicated that the Cambodian government was not "awaiting [an] explanation for US actions" in the Dap Chhuon plot. This dubious, far-reaching conclusion was communicated to Trimble in a brief, top-secret, "limit distribution" cable from Parsons, informing him that the State Department would not be approaching Ambassador Nong Kimny to explain Matsui's activities: the potential benefit of such an awkward conversation was "outweighed by [the] disadvantages."[66]

Contributing to this decision, Parsons wrote, was the desirability of assessing a new development in Cambodian politics—a national referendum to decide whether Sihanouk or Son Ngoc Thanh and Sam Sary should lead Cambodia. Proposed by the prince, who was reportedly brooding and seeing no one, the referendum was similar to the election idea he had suggested to President Eisenhower. If Sihanouk lost, he would either go into exile or stand trial before a "Supreme Court." If he won, any country that supported Son Ngoc Thanh and Sam Sary "would be considered hostile" to Cambodia and its people.[67]

Sihanouk shelved the referendum after the ICC refused to oversee the election. The prince did, however, continue his efforts to stop foreign support for Son Ngoc Thanh and Sam Sary. An article in the October 9 issue of *Réalités Cambodgiennes* contained new details about Victor Matsui, including his affiliation with the CIA.[68] Jean Barré, the publication's editor, told a French employee of the US Information Service that he had prepared another article on CIA activities in Cambodia. Although vague about when and in what publication the story might appear, Barré said that it would identify the CIA station chief and four or five other agency operatives. In what US mission officials described as an "ostensibly unrelated statement," Barré observed that turning over Sam Sary to the Cambodian government and ending Khmer Serei broadcasts and dissident activity along the six-hundred-mile border with South Vietnam would improve the political environment in the kingdom. Trimble and his colleagues concluded that Barré's "threat" to expose CIA officers was sanctioned by Sihanouk and "intended [to] lead [the] US [to] increase pressure on [the] GVN [to] cease support [of the] dissidents."[69]

Although Sihanouk generally tried to avoid simultaneous crises with Saigon and Bangkok, he chose this moment to refer the long-standing Preah Vihear temple dispute to the International Court of Justice. In a legal move certain to antagonize Thai prime minister Sarit Thanarat and his military colleagues, the prince sought a judgment to compel the withdrawal of Thai troops from Preah Vihear and to establish Cambodian ownership of the temple. Surachit Charuserani, director general of Thailand's Public Relations Department, declared that the Thai people were "prepared to shed blood and sacrifice lives" to maintain control of the ruins. Trimble, commenting on Sihanouk's referral of the temple dispute to the International Court of Justice, speculated that this "precipitate" action reflected Sihanouk's "present depression and concern [over] GVN-supported dissident activities. When in such moods, he tends [to] act impulsively and to disregard normal diplomatic procedures in [the] belief that they are too time-consuming."[70]

Sihanouk's frame of mind concerned Dr. Armand Riche, a French military officer and the prince's personal physician. In a conversation with a US embassy official, Dr. Riche commented about Sihanouk that "since the August 31st bomb attempt, worries about his own personal security and that of his parents had caused a psychological mood which was not conducive to good health."[71]

In Saigon, Durbrow continued his effort to stop South Vietnam's "irresponsible plotting" against Sihanouk. To rebut Diem's denial of South Vietnamese involvement in anti-Cambodian activities, the State Department authorized Durbrow to reveal certain details about US knowledge of Khmer Serei activities—for example, the location of a mobile radio transmitter within South Vietnam on a specific date. On October 7, the ambassador provided Diem with this and other information about Khmer Serei propaganda, including South Vietnamese "guidance" to Sam Sary and Son Ngoc Thanh in preparing anti-Sihanouk broadcasts and tracts. With diplomatic insincerity, Durbrow assured Diem that the United States believed he was unaware of such activities. Otherwise he "would have stopped them." Diem, responding in kind, said that he "would be greatly astonished" if the ambassador's allegations were true.[72]

Although Diem later claimed he was unable to confirm Durbrow's information, the ambassador's démarche may have been the impetus for a conversation on October 15 between Dang Duc Khoi, counselor of the South Vietnamese embassy in Bangkok, and Leonard S. Unger, his counterpart in the American embassy. Khoi, who was reportedly close to SEPES chief Dr. Tran Kim Tuyen, mentioned Sihanouk's preoccupation with Sam Sary, who was then living in Thailand, and with Son Ngoc Thanh. Khoi said that "he could see the value of getting one or both of these Cambodian exiles far away from the scene of the action." In his report of the conversation to the State Department, Unger commented: "It appeared clear that if this project ever comes up for serious consideration, the South Vietnamese will in all probability be asking Uncle Sam to foot the bill for transportation and continuing support."[73]

Unger further reported that Ambassador Johnson; Robert J. Jantzen, the CIA chief of station in Bangkok; and Desmond FitzGerald, the head of the agency's Far East Division, subsequently discussed the relocation of Son Ngoc Thanh and Sam Sary. Japan, which had long-standing ties to Son Ngoc Thanh, might take the dissidents, these officials concluded. A drawback of pro-US Japan providing asylum to the exiles was that Sihanouk would undoubtedly assume they "were regrouping and planning further dissident activities." Neutral India, however, might "not raise apprehension on Sihanouk's part." The Americans thought that Thai officials "would be happy to see Sam Sary on his way." They were "not so sure" about South Vietnam's attitude toward Son Ngoc Thanh.[74]

When FitzGerald returned to Washington, he discussed asylum for the dissidents with Parsons. "CIA," said FitzGerald, "would pick up [the] tab." (He also reported the contrarian view presented by Phnom Penh chief of station Roger Goiran, who believed that Sihanouk "welcomed" the nearby presence of Sam Sary and Son Ngoc Thanh because, posing little real danger to the regime, they were a useful symbolic threat that helped unify the nation behind the prince.) FitzGerald said that India would be the "best haven" for the exiles, with Japan a "poor second." Because the agency did not want to approach Nehru's government about relocating the dissidents, FitzGerald offered to speak with his UK contacts in Washington to "get them [to] carry [the] ball with India." According to notes of the conversation, FitzGerald believed that if the United States successfully pulled off the "operation" to relocate Sam Sary, then the South Vietnamese government "might be willing [to] give up SNT [Son Ngoc Thanh] in [the] same [manner]."[75]

While officials in Washington considered clandestine means of removing Sam Sary and Son Ngoc Thanh from Southeast Asia, Trimble put the matter squarely to Ambassador Cheed Sreshthaputra, his Thai counterpart in Phnom Penh. On November 28, Trimble offered the "personal suggestion" that the expulsion of the two dissidents by the Thai government "might do much to ease" regional tensions. Ambassador Cheed apparently agreed but claimed he could not make such a proposal to his government, presumably because it would infuriate Sarit and other Thai officials. Cheed suggested that Ambassador Johnson raise the issue with Thai leaders. He also opined that expelling Sam Sary and Son Ngoc Thanh from Thailand would require a "Cambodian quid pro quo"—for example, an alternative to the International Court of Justice for resolving the Preah Vihear dispute.[76]

State Department officials, disturbed by Thai intrigues with Cambodian dissidents, proposed to Ambassador Johnson that he make a detailed presentation of US views to Sarit. The points to be stressed included Sihanouk's firm grip on power, his growing appreciation of the internal communist threat, and the likelihood of a communist takeover should the prince "disappear." Because reducing Sihanouk's fears of US, Vietnamese, and Thai pressure offered the best hope of strengthening his resistance to communism, the State Department declared, "[The] most important initial step would be [to] effectively dissolve real and apparent free world associations with Cambodian dissidents."[77]

Johnson, who shared the Thais' dislike of Sihanouk and was reluctant, as Trimble put it, to "to task" them for supporting Cambodian rebels,[78] disagreed with his Washington colleagues' analysis. In his view, the department had "put the cart before the horse." Before appealing for Thai cooperation in reducing tension with its neighbor, the United States "must be able to prove there has been a definite improvement in Cambodia." The State Department deferred to Johnson's opposition to "a full scale démarche" to Thai officials. There was no instruction to the ambassador to urge the Thai government to "dissolve" its relationship with Sam Sary and Son Ngoc Thanh.[79]

In January 1960, Parsons discussed with officials of the South East Asia Department of the UK Foreign Office the "removal of Sam Sary from [the] immediate neighborhood" of Cambodia. "The Philippines, for example, would still be too close to be healthy," Parsons said.[80] With India refusing to provide asylum for the dissident, South East Asia Department diplomats suggested relocating him to France. Acknowledging uncertainty about the French reaction to such a proposal, the British subsequently received a reply from Pierre Millet, director of Asian affairs at the Quai d'Orsay. Using a direct if undiplomatic English colloquialism, Millet said that France "would not touch Sam Sary with a barge pole."[81]

The effort to relocate Sam Sary was further complicated by the publication of a letter that he had allegedly written to former DCM Edmund Kellogg in September 1959. Reproduced in *Blitz*, a notoriously anti-American Indian tabloid, in January 1960 and reprinted in Cambodia on February 5, the letter implicated the United States in plotting against Sihanouk by thanking Kellogg "for his support and expressing gratitude for [the] Thai and Vietnamese efforts on his behalf."[82] Ambassador Trimble, who insisted that the letter was a forgery planted by the Soviets, had appealed to Sihanouk to suppress its publication in Cambodia. Sihanouk refused. According to Australian diplomat Francis Stuart, Trimble was "incensed by what he regards as an 'unfriendly act' by the Prime Minister in allowing the document to be published."[83]

Sihanouk's public response to the Sam Sary letter was ambiguous—either inadvertently or, more probably, deliberately. The day after the letter's publication in Cambodia, he wrote an editorial in the *Nationalist*, a semiofficial weekly, that referred to the traitorous relationship between Slat Peau and Victor Matsui and that gave "credence to [the] Blitz accusations," according to the US embassy. Yet in a flyleaf attached to the same issue of the *Nationalist*, the prince declared that since writing the editorial he had received assurances from Ambassador Trimble that the *Blitz* allegations were "without basis." Although he told *Nationalist* readers that "the attack on Cambodian–American friendship" was without foundation, he also suggested that handwriting experts examine the Sam Sary letter.[84]

As historian Kenton Clymer notes, "Washington went to unusual lengths" to discredit the letter's authenticity. Handwriting experts from the US Postal Service examined the letter and concluded that it was a forgery. French experts, however, said that that the document was genuine. Whatever the letter's provenance, its publication apparently prompted the US government to end its attempt to secure political asylum for Sam Sary. "The United States," said Laurin Askew of the State Department, "could not risk being associated with Sam Sary in any way."[85] Every other country seemed to feel the same way: none offered him asylum.

Sam Sary, after a falling out with his co-conspirator Son Ngoc Thanh, vanished under circumstances that remain unclear to this day. Around January 1, 1961, Madame Sam Sary said that she had heard a rumor of her husband's recent death in an automobile accident in Japan. This account of his demise turned out to be false. On March 16, 1961, Diem told Ambassador Durbrow that he had not heard anything about Sam Sary for several months. "Maybe he is dead or might have left the area," said Diem. There was a rumor "that Sam Sary had been removed from [the] scene by 'American Special Services.'" Durbrow responded that he, too, had heard nothing about Sam Sary for months. He could, however, assure Diem that the rumor about "American Services" was incorrect.[86]

According to Sihanouk biographer Milton Osborne, Sam Sary "disappeared in 1962, probably put to death by one or another of his foreign paymasters." In 1965, the CIA *National Intelligence Survey* briefly discussed Sary's uncertain fate, citing an unconfirmed report that he was "murdered in South Vietnam in 1963." Sam Sary's son, Sam Rainsy, alleges that Son Ngoc Thanh "ordered" the death of his father. Relying on the "painstaking research" of his brother, Rainsy writes: "Sam Sary died in the southern Lao province of Pakse in late 1962 or early 1963, shot in the back at the age of forty-three."[87]

10

"Getting Along with Sihanouk" (1960)

On February 10, 1960—just five days after the Cambodian publication of the alleged Sam Sary letter to Edmund Kellogg—a ninth-grade student named Reath Vath arrived at the US chancery in Phnom Penh with a note protesting Prince Sihanouk's foreign policy and seeking American assistance in a plot to assassinate him. The attempt would be made the next day in Svay Rieng, where the prince was scheduled to speak at a youth rally. The inexperienced conspirator showed the note to two of the embassy's Cambodian employees to find out whom he should see. US officials spoke with the boy while simultaneously alerting the Cambodian police, who came to the chancery and arrested him.[1]

Ambassador William Trimble and his mission colleagues did not know what to make of this bizarre incident, which might have seemed comical had Cambodian distrust and suspicion of the United States been less intense. Was the young man deranged? He did not seem so to the embassy officers who spoke with him. Was he a communist-controlled provocateur? The amateurish nature of the approach suggested otherwise. A third possibility, the embassy speculated, was that he was a "sincere but naive youth who was genuinely disillusioned with Sihanouk's policies." Whatever Reath Vath's motivation, Trimble quickly concluded that the proposed plot was a "windfall" for the United States that he intended to "exploit" fully.[2]

The diplomatic benefits of the foiled assassination plan included a grateful Cambodian government, an opportunity to criticize the publication of the alleged Sam Sary letter, and an occasion to denounce the local press for unfairly attacking the United States. Within hours of Reath Vath's arrest, Foreign Minister Son Sann and other Cambodian officials came to Trimble's home, where the ambassador charged that the would-be assassin's approach to the embassy was the direct result of the "campaign of calumnies against [the] US being carried on by [the] Cambodian press." The so-called revelations initially published in *Blitz* were "completely false," said Trimble, and they "had poisoned [the] atmosphere here to [the] serious detriment [of] US–Cambodian relations." Son Sann, who had expressed deep appreciation for the embassy's response to the Reath Vath incident, "grimaced" while listening to Trimble's indignant protest.[3]

In his memoirs, Sihanouk charged that the CIA and Son Ngoc Thanh were behind a thwarted assassination attempt by "Rat Vat [*sic*]."[4] At the time of the incident, however, the prince blamed the communists. Sihanouk declared in a front-page editorial in the *Nationalist* that the leaders of the plot were "members of the editorial staff of *Pracheachon,* the mouthpiece of the Communist group of the same name." He explained that "the plot to kill him had been prepared by the Communist Cambodian–Vietnamese group which wished to profit from the Cambodians' present distrust of the United States[,] to place the onus of his assassination on the Americans, and to sow disorder favorable to communism." *Pracheachon* printed an open letter denying complicity in the affair, and *La Dépêche du Cambodge* ridiculed the notion of communist participation in such a crude plan.[5]

The public trial of Reath Vath did little to clarify the origins of the plot. An apparent victim of torture, he had reportedly confessed to the police that he belonged to the Khmer Serei, that he was a member of an assassination committee led by "a friend of Ho Chi Minh," and that the Pracheachon supported this committee. The leader of the assassination committee, Kol Sy, had allegedly confirmed its existence before he was shot and killed while "trying to escape" from Sihanouk's security forces. At his trial, Reath Vath testified that he "did not do anything." He said that he was simply trying to "roll" the Americans for some money.[6]

On December 7, 1960, a special military court convicted Reath Vath of treason, attempted uprising, and attempted coup d'état. He was condemned to death, but the sentence was subsequently commuted to imprisonment. On April 2, 1970—two weeks after Sihanouk's overthrow—Lon Nol released Reath Vath and 485 other political prisoners. "I tried to kill Sihanouk because he was a dictator," Reath Vath told reporters. "I wanted a republic."[7]

On the same day as Reath Vath's approach to the US embassy in Phnom Penh, the OCB in Washington acknowledged that the Eisenhower administration's policy of encouraging Sihanouk's anticommunist opposition had been counterproductive. In a special report on Southeast Asia, the OCB concluded that the prince had emerged from the failed Dap Chhuon coup with added power and prestige, that many anticommunist dissidents had been eliminated, and that "the revelation of their real or fancied association with the United States and other free world countries undermined Cambodian confidence in US motives and became an obstacle to the pursuit of our objectives." OCB staffer Kenneth P. Landon put the matter more directly when he wrote: "The major reason for recommending [a] review of policy is the need for guidance for dealing with Sihanouk and to eliminate language which might provide a basis for further abortive coup plots."[8]

In a related recommendation, the OCB suggested strengthening policy guidance on Cambodia's relations with South Vietnam and Thailand. Noting that this problem had assumed greater significance in recent months, the OCB perceived a "more urgent need for the U.S. to exert a moderating influence" on its anticommunist allies in Southeast Asia. At the March 10 meeting of the NSC, OCB vice chairman Karl G. Harr told the president and his advisers, "The operators now feel that we must direct our policy toward getting along with Sihanouk, who has survived a number of attempts to unseat him." The minutes of the NSC meeting indicate that the OCB report was "discussed"—though the only recorded comments are Harr's—and that the paper was referred to the NSC planning board.[9]

While the planning board began to formally revise the language guiding policy in Southeast Asia—a bureaucratic process that took four months—State Department officials wrestled with the immediate problem of preventing "eruptions in Cambodia's relations with its neighbors." A CIA report on anti-Sihanouk plotting in 1959, dated March 4, prompted an analysis of the current "attitudes of the participants" by Richard Usher, deputy director of the Office of Southeast Asian Affairs. He wrote that South Vietnam, based on its material and moral support for the Khmer Serei, was "appreciably more sanguine" than Thailand about the rebels' prospects. Dismissing the notion that Ngo Dinh Diem was unaware of South Vietnamese support for the Khmer Serei, Usher declared: "President Diem and Brother Ngo Dinh Nhu are fully cognizant of Vietnamese aid to the dissidents." Although he characterized Thailand as "relatively responsive" to US appeals, Usher predicted that "Vietnam will deliberately disregard Western advice and US requests to desist in its support of the Son Ngoc Thanh movement; the Vietnamese will respond only to unrelenting pressure with teeth in it."[10]

An "eruption" US officials did not anticipate, much less prevent, occurred on March 9, 1960, when South Vietnam provoked Sihanouk with a diplomatic note demanding that Cambodia renounce its claim to several small offshore islands in the Gulf of Thailand. (The ownership dispute was rooted in an administrative boundary adjustment by the French in 1939.) Since 1958, Cambodia had maintained a modest military presence on some of the disputed islands, which were adjacent to the larger Vietnamese-controlled island of Phu Quoc. According to a CIA report, Sihanouk said that Cambodia would fight to keep the islands and that he would seek assistance from China if necessary. Son Sann declared that Diem's diplomatic maneuver revealed "the annexationist aims of Vietnam."[11]

The wrangling over the islands escalated in April, when Cambodia landed troops on two uninhabited islets. The Diem government called that action a "premeditated act of aggression" and accused Cambodia of creating an "extremely dangerous situation for peace in this part of the world." South Vietnam sent two patrol craft to the islands and placed a company of marines on alert. Foreign Minister Vu Van Mau of South Vietnam assured Ambassador Elbridge Durbrow that South Vietnam had "no intention of dislodging the Cambodians by force." Mau admitted, however, that such an operation was "considered" at a special meeting of the cabinet. "Mau," Durbrow wrote, "complained that the West did not understand Cambodian leader Sihanouk's 'real game, which is one of continual aggressive jabs.'"[12]

Durbrow had little sympathy for South Vietnam's view of the island dispute. To him, the Diem government's diplomatic and military moves were part of a larger pattern of actions that jeopardized the fight against the growing insurgency in South Vietnam. Diem and Nhu had ignored US advice on winning the allegiance of the population, on using South Vietnamese security forces more effectively, and on ending the corrupt practices of the regime's Can Lao party. And instead of trying to work cooperatively with Cambodia on border-control measures, the Ngo brothers had continued to support the Khmer Serei and instigated a crisis over the ownership of some small offshore islands. In a cable to the State Department, Durbrow declared that the time had come for the United States to "force [the] GVN [to] desist from taking such irresponsible actions."[13]

Observing that US officials had never "put any teeth into our 'persuasion,'" Durbrow sought a sanction that would "hurt" but not "vitally" damage the Diem regime. "Diem could not care less if we cut off some economic development aid," the ambassador wrote. He therefore recommended informing Diem that the United States had reconsidered its decision to provide supplemental military equipment requested by the South Vietnamese government. Diem should be told that unless the United States was convinced that South Vietnam was making a "serious and sincere effort to settle basic outstanding problems" with Cambodia, there would be no equipment above and beyond normal military-assistance deliveries: "While I realize that this is [a] rather drastic suggestion[,] I am firmly convinced that unless we [are] prepared to stick by our guns and refuse to give extra help at this time[,] Diem will not come to his senses, relations with Cambodia will become worse and the latter might well aggravate [the] situation further by some stupid short-sighted deal with [the] ChiComs."[14]

With Walter Robertson no longer in charge of far eastern affairs, working-level State Department officials agreed with the proposed pressure tactic and drafted an affirmative reply to Durbrow. But Colonel Edward Lansdale, who had left the CIA in 1957 and resumed his military intelligence career in the Pentagon's Office of Special Operations, raised objections. An operator in the bureaucracy as well as in the field, Lansdale warned senior Defense Department officials that Durbrow's proposal could have "serious consequences for our national security." Diem, Lansdale wrote, was a "leader in a combat situation," and his forces were "starting to gain success. Is this the time, then, to threaten to withdraw our support? Defense, with its generations of experience in the needs of combat leadership, should have some opinion worth heeding on this point."[15]

Lansdale, who had worked in advertising before joining the Office of Strategic Services during World War II, made an emotional appeal to senior Pentagon officials, characterizing the State Department's "negative approach" to Diem as a threat to the prestige of the United States. Without mentioning the island dispute or South Vietnam's support for Cambodian dissidents—the actions that triggered Durbrow's request for limited military sanctions—Lansdale asked, "Would the few items involved portray the United States as a petty, nagging child, or as the world's leading nation?" Apparently intending to inflame Pentagon passions, he referred to the criticism that US military assistance to South Vietnam placed too much emphasis on conventional warfare rather than on antiguerrilla operations: "The U.S. military man and his thinking remain very much on trial in Vietnam. Defense should acknowledge realistically this situation it finds itself in, by insisting upon using its full, rightful voice in any further decisions affecting Vietnam."[16]

Lansdale's broadside led to a "serious [and] exhaustive" interagency assessment of the coercive diplomacy proposed by Durbrow. On May 9, the State Department informed the ambassador that the US government was currently "reluctant" to threaten Diem with military sanctions. Department officials explained that if Diem did not respond to the recommended threat, curtailing military aid risked "weakening our over-all security posture in Asia." The State Department praised Durbrow's analysis as "most convincing" but only authorized further jawboning—without the "teeth" requested by the ambassador: "You should emphasize in [the] strongest manner possible that we mean business with respect [to] Diem's anti-RKG activities." Durbrow's instructions included a warning to South Vietnamese officials that if they continued to misuse US military assistance for plots against Sihanouk, "we will give serious consideration to backing our words with action."[17]

Durbrow, reading from a prepared text to emphasize the seriousness of his presentation, spoke with Diem for thirty minutes on May 13 about "grave, serious and important" reports the US government had received. When discussing anti-Sihanouk activities, Durbrow said that Sam Sary had traveled from Bangkok to South Vietnam in April and that the

Diem government had recently furnished arms to Khmer Serei forces in Thailand. The US government, the ambassador said, was "particularly disturbed to learn" that Khmer Serei radio broadcasts had resumed. Durbrow's protest appeared to have little impact on Diem, who said that he was "deeply hurt" the United States believed such "rumors." Diem did, however, indicate that he might send a high-level delegation to Phnom Penh to negotiate the disputes between Cambodia and South Vietnam.[18]

Durbrow's démarche may also have contributed to an unspoken but more significant concession from Diem. Within weeks of their meeting, Khmer Serei propaganda broadcasts went off the air.

As was often the case, the catalyst for a new anti-American outburst by Sihanouk was an article in the Western press. On May 1, 1960, the *New York Times* published a long report on authoritarian noncommunist regimes in Asia that included a three-sentence paragraph on Cambodia. After discussing anticommunist governments in South Korea, Nationalist China, South Vietnam, and Thailand, reporter Tillman Durdin wrote, "In Cambodia mercurial Prince Sihanouk Norodom runs still another kind of authoritarianism. He maintains his dominance through a mass party that exercises a monopoly of political activity and demagogy. Prince Sihanouk remains widely popular but his abridgements of democracy, his neutralism and his tolerance toward communism are disliked in some quarters and there have been sporadic flareups against his regime."[19]

Sihanouk—who hated being characterized as "mercurial"—was outraged that the article equated neutral Cambodia with anticommunist regimes supported by the United States. In the May 21 issue of the *Nationalist,* Sihanouk responded with an open letter to the "imperialist milieux," an appellation the American embassy considered an unmistakable reference to the United States. The prince not only denounced the *New York Times* article but also attacked *A Short History of Cambodia,* a book written by diplomat Martin Herz and published in 1958. An informed introduction to the country, the book contained mild criticism of Sihanouk and observed that Son Ngoc Thanh had once been "a symbol of the fight for complete independence and sovereignty."[20]

Sihanouk had been deeply disturbed by Herz's book, publicly attacking the author as an American friend of Son Ngoc Thanh. (Before Trimble arrived in Phnom Penh, Parsons warned him, somewhat facetiously,

"Don't ever let Prince Sihanouk know you have read Martin Herz' book or that you know him.")[21] Sihanouk, in his open letter to the "imperialist milieux," lashed out at the "bad faith which is habitual to you," charging US "partisans" with disseminating Herz's book "with the sole intent of sullying me, misrepresenting our neutrality and glorifying Son Ngoc Thanh." In an indirect reference to Dap Chhuon's attempted coup, the prince wrote that any "discontented" movements in Cambodia—"and you know it better than any other"—"do not belong to the Khmer people but are groups artificially created by imperialists for the price of gold."[22]

The prince's open letter echoed speeches that he had been making across the kingdom. Basic Sihanouk themes noted by the US embassy included "excoriating Son Ngoc Thanh, stigmatizing [South Vietnam] and Thais and condemning [the] Western press, as well as boasting of CHICOM appreciation [of] Cambodian progress and [the] promise of support in case of aggression." (Zhou Enlai, who had recently visited Cambodia, praised the kingdom's neutrality and offered moral support for its disputes with its neighbors.) At the dedication of a library in the provincial capital of Kompong Cham, Sihanouk said that the "perfect orchestration" of Khmer Serei propaganda and the press in South Vietnam, Thailand, and the West was proof of their "one inimical aim against Cambodia."[23]

Ambassador Trimble responded to Sihanouk's open letter with a private one. "I was puzzled and saddened by the tone of your article," he wrote. It "contained many points of criticism which I feel are unjust." Reminding Sihanouk of US efforts to improve Cambodia's relations with its neighbors, Trimble admitted that he was "frankly discouraged by your accusation of bad faith on our part." He reiterated US respect for Cambodian independence and neutrality. As evidence of this attitude, he cited the substantial amounts of American military and economic assistance, "which in magnitude is many times greater than those of all other aid-donating countries put together." Trimble, who was about to leave Cambodia for home leave and consultations with the State Department, concluded his letter by observing, "It will be difficult for me upon my return to Washington to explain to my government just what Cambodian attitudes and intentions might be. I am afraid that the apparent lack of confidence by your Royal Highness in the good faith of the US in its relations with Cambodia will come as a considerable disappointment to President Eisenhower who has great personal esteem for your Royal Highness."[24]

Trimble's letter, written more in sadness than in anger, produced an aggrieved public reply from Sihanouk, who ruminated on "the tragic misunderstanding which has always characterized my relations with Americans." In a special French-language editorial in the *Nationalist,* he denied that the "imperilaist milieux" referred to the US government. "But this America, its president, its government, its ambassadors, are they sure of all those who serve 'under' them?" Such hostile elements, he wrote, also existed in the "journalistic and literary milieux and others specializing on Asian questions." Commenting on American diplomacy, Sihanouk admitted that he "always had difficulties with all ambassadors who represented [the] U.S. in Cambodia." The prince also mocked the concluding remark in Trimble's letter: "He promises to report my bad conduct to President Eisenhower[,] who should withdraw his esteem."[25]

US embassy officials in Phnom Penh viewed Sihanouk's latest comments on Cambodian–American relations as a "vicious attack on the Ambassador." They recommended that the State Department either publish Trimble's letter or plant a question about the "misunderstanding" at Secretary of State Christian Herter's next press conference. But Daniel V. Anderson, director of the Office of Southeast Asian Affairs, disagreed. "Under present conditions," Anderson concluded, "any further move on our part is apt not to produce constructive results and is more likely to add fuel to the fire." Parsons concurred, and the State Department made no public response to Sihanouk's outburst. In a private meeting with Ambassador Nong Kimny, Parsons did say that the United States was "sorry [that] Sihanouk felt it necessary [to] adopt this tone."[26]

C. Robert Moore, the American chargé in Trimble's absence, thought that redressing Sihanouk's "anti-US bias" would require something more than merely reiterating US sympathy for Cambodia's neutrality and independence. The United States, Moore advised the State Department, would have to convince the prince of its "dissociation from forces opposed to him and his neutrality." Many "observers"—a group that presumably included Western diplomats and Moore himself—found it "striking" that the United States had never really addressed the "direct and indirect charges of sympathy and support for the 'traitors.'" Moore acknowledged that "any disavowal runs squarely into [the] problem of [the] Matsui allegations," but he doubted there would be any improvement in US–Cambodian relations until this issue was "squarely faced."[27]

Moore was unsure about the most effective timing for his proposed "dissociation" statement—in part, because of "Sihanouk's upset state of mind." Washington officials, who continued to oppose providing the Cambodians with an explanation for Matsui's contact with Dap Chhuon, shared the chargé's concern over the prince's troubled mood. Deputy Assistant Secretary of State John Steeves, for example, characterized Sihanouk as "disturbingly paranoiac." The prince, in addition to being distressed by South Vietnam, Thailand, and the "imperialist milieux," had been agitated by a succession crisis created by the death of King Suramarit on April 3. Sihanouk resigned as prime minister, ostensibly to rest and mourn. He did not, however, want to become king again or have anyone else succeed his pliant father. According to the CIA, Sihanouk "successfully blocked efforts to place his mother or his uncle Monireth on the throne."[28]

A regency council including Sihanouk, the queen, and Prince Monireth reigned over Cambodia from April to June. On June 5, the kingdom held a national referendum intended to show the "world in general and our imperialist neighbors in particular" that Sihanouk enjoyed popular support.[29] To no one's surprise, he won 99.98 percent of the vote against condemned-in-absentia Son Ngoc Thanh and unnamed communists. The regency council was dissolved, and the National Assembly amended the Cambodian Constitution to allow the prince to become "chief of state." This newly created position permitted him both to govern as a politician and to reign as a royal. In a memorandum to Herter, Steeves speculated: "Sihanouk's reassertion of his domestic political power as the new 'Chief of State,' a recently reported reconciliation with his family, and his forthcoming rest cure in France may serve to calm his emotional agitation."[30]

Despite hopeful prospects for soothing Sihanouk's state of mind, there would be little tranquility in US–Cambodian relations. On June 20, 1960—the same day as the prince's investiture as chief of state—the Cambodian Foreign Ministry circulated a confidential note to diplomatic missions in Phnom Penh. "Dissidents, supported by neighboring countries, [are] assembling for an incursion into Cambodia," the note declared. "Any such incursion from a foreign country would be regarded as an act of aggression by that country." American officials, relieved that this latest allegation was a confidential diplomatic communication rather than a public accusation, perceived an opportunity for the United States, South Vietnam, and Thailand to dissociate from rebel activity and to halt Sihanouk's leftward drift. The State Department instructed chargé Moore to assure the Cambodian government in the "most categoric terms of firm US opposition to any rebel activities directed against [the] RKG from foreign countries."[31]

Moore, then forty-five, was a Harvard graduate who had worked for the Bank of New York in the 1930s and served as a Lend-Lease administrator during World War II. Entering the Foreign Service in 1947, he was assigned to Ankara, Paris, and Washington before becoming the DCM in Cambodia. Historian David Chandler, who began his career as a language officer in the US embassy in Phnom Penh, characterized Moore as sharp and approachable: "Bob Moore, although intellectually demanding, was a joy to work for."[32]

On June 29, 1960, Moore assured Foreign Minister Tep Phan of US opposition to rebel activities and expressed American willingness to discuss ways of addressing them. The State Department, said Moore, had been surprised by Cambodia's concern over the Khmer Serei, which did not appear to represent "any appreciable threat" to the kingdom. "Several months ago," Tep Phan replied, approximately three hundred dissidents had crossed the South Vietnamese border into Kratie Province. This incursion had "made the Cambodians particularly aware of their own weakness." Moore commented that three hundred or even one thousand rebels might be "disquieting," but they could not seriously threaten Cambodia's territorial integrity. Tep Phan responded that perhaps the incident had been "a probing effort, a forerunner of a more serious incursion. In any event, it was unprecedented in its magnitude."[33]

Raising a new though related topic, Tep Phan referred to a recent editorial in the *Nationalist* criticizing US military assistance to Cambodia as "poor, antiquated and insufficient." Unsigned but presumably approved, if not written, by Sihanouk, the editorial charged that South Vietnam and Thailand "used American military aid to threaten Cambodia, to try to seize parts of Cambodia's territory and to equip and train groups of traitors and guerrillas to ravage its provinces." Pointing out the disproportionate amounts of military aid received by South Vietnam and Thailand, the article called for Cambodian officials to negotiate an increased and improved program of US military assistance. According to a memorandum of their conversation, Tep Phan told Moore that the *Nationalist* editorial "reflected the views of many Cambodians—intellectuals, deputies, members of the government, etc.—and [that] he hoped that the US would be able to be responsive."[34]

Moore doubted that Cambodians had a precise idea of the enhanced military capabilities they sought. He did, however, know that the Defense Ministry had a pending request to the United States for eight jet fighters and training for pilots. Because the aircraft would have little impact on the military balance between Cambodia and its more powerful neighbors, US officials concluded that the desire to acquire jets was a matter of national prestige. The State Department's Bureau of Intelligence and Research thought that Sihanouk would likely regard the provision of jets as "an indication of Washington's sincerity" in supporting Cambodia. A refusal would probably lead Sihanouk to request jet aircraft from a communist country.[35]

This prediction was confirmed by an interview with Sihanouk in the July 3 edition of the *Observer* (London). "If the United States did not radically revise its anti-Communist military aid policy in South-east Asia in the next few months he would ask the Soviet bloc to send aircraft and arms to this neutral enclave in the heart of the Seato defence area," wrote Dennis Bloodworth, the newspaper's chief Asian correspondent. Sihanouk charged that "certain American elements" had been actively supporting rebel Cambodian leaders, who "move freely between Bangkok and Saigon" and whose "forces are being raised and based on Thailand and South Vietnam." The prince faulted the United States for failing "to apply real pressure" on Cambodia's neighbors, who constantly threatened the kingdom's territory. "It is a vicious circle from which we must find an exit," he said.[36]

Removing any doubt about his responsibility for the earlier unsigned editorial in the *Nationalist,* Sihanouk told Bloodworth that the United States had not provided Cambodia with sufficient means for self-defense: "While Thailand and Vietnam receive modern arms, we are getting superseded and worn-out equipment, including guns which are as much a menace to their users as to the enemy, and aircraft that can be described as 1914–18 taxis." The prince declared: "[The] American failure to restrain our enemies and to give us adequate arms can be explained by a desire to sink us."[37]

Sihanouk's warning that he might seek military aid from "the Socialist camp" concerned US officials. In a memorandum to President Eisenhower, Secretary Herter wrote: "The United States position in neutral Cambodia is being threatened by an accelerated tendency on the part of Cambodia's Chief of State, Prince Sihanouk, to seek closer relations with the Sino–Soviet bloc. We believe this tendency stems in large part from a decline in Cambodia's confidence in our willingness to protect it in the face of real or imagined threats from neighboring anti-communist Thailand and Viet-Nam."[38] Herter's unwillingness to discuss Sihanouk's possible reasons for losing confidence in the United States is striking. The secretary apparently thought that the Dap Chhuon affair was either diplomatically insignificant or too sensitive a topic to be included in a memorandum to the president.

Herter informed Eisenhower that Cambodia wanted military aid comparable to the assistance the United States provided to Thailand and South Vietnam. "It would appear, however, that basically he is seeking additional assurances of US interest and support."[39] The State Department instructed Moore to reiterate to Foreign Minister Tep Phan the willingness of the United States to discuss threats faced by the kingdom and ways of countering them. Moreover, the chargé should say that the MAAG commander, Brigadier General Charles H. Chase, was available to discuss the kind of equipment required by Cambodia's military. Irritated by Sihanouk's latest act of public diplomacy, the State Department's leaders wanted Moore to urge the royal government to "state its official views through normal diplomatic channels."[40]

Ambassador Trimble, who was on leave in the United States, emphasized this latter point to Nong Kimny. Although Trimble had no intention of formally protesting Sihanouk's complaints about US policy—which would almost certainly trigger an anti-American rejoinder from the prince—he informed Kimny that this public approach to diplomacy "did not make a good impression in Washington and certainly did not evoke confidence." Commenting on allegations of US involvement with anti-Sihanouk plotters, Trimble denied reports in the Cambodian press of American backing for Major General Lon Nol as a replacement for the prince. "There had never been an effort by the US to find an alternative 'strong man' in Cambodia," said Trimble. Nong Kimny replied that there was "positive proof" of the involvement of "certain Americans" with Cambodian dissidents.[41]

A revision of US policy in mainland Southeast Asia was the first item discussed at the NSC meeting of July 21, 1960. "The most important change in the new draft policy," wrote NSC staffer Samuel E. Belk, "is the U.S. attitude toward Prince Sihanouk." The amended directive, originally proposed by the OCB in February, formally changed US policy from "encouraging anti-Sihanouk groups and individuals" to trying "to establish an effective working relationship" with him. Although acknowledging the prince's popularity and political power, the new policy did not mean that senior Eisenhower administration officials viewed him with any more sympathy. In his background briefing for the council, Allen Dulles said: "We continue to have to deal with Sihanouk[,] who is a difficult character."[42]

Dulles reported to the NSC that Sihanouk had threatened to seek military assistance from the communists unless the United States provided more and better equipment. Commenting on the prince's concerns about his neighbors, the DCI said that Sihanouk suspected the United States of having "secret designs to 'sink' Cambodia." Dulles speculated that the motivation for Sihanouk's threat to seek communist military aid was to "frighten" South Vietnam and Thailand into ending their support of Cambodian dissidents. "Thailand," said Dulles, "has shelved its anti-Sihanouk campaign. Vietnam, however, is still planning anti-Sihanouk activities."[43]

Secretary of State Herter, who presided over the NSC meeting in Eisenhower's absence, said that "he could not agree more with Mr. Dulles' view of Sihanouk." Herter had expressed similar sentiments in a background interview for *Newsweek* earlier in July: "The situation in Cambodia is disturbing. Sihanouk is completely unpredictable, and he is still in full control."[44]

In an oral history recorded in 1964, Herter admitted that he had never achieved John Foster Dulles's "extraordinarily close" relationship with President Eisenhower. Although liked and respected by his colleagues at the State Department, Herter lacked the policy influence and forceful personality of his predecessor, who had succumbed to cancer on May 24, 1959. In an unpublished memoir, J. Graham Parsons characterized Herter as "almost a lame duck." Noting the loss of the State Department's preeminence in formulating foreign policy, Parsons wrote that, "unmistakably, a decline from the Department's traditional role set in gradually after Mr. Dulles' death and the Administration grew obviously older and less decisive."[45]

Herter had limited experience with Asian affairs, and his views on Southeast Asia generally echoed the anticommunism of John Foster Dulles and Walter Robertson. Although he supported the policy of providing "modest" military aid to Cambodia, he was reluctant to recommend an increase in such assistance. "Thailand and Vietnam," he told the NSC, "would soon be crying that Cambodia planned to use the military equipment the U.S. provided against them rather than against Communist China."[46]

Herter and other Washington-based officials were particularly leery of granting Cambodia's request for jets and pilot training. There seemed to be no military justification for the aircraft. If the United States provided them for political purposes, South Vietnam would inevitably request jets, which would violate the Geneva accords. Moreover, Thailand and other Asian allies would likely perceive the provision of jet aircraft as giving in to neutralist blackmail. The administration's new policy statement, NSC 6012, sought "to discourage Cambodia from accepting substantial military aid from the Sino–Soviet Bloc" but deferred a decision on providing jets to the kingdom.[47]

Although specialists in the national security bureaucracy remained deeply engaged with the festering political and military problems in Southeast Asia, the region neither demanded nor received much attention from President Eisenhower at this time.[48] On July 25, Gordon Gray, Eisenhower's special assistant for national security affairs, traveled to Newport, Rhode Island, where the president had been vacationing. Among the topics Gray discussed with Eisenhower was the recent NSC meeting. "I told him that the principal item involved was the revision of U.S. Policy in Mainland Southeast Asia which was unanimously agreed to," wrote Gray a few days later. "I said I did not feel the need to take his time to describe the language changes[,] which really involved no startling change of policy. He authorized me to approve the Record of Actions."[49]

On July 21, the Cambodian Foreign Ministry informed the embassies in Phnom Penh that Sihanouk, as chief of state, would receive only those diplomats bearing personal messages from leaders of equivalent rank. Communications from prime ministers or foreign ministers should be directed to Tep Phan. The Foreign Ministry's announcement merely confirmed what had been evident for many weeks: Sihanouk did not want to meet with the local diplomats, who often raised disagreeable topics. He was, however, willing to speak with his *grand ami* Malcolm MacDonald, then the UK high commissioner in India. On August 9, MacDonald was the prince's personal guest for a tour of the recently completed port of Sihanoukville. The only other westerners in attendance were Frederick Francis Garner, the British ambassador to Cambodia, and Sol H. Brown, a US public-works official who advised the Cambodian government on dredging operations. In a backhanded swipe at American diplomats, Sihanouk said that Brown was the kind of technician who "instilled a feeling of sincerity" in Cambodian officials.[50]

During a conversation at lunch, Sihanouk stressed that he was not pro-communist and that he preferred Western military assistance. His difficulties with the British and US governments, he said, were caused by their failure "to evaluate the feelings of the Cambodians properly." Sihanouk spoke of "a certain fear" of the West, which was building up the military strength of Thailand and Vietnam while providing relatively small amounts of military assistance to his country. His neighbors, the prince said, were threatening to take territory from Cambodia, which intended "to keep every square centimeter" of its land. He argued that it was "incumbent on the western bloc to act in such a manner that the Cambodians would feel that their borders will be secure," adding that he was "ready and willing at any moment to sign treaties with his neighbor countries that will include a guaranty of the present existing borders."[51]

Sihanouk emphasized to MacDonald that he did not believe Cambodia needed a large military force. Moreover, the kingdom did not require "jet planes at the present time." What was necessary, "both morally and psychologically," was a small corps of Cambodian officers who had jet training. This simple request, said Sihanouk, was a matter of national prestige. If the UK and US governments refused to train Cambodian pilots, "[I] would have no alternative but to ask Russia and Red China to perform this service."[52]

When asked about his future travel plans, Sihanouk said that he would be visiting China in the near future. The West would undoubtedly conclude that the trip was evidence of pro-communist leanings, but his only reason for going was that the Chinese had extended an invitation. The prince added that, to date, he had not received an invitation for an official state visit from either the British or the Americans. He volunteered that he would likely sign "a friendship treaty" with China to encourage continued "understanding and exchange of cultural activities." When MacDonald asked whether this treaty might include a pargraph that would "guarantee" Cambodia's current borders, Sihanouk replied that there was no present intention to include such language. He would, however, accept a Chinese guarantee if the West were unwilling to help secure Cambodia's borders.[53]

MacDonald reported to London that Cambodia's "fears of Vietnam and Thailand are genuine, deep-seated, and (in my opinion) the root of the present trouble." If the prince were not reassured about Vietnamese and Thai intentions and about US military assistance, MacDonald thought there was "a distinct danger that he will fall to the temptation of accepting some Communist military aid and a Chinese guarantee of his frontiers." Commenting on US military aid to Cambodia, MacDonald wrote that Sihanouk's criticism of inadequate, out-of-date equipment appeared to have some justification: "I greatly hope the Americans (or other Western friends) will be sufficiently forthcoming about his present requirements for more help."[54]

US chargé Moore, commenting to the State Department on Sihanouk's conversation with MacDonald, expressed concern over Washington's reluctance to provide Cambodia with "sophisticated weapons"—that is, jets. Sihanouk was determined to have Cambodia enter the jet age, and an agreement by the United States to train his pilots would forestall a similar request to the communists. The US government, cabled Moore, "must obviously be prepared to be reasonably responsive to [the] Cambodian request for jet aircraft which will inevitably follow." Summarizing the views of the country team in Phnom Penh, Moore wrote: "We believe [the] US must reconcile itself to [the] fact that increased military aid in itself will lack [the] necessary impact unless some items of equipment are included which are identified in Sihanouk's view with more modern and more effective forces."[55]

Ambassador Trimble, who held similar views, returned to Phnom Penh by way of London and Paris, where he informed the UK and French

Foreign Ministries of US reluctance to provide Cambodia with jet air-craft. Frederick Warner, head of the South East Asia Department in the UK Foreign Office, "was convinced that Sihanouk would put the [US government] on the spot and press his claim to be given jets." Such a request would be a "test" of US intentions, Warner predicted. Sihanouk "would point out that Thailand had American jets and would demand equal treatment in principle, if not in quantity."[56]

Among the topics Trimble and Warner discussed was India's waning influence in Cambodian affairs. One reason for this reduced authority was India's unwillingness to intervene with Sihanouk's anticommunist neighbors. Another was the border fighting between India and China in 1959, which had revealed the former's weakness and the latter's strength. Trimble, commenting on Sihanouk's belief that communism was the "wave of the future" in Southeast Asia, said that "the main job of the Free World was to convince Sihanouk that his greater interests still lay with the Free World and [that] he had no need to invite Chicom assistance in sup-port of his position."[57]

During his talks with Trimble, Warner raised an issue of sufficient sensitivity to require a separate "limit distribution" memorandum of con-versation: Sihanouk's charges of "US complicity" in the attempted coup by Dap Chhuon. Trimble's initial statement was general. The United States, he said, "had given Sihanouk assurances many times that no US officials had supported Dap Chhuon." When Warner mentioned Siha-nouk's repeated comments to "British sources that a particular individual in the American Embassy with a Japanese name had been involved with the coup," Trimble "clarified the matter," according to notes prepared by a US embassy officer in London. "While the US did have intelligence nets working in Cambodia," said Trimble, "they were not directed at Siha-nouk. They were, on the contrary, operating to keep a line on what moves were on foot against him in an effort to discourage such moves." Warner then asked if this explanation had ever been given to the prince. "Siha-nouk would never believe it," Trimble replied.[58]

Trimble met with Sihanouk on September 2, 1960, an audience that had been delayed by the weeklong ceremonies associated with the cremation of King Suramarit. Sihanouk initially appeared nervous but gradually relaxed. To take advantage of the prince's stated admiration for Eisen-

hower, the ambassador delivered a message from the president congratulating Sihanouk on becoming chief of state, assuring him of US respect
for his policy of neutrality, and expressing regret at being unable to accept
an invitation to visit Cambodia. He read the letter with "obvious plea-
sure," according to Trimble. Sihanouk said that he wanted to release the
message to the press and broadcast it over the radio.[59]

A more substantive topic of conversation was military aid. After Sihanouk's acrimonious accusations earlier in the summer, US officials had
been perplexed by the absence of a specific, official request for enhanced
military assistance. When Trimble reiterated US willingness to discuss
Cambodia's military requirements, Sihanouk made the surprising and
disingenuous observation that MAAG commander Chase appeared to
be "awaiting some further authority [to] conduct discussions." It seemed
advisable, said Sihanouk, to send Lon Nol and other Cambodian officials to Washington for direct talks with the Pentagon and State Department. Trimble replied that there must be some misunderstanding, but if
Sihanouk wanted Lon Nol to visit Washington, then the ambassador was
"sure he would be welcome there."[60]

Sihanouk's decision to send his defense minister to Washington
seemed to indicate the prince's eagerness to modernize Cambodia's military. In a cable to the State Department, Trimble declared that the time
had come to grant Cambodia's request for training pilots to fly jets.
Detecting a fragile improvement in US relations with Cambodia, Trimble thought that such training would go a "long way in satisfying Sihanouk that his needs are understood by [the] West and in strengthening
his resistance to attractive bloc offers." In a subsequent letter to Parsons,
Trimble wrote that training six to eight pilots "should do much to assuage
the little man's disappointment when he find[s] out we cannot fully meet
his requests for additional military aid."[61]

Trimble's appeals did not change Washington's reluctance to provide
jet training or aircraft. The State Department also rejected a protocol suggestion by the ambassador for Sihanouk's upcoming visit to the United
States, where he would lead the Cambodian delegation at the fifteenth
session of the UN General Assembly. Trimble, urging "appropriate high-
level attention to Sihanouk," proposed that the prince receive full military
honors when he landed at the airport and be met by "at least" the secretary of state. Both Trimble and Sihanouk were undoubtedly disappointed

to learn that Mac Godley, the former DCM in Phnom Penh, would be greeting the prince upon his arrival in the United States. (When Diem had visited America in 1957, President Eisenhower had met him at the airport.) Sihanouk's sensitivity to protocol slights concerned Ambassador Nong Kimny, who told the State Department that he hoped "an official car or some police motorcycles would be assigned to escort the Prince to the hotel."[62]

The State Department and White House did accede to Trimble's request for Sihanouk to speak with the president—although not for the full hour recommended by the ambassador. On September 27, 1960, Sihanouk talked with Eisenhower for twenty-two minutes at the president's suite at the Waldorf Astoria, a convenient location for meeting with many of the world leaders attending the opening of the UN General Assembly. After introductory pleasantries, Sihanouk made his pitch for more military aid. Downplaying his usual rationale for enhanced military assistance—self-defense from his anticommunist neighbors—Sihanouk claimed that his army had considerable difficulty stopping guerrillas who used Cambodian territory to infiltrate into South Vietnam. Although the Diem regime greatly exaggerated infiltration, said Sihanouk, Cambodia needed additional aircraft, helicopters, and arms to "remove" this threat.[63]

Eisenhower replied that the US government would study Cambodia's appeal "sympathetically." According to a summary of the meeting, he "stressed that we sometimes find difficulty in meeting requests for arms aid." During the rest of their conversation, which was notably cordial, the president and prince appeared to be of one mind on such topics as the importance of the UN to smaller nations, the inadvisability of Nikita Khrushchev's proposal to replace the secretary-general with an ideologically balanced triumvirate, and the dignified nature of Eisenhower's speech to the General Assembly. Flattering Sihanouk, the president said that small nations may not possess great military and economic strength, but they could exert a spiritual and moral force: "In this regard," the summary of their meeting stated, "the President said that Prince Sihanouk can be as effective as the President himself. The Prince expressed his delight at this idea."[64]

Sihanouk tried to exercise Cambodia's moral authority two days later in a speech to the UN General Assembly. Acknowledging the "feebleness" of his country's influence, he advocated for nuclear disarmament and condemned the proliferation of conventional weapons, sardonically characterizing them as "old playthings which destroyed only a few tens of millions of people during the second world war." Calling the exclusion of the PRC from the United Nations "futile and absurd," Sihanouk observed that "certain members of the United Nations are far from behaving towards their weaker neighbors in a better fashion than China, and that it has never occurred to anyone to consider them unworthy to sit amongst us."[65]

Sihanouk's statement to the UN included condemnation of foreign interference in Laos, where the country's left, right, and center factions were descending into civil war. He said that the neutralization of Laos, backed by international guarantees, was "the only reasonable and valid solution to eliminate this new and dangerous trouble spot." To reduce "the risk of friction between the opposing blocs" in Southeast Asia, Sihanouk proposed the establishment of a neutral zone made up of Laos and Cambodia. Envisioning the two countries as "buffer states," he called for the major powers to guarantee the strict neutrality of this zone and to remove Laos and Cambodia from the global ideological struggle.[66]

Near the end of his seven-thousand-word speech, which touched on a wide range of international issues, Sihanouk made a veiled reference to US interference in Cambodia's internal affairs. A recent article in *Time* magazine had characterized his approach to foreign aid as "always bite the hand that feeds you."[67] Responding to this "dubious humor," Sihanouk declared:

Too often a friendly aid, provided for in official agreements, is accompanied by a secret and far less friendly kind of aid. This latter kind of aid, which is never mentioned, and which arouses indignation if one mentions it, can take several forms: either direct subversion, the totally artificial support or the creation of opposition groups, or the purchase of the consciences of men considered strong enough to achieve the secession of certain provinces, and torpedo neutrality and [the] national regime. . . . In brief, it should be known that I do not bite the hand of those who come to our people's aid, but the other hand, the one which is trying to put us to death.[68]

Sihanouk's UN remarks received scant attention in the Western press. Disappointed by his visit to the United States, he returned to Cambodia, where he expressed unhappiness with President Eisenhower's "rather vague" response to his request for military aid. Criticizing the treatment he received in New York, the prince complained that Sukarno of Indonesia, Gamal Abdel Nasser of Egypt, and other dignitaries from Asia and Africa attending the General Assembly had more elaborate security arrangements and police escorts. He also resented the disproportionate public attention focused on the Soviet Union and other major powers. "America showed its true face," wrote Sihanouk. "It is far from recognizing in fact the equality of the big and small."[69]

Although Sihanouk sought friendly relations with China and other communist countries, he did not tolerate Cambodian leftists who opposed his social, economic, or foreign policies. In the summer of 1960, for example, the Pracheachon criticized the prince's plan to expand French-language training in elementary schools. The government responded by closing four left-wing newspapers and arresting their editors. Speaking to Phnom Penh's diplomatic corps on the eve of the cremation of his father, Sihanouk said that his government had known for a long time that the Pracheachon was working with foreigners, sabotaging the regime, and attempting to divide the Cambodian people.[70]

Sihanouk could suppress the overt propaganda of the Pracheachon front organization, but his security forces had more difficulty detecting the clandestine KPRP and its political organizing. In late September 1960, twenty-one KPRP leaders met secretly on the grounds of the Phnom Penh railroad yards for the first party congress since 1951. The gathering of Cambodian communists included rural veterans of the war with France and urban radicals educated in Paris. "Had the enemy discovered the site of the congress," Pol Pot later wrote, "the entire leadership of the Party would have been destroyed."[71]

The KPRP remained strongly influenced by Hanoi, which had ordered the convening of the Cambodian party's congress. Earlier in September, the Vietnamese Workers' Party held its third congress, which named southern revolutionary Le Duan as first secretary and which "laid the foundation for the creation of the National Liberation Front" in South Vietnam.[72] The party opposed armed struggle against Sihanouk at this time. Among the more likely reasons: the KPRP was small and weak, the prince's neutrality kept US military-training teams out of Cambodia, and his hostility toward Diem could only help the DRV achieve its ultimate goal of a reunified Vietnam ruled by Hanoi.

Within the KPRP, opinions about Sihanouk were divided. The veterans of the French war, according to Ben Kiernan, "were much more inclined to see Sihanouk's neutrality and his increasingly anti-imperialist stance as positive factors in the Indo-China-wide struggle for socialism, while at the same time also giving the Prince credit for maintaining the country's independence, a goal for which they themselves had sacrificed much in the past." Pol Pot and other French-educated radicals, however, viewed the Sihanouk regime as a "backward, dictatorial monarchy." Eager to take up arms against the government, they considered Cambodia "a satellite of imperialism, of US imperialism in particular."[73]

The KPRP congress endorsed a continuation of overt and clandestine political struggle. A new central committee was formed, with Tou Samouth serving as party secretary. Pol Pot moved up to the party's number-three position, and Son Ngoc Minh, who had remained in Vietnam after the Geneva conference, was elected to the central committee in absentia. The party congress also changed the party's name to the Khmer Workers' Party, which implied equivalency with the Vietnamese Workers' Party. The new name "facilitated propaganda activities among non-Communists, by allaying their fears of Communism," writes Steve Heder. "The term Communist Party would be used once conditions were more favourable."[74]

11

"Definite Political Problems" (1960–1961)

In a cable to the State Department, dated October 1, 1960, the US mission in Phnom Penh summarized its recommendations for military and police aid to Cambodia. The program included jet training for six pilots and funding to increase the size of the army from twenty-eight thousand to thirty-one thousand men. Having pared back a Cambodian request for $120 million over five years to $41 million, Ambassador William Trimble and his mission colleagues were convinced that their aid program was the minimum necessary to prevent Sihanouk from turning to China or other communist countries for military assistance. Trimble and his country team urged senior Washington officials to approve "immediate implementation" of its proposal and to inform Sihanouk of the military aid before his trip to China later in the year.[1]

The recommendations from Phnom Penh encountered stiff resistance from the Commander in Chief, Pacific (CINCPAC) headquarters, the Pentagon, and the State Department office responsible for coordinating military and economic aid. At a time when the Eisenhower administration and Congress sought ways of reducing the economic burden of foreign assistance, the country team's recommended program, not to mention Cambodia's extravagant request, seemed a wasteful and possibly dangerous use of limited military resources. John O. Bell, the State Department's deputy coordinator for mutual security programs, opposed both the provision of jet training and the request for aircraft, which would inevitably follow. Among his concerns was the possibility that jets controlled by Sihanouk would "eventually be used against free world interests."[2]

Yet within the State Department's Bureau of Far Eastern Affairs, a less negative view of Sihanouk's Cambodia was emerging. Assistant Secretary J. Graham Parsons concluded that Cambodia, compared to Laos and South Vietnam, was "by far" the most stable state in Indochina. Its people appeared united in their support of Sihanouk, a leader who had no intention of ceding power to communists or anyone else. With the prince having the best prospects of survival of any ruler in mainland Southeast Asia, Parsons commented to his State Department colleagues, "Cambodia oddly appears at [the] moment more as [an] asset and less as [a] threat to U.S. interests in [the] area." In an indirect admission of Washington's limited understanding of Cambodian affairs, Parsons noted that the facts and analyses underlying his conclusion had not "gone unreported over the years." He attributed policymakers' inability to grasp Cambodian realities to "spectacular and irritating Sihanouk moves on [the] international checkerboard."[3]

Parsons made these observations in October 1960, when he traveled to Southeast Asia with John N. Irwin II, assistant secretary of defense for international security affairs, and Vice Admiral Herbert D. Riley, CINCPAC's chief of staff. The primary purpose of their visit was to reconcile the conflicting views of senior officials in Washington and their subordinates in Vientiane about policy and personalities in Laos. As in Phnom Penh, the US mission in Vientiane had a surer grasp of the complex political and historical forces at work locally than did top officials in Washington, who tended to be more knowledgeable about Europe than Asia. One consequence of the differing US perspectives on Laos was the "untenable" policy of nominally supporting the internationally recognized government of neutralist Souvanna Phouma while simultaneously providing military aid directly to Phoumi Nosavan, the Lao general who openly sought to overthrow him.[4]

During his trip to Southeast Asia, Parsons met with ambassadors U. Alexis Johnson (Thailand), Elbridge Durbrow (South Vietnam), and Trimble in Bangkok. Among the topics discussed was Sihanouk's suggestion that both "blocs" guarantee the independence and neutrality of Laos and Cambodia. Prime Minister Souvanna Phouma of Laos supported the idea, and his foreign minister asked the major powers "to ponder seriously this proposal." Parsons and the three US ambassadors, however, were skeptical. Although a neutral Laos was deemed preferable to communist rule, Sihanouk's plan "would inhibit Free World support of Laos without exercising any effective restraint on the communists with their very advantageous geographical position in North Vietnam."[5]

Parsons returned to Washington with little to show for his visit to Southeast Asia. His trip to Laos with Irwin and Riley—"a virtual disaster," Parsons later wrote[6]—failed to unify US opinions about that country. He seemed determined, however, to persuade the leaders of the State Department to modify some of their "basic concepts" about Cambodia. In a memorandum to Under Secretary C. Douglas Dillon, Parsons wrote: "I believe we may not have given Cambodia the importance it merits from the standpoint of US and free world security in the area. Despite Sihanouk's noisy neutrality-mongering, Cambodia's political stability and its resistance to internal Communist subversion represents a significant element of strength in the free world position in Southeast Asia. I believe we should devote care to cultivating this asset and should by all means avoid losing it."[7]

Increasing US miltary assistance to Cambodia, Parsons argued, was an "opportunity" to strengthen the kingdom's confidence in the United States and in its own ability to meet real or imagined threats from Thailand and South Vietnam. Since the United States would be "hard put" to meet all of Cambodia's military requests, Parsons thought that training for six to eight Cambodian pilots and planning for the provision of US jet aircraft were part of "the minimum response required." Such a decision, he acknowledged, would be "a major departure from our previous position."[8]

While the national security bureaucracy tried to develop a Cambodian aid program that would forestall a military assistance request to the communists, Lon Nol arrived in Washington as a guest of the Department of Defense. The commander in chief of Cambodia's armed forces as well as the minister of defense, Lon Nol was presumably still loyal to Sihanouk. Ambassador Trimble had told the British in August that Cambodian newspaper reports of US backing for Lon Nol as a possible alternative to Sihanouk were "clearly a case of a Soviet plant." Nonetheless, the stories had "evoked a sharp reaction from Sihanouk." The prince's response was probably the reason that Parsons observed, "Lon Nol is basically more favorable to [the] free world and [the] U.S. particularly than he can afford openly to indicate."[9]

The US government was trying to cultivate good relations with Lon Nol. In November 1959, the general had attended a ten-day CINCPAC "weapons demonstration." Observed by top military officers of US allies, the demonstration featured impressive displays of firepower by American air, ground, and naval forces. Admiral Harry D. Felt, commander of all US forces in the Pacific, and Admiral Herbert G. Hopwood, commander of the Pacific fleet, "took particular pains to extend their personal hospitality to General Lon Nol," an escort officer reported. "It was apparent that he was gratified and pleased."[10]

On October 31, 1960, Pentagon officials attempted to persuade Lon Nol that Cambodia's request for $120 million in US military assistance was neither necessary nor desirable. A financial objection to the Cambodian proposal was the cost of maintaining and providing spare parts for the requested materiel, which would run into hundreds of millions of dollars over five years. Such a sum, Pentagon officials said, was an unrealistic economic burden for either the United States or Cambodia. The Defense Department was also unenthusiastic about a request for fifty thousand rifles to arm Cambodian paramilitary forces. Although Sihanouk maintained a sentimental attachment to the armed peasants mobilized for the crusade for independence in 1953, US military officials thought a well-trained regular army was the most effective means of self-defense. They were also worried about arming irregulars who "may be subjected to subversive influences." Lon Nol, unmoved by US arguments, declared that "the Cambodian demands were fully justified."[11]

At the State Department, Deputy Assistant Secretary John Steeves tried to reduce Lon Nol's expectations of a large increase in US military assistance. Mentioning the privilege of being present at Sihanouk's recent meeting with Eisenhower in New York, Steeves repeated the president's message to the prince: our resources were "not unlimited," but we would consider Cambodian proposals "with sympathy and interest." Steeves also described the US budget process of annually appropriating foreign aid, which precluded the multiyear commitment sought by Cambodia. Lest Lon Nol suspect political motives for US parsimony, Steeves stressed that Cambodia's policy of neutrality was "entirely acceptable to us and we have no quarrel with it."[12]

Lon Nol, who wanted a reply to the Cambodian aid proposal before he met with Sihanouk later in November, made "two emphatic requests" to Joseph V. Charyk, acting secretary of the US Air Force. The first was jet training for eight Cambodian pilots. The second was two "reasonably high performance" jet fighters, which the newly trained pilots would fly in 1961 at a celebration of Cambodian independence. In a memorandum to Secretary of Defense Thomas S. Gates Jr., Charyk noted that fulfilling Lon Nol's requests presented "definite political problems"—that is, anticommunist countries in Southeast Asia would object to the United States providing Cambodia with jet training and aircraft. Nevertheless, Charyk recommended a prompt affirmative response both to promote Cambodian goodwill and to prevent a similar request to the Soviet Union or China.[13]

Assistant Secretary of Defense Irwin had already reconciled himself to providing jet training for a limited number of Cambodian pilots. But giving Cambodia jet aircraft was another matter. In interagency meetings, Irwin argued that Cambodia should purchase jets from France or some other free-world nation. This arrangement would share the mutual-defense burden and deflect Thai and South Vietnamese anger away from the United States. As a last resort, Irwin would be willing to agree to partial US financing of the sale of French aircraft to Cambodia.[14]

State Department officials thought that Irwin's position posed "the political risk of confusing and irritating the Cambodians, without having sufficient compensating advantage." The OCB sought to resolve the State–Defense split but merely finessed it. On November 9, the OCB recommended informing the Cambodians that the United States was prepared to provide pilot training, but if the Cambodians asked about jets, they should "be told the provision of jet aircraft [would] be given sympathetic consideration at an appropriate time." Left unresolved was whether the United States or some other country would provide the airplanes.[15]

Secretary of State Christian Herter concurred with the OCB position, but Secretary of Defense Gates opposed both training pilots and providing jets. More of a policy activist than his immediate predecessors, who focused on efficiently managing the vast US defense establishment, Gates admired John Foster Dulles but found the State Department shockingly undisciplined. In an oral history interview, he recalled: "You sent out an order—you'd finally agree on a position with the State Department—and sent out an order to an Ambassador, and he'd write a novel back to you, telling why he wasn't going to obey the order." Gates's objection to providing training and aircraft, which presumably reflected the views of the Joint Chiefs of Staff, included the hyperbolic observation that Cambodian jets "couldn't take off without over-flying the borders" of its neighbors. The Treasury Department also had a problem with the OCB proposal: the possibility of financing Cambodia's purchase of airplanes from another country would negatively impact the US balance of payments.[16]

On November 11, National Security Adviser Gordon Gray discussed the State–Defense split with President Eisenhower, who was vacationing in Augusta, Georgia. Because the decision about jets was fundamentally political rather than military, Eisenhower approved the State Department position. He decided that the Cambodian government should immediately be informed of the US decision to provide jet training for ten pilots. (The president's higher-than-requested number of pilots allowed for the inevitable rejection of some individuals.) Eisenhower's decision included an instruction to US officials to "evade a definitive reply to the Cambodians" on providing jets. Sympathetic to Treasury's balance-of-payments concerns, the president vetoed the idea of offshore procurement of the aircraft.[17]

The next day Parsons handed Ambassador Nong Kimny a paper summarizing the US response to Cambodia's military-assistance proposal. Explaining the difficulties in meeting such a surprisingly large request, Parsons said that the United States "would be glad to start the training program for Cambodian jet pilots as promptly as possible." The US materiel offered to Cambodia included equipment for an engineer construction battalion, three mechanized landing craft, three M-24 light tanks, and "modern small arms and crew-served weapons for existing regular units." Ten thousand carbines were earmarked for Cambodian paramilitary forces "on the understanding that such forces are effectively under the control of the Royal Government."[18]

Parsons told Nong Kimny that a 10 percent reduction in pay and allowances for Cambodia's armed forces had been planned, but the United States was willing "to meet the Cambodians half way by splitting the difference"—that is, reducing pay and allowances by only 5 percent. The overall military-assistance package, although far smaller than the one requested by the Cambodian government and less than the US mission in Phnom Penh recommended, was a modest addition "to the regular United States aid programs for the Cambodian military and police forces already approved for the current fiscal year." The aid increase, said Parsons, "was the best we could do under the circumstances."[19]

Sihanouk made no immediate official comment about the adequacy of the proffered US military assistance. He did, however, discuss military aid during a rambling, informal talk with Cambodian students in Paris on November 19. "It is best to ask America to furnish the pay for our troops," he said. "Although China, the USSR, Czechoslovakia and other Red countries furnish us with equipment and technical aid, they are unwilling to give us troop pay. America, on the other hand, is willing to furnish troop pay, and we may as well ask Uncle Sam to furnish it." Voicing frustration with the gradual reductions in US support for military pay and allowances, Sihanouk implied that Lon Nol's visit to Washington had at least temporarily halted these cuts. "Uncle Sam," the prince said, "is afraid that we will go to the other side and will release quite a lot." Summarizing the results of the general's negotiations with US officials, he observed: "Figure it up, and it's not bad; for the time being we can continue to go along with these people."[20]

Lon Nol was disappointed by the small increase in US military assistance to Cambodia. "While he naturally did not expect that their demands would be met in full," Trimble commented, "he was unquestionably counting on considerably more than we have offered to give."[21] The general did, however, seem pleased by the VIP treatment he received in Washington, which included a formal dinner and Potomac cruise hosted by Secretary Gates and attended by the highest-ranking officers of each military service. Such attention, Trimble wrote to Admiral Felt, was "producing useful results. There has been, I feel, a greater warmth on his part towards the United States, as well as a greater understanding of the interest and good intentions of the United States toward Cambodia and its armed forces. The result may not be a conspicuous change in our relationship with FARK, as I am sure you will appreciate, but I believe the influence is a subtle one which justifies the effort that has been made to develop General Lon Nol."[22]

In November 1960, the United States turned decisively against Prime Minister Souvanna Phouma of Laos. Secretaries Herter and Gates agreed that "a neutralist Laos was an unacceptable goal [and] that Souvanna would have to be replaced."[23] Ignoring a request by Souvanna to stop all aid to rebel general Phoumi Nosavan, the US government made covert payments to the general's troops, fulfilled his requests for weapons and airlift, and assigned elite, CIA-controlled Thai paramilitary forces to each of his five battalions. US Army personnel advised Phoumi's troops, and CIA officers provided political advice and support.[24]

With the Laotian civil war intensifying, Sihanouk sought support for a UN resolution guaranteeing the neutralization of Laos and Cambodia. The US government opposed the resolution but did not want to appear hostile to the peaceful gesture. Phoumi's military position appeared to be improving, and his eventual assumption of power would ensure a more reliably anticommunist government in Vientiane. On November 26, the State Department informed the US delegation at the UN, "[The] Department would strongly prefer delaying further action on Cambodian proposals pending clarification [of the] fluid political situation [in Laos]. Highly doubtful [that] any declaration of neutrality [the] Souvanna Phouma government might make under [the] present circumstances would be acceptable to us. However it is not desirable [to] convey these sentiments to [the] Cambodians or other foreign representatives."[25]

Phoumi's Lao supporters also preferred delaying any action by the UN. On December 3, Sisouk na Champassak, the Laotian delegate, received instructions from Souvanna to ask the UN to intervene in the civil war. The appeal would be based on Thai intervention in Laos on behalf of General Phoumi. Sisouk, who was a relative of Phoumi's front man, Prince Boun Oum, planned "to take no action on Souvanna's order, and if again ordered to comply, will refuse," according to a US Army intelligence report. Major General John M. Willems, assistant chief of staff for intelligence, concluded that Sisouk "hopes to delay UN intervention in order to allow Phoumi time to seize Vientiane and thus present the UN with a fait accompli."[26]

With Phoumi's forces closing in on Vientiane, Souvanna and most of his cabinet fled to Phnom Penh on December 9. Leftist minister Quinim Pholsena, neutralist commander Kong Le, and representatives of the communist-led Pathet Lao flew to Hanoi to request additional military assistance from the DRV and the Soviet Union. The US government, recalled Winthrop G. Brown, the American ambassador in Vientiane, "simply pushed Souvanna into the arms of the Soviet Union and the Chinese and the Pathet Lao. We were always complaining that he was too weak, that he couldn't control his forces, he couldn't control the Pathet Lao, and yet we've always denied him the resources and the political support which would be necessary to enable him to do so."[27]

Following a vote of no confidence in Souvanna in the National Assembly, King Savang Vatthana stripped the prime minister of his powers on December 12 and authorized Boun Oum and General Phoumi to form a provisional government. The next day Phoumi's forces, stiffened by Thai paramilitary units and US advisers, began their successful assault on Vientiane. The three-day battle was largely an artillery duel, with indiscriminate shelling of the town by both Phoumi's and Kong Le's forces. Some six hundred civilians were killed, whereas the combined losses for the combatants were no more than forty.[28]

Sihanouk thought that the United States was "forcing an unpopular Western-oriented regime on [the] Lao people," Trimble wrote to the State Department. Moreover, American backing for General Phoumi reinforced the prince's belief that the United States "would prefer and hence is probably working for a regime in Cambodia favorable toward SEATO." The ambassador added that the United States "continues to be judged not only by actions in Cambodia but elsewhere, and particularly in [the] neighboring countries [of] Thailand, Laos and Vietnam."[29]

Sihanouk, seeking political and economic support from communist countries, visited the Soviet Union and the PRC in December. His hosts were, of course, hostile to Phoumi and the US presence in Laos. They did not, however, support the prince's plan to neutralize Laos and Cambodia under the auspices of the UN. Nikita Khrushchev found the leadership of UN secretary-general Dag Hammarskjöld biased toward the West, and the PRC was still blocked from joining the world body. Following talks between Khrushchev and Sihanouk, the Soviet Union and Cambodia issued a joint communiqué that included recognition of Souvanna's government in exile, opposition to "foreign interference" in Laos, and advocacy for "a return to the Geneva agreements of 1954." The document also endorsed Soviet proposals for disarmament and for modifying the secretariat of the UN. (The prince's support for Khrushchev's UN plan was a reversal of the statements he had made to the General Assembly and to President Eisenhower two months earlier.) In exchange for Sihanouk's backing, the Soviet Union agreed to construct a technology institute in Cambodia, to deliver a twelve-passenger helicopter, and to provide loans repayable in produce.[30]

Like his declarations in the Soviet Union, Sihanouk's public statements in China did not mention a Cambodia-Laos neutrality zone guaranteed by the UN. The prince instead proposed an international meeting of eight countries to save "Laos and peace in Southeast Asia." The communist attendees would be the PRC, the Soviet Union, and North Vietnam, and the anticommunists would be represented by the United States, Thailand, and South Vietnam. The neutral nations would be India and Cambodia. "Although theoretically evenly balanced with three participants each from [the] East and West blocs plus two neutrals," Ambassador Trimble observed, "[the] suggested composition [is] actually weighted against [the] West by [the] omission [of the] UK and France and [the] inclusion [of] 'neutral' Cambodia."[31]

As expected, Sihanouk's trip to China included the signing of a Treaty of Friendship and Mutual Non-Aggression. Among its reciprocal commitments were adhering to the five principles of peaceful coexistence and establishing stronger economic and cultural ties. Notably absent from the treaty was any mention of Chinese military assistance to Cambodia or a PRC commitment to defend the kingdom's borders. The prince, Trimble concluded, "seems to have been aware of [the] danger of going too far."[32]

Sihanouk, who publicly supported the PRC's admission to the UN and its claim to Taiwan, returned to Phnom Penh on December 26 with a new $40 million program of Chinese economic aid and technical assistance. At the airport, he declared that his endorsement of the PRC's "legitimate rights" was worth as much to China as all of the aid that country provided to Cambodia. Foreign newspapers, he said, would probably claim that Cambodia had been "duped" by the communists. Sihanouk, however, suggested that his statements on behalf of Soviet and Chinese political positions were simply a self-interested quid pro quo. "Let everyone know," he said, "we understand perfectly [that] all powers try [to] defend their national interests, just as we defend ours."[33]

Sihanouk refined his thinking about ending the civil war in Laos in a letter to the UK and Soviet cochairs of the Geneva conference and to other world leaders. Dated January 1, 1961, the letter called for an international meeting to restore peace, remove foreign influence, and establish self-determination in a country where US and Soviet military personnel were in dangerously close proximity. The conference participants should include signatories of the Geneva accords of 1954 (France, Great Britain, Soviet Union, PRC, DRV, Cambodia, and Laos); countries serving on the ICC (Canada, India, and Poland); and nations bordering Laos (Thailand, South Vietnam, and Burma). The United States, Sihanouk wrote, was among the nations whose participation was "indispensable."[34]

Sihanouk's proposal, which became the basis for the fourteen-nation Geneva conference on Laos (from May 1961 to July 1962), was promptly supported by the Soviet Union, China, and the DRV. The United Kingdom and France thought a more practical step for stopping the fighting was reactivating the ICC in Laos, which had been suspended indefinitely in 1958. The Europeans did not, however, object to convening the conference proposed by Sihanouk. The United States, seeking to strengthen Phoumi's military position and contemplating SEATO or unilateral American intervention to prevent his defeat, opposed the idea of an international conference. For senior officials in Washington, the problem with Sihanouk's proposal and other international initiatives to end the fighting in Laos was the likely outcome of "bringing the Communists into the government and thus leading to the probable loss of the country peacefully instead of militarily."[35]

In a memorandum to President Eisenhower, Herter wrote: "I believe it most unlikely that a conference such as proposed by Prince Sihanouk would contribute to a satisfactory resolution of the Lao problem." Rather than reject Sihanouk's idea outright, Herter recommended a reply by Eisenhower that expressed his appreciation for a constructive suggestion and his intention to give the conference proposal "serious study." On January 16, four days before leaving office, the president approved the State Department's temporizing response to Sihanouk without changing a word.[36]

Robert A. Divine, Stephen E. Ambrose, and other historians have documented President Eisenhower's moderation, prudence, and restraint in managing the nation's foreign affairs. These qualities, however, were often lacking in his administration's relations with Cambodia, which were defined largely by hostility to Sihanouk's conception of neutrality, by contempt for the prince personally, and by a covert effort to encourage his overthrow—"change from the top." The failure of the Dap Chhuon coup and the subsequent stonewalling about US involvement in the conspiracy not only marked the point of no return in American relations with the prince but also contributed to Eisenhower's dubious legacy of relying heavily on the CIA to remove worrisome national leaders.

Early in his administration, President Eisenhower authorized agency operations that toppled Prime Minister Mohammad Mosaddegh in Iran and President Jacobo Árbenz Guzmán in Guatemala. These two coups, according to historian Richard H. Immerman, created an unrealistic, reckless "legend of invincibility that came to define the CIA by the end of Eisenhower's two terms in office."[37] In Southeast Asia alone, agency operations to depose insufficiently anticommunist leaders included covert support to rebels opposing President Sukarno in Indonesia in 1958 and to a Laotian front group that first ousted Prime Minister Souvanna Phouma in 1958 and then his insufficiently dynamic successor, Phoui Sananikone, one year later.[38]

"President Eisenhower approved every covert action undertaken during his administration," according to Immerman.[39] Eisenhower's organizational mechanism for reviewing covert operations was the special group established by NSC 5412/2. The group's members included representatives of the State Department and the Pentagon, DCI Allen Dulles, and the president's national security adviser. The special group met infrequently from 1954 to 1958, when CIA operations were often authorized in conversations between the Dulles brothers and the president. On December 26, 1958, Eisenhower changed this practice, telling Allen Dulles and National Security Adviser Gordon Gray that he wanted the special group "to meet regularly, probably weekly." The reason for this change was that the President's Board of Consultants on Foreign Intelligence Activities had "'severe misgivings' about the entire NSC 5412/2 program" and the special group's ability to oversee covert operations.[40]

The President's Board, a committee of distinguished civilians and retired military officers who advised the president on intelligence matters, questioned the efficacy of covert political and paramilitary operations. In a final report submitted to President Eisenhower in January 1961, board chairman John E. Hull wrote, "We have been unable to conclude that, on balance, all of the covert action programs undertaken by CIA up to this time have been worth the risk or the great expenditure of manpower, money and other resources involved. In addition, we believe that CIA's concentration on political, psychological and related covert action activities have tended to detract substantially from the execution of its primary intelligence gathering mission."[41]

In Southeast Asia and elsewhere, exposed CIA operations inspired hostility toward the United States and its interests—even among allies. In Laos, where the agency maintained a conspicuously large presence in the late 1950s, ostensibly clandestine US efforts to undermine Souvanna and promote General Phoumi appalled French and British officials. In an "eyes only" cable to President Kennedy in May 1961, Secretary of State Dean Rusk commented on the "deep-seated" impression at the Geneva conference that the United States had "earned" the communist attacks against Phoumi's government: "I had not fully appreciated [the] extent to which [the] US had become isolated on Laos by [the] acts [of the] previous administration seen both by friends and neutrals as overplaying our hand."[42]

As in Cambodia and Laos, the unintended consequences of CIA interference in Indonesian affairs were counterproductive. Sukarno, a nonaligned nationalist described by John Foster Dulles as "dangerous and untrustworthy and by character susceptible to the Communist way of thinking," emerged from the failed rebellion of 1958 in a stronger political position. So did the Indonesian communists. Sukarno eventually became obsessed with the notion that the CIA was "plotting to kill him." His concern was not unreasonable. Richard M. Bissell Jr., a senior agency official who participated in planning the covert support to the Indonesian rebels, subsequently told a presidential commission that an attempt to assassinate Sukarno had "progressed as far as the identification of an asset [agent] who it was felt might be recruited for this purpose. The plan was never reached, was never perfected to the point where it seemed feasible. The difficulty concerned the possibility of creating a situation in which the potential agent would have access to the target."[43]

CIA support for the unsuccessful Indonesian rebellion provided Sukarno with fodder for anti-American speeches. In Cambodia, Sihanouk not only delivered similar addresses about US covert action but also utilized a unique propaganda tool to discredit CIA activities: a feature-length film titled *Shadow over Angkor*. Sihanouk, who made several films in the 1960s, was the producer, director, and writer of *Shadow over Angkor*. He also played the role of Prince Dhanari, an admiral assigned to Cambodian counterintelligence to infiltrate a plot by the United States and its "satellites," South Vietnam and Thailand. Sihanouk's wife, Princess Monique Izzi, starred in the film as an ambassador and the admiral's romantic interest.[44]

Loosely based on the Dap Chhuon coup, *Shadow over Angkor* portrays "Colonel Lansdale" as the puppeteer behind the conspiracy. Played by an actor who bore a reasonable resemblance to the intelligence officer, Lansdale is depicted as both a malevolent operative and an uncultured buffoon. The Dap Chhuon character delivers such lines as "The agents of the CIA are loaded with money. The USA is rich and Cambodia will be on its side and receive important credits to equip the army and enrich our officers." When army loyalists foil the conspiracy, the disgraced traitor accepts both a revolver from Prince Dhanari and his suggestion to commit suicide.[45]

On November 17, 1968, *Shadow over Angkor* opened the first—and second to last—Phnom Penh International Film Festival. Twenty-four countries, including twelve communist nations, were represented at the competition. Because of its political content, Sihanouk did not enter *Shadow over Angkor* for an award. He did, however, win the grand prix for another of his movies, *The Little Prince*. It starred his son, Prince Norodom Sihamoni, who thirty-five years later became the king of Cambodia. Sihanouk also received a special award for his short documentary *Royal Procession*. Milton Osborne accurately characterizes the so-called competition as "a charade."[46]

The Western press reported but did not dwell on the political content of *Shadow over Angkor*. *Time* magazine, which ridiculed the prince's multiple filmmaking roles, did mention the movie's "striking parallels to an alleged anti-Sihanouk plot of 1959." In his memoirs, Sihanouk understated his many contributions to the film—perhaps embarrassed by the time and resources expended on filmmaking during a period of national peril. What remains unclear is the degree to which he overstated the threat posed by the United States and the CIA. "The Dap Chhuon plot," he wrote, "was used as the theme for a film I produced, *Shadow over Angkor*. Many Westerners thought it was the product of an overly active imagination. Alas, I did not at that time possess an imagination sufficiently fertile to foresee the grotesque and fantastic schemes which the CIA was dreaming up."[47]

Epilogue

"Forebodings and Potential Opposition"

When John F. Kennedy became president, Cambodia was a relatively peaceful front in the cold war. He initially identified Cuba, the Congo, Laos, and South Vietnam as the four developing countries most vulnerable to communism. Two weeks before Kennedy took office, Nikita Khrushchev had delivered a speech that included a pledge to support "wars of national liberation." Disturbed by the threat posed by subversive insurgency, Kennedy encouraged his advisers to read Khrushchev's remarks and subsequently described them as "possibly one of the most important speeches of the decade." In Cambodia, the Kennedy administration's basic policy objective was to prevent the country from "falling under Communist control."[1]

During the initial months of Kennedy's presidency, US relations with Cambodia were largely untroubled by disruptive incidents involving Sihanouk and his neighbors. There was, however, one new irritant in Ngo Dinh Diem's relations with Sihanouk: Cambodia retained a South Vietnamese C-47 aircraft that had transported the leaders of an unsuccessful ARVN coup to Phnom Penh in November 1960. "[The] GVN does not believe [the] RKG has [a] shadow of justification under international law in keeping this aircraft," reported Ambassador Frederick E. Nolting Jr., Elbridge Durbrow's successor in Saigon. "Unless we can get this problem settled it will undoubtedly be raised as [the] first obstacle by Diem in any conversation with him on relations with Cambodia."[2]

President Kennedy discussed Cambodian–South Vietnamese relations with Sihanouk in New York on September 25, 1961. Like Eisenhower's meeting with the prince one year earlier, the talk with Kennedy coincided with the opening of the UN General Assembly session. According to notes of their conversation, "the Prince recounted in great detail the points of friction between Cambodia and Viet-Nam." These disagreements included the treatment of the Khmer minority in South Vietnam, incidents along the border, and ownership of offshore islands. Sihanouk assured Kennedy that "there was absolutely no truth to the Vietnamese accusation that he assisted the rebels in making trouble in Viet-Nam."[3]

Walt W. Rostow, the deputy national security adviser and White House aide responsible for Southeast Asia, had advised Kennedy to give "special attention" to Sihanouk's susceptibility "to flattery and lavish display of protocol from foreign powers." A biographical sketch prepared by the State Department observed: "Highly desirous of world statesman status, [Sihanouk] seeks meetings with world leaders as often as possible."[4] In his conversation with Sihanouk on September 25, Kennedy mixed flattery with a sincere interest in the prince's views on regional security. The two leaders engaged in a long, substantive discussion of the feasibility of a neutral solution for Laos, the consequences of SEATO intervention in that country, and Souvanna Phouma's political orientation. According to the minutes of the meeting, Sihanouk "obviously appreciated the President's deep interest in his opinion and the conversation ended on a most cordial note."[5]

This promising interlude in US–Cambodian relations did not last long. One month after Kennedy's talk with Sihanouk, the prince's view of the United States had become so hostile that Ambassador William Trimble considered evacuating embassy personnel to Manila. The crisis began with a story in the *Times of Japan* quoting Sihanouk's belief that Cambodia would more likely use its armed forces against Thailand and South Vietnam than against the communists. Prime Minister Sarit Thanarat of Thailand, fed up with Sihanouk's "provocations," publicly accused the "head of a certain country" of harboring communist aggressors and referred to that leader as a "pig." Thailand, said Sarit, would be forced to take steps that would "preserve the safety and honor of our nation."[6]

Sihanouk, deeply insulted by Sarit's name-calling, responded to the prime minister's vaguely worded threat by convening a special session of both houses of Parliament on October 23. In a two-hour address, he attacked his neighbors, urged self-defense preparations, and obtained the legislators' consent to sever relations with Thailand. Comparing past plots with the current crisis, Sihanouk observed that in 1958, while President Eisenhower entertained him in the White House, US "intelligence services" had recruited Dap Chhuon's brother. President Kennedy, said Sihanouk, had recently shown him understanding, while the "American lackey" Sarit prepared for war against Cambodia.[7]

An editorial in the *New York Times* intensified Sihanouk's anger: "The Cambodian Chief of State has acted with characteristic excitability and imperiousness in initiating a break in relations between Thailand and Cambodia." Although mildly rebuking Sarit for an unwise outburst, the editorial sympathized with his and Diem's security concerns: "Vietnamese Communists have profited from Cambodian neutrality by crossing through Cambodian territory in the course of their military operations against South Vietnam."[8]

Sihanouk responded to the editorial by redoubling his verbal attacks against the United States and his anticommunist neighbors. During an official tour of Kompong Speu, he declared that American leaders were "the most stupid people in the world." He also misrepresented his conversation with Kennedy—for example, stating that the president had "accused me of being directed by the Communists." Reporting to Washington, Ambassador Trimble summarized Western and neutral diplomats' reaction to the prince's remarks: "Sihanouk [is] at least temporarily mentally deranged, [a] view which I share."[9]

Secretary of State Dean Rusk called Ambassador Nong Kimny to the State Department to discuss Sihanouk's Kompong Speu speech. Calling the remarks "quite incomprehensible," Rusk said that he had hoped the prince's discussion with President Kennedy was the opening of a "new chapter" in relations between Cambodia and the United States, yet Sihanouk's speech went beyond the "bounds of rational discussion between friends" and "deeply disturbs us." Kimny, who had not read the speech, said that if reports of it were accurate, he "understood perfectly our feeling." While Kimny sought "clarification" of Sihanouk's comments, he asked Rusk to "be good enough to understand [the] Prince at this precise moment has a sort of complex that [the] world does not understand him and his policy."[10]

Sihanouk explained himself in a national radio address broadcast on

October 28. He characterized the speech as a "final warning" to the West. Calling the *New York Times* editorial "the last straw," he said that the American press had opposed Cambodian neutrality since 1956 and had "lost no opportunity [to] falsely interpret my intentions or to slander and discredit me." US reporters, he claimed, were "responsible for [the] legend of [a] 'shifting, unstable and inconstant' Prince given to unforeseen and inexplicable decisions." The prince's criticism of the press was on firmer ground, however, when he noted the absence of reporting on his "single-mindedness" in pursuing neutrality and other national goals.[11]

Sihanouk expressed "profound gratitude" for American aid but criticized the US government for refusing to "arbitrate" the disputes between Cambodia and its neighbors and for having the "audacity" to dismiss the threat posed by South Vietnam and Thailand. Commenting on the CIA's activities, he repeated his earlier remarks to Parliament:

> In 1958 and 1959 some "operators" of American nationality, such as diplomat Victor Matsui, were involved (to avoid saying they participated) in [the] Dap Chhuon, Sam Sary and Son Ngoc Thanh plots against our neutrality, independence and territorial integrity. In September 1958, more particularly, when I was being received with touching deference by President Eisenhower at [the] White House, agents of Mr. Allen Dulles were succeeding at the same time in New York in corrupting and buying the treason of one of our delegates to [the] 13th session of [the] U.N., namely Slat Peau.[12]

Despite President Kennedy's "unqualified homage" to Cambodian neutrality, Sihanouk said, "certain American circles" encouraged Thailand and South Vietnam "to seek fallacious pretexts to occupy our country." The prince, who feared communist domination of Cambodia but preferred that fate to territorial encroachment by his neighbors, declared that Sarit and other free world leaders "have nearly succeeded in causing us [to] abandon our neutrality and go over to [the] socialist camp." Expressing a desire to maintain peaceful, friendly relations "with all blocs," Sihanouk concluded his address with a warning: "This appeal to the understanding of the free world is my last appeal."[13]

Sihanouk undoubtedly considered his speech an accurate summary of Cambodia's circumstances, a reasoned critique of US policies and practices, and an earnest plea for comprehension of the kingdom's foreign policy. Trimble, however, had a different perception of the address. In a cable to the State Department, he wrote that it falsely depicted a "small, neutral and peace-loving Cambodia," victimized by the aggressive intentions of Thailand and South Vietnam and by the American obsession with the "commie menace." Trimble thought there were two possible explanations for such a speech: (1) Sihanouk was trying to justify some new move toward the communists, or (2) the prince was depressed, and his leftist advisers had manipulated his "persecution complex."[14]

On October 30, Trimble commented to the State Department on the "nervousness" in Cambodia. FARK had canceled all military leaves, Sihanouk had warned that invaders might soon attack the kingdom, and the government had asked the population to dig air-raid trenches. Among the political rumors circulating in Phnom Penh was the improbable notion that the prince was planning to sever relations with all SEATO countries. "While there have been no incidents involving US citizens and [the] attitude of Cambodian friends and associates continues to be one of friendship," wrote Trimble, "[this] picture could change overnight should Sihanouk whip up [an] anti-American campaign. Therefore, [I] propose to initiate [the] first phase [of the embassy] evacuation plan tomorrow."[15]

In the days that followed, Trimble's worries about a violent upheaval in Phnom Penh abated. Yet divisions remained within the US government over the meaning of Sihanouk's radio address and the official press attacks against America. Were they part of a carefully conceived strategy to curry favor with China or a typical overreaction by the prince to criticism? How should US officials conduct themselves with Sihanouk going forward? "Essentially we are dealing with a child and a spoilt one at that," Trimble concluded. "Infinite patience is called for but this should be tempered from time to time by a judicious display of firmness."[16]

Sihanouk's anti-American comments surprised President Kennedy. "Have we done anything to him?" Kennedy asked George W. Ball, under secretary of state and acting secretary while Dean Rusk was in Tokyo. Ball provided a blunt, simplistic answer: "[Sihanouk is] crazy, we have done nothing." According to the notes of their telephone conversation, Kennedy asked again: "Nothing we have done or said" provoked the outbursts? "No," Ball replied. "He has always been a curious fellow. He is in bad health and apparently has gone off the deep end." When Kennedy asked about the department's instructions to Trimble, Ball said that the ambassador was trying to "patch up" US relations with Cambodia.[17]

In Phnom Penh, US officials maintained an attitude of "courteous aloofness" with their Cambodian counterparts, and the tension between the two countries dissipated. In a meeting with Trimble on December 5, Sihanouk said that he had been "very worried" about the possibility of an attack by Thailand. Now, however, he thought that an invasion was "much less likely" and that the situation was "returning to normal." Trimble assured the prince of US opposition to aggression against Cambodia from any source. The only concern of the United States, Trimble said, was Cambodia's freedom, independence, and economic and social progress. "Sihanouk," the ambassador reported to Washington, "received these assurances most warmly and, throughout [the] conversation, was very temperate in [his] statements re Thailand and Vietnam."[18]

Despite the apparent improvement in Cambodia's relations with South Vietnam and Thailand, plotting against Sihanouk by his neighbors increased in 1962. One incident that undoubtedly intensified Diem's hostility toward the prince occurred on February 27 when two South Vietnamese AD-6 attack aircraft bombed the presidential palace in Saigon. Diem was not harmed by the attack, and one of the fighter-bombers was forced down by antiaircraft fire. The other pilot, however, flew to Phnom Penh, where he received asylum. According to the US embassy, Sihanouk said, "half-jokingly, that he might consider exchanging [the] pilot for Cambodian 'traitors' Son Ngoc Thanh and Chau Bory," a Khmer Serei rebel who had also received a death sentence in absentia. Many world leaders sent messages of sympathy to Diem, but Sihanouk did not. Apparently finding humor in the failed attack, he commented on national radio: "Before dropping bombs it should be determined whether Mr. Diem is at home. If he is out it would be useless to drop bombs on his house."[19]

Another incident exacerbating Saigon's relations with Sihanouk was the massacre of fifty-two civilians in the South Vietnamese village of Vinh Lac on April 20. South Vietnam charged that Cambodian forces were responsible for the attack and "demanded indemnities for the families of the victims and punishment for the raiders." Cambodia denied any responsibility for the slaughter, charging the Diem government with "slander." (US officials concluded that aggrieved Khmer Krom—ethnic Cambodians who lived in the border areas of Vietnam—were the probable attackers.) South Vietnam threatened economic sanctions if Cambodia did not take "satisfactory action." State Department officials speculated that "some elements" of the Diem government might use the Vinh Lac incident to "further [a] plot [to] overthrow Sihanouk."[20]

During the spring, the US government received "reports from many different sources that dissident Cambodians [were] being armed and trained on Thai and Vietnamese soil for return to Cambodia." According to a paper by the interagency Vietnam Task Force, dated May 15, Ngo Dinh Nhu said that South Vietnam "intended to take a hard line toward Cambodia." The hardness of that line was discussed in the CIA's *Central Intelligence Bulletin:* "Nhu reportedly stated in mid-May that he intended to send small political action/guerrilla teams into Cambodia, having as one of their objectives the assassination of Sihanouk."[21]

On May 19, Leonard Unger, the DCM in Bangkok, learned from General Chairatanta Inthaputi that Khmer Serei units would probably "be moving soon into Cambodia from South Vietnam and Thailand." The Thai general, Unger reported, "was not at all specific as to what the mission of these groups would be, whether they would be infiltrators making contact with the insurgent rebels already in Cambodia or whether they would be operating under deep cover. The implication, nevertheless, was that these were dissidents whose objective was removing Sihanouk."[22]

The multiple reports of plotting by Son Ngoc Thanh alarmed State Department officials, who thought that the plans to remove Sihanouk were "unrealistic and dangerous to free world interests." The prince maintained a firm grip on power, and he would likely call for communist assistance in the event of aggressive acts by South Vietnam and Thailand. With the civil war in Laos still unsettled and the insurgency in South Vietnam intensifying, department officials found it "unthinkable that our allies should encourage or allow actions which might create new and serious dangers in [the] area." The US ambassadors in Bangkok and Saigon were instructed to seek assurances from the Thai and South Vietnamese governments that Khmer Serei activities would be "kept under firm control and prevented from threatening Cambodian security."[23]

The diplomatic message for Sihanouk was less straightforward. Officials in Washington and Phnom Penh were well aware of the damaging consequences of not informing Sihanouk of the plots against him in 1959.

Moreover, there were indications that Sihanouk had learned of the Khmer Serei's current plans, either from Cambodian agents who had penetrated the rebel group or from communist intelligence passed on to him. On May 25, an editorial in *La Dépêche du Cambodge* alleged that planning was under way for an attack by Khmer Serei forces supported by South Vietnam. Sihanouk echoed that charge at the national Sangkum congress five days later. And during a toast at a farewell dinner for Ambassador Trimble, who was finishing his three-year assignment in Phnom Penh, Sihanouk "made thinly veiled accusations against [his] neighbors for plotting against Cambodia and even alluded to [the] possibility that Cambodia might be [the] victim of [an] unjustified attack."[24]

State Department officials thought it might be desirable to confidentially inform the Cambodian government that the United States had also heard about impending dissident activity and disapproved of it. Trimble, however, did not believe that it was the "proper moment" to share this information with Sihanouk: "It would be extremely difficult for him to resist making public mention that [the] U.S. had 'confirmed' such reports." Moreover, if the United States revealed its knowledge of plotting by Cambodia's neighbors, a confidential expression of "disapproval" would be insufficient. Sihanouk, Trimble wrote, would expect a strong statement putting South Vietnam and Thailand on notice that the United States "would not tolerate" their conspiring with Cambodian dissidents.[25]

To reduce the likelihood of a public incident, Trimble suggested an alternative approach to the Cambodian government. In his farewell interview with Sihanouk, he would acknowledge the prince's stated concerns about an attack by his neighbors but would not indicate that the United States had heard similar reports. The ambassador would then "state categorically that [the] U.S. would strongly disapprove of any plot against [the] Royal Government." Moreover, if Cambodia could provide evidence of a conspiracy by Khmer dissidents, the United States "would take whatever step it could to squash such a move."[26]

The State Department approved Trimble's proposed line with Sihanouk. On June 5, the ambassador made the agreed-upon representations to the prince, who said that he was grateful for the US assurances. (Trimble also presented Sihanouk with a valedictory gift—a Sears barbecue set, "which seemed [to] appeal [to] his love [of] gadgetry." Whether the gift appealed to his love of haute cuisine is more doubtful.) At the end of a cordial forty-five-minute conversation that covered a range of diplomatic and security matters, Sihanouk returned to the topic of "strong U.S. disapproval [of] action by Khmer dissidents." He reiterated that Trimble's statement "was most reassuring." The two men parted with mutual expressions of high regard. The ambassador's work, said Sihanouk, "had contributed much to [a] better understanding between [the] U.S. and his own country."[27]

The prince's kind words for Trimble were likely no more sincere than similar remarks made to the departing Robert McClintock in 1956. Although America's standing in Cambodia had nowhere to go but up after Carl Strom's final days in Phnom Penh, the rebound in relations after the failed Dap Chhuon coup was neither very high nor very stable. Trimble, who saw the prince infrequently, had been directly associated with many troubling episodes in US–Cambodian relations, including the unconvincing denials of American involvement in Dap Chhuon's plot, the alleged letter from Sam Sary to Edmund Kellogg, and the US unwillingness to take meaningful steps to restrain South Vietnam and Thailand from interfering in Cambodia's internal affairs.

The final US–Cambodian misunderstanding of Trimble's term as ambassador surfaced about a month after he left Phnom Penh. In an article in *Réalités Cambodgiennes,* Sihanouk wrote: "Ambassador Trimble informed me before his departure that he was authorized by his government to give formal assurances that [the] U.S. would not permit her Thai or SVN friends to attack or invade Cambodia and that [the US] would be able to prevent them from doing do." Chargé C. Robert Moore, who distinguished between quashing plots by Khmer dissidents and controlling the actions of US allies, informed the State Department that Sihanouk's statement was a "gross distortion of [the] Ambassador's actual remarks." Unwilling to comment publicly on "privileged communications" between Trimble and Sihanouk, Moore thought that the prince's claim would cause more problems in South Vietnam and Thailand than in Cambodia.[28]

For the US ambassadors in Saigon and Bangkok, persuading their host governments to abandon plots against Sihanouk seemed a futile undertaking that complicated the central task of containing communism in Southeast Asia. On June 6, 1962, Ambassador Nolting reported to the

State Department that he had received "categoric assurances" from President Diem and Foreign Minister Vu Van Mau: South Vietnam was "not aiding or abetting any attempt, by Khmer dissidents or anyone else, to overthrow Sihanouk or to invade Cambodia, or to make trouble for [the] RKG." Diem even denied any South Vietnamese involvement in the Dap Chhuon plot. Nolting informed Washington that he believed Diem and Mau.[29] One explanation for the ambassador's credulity was his standing instruction to rebuild Diem's confidence in the United States, which had been undermined by Durbrow's criticism of the Ngo family.

Ambassador Trimble, in one of his final cables from Phnom Penh, wrote that he appreciated Nolting's démarche but found Diem's attempt to dissociate from the Dap Chhuon conspiracy "surprising and even disturbing in view of [the] irrefutable evidence" of South Vietnamese participation. State Department officials apparently shared Trimble's reaction. Nolting, likely acting under instructions, told Diem that he had reported to Washington Diem's "categoric denial" of engaging in anti-Sihanouk activities. But since their earlier conversation, the ambassador said, he had received numerous disturbing reports of South Vietnamese plots.[30]

This evidence, Nolting stated, indicated that "certain cadres" from South Vietnam were receiving training "in Taiwan for subversive political activity in Cambodia" and that the Diem government had helped Son Ngoc Thanh travel to Taipei "to take part in or to direct such plotting."[31] (According to one CIA source, SEPES chief Dr. Tran Kim Tuyen in South Vietnam "had been in almost constant touch" with his Nationalist Chinese counterpart planning the overthrow of Sihanouk.)[32] Nolting asked Diem to verify that no part of his government was engaged in anti-Sihanouk activities. "Diem," Nolting wrote, "responded immediately and without any hesitation that he had, after our last talk, checked into the matter thoroughly." Diem said that he could not guarantee what Taiwan and Thailand might be doing but that he stood behind his earlier denial of South Vietnamese plotting.[33]

What Thailand was doing overtly in June 1962 was denouncing a ruling by the International Court of Justice that the Preah Vihear temple belonged to Cambodia. Perhaps because former secretary of state Dean Acheson argued Cambodia's case before the court, furious Thai officials threatened to withdraw from SEATO and to boycott the Geneva conference on Laos. Kenneth Young, the US ambassador in Bangkok, wrote to

Washington that Thai support for "anti-Sihanouk elements" would not be a surprising reaction to the court's decision.[34]

Reports of plotting against Sihanouk continued throughout the summer. On July 14, for example, the CIA's *Current Intelligence Bulletin* reported that Ngo Dinh Nhu "remains opposed to any rapprochement with Cambodia and believes South Vietnam should take covert action to overthrow Sihanouk." The *President's Intelligence Check List*, the agency's concise daily summary of important foreign developments, informed Kennedy: "We are hearing once more that Diem's brother Nhu may be getting ready to go gunning for Sihanouk." In a memorandum to the special group, CIA analysts wrote: "Sihanouk takes the view that Washington condones such plotting."[35]

On August 13, State Department officials wrote to the embassies in Saigon, Bangkok, Taipei, and Phnom Penh: "Department disturbed at [the] continuing reports of Thai and [South Vietnamese] support for possible imminent action against Sihanouk by Son Ngoc Thanh." The Cambodian dissident was not only increasing his contacts with "low level" officials but also meeting with leaders of the intelligence agencies in South Vietnam, Thailand, and Nationalist China. These officials, the department added, were "acting with [the] knowledge of upper echelons" of their governments.[36]

Although Washington considered such plotting "unrealistic," "unreliable," and "dangerous," there was little enthusiasm within the State Department or the embassies in Saigon and Bangkok for taking a firm stand toward Diem and Sarit. Like US officials at the end of Eisenhower's presidency, Kennedy's foreign policy advisers wanted South Vietnam and Thailand to stop conspiring against Sihanouk, but they refused to back their ineffectual diplomatic appeals with stronger threats or action. They always subordinated the prince's security concerns to fighting communism and to maintaining good relations with Diem and Sarit.

Nolting stressed to Dr. Tran Kim Tuyen the "dangers of plotting against Sihanouk," but the ambassador did not think there was "much to be gained by [a] further formal démarche to President Diem at this time." Ambassador Young commented to the State Department that the Thai leaders' "emotional" and "intractable fixation" on Cambodia made rational conversation about that country difficult. He further observed that when discussing ways of reducing friction between Thailand and Cambodia, "we must constantly keep in mind that Thailand is still [a] firm US ally, [the] only such ally in [the] area with strong [military] assets and [the] only firm base in [Southeast Asia] for all contingency planning."[37]

Ambassador Trimble's successor was Philip Dodson Sprouse. Then fifty-five, Sprouse was one of the State Department's China specialists whose careers had either been destroyed or damaged by the "loss" of China to communism in 1949. Having worked on Chinese affairs for fifteen years, Sprouse was assigned to the embassy in Paris from 1950 to 1954. His principal responsibility in Paris was to follow the war in Indochina. After serving in Brussels and as a Foreign Service inspector, Sprouse was appointed ambassador to Cambodia on June 16, 1962. "This was something that would never have been possible, I think, under a Republican administration," Sprouse later recalled, "because the names of the China specialists were never sent up for nomination as ambassador to anywhere. I was on the verge of retiring when Kennedy became President."[38] Although a capable manager of the US mission in Cambodia, Sprouse established no better rapport with Sihanouk than had his predecessors. Assistant Secretary of State W. Averell Harriman, who supported Sprouse's appointment as ambassador, later criticized him for lacking imagination in dealing with Sihanouk. "I kick myself around the room," said Harriman, "because we sent the wrong guy [to Cambodia]."[39]

Upon his arrival in Phnom Penh on August 11, Sprouse found himself in the middle of a crisis involving the CIA station. Agency operative Kwang P. Chu, ostensibly employed by the US economic aid mission, had disappeared on August 7. Six days later, during Sprouse's introductory meeting with the Cambodian foreign minister, Huot Samboth, the ambassador learned that the royal police had detained Chu for "flagrant espionage activities." The police also wanted to question Samuel B. H. Hopler, the alleged leader of the espionage ring. A World War II veteran, Hopler had joined the CIA after graduating from the Citadel in 1950. Like his subordinate, Chu, Hopler ostensibly worked for the US economic aid mission.[40]

Sprouse and other embassy officers demanded the immediate release of Chu, insisting that all non-Cambodian employees of the US mission were entitled to diplomatic immunity. The Americans also protested the Cambodian government's failure to notify the embassy immediately of

Chu's detention and its unwillingness to allow US officials to speak with him. The Cambodians, however, did not recognize Chu's or Hopler's diplomatic immunity, observing that they were not on the Foreign Ministry's list of accredited diplomats. Threatening to "publicly declare them *persona non grata*," Huot Samboth made a suggestion: if Hopler submitted to questioning by the police, then both men "would be permitted to leave the country quietly with no publicity of any kind."[41]

Huot Samboth's proposal was "an outrageous form of pressure not customary between friendly nations," according to Robert G. Cleveland, deputy director of the State Department's Office of Southeast Asian Affairs. In a memorandum to Harriman describing the incident, Cleveland suggested that the US government should respond with a threat of its own: public expulsion of the two officials "would be detrimental" both to American public opinion and to US relations with Cambodia.[42]

Harriman conveyed this message to Ambassador Nong Kimny. Naturally, said Harriman, the United States would be prepared to withdraw Chu and Hopler from Cambodia, but it would be best if there were "no publicity." The diplomatic crisis was resolved on August 18, when Chu and Hopler were allowed to leave Cambodia quietly. "Chu was in very bad condition upon his release and scarcely able to walk," Cleveland informed Harriman. "The Embassy's doctor reported him as suffering from severe malnutrition, deep mental shock, great fatigue, strep throat, possible kidney infection, and possibly pneumonia. Aside from having been subjected to inhuman imprisonment, painful torture (whipping and 'chopsticks') and drugs were used on him during the time he was held by the Cambodian police."[43]

Two days after Hopler and Chu left Cambodia, Sihanouk was friendly and voluble at the ceremony for the presentation of Ambassador Sprouse's diplomatic credentials. Providing Sprouse with an extended overview of Cambodia's foreign policy, the prince made one comment the ambassador found "disturbing and surprising." Referring to the large nations that provided assistance to Cambodia, he said, "They sometimes confront us with near ultimatums, and we accept them because we are grateful for [the] aid they give us." After a slight pause, the prince mentioned Chu by name and his "extra-diplomatic activities." Sihanouk said that he had been willing to grant the US request to release him "because we are grateful to you for [the] aid you give us."[44]

In his subsequent public denunciations of CIA activities in Cambodia, Sihanouk frequently mentioned Victor Matsui's involvement with Dap Chhuon but rarely discussed the Hopler-Chu affair. An explanation for the prince's silence about the latter incident was that the espionage by Hopler and Chu apparently targeted the PRC, not Cambodia. In other words, their spying lacked the domestic political advantage of a direct threat to the prince and Cambodia's security, which would have helped unify the people behind Sihanouk. Ambassador Sprouse, disturbed by his inauspicious introduction to intrigue in Cambodia, responded to the Hopler-Chu incident by reducing the number of agency personnel in Phnom Penh. "He virtually shut down the CIA Station in the Embassy," recalled James Lilley, "but some of us were able to stay on and continued to work."[45]

During the second half of 1962, US diplomats concerned with Cambodia sought to deflect appeals by Sihanouk for an international agreement to guarantee the kingdom's neutrality and borders. After fourteen nations signed the Geneva accords on Laos in July, Sihanouk wrote to President Kennedy and other world leaders proposing a similar conference on Cambodia. In a speech in Svay Rieng Province, Sihanouk linked his proposed conference to US responsibility for plots against Cambodia: "We have long held strong suspicions about [the] covert support given Thailand and SVN by certain powers, support which largely accounts for wrongs thus far done to us by those two countries. Should we consider reluctance or even eventual refusal of certain powers to approve [the] conference proposal as confirming our suspicions? Would it be illogical or unjust to draw this conclusion?"[46]

Moscow, Beijing, and Hanoi promptly endorsed Sihanouk's idea for a conference on Cambodia, which would provide a platform for denouncing the United States and its Southeast Asian allies. The reaction in anticommunist capitals was less welcoming. One objection was that the circumstances in Laos and Cambodia were very different. On the one hand, Laos had been engaged in a civil war involving communist, anticommunist, and neutral factions as well as their international supporters. Cambodia, on the other hand, was a peaceful country that was already neutral. From the US perspective, there were other problems with Sihanouk's proposal, but the "chief reason for opposing [the] conference idea is [the] danger

[that] Sihanouk might be encouraged [to] press for [a] similar conference [on] Viet-Nam."⁴⁷

The US government wanted Sihanouk to resolve his problems with his neighbors through bilateral negotiations or through the United Nations. The United Kingdom and India were also opposed to a conference on Cambodia. The former did not want to become involved in every Sihanouk complaint against Thailand and South Vietnam, and the latter noted that the effectiveness of the recently concluded Laos conference was still unknown. The discouraging responses to his conference proposal caused Sihanouk to temporarily drop the idea. He did, however, pursue an alternative: written commitments from the Geneva powers guaranteeing Cambodia's neutrality and borders. Similar in form to the Laos accords, the agreements Sihanouk contemplated included the withdrawal of MAAG, an outcome opposed by both the United States and FARK. "Cambodian military leaders," the CIA reported, "have expressed serious concern over the threatened loss or curtailment of Western military assistance."⁴⁸

Although Sihanouk's neutrality plans envisioned a withdrawal of US military advisers, MAAG commander Brigadier General E. C. D. Scherrer wanted to increase his advisory mission from sixty-three to eighty-three personnel. Minister of Defense Lon Nol held "MAAG in considerable esteem," and US advisers were moving farther out into the countryside. Among the justifications for the personnel increase was a new "intelligence function" assigned to MAAG—perhaps a consequence of the reduction in CIA officers in Cambodia. Ambassador Sprouse endorsed the proposed MAAG increase, "which would provide greater opportunities for U.S. military personnel to establish good relations with their counterparts at all levels of the Cambodian military establishment. These relationships would obviously furnish greater opportunities for the collection of intelligence and might prove extremely useful in some future political or military contingency."⁴⁹

The suggested increase in US military advisers was a nonstarter, however, and Sihanouk threatened to turn to Beijing for protection if the West did not agree to his neutrality proposal. Ambassadors Nolting and Young warned the State Department that giving in to the prince's "blackmail tactics" would undermine the US position in South Vietnam and Thailand. Nolting, who urged the State Department to reject Sihanouk's proposal "flatly and promptly," wondered how the anticommunist efforts in South Vietnam and Thailand could succeed if the United States and its "principal western allies put themselves in [the] position of 'defending' Cambodia against [the] two anchors of our line of defense in this area." Young, who agreed with Nolting's overall analysis, observed that the Thai government was "hypersensitive to any implication [that the] US places credence in Sihanouk's ceaseless charges of aggression."[50]

On November 21, 1962, Sihanouk formally submitted his neutrality agreement to President Kennedy and the leaders of other Geneva powers. The State Department found "many legal, technical and textual weaknesses" with the accord. For example, the proposed agreement required the signatories "to undertake at the request of the Royal Government of Cambodia all necessary steps to ensure effective respect" for the kingdom's neutrality, independence, and territorial integrity. Moreover, the signatories "will in no wise permit any act that may endanger" Cambodia's security. Such sweeping guarantees were unacceptable to department officials: "However, outright rejection is not advisable in view of the likelihood of an irrational reaction by Sihanouk."[51]

Kennedy made a temporizing response to Sihanouk that suggested limited US interest in his neutrality agreement. Although assuring the prince that his proposal would receive "urgent attention," the president alluded to the "radically different" situations in Laos and Cambodia. He also referred to the recent border war between China and India: "We have just witnessed flagrant aggression against neutral India by one of the parties to [the Laos] agreements, which raises the question of how much reliance should be placed on the word of this party to respect the independence, neutrality and territorial integrity of any country."[52]

The United Kingdom, according to Harriman, shared the US view of Sihanouk's neutrality agreement "in most important respects." French officials objected to specific aspects of the prince's proposal but thought that the West should try to change them through negotiations. In a moderate, year-end state-of-the-kingdom speech Sihanouk acknowledged international "reservations" about guaranteeing Cambodia's security and admitted that a signed neutrality agreement was "far off." Yet if relations with South Vietnam and Thailand could be stabilized, he would wait "patiently" for an international accord.[53]

How long the Kennedy administration would remain patient with

Sihanouk was unclear. At the end of 1962, the objectives of US policy remained unchanged: "the continued independence of Cambodia from all external influence or control, respect for its neutrality and territorial integrity, and the provision of necessary assistance to achieve these objectives." Yet "change from the top" still remained an option. In a memorandum to Harriman suggesting future courses of action in Cambodia, Henry L. T. Koren, the director of the State Department's Office of Southeast Asian Affairs, wrote: "Ultimately, consideration might be given to whether in the not too distant future some successor to Sihanouk should be found."[54]

Cambodia's chronically bad relations with Saigon and Bangkok suffered a further setback in February 1963, when PRC officials informed Sihanouk that his neighbors and Taiwan had "relaunched" Son Ngoc Thanh to either overthrow or assassinate him. Expressing gratitude for Beijing's earlier warnings about the Dap Chhuon coup, Sihanouk publicly charged that Thanh's supporters included an unnamed "imperialist power." The prince's obvious reference to the United States prompted a confidential message from Ambassador Sprouse to Foreign Minister Huot Samboth: the US government "strongly disapproved of anti-Cambodian subversion on [the] part of Khmer dissidents and if provided with information on which [the] RKG concern [is] based would do all in its power to quash them."[55]

The démarche was a virtually verbatim restatement of Trimble's valedictory assurance to Sihanouk. When Sprouse asked whether he should repeat the declaration to Sihanouk, Huot Samboth quickly replied that the ambassador's statement to him was "sufficient." Likely fearing another diplomatically destructive dispute with the United States, Samboth said that he would deliver the ambassador's message to the prince. Embassy officials observed to the State Department that the report of the "alleged Son Ngoc Thanh plot has unquestionably reinflamed [Sihanouk's] suspicions of the US and will probably condition his attitude toward us for some time to come."[56]

In a cable to the embassy in Saigon, department officials acknowledged that there was "some factual basis for Sihanouk's allegations on Thanh's activities." Noting both the PRC's "eagerness" to keep the prince apprised of plotting against him and the likely penetration of the Khmer Serei by Sihanouk's agents, the department instructed Nolting to "raise again with Diem the dangers implicit in Son Ngoc Thanh's continued conspiratorial activities in Viet-Nam." Washington further suggested that Diem consider declaring Son Ngoc Thanh an "undesirable alien" and "expelling" him from South Vietnam.[57]

On March 13, Nolting replied that he had spoken with the South Vietnamese about Son Ngoc Thanh. The conversations persuaded him that the Diem regime had "changed its tactic" with the Cambodian dissident. Instead of supporting Son Ngoc Thanh as "an agent provocateur against Cambodia," the government was using him "as a means of rallying and ensuring the support of ethnic Cambodians in South Vietnam." Nolting's willingness to accept this dubious explanation seems to have been motivated, in part, by his reluctance to make another futile protest to Diem. A talk with the South Vietnamese president about allegations of plotting against Sihanouk, Nolting wrote, "would merely elicit a denial and might give Diem an occasion to complain about Cambodian activities directed against him."[58]

A more complete understanding of Nolting's thinking would require declassification of a companion cable, sent through CIA channels, that discussed "alternative proposals for handling the matter."[59] This second telegram may have mentioned Son Ngoc Thanh's involvement with South Vietnamese counterinsurgency efforts. The Khmer Serei, according to the CIA, "often became home guards in many South Vietnamese villages along the Cambodian border." Thanh's brother, Son Thai Nguyen, received support from the Diem government to promote national loyalty among the ethnic Cambodians living in South Vietnam. Son Thai Nguyen used "his contacts with the Khmer Krom to drum up support for his brother and the Khmer Serei."[60]

Nolting may have also discussed the link between the Khmer Serei and the Citizens Irregular Defense Groups (CIDG), a rapidly expanding counterinsurgency program conceived by the CIA in 1961. Comprising a range of intelligence and paramilitary activities, the CIDG program recruited members of tribal and ethnic groups, including the Khmer Krom, who had largely been excluded from South Vietnam's regular army. CIDG "strike forces" were full-time paramilitary troops trained by US Army Special Forces. The CIA selected the "most promising" CIDG personnel for border-surveillance units, which monitored and harassed infiltration from Laos and Cambodia into South Vietnam.[61]

Some of the ethnic Cambodians recruited for the CIDG program were Khmer Serei. In March 1964, the US Military Assistance Command, Vietnam, estimated that about 1,000 of the 1,677 Khmer Krom in CIDG strike forces were Khmer Serei.[62] Yet later that same year a Pentagon officer who reviewed the program reported that the number of Khmer Serei in CIDG strike forces "has not been determined . . . but is receiving careful study." The reporting officer did observe that at least one of the twenty-one Khmer Krom strike-force companies was composed entirely of Khmer Serei.[63] Although the numbers of Cambodian dissidents in the CIDG program are imprecise, one fact is indisputable: during the Kennedy and Johnson administrations paramilitary forces responsive to orders from Son Ngoc Thanh received weapons, training, and pay from the CIA and the US Army.

To be sure, American support for Son Ngoc Thanh's forces was an incidental consequence of the CIDG program, not an objective. Yet within the US government there was little urgency to resolve the policy contradiction of seeking to improve Sihanouk's relations with South Vietnam while simultaneously providing assistance to the Khmer Serei. Like the weak appeals to Diem and Sarit to stop plotting against Sihanouk, US policy calculations about the CIDG program subordinated the prince's concerns about dissidents to defeating communists in South Vietnam.

The Buddhist crisis in South Vietnam was the beginning of the end not only for the Diem regime but also for US military and economic assistance to Cambodia. After the initial bloody demonstration in Hue on May 8, 1963, Sihanouk criticized Diem for mistreating South Vietnamese Buddhists. After the first self-immolation of a Buddhist monk—who died in front of the Cambodian embassy in Saigon—the prince asked President Kennedy and other world leaders to intercede with Diem on behalf of Vietnamese Buddhists: "It rests with the great powers to bring back to reason a government that has revived religious conflicts that had been quiescent for more than a century."[64]

Sihanouk's criticism of Diem was the likely catalyst for the resumption of Khmer Serei broadcasts into Cambodia, which had been off the air for three years. According to the CIA, the prince interpreted the thrice-daily propaganda blasts "as an indicator of renewed South Vietnamese–Thai–Khmer Serei anti-Cambodian machinations."[65] The resumption of

Khmer Serei broadcasts was soon followed by a South Vietnamese aircraft attack against a Cambodian guard post near the border. On August 24, Sihanouk announced his intention to sever relations with South Vietnam, presciently observing: "Diem [will] last only two–three months more." That same day the State Department sent an infamous cable to the US mission in Saigon that initiated an unsuccessful weeklong effort to stimulate a coup d'état in South Vietnam. Reports of CIA intrigues against the Ngo family soon appeared in the Vietnamese and international press, which almost certainly increased Sihanouk's fears of US plotting in Cambodia.[66]

In October, Sihanouk made speeches and wrote an editorial for the *Nationalist* alleging that the CIA was conspiring with the Khmer Serei. Embassy chargé Herbert D. Spivack, acting under instructions from the State Department, expressed to the acting Cambodian foreign minister, Prince Norodom Phurissara, the US government's "deep concern" over these accusations. The United States, said Spivack, deplored dissident activities, which threatened Cambodia's stability and unity. In his report of the conversation to the State Department, he wrote: "I stated that no agency of the United States Government was in any way aiding the Khmer Serei."[67]

The Cambodian Foreign Ministry made a formal request to Spivack to meet with royal adviser Penn Nouth, who said that Sihanouk had asked him to communicate the prince's views on US–Cambodian relations. Referring directly to the Dap Chhuon coup and indirectly to the Hopler-Chu incident, Penn Nouth said that the Cambodian government was "convinced" of CIA support for the Khmer Serei. He stressed, however, that Sihanouk's charges were directed only at the CIA and not at the government of the United States or its people. Spivack replied that the agency was part of the US government and that "accusations directed against the CIA were, in effect, directed against the United States Government."[68]

In Spivack's account of the meeting, the conversation ended with Penn Nouth repeating his belief that the CIA did not always act "in accordance with overall United States Government Policy." According to Sihanouk, however, Spivack's admission that the CIA operated under the direct orders of the US government had elicited this response from Penn Nouth: "If you say so, the affair will become more grave as far as the United States is concerned because in saying so you imply that the Victor Matsui–Slat Peau case, the arrest of two Vietnamese in possession of a transmitter in Dap Chhuon's house, and the existence of Son Ngoc Thanh and Sam Sary's transmitters are proof of the U.S. Government's [involvement]." Spivack was reportedly "at a loss for [a] reply and the conversation ended at that point."[69]

The coup d'état in South Vietnam on November 1 and the assassination of Diem and Nhu confirmed Sihanouk's worst fears about the United States. "Sihanouk was utterly convinced that Americans had engineered the coup," according to the State Department. In a radio address broadcast on November 5, the prince dismissed US denials of connections with the Khmer Serei and reminded his audience that Cambodia had caught Victor Matsui and Slat Peau with their "hands in the bag" during the Dap Chhuon coup. Alleging that "Nhu died immediately after informing the Americans that he would not carry out their orders," Sihanouk issued an ultimatum: "If on 31 December 1963 the Khmer Serei radio is still functioning, I will ask the United States to cut off economic and military aid and to withdraw its aid missions from our country."[70]

State Department officials were shocked by Sihanouk's threat, finding it "inconceivable" that Cambodia would abandon US assistance "in response to the activities of a small dissident group that has no popular support in Cambodia and represents no threat to [the] RKG, no matter how irritating its propaganda may [be]." US efforts to dissuade the prince from carrying out his threat included a renewed attempt to end the Khmer Serei broadcasts. At least one secret transmitter was almost certainly in Thailand, but the Sarit regime was not inclined to be helpful. Foreign Minister Thanat Khoman told Alfred Puhan, the US chargé in Bangkok, that Sihanouk's ultimatum would "cause some people in Washington to get the jitters." Thanat stated preemptively that he did not want to be pressured by the United States to do something about the Khmer Serei. "He asked me if I got his message," Puhan reported to the State Department. "When I replied 'loud and clear,' he repeated 'you read me loud and clear.'"[71]

In Saigon, the new military government shared Diem's "distaste" for Sihanouk and believed that Cambodia was a major operating base for Vietnamese communists. The junta's view of US methods of operation may be inferred by a question Brigadier General Le Van Kim posed to Henry Cabot Lodge, who had replaced Nolting as the American ambassador to South Vietnam: "If Sihanouk is proven to be a Communist, will the United States put a nationalist in power in Cambodia?"[72]

Son Ngoc Thanh may have had a similar question for Lodge, who was locally perceived as more of a proconsul than an ambassador. On November 18, an unnamed Khmer Serei representative asked an embassy employee in Saigon to inform Lodge that "Son Ngoc Thanh wished to see [the] ambassador urgently." The request was refused. State Department officials thought Thanh's approach to Lodge was an "example [of the] boldness with which he is acting."[73]

A widespread rumor in Saigon of an imminent "anti-Sihanouk coup" was the likely reason that the prince advanced his year-end timetable for ending US aid. At a hastily arranged public meeting of the Sangkum on November 19, Sihanouk personally questioned two of Son Ngoc Thanh's followers, who "confessed" that South Vietnam and the United States were arming and financing the Khmer Serei. After this kangaroo court, which condemned one of the prisoners to death, Sihanouk asked for and received the Sangkum's approval for the immediate withdrawal of all US military, economic, and cultural assistance. In a diplomatic note to the US government dated November 20, the Cambodian Foreign Ministry alleged "flagrant American participation in a plot against our people and our liberties" and requested "the initiation without delay of bilateral conversations on the liquidation of current [US aid] programs."[74]

Ambassador Nong Kimny was summoned to the State Department, where Harriman's successor, Assistant Secretary of State Roger Hilsman, restated the American position: the US government was not conspiring with the Khmer Serei and "could not control South Vietnam or Thailand." During his meeting with Kimny, Hilsman stepped away to take a telephone call from President Kennedy. This was the call recorded by Kennedy on November 20. The president, whose preoccupations in Southeast Asia had been Laos and Vietnam, did not seem well informed about Cambodia. When Hilsman mentioned the Khmer Serei, Kennedy asked: "What's the Khmer Serei?" During their conversation, Hilsman told the president about Sihanouk's "fear of what's happened to Diem and Nhu" and "fear of his own military."[75]

A subsequent CIA report discussed Sihanouk's "great unease concerning the cordial relationship existing between US officials and the Cambodian military."[76] The prince's discomfort was hardly irrational.

On November 21, Lon Nol made conspiratorial comments to Brigadier General Robert C. Taber, the MAAG commander. Sounding much like Dap Chhuon during his initial approach to Ambassador McClintock in 1956, Lon Nol declared, "Cambodian nationalists [are] not communists and would never become communists." He added that if the communists increased their strength in Cambodia, then "necessary action" would be taken, including perhaps "calling on the West for help." Although US military and economic assistance was ending, he said, the United States might someday "wish to aid Cambodia again, perhaps in a different way."[77]

In a top-secret cable to the State Department, Ambassador Sprouse described Lon Nol's veiled remarks to General Taber as the "most reassuring note we have yet encountered in this otherwise disquieting situation." Sihanouk's policies, the ambassador wrote, were "beginning [to] generate forebodings and potential opposition in that one sector which has [the] organization and means [to] make such opposition effective."[78]

Acknowledgments

I am grateful for the assistance of archivists at the National Archives and Records Administration in College Park, Maryland; the Dwight D. Eisenhower Library in Abilene, Kansas; the John F. Kennedy Library in Boston; the Library of Congress in Washington, DC; the Seeley G. Mudd Manuscript Library at Princeton University; and the Special Collections Research Center at Georgetown University Library. I am especially thankful for the help provided by Stanley Fanaras and Jeffery Hartley at the National Archives; Mary Burtzloff, Chalsea Millner, and Kathy Struss at the Eisenhower Library; and Stacey Chandler and Michael Desmond at the Kennedy Library.

I owe a particular debt to Kenton Clymer, distinguished research professor of history at Northern Illinois University. Author of three books on US relations with Cambodia, he was kind enough to read an early draft of the manuscript and offered many helpful suggestions for improving it. Merle L. Pribbenow II, a retired CIA official and an independent scholar specializing in the Vietnam War, generously shared his own translations of documents from the Democratic Republic of Vietnam. Ang Cheng Guan, author of international histories of Southeast Asia and the Vietnam War, suggested useful sources for my research. Anonymous reviewers selected by the University Press of Kentucky offered constructive suggestions for strengthening the manuscript.

I am pleased to continue my association with the University Press of Kentucky and its team of editorial, production, and marketing professionals. Acquisitions editor Allison B. Webster has been a particularly helpful colleague, and copyeditor Annie Barva has made my prose more readable. I am delighted that this book is a volume in the press series Studies in Conflict, Diplomacy, and Peace. Among its series editors and advisory board members are many of the leading historians of the Indochina wars.

Finally, Kristin Coffey, my partner in work and life, provided research assistance and editing suggestions that have made this book better. Any errors of commission or omission are, of course, mine alone.

Notes

Abbreviations Used in the Notes and the Bibliography

ASFEA	Assistant Secretary for Far Eastern Affairs
AWF	Ann Whitman File
BFEA	Bureau of Far Eastern Affairs
CDF	Central Decimal File
CFPF	Central Foreign Policy Files
CIB	*Current Intelligence Bulletin*
CID	*Current Intelligence Digest*
CIWS	*Current Intelligence Weekly Summary*
CREST	CIA Records Search Tool
DCER	Canadian Department of Foreign Affairs and International Trade, *Documents on Canadian External Relations*
DDEL	Dwight D. Eisenhower Library
ESRCOF	Executive Secretariat, Regional and Country Operations Files
FO	Foreign Office
FRUS	US Department of State, *Foreign Relations of the United States*
ICC	International Commission for Supervision and Control
JFKL	John F. Kennedy Library
JGPP	J. Graham Parsons Papers (Georgetown University, Special Collections Research Center, Washington, DC)
KARC	Kennedy Assassination Records Collection
LOC	Library of Congress
MFS	Microfiche Supplement
NAA	National Archives of Australia
NARA	National Archives and Records Administration
NIE	National Intelligence Estimate
NSC	National Security Council
NSF	National Security Files
OCB	Operations Coordinating Board
OSAA	Office of Southeast Asian Affairs
RG	Record Group
RG 59	General Records of the Department of State
RG 84	Records of the Foreign Service Posts of the Department of State

RG 319	Records of the Army Staff
RG 469	Records of the US Foreign Assistance Agencies
RG 472	Records of the US Forces in Southeast Asia, 1950–1976
SWJN	Jawaharlal Nehru, *Selected Works of Jawaharlal Nehru*
UKNA	National Archives, United Kingdom
USVR	US Department of Defense, *United States–Vietnam Relations, 1945–1967*
WAHP	W. Averell Harriman Papers
WCTP	William C. Trimble Papers (Princeton University, Department of Rare Books and Special Collections, Princeton, NJ)
WHOF	White House Office Files

Prologue

1. Kennedy–Hilsman conversation, November 20, 1963, JFKL, Telephone Recordings: Dictation Belt 34 (also available at http://www.millercenter.org). The Kennedy Library identifies neither Hilsman nor the date of the telephone conversation. A draft memorandum of conversation paraphrasing the telephone call (JFKL, Roger Hilsman Papers, box 1) confirms Hilsman's identity.

2. Philip D. Sprouse to State Dept., November 13, 1963, *FRUS, 1961–1963,* XXIII, d. 111.

3. Kennedy–Hilsman conversation, Telephone Recording, November 20, 1963.

4. John F. Kennedy, November 4, 1963, JFKL, Telephone Recordings: Dictation Belt 52.1.

5. Smith, *The Unknown CIA,* p. 15.

6. US Senate, *Alleged Assassination Plots Involving Foreign Leaders,* p. 10.

7. Samuel Belk, "Briefing Note for NSC Meeting," July 20, 1960, DDEL, AWF, NSC Series, box 12.

8. OCB, "Special Report on Southeast Asia," February 10, 1960, *USVR,* V-B-3d, p. 212; Trimble interview by Kennedy, February 24, 1990.

9. Kenneth Landon to Bromley Smith, January 27, 1960, DDEL, WHOF, NSC Staff Series, OCB Secretariat Series, box 7.

10. Robert McClintock to State Dept., May 3, 1956, NARA, RG 59, CDF, 1955–1959, box 3354; John Foster Dulles, "The Cost of Peace," *Department of State Bulletin,* June 18, 1956, p. 999.

11. Memorandum of conversation, January 31, 1956, *FRUS, 1955–1957,* XXI, d. 80.

12. Memorandum of conversation, February 10, 1956, *FRUS, 1955–1957,* XXI, d. 225.

13. Robert M. McClintock, "United States Policy toward Cambodia," May 8, 1957, NARA, RG 59, BFEA, OSAA, Cambodia, 1958–1963, box 6; memorandum of conversation, April 6, 1956, NARA, RG 59, CDF, 1955–1959, box 3354; Parsons, unpublished memoir, JGPP, box 12.

14. Haverkamp interview by Kennedy, April 11, 1994.

15. Sihanouk, radio address, December 9, 1963, *FRUS, 1961–1963,* XXIII, d. 132.

16. Taylor, "Prince Sihanouk and the New Order in Southeast Asia," p. vii; John S. Thomson, "Background Paper: US/Cambodia Relations," December 24, 1964, NARA, RG 59, Entry 5415-A, box 1.

17. Clymer, *The United States and Cambodia, 1870–1969*, p. 3; CIA, "Political Dynamics," p. 53-3.

18. Osborne, *Sihanouk*, pp. 21–22; State Dept., biographical sketch of Sihanouk, March 13, 1969, NARA, RG 59, Bureau of East Asian and Pacific Affairs, Office of the Country Director for Laos and Cambodia, Cambodia records, box 5.

19. Osborne, *Sihanouk*, p. 38.

20. Chandler, *The Tragedy of Cambodian History*, p. 20.

21. Jefferson Caffery to State Dept., November 28, 1945, *FRUS, 1945*, VI, p. 315; Strategic Services Unit (Kandy) to War Dept., November 6, 1945, NARA, RG 226, Entry NM 54-6, box 8.

22. Taylor, "Prince Sihanouk and the New Order in Southeast Asia," p. 4.

23. CIA, "The Pan-Thai Movement," August 11, 1953, NARA, CREST.

24. Edwin Stanton to State Dept., December 17, 1946, *FRUS, 1946*, VIII, pp. 1104–1105.

25. Goscha, *Thailand and the Southeast Asian Networks of the Vietnamese Revolution*, p. 123.

26. CIA, "Communism and Cambodia."

27. Kiernan, *How Pol Pot Came to Power*, p. 57.

28. Goscha, *Thailand and the Southeast Asian Networks of the Vietnamese Revolution*, p. 399.

29. Kiernan, *How Pol Pot Came to Power*, pp. 79–80.

30. State Dept. Working Group, February 1, 1950, and memorandum of conversation, February 3, 1950, *FRUS, 1950*, VI, pp. 714 and 719.

31. George M. Abbott to State Dept., February 13, 1950, *FRUS, 1950*, VI, pp. 728–730.

32. Memorandum of conversation, November 27, 1950, NARA, RG 59, CDF, 1950–1954, box 3696.

33. Don V. Catlett to State Dept., July 31, 1951, NARA, RG 59, CDF, 1950–1954, box 3696.

34. Chandler, *The Tragedy of Cambodian History*, p. 58.

35. Osborne, *Sihanouk*, p. 67.

36. Philip Bonsal to State Dept., March 21, 1952, and Catlett to State Dept., February 11, 1952, NARA, RG 59, CDF, 1950–1954, boxes 3698 and 2924.

37. Catlett to State Dept., March 20, 1952, and Donald R. Heath to State Dept., March 24, 1952, NARA, RG 59, CDF, 1950–1954, box 3696.

38. Memorandum of conversation, March 28, 1952, NARA, RG 59, CDF, 1950–1954, box 3696.

39. CIA, "The Khmer–Issarak Movement," September 14, 1948, NARA, CREST; memorandum of conversation, March 28, 1952.

40. CIA, *CID*, May 9, 1952, NARA, CREST.

41. Heath to State Dept., May 2, 1952, NARA, RG 84, US Embassy, Phnom Penh, Classified General Records, 1950–1963, box 1; CIA, *CID,* May 15, 1952, NARA, CREST.

42. Heath to State Dept., March 3, 1953, and June 2, 1952, NARA, RG 59, CDF, 1950–1954, box 3696.

43. C. D. Jackson, memorandum, January 18, 1954, and Charlton Ogburn to John Allison, December 29, 1952, *FRUS, 1952–1954,* XIII, part 1, d. 512 and d. 157 n.

44. Heath to State Dept., June 2, 1952.

45. Heath to State Dept., March 3, 1953; Edmund Gullion to State Dept., June 15, 1952, NARA, RG 59, CDF, 1950–1954, box 3698.

46. Thomas J. Corcoran to State Dept., June 17, 1952, *FRUS, 1952–1954,* XIII, part 1, d. 81; CIA, *CID,* June 19, 1952, NARA, CREST; Charles Spinks to State Dept., June 16, 1952, NARA, RG 59, CDF, 1950–1954, box 3698.

47. Chandler, *Brother Number One,* Kindle locations 905–913.

48. Joseph J. Montllor to State Dept., January 21, 1953, NARA, RG 59, CDF, 1950–1954, box 3696.

49. Montllor to State Dept., February 3, 1953, NARA, RG 59, CDF, 1950–1954, box 3696.

50. Montllor to State Dept., February 9, 1953, NARA, RG 59, CDF, 1950–1954, box 3698.

51. Memorandum of conversation, February 12, 1953, NARA, RG 59, Office of the Chief of Protocol, Visits by Heads of Government, 1928–1977, box 13.

52. State Dept. to Saigon, February 17, 1953, NARA, RG 59, CDF, 1950–1954, box 3696.

53. Heath to State Dept., February 27, 1953, NARA, RG 59, CDF, 1950–1954, box 3696.

1. "A Shrewd Move"

1. John Getz to Bonsal, April 10, 1953, and April 14, 1953, NARA, RG 59, CDF, 1950–54, box 2924.

2. Heath to Walter Robertson, April 20, 1953, *FRUS, 1952–1954,* XIII, part 1, d. 226.

3. Ibid.; Nixon, *The Memoirs of Richard Nixon,* p. 125.

4. Montllor to State Dept., May 17, 1953, and May 19, 1953, NARA, RG 59, CDF, 1950–54, boxes 3698 and 3696.

5. Michael James, "King, Here, Warns Cambodia May Rise," *New York Times,* April 19, 1953.

6. Heath to John Foster Dulles, April 28, 1953, *FRUS, 1952–1954,* XIII, part 1, d. 250.

7. As described in Heath to W. Robertson, April 20, 1953.

8. Heath to State Dept., May 3, 1952, NARA, RG 84, US Embassy, Phnom Penh, Classified General Records, 1950–1963, box 1.

9. Montllor to State Dept., April 30, 1953, NARA, RG 59, CDF, 1950–1954, box 3696.

10. McClintock to State Dept., April 27, 1953, NARA, RG 59, CDF, 1950–1954, box 3696.

11. Ibid.; J. F. Dulles to Sihanouk, April 28, 1953, *FRUS, 1952–1954,* XIII, part 1, d. 249.

12. Memorandum of conversation (de Langlade), April 28, 1953, and memorandum of conversation (Risterucci), April 28, 1953, NARA, RG 59, CDF, 1950–1954, box 3696.

13. Robert D. Murphy to State Dept., April 29, 1953, NARA, RG 59, CDF, 1950–1954, box 3696.

14. C. Douglas Dillon to State Dept., April 30, 1953, NARA, RG 59, CDF, 1950–1954, box 2924.

15. Dillon to State Dept., April 30, 1953, *FRUS, 1952–1954,* XIII, part 1, d. 255.

16. Montllor to State Dept., June 4, 1953, NARA, RG 59, CDF, 1950–1954, box 3698.

17. Montllor to State Dept., no. 75, June 15, 1953, NARA, RG 59, CDF, 1950–1954, box 3698.

18. Ibid.; Montllor to State Dept., no. 74, June 15, 1953, *FRUS, 1952–1954,* XIII, part 1, d. 305.

19. Paris to State Dept., June 15, 1953, and Edwin F. Stanton to State Dept., June 18, 1953, NARA, RG 59, CDF, 1950–1954, boxes 3696 and 3698.

20. CIA, "Comment on Cambodian King's Flight to Thailand," June 14, 1953, NARA, CREST.

21. McClintock to State Dept., June 17, 1953, and Heath to State Dept., June 19, 1953, NARA, RG 59, CDF, 1950–1954, box 3698.

22. Stanton to State Dept., June 18, 1953.

23. Memorandum of conversation, July 2, 1953, and Charles N. Spinks to State Dept., July 6, 1953, NARA, RG 59, CDF, 1950–1954, box 3697.

24. Heath to State Dept., July 3, 1953, NARA, RG 59, CDF, 1950–1954, box 3696.

25. Ibid.

26. Henry Day to U. Alexis Johnson, July 1, 1953, NARA, RG 59, BFEA, Subject Files, 1953, box 5.

27. Heath to State Dept., July 2, 1953, NARA, RG 59, CDF, 1950–1954, box 3696; Johnson to J. F. Dulles, July 1, 1953, NARA, RG 59, BFEA, Subject Files, 1953, box 5.

28. State Dept. to Saigon and Paris, July 1, 1953, *FRUS, 1952–1954,* XIII, part 1, d. 318.

29. Dillon to State Dept., July 2, 1953, *FRUS, 1952–1954,* XIII, part 1, d. 320.

30. Dillon to State Dept., July 3, 1953, *FRUS, 1952–1954,* XIII, part 1, d. 323; CIA, "The Associated States Situation," July 9, 1953, NARA, CREST.

31. State Dept., biographical sketch of Nong Kimny, September 21, 1961, NARA, RG 59, ESRCOF, 1953–1961, box 16; memorandum of conversation, July 6, 1953, *FRUS, 1952–1954,* XIII, part 1, d. 325.

32. Memorandum of conversation, July 12, 1953, *FRUS, 1952–1954,* XIII, part 1, d. 337.

33. State Dept. to Heath, July 17, 1953, *FRUS, 1952–1954,* XIII, part 1, d. 347.

34. Ibid.

35. Montllor to State Dept., July 20, 1953, NARA, RG 59, CDF, 1950–1954, box 2924.

36. Heath to State Dept., July 22, 1953, NARA, RG 59, CDF, 1950–1954, box 3697; Montllor to State Dept., July 20, 1953.

37. Heath to State Dept., July 22, 1953.

38. Heath to State Dept., no. 170, July 25, 1953, NARA, RG 59, CDF, 1950–1954, box 2924.

39. Heath to State Dept., no. 171, July 25, 1953, *FRUS, 1952–1954,* XIII, part 1, d. 355.

40. Heath to State Dept., no. 171, July 25, 1953 (unredacted), NARA, RG 59, CDF, 1950–1954, box 2924.

41. Heath to State Dept., July 26, 1953, NARA, RG 59, CDF, 1950–1954, box 2924.

42. In 1953, the Cambodian army was called "Armée Royale Khmèr." This name was soon replaced by the more encompassing one "Forces Armées Royales Khmères." For reading ease and consistency, I use only the latter designation in this book.

43. CIA, *CIB,* September 1, 1953, NARA, CREST.

44. Rudolphe Duder to External Affairs Dept. (Canada), October 27, 1954, *DCER,* XX, d. 784.

45. Heath to State Dept., September 12, 1953, *FRUS, 1952–1954,* XIII, part 1, d. 402 n.

46. Dillon to State Dept., September 14, 1953, NARA, RG 59, CDF, 1950–1954, box 3697.

47. Heath to State Dept., September 12, 1953.

48. State Dept. to Heath, September 12, 1953, *FRUS, 1952–1954,* XIII, part 1, d. 403.

49. Dwight D. Eisenhower to Alfred Gruenther, July 2, 1954, in Eisenhower, *The Papers of Dwight David Eisenhower,* 15:1157.

50. Heath to State Dept., September 15, 1953, *FRUS, 1952–1954,* XIII, part 1, d. 406.

51. Ibid.

52. Montllor to State Dept., September 17, 1953, *FRUS, 1952–1954,* XIII, part 1, d. 408.

53. Oberdorfer, *Senator Mansfield,* p. 112; Heath to State Dept., September 24, 1953, *FRUS, 1952–1954,* XIII, part 1, d. 410.

54. Getz to Bonsal, April 10, 1953; Heath to State Dept., September 24, 1953.

55. Memorandum of conversation, October 12, 1953, *FRUS, 1952–1954,* XIII, part 1, d. 419; Mansfield, *Report of Senator Mike Mansfield on a Study Mission to the Associated States of Indochina,* p. 6.

56. Heath to State Dept., October 6, 1953, NARA, RG 59, CDF, 1950–1954, box 2924; CIA, *CIB,* October 8, 1953, NARA, CREST.

57. Gerald Warner to State Dept., September 28, 1953, NARA, RG 59, CDF, 1950–1954, box 3697.

58. Ibid.

59. Ibid.

60. Ibid.

61. Ibid.

62. Montllor to State Dept., October 19, 1953, NARA, RG 59, CDF, 1950–1954, box 2924.

63. Ibid.

64. Ibid.

65. McClintock to State Dept., December 28, 1953, and Montllor to State Dept., November 16, 1953, NARA, RG 59, CDF, 1950–1954, boxes 3697 and 3698.

66. Heath to State Dept., November 11, 1953, *FRUS, 1952–1954,* XIII, part 1, d. 445.

67. Montllor to State Dept., November 15, 1953, *FRUS, 1952–1954,* XIII, part 1, d. 448.

68. McClintock to State Dept., December 28, 1953, NARA, RG 59, CDF, 1950–1954, box 3697.

69. Chandler, *The Tragedy of Cambodian History,* p. 71; CIA, "Communism and Cambodia," p. 7; Heath to State Dept., February 22, 1954, *FRUS, 1952–1954,* XIII, part 1, d. 574; NIE, June 1, 1954, *FRUS, 1952–1954,* XVI, d. 677; Herbert Goodman to State Dept., June 12, July 2, and July 27, 1954, NARA, RG 59, CDF, 1950–1954, boxes 3698 and 3680.

70. Kiernan, *How Pol Pot Came to Power,* p. 133.

71. Goodman to State Dept., July 2, 1954.

72. Montllor to State Dept., April 22, 1954, *FRUS, 1952–1954,* XIII, part 1, d. 772; CIA, *CIB,* April 24, 1954, www.foia.cia.gov.

73. McClintock to State Dept., April 23, 1954, NARA, RG 59, CDF, 1950–1954, box 3697.

74. McClintock to State Dept., April 24, 1954, NARA, RG 59, CDF, 1950–1954, box 3697.

75. McClintock to State Dept., April 27, 1954, NARA, RG 59, CDF, 1950–1954, box 3697.

76. Montllor to State Dept., April 29 and May 7, 1954, NARA, RG 59, CDF, 1950–1954, box 3697.

2. "Not a Happy Omen"

1. W. Park Armstrong to J. F. Dulles, March 31, 1954, *FRUS, 1952–1954,* XIII, part 1, d. 664; State Dept. press release, February 19, 1954, *FRUS, 1952–1954,* XIII, part 1, d. 568.

2. Geneva conference, first plenary session, May 8, 1954, NARA, RG 59, Conference Files, 1949–1963, box 44.

3. Ibid.; Walter Bedell Smith quoted in Shuckburgh, *Descent to Suez,* p. 190.

4. Geneva conference, first plenary session, May 8, 1954.

5. Geneva conference, third restricted session, May 19, 1954, and fourth restricted session, May 21, 1954, NARA, RG 59, Conference Files, 1949–1963, box 44.

6. Zhai, *China and the Vietnam Wars,* p. 56.

7. Zhou Enlai to Mao Zedong et al., June 18, 1954, http://digitalarchive .wilsoncenter.org/document/111501; Walter Bedell Smith to State Dept., June 17, 1954, *FRUS, 1952–1954,* XVI, d. 779; CIA, *CIB,* June 23, 1954, www.foia.cia.gov.

8. CIA, *Indochina Report,* June 23, 1954, NARA, CREST.

9. Goodman to State Dept., June 24, 1954, NARA, RG 59, CDF, 1950–1954, box 3698.

10. Biographical sketch of Nhiek Tioulong, June 14, 1956, NARA, RG 59, OSAA, Cambodia and Vietnam, 1953–1958, box 5; Goodman to State Dept., June 24, 1954.

11. McClintock to State Dept., June 24, 1954, no. 2892, NARA, RG 59, Conference Files, 1949–1963, box 48.

12. Goodman to State Dept., July 7, 1954, NARA, RG 59, CDF, 1950–1954, box 3697.

13. George M. Widney to William Donovan, June 7, 1954, NARA, RG 59, CDF, 1950–1954, box 3698.

14. Goodman to State Dept., June 29, 1954, NARA, RG 59, CDF, 1950–1954, box 3697.

15. Widney to Donovan, June 7, 1954.

16. Goodman to State Dept., July 7 and July 8, 1954, NARA, RG 59, CDF, 1950–1954, box 3697.

17. Heath to State Dept., no. 111, July 9, 1954, NARA, RG 59, CDF, 1950–1954, box 3697; memorandum, C. D. Jackson, January 18, 1954, *FRUS, 1952–1954,* XIII, part 1, d. 512; NSC 5429/2, August 20, 1954, *USVR,* Part-V-B-3c, p. 731.

18. Heath to State Dept., no. 113, July 9, 1954, *FRUS, 1952–1954,* XIII, part 2, d. 1035.

19. Ibid.; McClintock to State Dept., June 24, 1954, no. 2894, NARA, RG 59, Conference Files, 1949–1963, box 48; Goodman to State Dept., June 18, 1954, NARA, RG 59, CDF, 1950–1954, box 3698.

20. W. B. Smith to State Dept., July 17, 1954, *FRUS, 1952–1954,* XVI, d. 961.

21. Minutes of conversation, July 17, 1954, http://digitalarchive.wilsoncenter .org/document/111072.

22. Geneva conference, eighth plenary session, July 21, 1954, *FRUS, 1952–1954,* XVI, d. 1039.

23. Ibid., d. 1038.

24. Declaration by the Royal Government of Cambodia, July 21, 1954, *FRUS, 1952–1954,* XVI, d. 1051.

25. W. B. Smith–J. F. Dulles phone call, July 21, 1954, *FRUS, 1952–1954,* XVI, d. 1028; CIA, *Indochina Report,* August 4, 1954, NARA, CREST.

26. Logevall, *Embers of War,* p. 612.

27. Johnson to State Dept., June 22, 1954, *FRUS, 1952–1954,* XVI, d. 808; Heder, *Cambodian Communism and the Vietnamese Model,* p. 37.

28. Memorandum of conversation, July 26, 1954, *FRUS, 1952–1954,* XII, part 1, d. 270.

29. Heath to State Dept., July 29, 1954, NARA, RG 59, CDF, 1950–1954, box 3680.

30. Memorandum, Bonsal, April 30, 1954, *FRUS, 1952–1954,* XVI, d. 405; J. F. Dulles to Eisenhower, May 17, 1954, *FRUS, 1952–1954,* XIII, part 2, d. 897.

31. Green interview by Kennedy, March 17, 1995; McClintock to W. B. Smith, August 12, 1954, NARA, RG 59, BFEA, OSAA, Cambodia Files, 1958–1963, box 5; Sihanouk, *My War with the CIA,* p. 86.

32. "Excerpt from OCB meeting minutes," August 4, 1954, NARA, RG 59, CDF, 1950–1954, box 3681.

33. McClintock to W. B. Smith, August 12, 1954.

34. Ibid.

35. Ibid.

36. Memorandum of conversation, July 24 and July 29, 1954, *FRUS, 1952–1954,* XII, part 1, d. 267 and 278.

37. Memorandum of conversation, August 17, 1954, and J. F. Dulles to Dillon, August 18, 1954, *FRUS, 1952–1954,* XIII, part 2, d. 1133 and d. 1136.

38. Dillon to State Dept., August 20, 1954, *FRUS, 1952–1954,* XIII, part 2, d. 1142.

39. State Dept. to Dillon, August 28, 1954, NARA, RG 59, CDF, 1950–1954, box 3681.

40. Memorandum of conversation, August 24 and September 1, 1954, NARA, RG 59, CDF, 1950–1954, box 3698.

41. W. Robertson to W. B. Smith, September 11, 1954, NARA, RG 59, CDF, 1950–1954, box 3698.

42. Steeves interview by O'Brien, September 5, 1969.

43. Heath to Bonsal, July 4, 1954, *FRUS, 1952–1954,* XVI, d. 864; Eden, *Full Circle,* p. 126.

44. W. Robertson to W. B. Smith, September 11, 1954.

45. State Dept. to Phnom Penh, September 29, 1954, *FRUS, 1952–1954,* XIII, part 2, d. 1236; Phnom Penh to State Dept., October 4, 1954, NARA, RG 59, CDF, 1950–1954, box 3698.

46. Phnom Penh to State Dept., October 4, 1954; McClintock to State Dept., December 18, 1954, NARA, RG 59, CDF, 1950–1954, box 3697.

47. McClintock to State Dept., October 23, 1954, NARA, RG 59, CDF, 1950–1954, box 3697.

48. Ibid.; Adrian Colquitt to State Dept., September 28, 1954, NARA, RG 59, CDF, 1950–1954, box 3697.

49. Colquitt to State Dept., September 9, 1954, NARA, RG 59, CDF, 1950–1954, box 3697; McClintock to State, October 23, 1954.

50. McClintock to State Dept., October 12, 1954, NARA, RG 59, CDF, 1950–1954, box 3682.

51. McClintock to State Dept., October 7, 1954, NARA, RG 59, CDF, 1950–1954, box 3682; Cambodian demand and ICC rejection reported in Duder to External Affairs Dept. (Canada), November 26, 1954, *DCER*, XX, p. 1801.

52. Dinesh K. Patnaik, "Sihanouk's Indian Connection," *Phnom Penh Post*, October 30, 2012.

53. Jawaharlal Nehru to Edwina Mountbatten, November 2, 1954, in Nehru, *SWJN*, 27:70.

54. Ibid.; Nehru, "The Situation in Cambodia," November 29, 1954, and "Implications of China Visit," November 14, 1954, in Nehru, *SWJN*, 27:104, 86.

55. Nehru, "The Situation in Cambodia," November 29, 1954, and speech, November 2, 1954, in Nehru, *SWJN*, 27:54–55; McClintock to State Dept., November 5, 1954, NARA, RG 59, CDF, 1950–1954, box 3697.

56. McClintock to State Dept., November 5, 1954.

57. McClintock to State Dept., November 12, 1954, NARA, RG 59, CDF, 1950–1954, box 3697.

58. Ibid.

59. Ibid.

60. Ibid.

61. Ibid.

62. ICC, *First Progress Report*, pp. 5–7.

63. Colquitt to State Dept., September 29, 1954, *FRUS, 1952–1954*, XIII, part 2, d. 1220; ICC, *First Progress Report*, p. 6; Engelbert and Goscha, *Falling out of Touch*, p. 46.

64. Duder to External Affairs Dept. (Canada), October 27, 1954, *DCER*, XX, d. 784; Duder to External Affairs Dept. (Canada), December 27, 1954, NARA, RG 59, OSAA subject files, 1950–1956.

65. ICC, *First Progress Report*, p. 17.

66. Ibid., p. 9; Duder to External Affairs Dept. (Canada), December 16, 1954, *DCER*, XX, d. 791.

67. R. M. Macdonnell to External Affairs Dept. (Canada), November 12, 1954, and Duder to External Affairs Dept. (Canada), November 26, 1954, *DCER*, XX, d. 785 and d. 787.

68. Duder to External Affairs Dept. (Canada), December 23, 1954, *DCER*, XX, d. 792.

3. "Time for Further Maneuvers"

1. McClintock to State Dept., January 30, 1955, NARA, RG 59, CDF, 1955–1959, box 3353; "Extracts from the Constitution of the Kingdom of Cambodia," in ICC, *Fourth Interim Report,* p. 28.

2. CIA, *CIB,* January 25, 1955, www.foia.cia.gov.

3. McClintock to State Dept., February 4, 1955, NARA, RG 59, CDF, 1955–1959, box 3358.

4. McClintock to State Dept., February 15, 1955, NARA, RG 59, CDF, 1955–1959, box 3353. Also see ICC, *Second Progress Report,* pp. 33–36; Nehru, February 23, 1955, in Nehru, *Letters to Chief Ministers,* 4:137; Taylor, "Prince Sihanouk and the New Order in Southeast Asia," p. 16.

5. Daniel Arzac to McClintock, February 19, 1955, NARA, RG 59, CDF, 1955–1959, box 3358.

6. Ibid.

7. McClintock to State Dept., February 20, 1955, NARA, RG 59, CDF, 1955–1959, box 3353; CIA, *CIB,* February 22, 1955, www.foia.cia.gov.

8. McClintock to State Dept., March 6, 1955, no. 704, NARA, RG 59, CDF, 1955–1959, box 3356.

9. Ibid.; McClintock to State Dept., February 28, 1955, NARA, RG 59, CDF, 1955–1959, box 3353.

10. McClintock to State Dept., February 28, 1955.

11. McClintock to Arthur Radford, July 26, 1956, NARA, RG 59, BFEA, OSAA, Cambodia Files, 1958–1963, box 4.

12. J. F. Dulles to State Dept., March 1, 1955, no. 49, NARA, RG 59, CDF, 1955–1959, box 3353; Kenneth T. Young to State Dept., March 3, 1955, and McClintock to State Dept., March 3 and March 8, 1955, NARA, RG 59, CDF, 1955–1959, boxes 3358 and 399.

13. McClintock to State Dept., March 3, 1955; J. F. Dulles to State Dept., March 1, 1955, no. 18, *FRUS, 1955–1957,* I, d. 48.

14. J. F. Dulles to State Dept., February 24, 1955, NARA, RG 59, CDF, 1955–1959, box 1408; J. F. Dulles to State Dept., March 1, 1955, no. 18.

15. Memorandum of conversation, February 14, 1955, NARA, RG 59, BFEA, Country File–1955, box 10.

16. Arthur Davis to Joint Chiefs of Staff, January 14, 1955, *FRUS, 1955–1957,* XXI, d. 179; "U.S. Training Mission for Cambodia," undated, c. February 5, 1955, NARA, RG 59, CDF, 1955–1959, box 3360.

17. Andrew Goodpaster, memorandum for the record, February 19, 1955, DDEL, WHOF, Office of the Staff Secretary, Subject Series, Department of Defense Subseries, box 1; J. F. Dulles to State Dept., March 2, 1955, *FRUS, 1955–1957,* XXI, d. 192; McClintock to Young, June 21, 1955, *FRUS, 1955–1957,* XXI, d. 206.

18. J. F. Dulles to State Dept., March 1, 1955, no. 18.

19. ICC, *Second Progress Report,* pp. 37–38.

20. Cunningham interview by Kennedy, March 17, 1997.

21. Colquitt to State Dept., March 2 and March 3, 1955, NARA, RG 59, CDF, 1955–1959, box 3358.

22. McClintock to State Dept., March 3, 1955, and Robert Hoey to William Sebald, March 3, 1955, NARA, RG 59, CDF, 1955–1959, box 3358.

23. McClintock to State Dept., March 5, 1955, NARA, RG 59, CDF, 1955–1959, box 3358.

24. McClintock to State Dept., March 6, 1955, no. 703, NARA, RG 59, CDF, 1955–1959, box 3358; McClintock to State Dept., March 5, 1955.

25. McClintock to State Dept., March 6, 1955, no. 710, NARA, RG 59, CDF, 1955–1959, box 3358.

26. ICC, *Second Progress Report,* pp. 39–40.

27. McClintock to State Dept., March 14, 1955, NARA, RG 59, CDF, 1955–1959, box 3358; CIA, "The Question of the Abdicated King," March 9, 1955, NARA, CREST.

28. "Talks with Norodom Sihanouk," March 17, 1955, in Nehru, *SWJN,* 28:184–187.

29. Ibid.

30. ICC, *Second Progress Report,* p. 39.

31. Nehru to Vijayalakshmi Pandit, March 19, 1955, in Nehru, *SWJN,* 28:597.

32. McClintock to State Dept., March 29, 1955, NARA, RG 59, CDF, 1955–1959, box 3358.

33. Nehru, speech to Indian Parliament, March 31, 1955, in Nehru, *SWJN,* 28:307; Josif interview by Kennedy, October 4, 1999.

34. Barnett, "Asia and Africa in Session," p. 8; "Text of Final Communiqué," NARA, RG 59, Policy Planning Staff/Council, Subject Files, 1947–1962, box 47.

35. Memorandum of conversation, January 7, 1955, *FRUS, 1955–1957,* XXI, d. 1.

36. NSC Meeting, March 3, 1955, minutes, DDEL, AWF, NSC Series, box 6.

37. Barnett, "Asia and Africa in Session," p. 8, ellipsis in original.

38. G. Kahin, *The Asian–African Conference,* p. 22.

39. "Texts of Chou's Speech and Statement," NARA, RG 59, Executive Secretariat, Subject Files, 1953–1961, box 35.

40. Sihanouk, *My War with the CIA,* p. 202.

41. Kahin, *The Asian–African Conference,* p. 22, ellipsis in original.

42. Paul Ely to Antoine Pinay, April 28, 1955, Centre virtuel de la connaissance sur l'Europe, www.cvce.eu.

43. Cable, *The Geneva Conference of 1954,* p. 17; State Dept., biographical sketch of Malcolm MacDonald, May 1961, LOC, WAHP, box 527; Sanger, *Malcolm MacDonald,* p. 358; Australian Commission, Singapore, to External Affairs Dept. (Australia), April 30, 1955, NAA, Cambodia—Relations with India, 1955–1970.

44. Lewis Purnell, "Cambodia's Drift toward Neutralism," May 9, 1955, NARA, RG 59, OSAA, Cambodia and Vietnam, box 1; CIA, *CIB,* May 5, 1955, NARA, CREST.

45. CIA, *CIWS*, May 5, 1955, NARA, CREST.

46. McClintock to Leng Ngeth, May 16, 1955, NARA, RG 59, CDF, 1955–1959, box 3360.

47. State Dept., "Indian Involvement, Cambodia," May 25, 1955, and Samuel Parelman to Young, April 7, 1955, NARA, RG 59, CDF, 1955–1959, box 3360.

48. ICC, *Third Interim Report*, pp. 17–19.

49. Martin F. Herz to State Dept., May 28, 1955, NARA, RG 59, CDF, 1955–1959, box 3354.

50. As reported in ICC, *Third Interim Report*, pp. 16–17.

51. Sihanouk communiqué, June 7, 1955, NARA, RG 472, Cambodian Background Files, 1955–1972, box 58.

52. Duder to External Affairs Dept. (Canada), June 13, 1955, *DCER*, XXI, d. 648.

53. Duder to External Affairs Dept. (Canada), June 10, 1955, *DCER*, XXI, d. 647.

54. "Visit of Krishna Menon to Ottawa," June 13, 1955, NARA, RG 59, OSAA, Cambodia and Vietnam, box 1.

55. Duder to External Affairs Dept. (Canada), June 10, 1955, *DCER*, XXI, d. 647.

56. State Dept., biographical sketch of V. K. Krishna Menon, May 1961, LOC, WAHP, box 527; J. F. Dulles to Eisenhower, March 14, 1955, DDEL, John Foster Dulles Papers, Chronological Series, box 11; Clark interview by Stern, January 11, 1994.

57. Memorandum of conversation, June 29, 1955, *FRUS, 1955–1957*, XXI, d. 208; J. F. Dulles to State Dept., December 17, 1954, *FRUS, 1952–1954*, XIII, part 2, d. 1386; State Dept., "Indian Involvement, Cambodia," May 25, 1955.

58. U Nu to J. F. Dulles, May 3, 1955, NARA, RG 59, Presidential and Secretary of State Correspondence with Heads of State, 1953–1964, box 21; State Dept., "Indian Involvement, Cambodia," May 25, 1955.

59. "Minutes of Talks," April 26, 1955, in Nehru, *SWJN*, 28:195–196.

60. Nehru to Nu, May 19, 1955, in Nehru, *SWJN*, 28:197; "Visit of Krishna Menon to Ottawa," June 13, 1955. Also see Nehru, May 20, 1955, in Nehru, *Letters to Chief Ministers*, 4:175–176.

61. Memorandum of conversation, June 29, 1955, *FRUS, 1955–1957*, XXI, d. 208.

62. McClintock to State Dept., June 19, 1955, NARA, RG 59, CDF, 1955–1959, box 3356.

63. McClintock to State Dept., June 17, 1955, *FRUS, 1955–1957*, XXI, d. 204.

64. McClintock to State Dept., June 19, 1955.

65. Duder to External Affairs Dept. (Canada), October 27, 1954, *DCER*, XX, d. 784; McClintock to Young, June 21, 1955, *FRUS, 1955–1957*, XXI, d. 206.

66. CIA, *CIWS*, June 23, 1955, NARA, CREST.

67. M. A. Hussain, "Minutes of Talks with Polish Leaders," June 24, 1955, in Nehru, *SWJN*, 29:232–237.

68. Nehru to Zhou Enlai, June 26, 1955, in Nehru, *SWJN,* 29:354–355.

69. ICC, *Third Interim Report,* pp. 8–11.

70. ICC, *Fourth Interim Report,* p. 11.

71. McClintock to State Dept., June 26, 1955, and October 25, 1955, NARA, RG 59, CDF, 1955–1959, boxes 3356 and 3354.

72. Department of the Army Intelligence Report, August 27, 1957, RG 319, "Who's Who Reports," 1956–1958, box 52; memorandum of conversation, March 7, 1953, NARA, RG 59, CDF, 1950–1954, box 3698; McClintock to State Dept., January 26 and August 9, 1955, NARA, RG 59, CDF, 1955–1959, boxes 3353 and 3354.

73. NIE, August 16, 1955, *FRUS, 1955–1957,* XXI, d. 217; G. McMurtrie Godley to State Dept., September 8, 1955, NARA, RG 59, CDF, 1955–1959, box 3354.

74. Intelligence Advisory Committee, NIE Post-Mortems, August 16, 1955, NARA, CREST.

75. ICC, *Fourth Interim Report,* pp. 8–16; Arnold Smith to External Affairs Dept. (Canada), September 27, 1955, *DCER,* XXI, d. 633.

76. McClintock to State Dept., August 9, 1955, NARA, RG 59, CDF, 1955–1959, box 3354.

77. McClintock to State Dept., October 25, 1955.

78. McClintock to State Dept., September 12, 1955, *FRUS, 1955–1957,* XXI, d. 218.

79. Herz to State Dept., February 14, 1957, NARA, RG 59, CDF, 1955–1959, box 3354.

80. A. Smith to External Affairs Dept., September 27, 1955.

81. CIA, *CIB,* August 4, 1955, NARA, CREST.

82. A. Smith to External Affairs Dept., September 27, 1955.

83. McClintock to State Dept., September 18, 1955, NARA, RG 59, CDF, 1955–1959, box 3356; CIA, *CIWS,* September 29, 1955, NARA, CREST.

84. McClintock to State Dept., October 25, 1955.

85. McClintock to State Department, September 12, 1955, October 9, 1955, and October 14, 1955, NARA, RG 59, CDF, 1955–1959, boxes, 3354, 3356, and 3361.

86. Joint Chiefs of Staff to Charles Wilson, October 19, 1955, *FRUS, 1955–1957,* XXI, d. 221; State Dept. to McClintock, November 28, 1955, NARA, RG 59, CDF, 1955–1959, box 3354.

87. McClintock to State Dept., November 29, 1955, NARA, RG 59, CDF, 1955–1959, box 3354.

88. McClintock to Allen Dulles, December 9, 1955, NARA, RG 59, Records of the Director, Office of Philippine and Southeast Asian Affairs, box 3.

89. Ibid.

90. Robert M. McClintock, "United States Policy toward Cambodia," May 8, 1957, NARA, RG 59, BFEA, OSAA, Cambodia Files, 1958–1963, box 6.

4. "Irresponsible and Mischievous Actions"

1. McClintock to State Dept., November 26, 1955, NARA, RG 59, CDF, 1955–1959, box 3356.

2. Herz to State Dept., January 6, 1956, NARA, RG 59, OSAA, Records Relating to Cambodia and Vietnam, 1953–1958, box 2; McClintock to Radford, July 26, 1956, NARA, RG 59, BFEA, OSAA, Cambodia Files, 1958–1963, box 4; McClintock to State Dept., June 14, 1956, NARA, RG 59, CDF, 1955–1959, box 3358.

3. William Walker to State Dept., February 13, 1956, NARA, RG 59, CDF, 1955–1959, box 3358.

4. Ibid.

5. Ibid.

6. McClintock to State Dept., May 3, 1956, NARA, RG 59, CDF, 1955–1959, box 3354; Sihanouk, *My War with the CIA,* pp. 77–79.

7. McClintock to State Dept., April 26, 1956, despatch 351 and no. 1448, NARA, RG 59, CDF, 1955–1959, box 2511; Office of the Press Secretary, Malacañang, January 31, 1956, NARA, RG 59, CDF, 1955–1959, box 3358.

8. Tarling, *Britain and Sihanouk's Cambodia,* p. 16.

9. A. Dulles to J. F. Dulles, May 24, 1955, www.foia.cia.gov.

10. Memorandum of conversation, February 7, 1956, NARA, RG 59, CDF, 1955–1959, box 3361.

11. Memorandum of conversation, October 5, 1955, *FRUS, 1955–1957,* I, d. 263.

12. Godley to State Dept., February 8, 1956, NARA, RG 59, CDF, 1955–1959, box 3358; Phnom Penh to State Dept., February 11, 1956, NARA, RG 59, BFEA, Country File–1955, box 9.

13. Walker to State Dept., February 13, 1956; McClintock to State Dept., January 19, 1956, NARA, RG 59, CDF, 1955–1959, box 3354.

14. CIA, *CIB,* February 2, 1956, www.foia.cia.gov.

15. Tucker, *China Confidential,* p. 91.

16. Memorandum of conversation, February 10, 1956, *FRUS, 1955–1957,* XXI, d. 225.

17. Memorandum of conversation, January 31, 1956, *FRUS, 1955–1957,* XXI, d. 80.

18. Memorandum of conversation, February 10, 1956.

19. State Dept., "Preliminary Biographical Notes on the Cambodian Delegation," May 11, 1954, NARA, RG 59, Executive Secretariat, Conference Files, 1949–1963, box 48; memorandum of conversation, February 10, 1956.

20. Ang, *Vietnamese Communists' Relations with China,* p. 17.

21. Phnom Penh to State Dept., February 26, 1956, NARA, RG 59, CDF, 1955–1959, box 3354; CIA, *CIB,* February 21, 1956, and April 5, 1956, www.foia.cia.gov.

22. McClintock to State Dept., February 21, 1956, NARA, RG 59, CDF, 1955–1959, box 3354.

23. McClintock to State Dept., February 24, 1956, NARA, RG 59, CDF, 1955–1959, box 3361.

24. McClintock to State Dept., February 21, 1956.

25. Phnom Penh to State Dept., March 4, 1956, NARA, RG 59, BFEA, Country File–1955, box 9.

26. Ibid.

27. Murphy to McClintock, March 12, 1956, NARA, RG 59, CDF, 1955–1959, box 3358.

28. McClintock to State Dept., February 22, 1956, NARA, RG 59, CDF, 1955–1959, box 3354.

29. A. Smith to External Affairs Dept. (Canada), February 16, 1956, NAA, Cambodia—Relations with South Vietnam, 1956.

30. Herz, *A Short History of Cambodia,* p. 129, ellipsis in original.

31. State Dept. to McClintock, March 3, 1956, NARA, RG 59, CDF, 1955–1959, box 2511.

32. Dean interview by Kennedy, September 6, 2000.

33. McClintock to State Dept., March 9, 1956, no. 1155, NARA, RG 59, CDF, 1955–1959, box 3361.

34. McClintock to State Dept., March 9, 1956, no. 1154, and McClintock to State Dept., March 13, 1956, NARA, RG 59, CDF, 1955–1959, box 3354.

35. Robert N. Magill to State Dept., March 7, 1956, NARA, RG 59, CDF, 1955–1959, box 3354.

36. Nehru to Commonwealth Secretary, March 16, 1956, in Nehru, *SWJN,* 31:352.

37. John E. Peurifoy to State Dept., August 4, 1955, NARA, RG 59, CDF, 1955–1959, box 3908.

38. Memorandum of conversation, February 23, 1956, NARA, RG 59, CDF, 1955–1959, box 3908.

39. Charles Spinks to State Dept., June 16, 1952, NARA, RG 59, CDF, 1950–1954, box 3698; NIE 63.2–55, August 16, 1955, *FRUS, 1955–1957,* XXI, d. 217.

40. John E. Peurifoy, "Thai Activity in Laos," December 23, 1954, NARA, RG 84, US Embassy, Bangkok, Top Secret General Records, 1954–1958, box 2.

41. James E. Cable, minutes, August 17, 1956, UKNA, FO 371/123651; McClintock to State Dept., March 2, 1956, NARA, RG 59, CDF, 1955–1959, box 3354.

42. McClintock to State Dept., March 9, 1956, no. 1154.

43. McClintock to State Dept., March 9, 1956, no. 1155.

44. McClintock to State Dept., March 15, 1956, NARA, RG 59, CDF, 1955–1959, box 3354.

45. Ibid.

46. Ibid.

47. Ibid.

48. Norbert Anschutz to State Dept., November 30, 1955, NARA, RG 59, CDF, 1955–1959, box 3908.

49. Memorandum of conversation, March 13, 1956, *FRUS, 1955–1957,* XXII, d. 489.

50. Ibid.

51. Godley to State Dept., March 18, 1956, NARA, RG 59, CDF, 1955–1959, box 3354.

52. "Cambodia: Honorable Comrade," *Time,* March 19, 1956.

53. Admiral Felix B. Stump to Brigadier General George O. N. Lodoen, March 22, 1956, and Lodoen to Stump, March 24, 1956, *FRUS, 1955–1957,* XXI, d. 227 and d. 228.

54. McClintock to State Dept., March 30, 1956, no. 1267, NARA, RG 59, CDF, 1955–1959, box 3358.

55. McClintock to State Dept., March 30, 1956, no. 1269, *FRUS, 1955–1957,* XXI, d. 229.

56. McClintock to State Dept., May 31, 1956, NARA, RG 59, CDF, 1955–1959, box 3354.

57. CIA, *CIB,* April 1, 1956, www.foia.cia.gov.

58. Robert M. McClintock, "United States Policy toward Cambodia," May 8, 1957, NARA, RG 59, BFEA, OSAA, Cambodia Files, 1958–1963, box 6.

59. CIA, NSC Briefing, April 4, 1956, NARA, CREST.

60. McClintock, "United States Policy toward Cambodia," May 8, 1957.

61. CIA, NSC Briefing, April 4, 1956.

5. "Change from the Top"

1. McClintock to State Dept., April 15 and April 13, 1956, no. 1362, NARA, RG 59, CDF, 1955–1959, boxes 3356 and 3358.

2. McClintock to State Dept., April 15, 1956; McClintock to State Dept., April 13, 1956, no. 1365, NARA, RG 59, CDF, 1955–1959, box 3358.

3. McClintock to State Dept., April 10, 1956, NARA, RG 59, CDF, 1955–1959, box 2511.

4. Godley to State Dept., March 17, 1956, NARA, RG 59, CDF, 1955–1959, box 2511.

5. McClintock to Young, June 21, 1955, *FRUS, 1955–1957,* XXI, d. 206; W. Robertson to J. F. Dulles, undated, c. April 10, 1956, NARA, RG 59, CDF, 1955–1959, box 2511.

6. External Affairs Dept. (Canada) to A. Smith, April 13, 1956, *DCER,* XXIII, part 2, p. 1275; John C. Cloake, minutes, April 28, 1956, UKNA, FO 371/123651.

7. Press conference, April 2, 1956, in Nehru, *SWJN,* 31:539; Nehru to Josip Broz Tito, April 2, 1956, in Nehru, *SWJN,* 31:365.

8. McClintock to State Dept., April 15, 1956; McClintock to State Dept., April 7, 1956, NARA, RG 59, CDF, 1955–1959, box 2511.

9. McClintock to State Dept., April 12, 1956, NARA, RG 59, CDF, 1955–1959, box 3358.

10. McClintock to State Dept., January 17, 1956, and May 31, 1956, NARA, RG 59, CDF, 1955–1959, box 3354.

11. McClintock to State Dept., April 17, 1956, NARA, RG 59, CDF, 1955–1959, box 2511.

12. Ibid.

13. J. F. Dulles, chiefs of mission conference, March 19, 1956, NARA, RG 59, BFEA, Conferences, Meetings, and Visits, 1956, box 1.

14. W. Robertson to J. F. Dulles, undated, c. April 10, 1956.

15. State Dept. to McClintock, April 17, 1956, *FRUS, 1955–1957,* XXI, d. 235.

16. McClintock to State Dept., April 20, 1956, no. 1411, NARA, RG 59, CDF, 1955–1959, box 2511.

17. Ibid.

18. McClintock to State Dept., April 20, 1956, no. 1422, NARA, RG 59, CDF, 1955–1959, box 2511.

19. McClintock to State Dept., May 31, April 28, and May 3, 1956, NARA, RG 59, CDF, 1955–1959, boxes 3354, 3356, and 3354.

20. McClintock to State Dept., April 24, 1956, NARA, RG 59, CDF, 1955–1959, box 2511; Robert Alden, "Cambodia Wary of U.S. Aid Policy," *New York Times,* March 1, 1956.

21. McClintock to State Dept., April 24, 1956.

22. McClintock to State Dept., April 26, 1956, NARA, RG 59, CDF, 1955–1959, box 2511.

23. McClintock to State Dept., May 8, 1956, NARA, RG 59, CDF, 1955–1959, box 2629.

24. McClintock to State Dept., April 26, 1956, NARA, RG 59, CDF, 1955–1959, box 2511.

25. McClintock to State Dept., April 25, 1956, NARA, RG 59, CDF, 1955–1959, box 2511.

26. McClintock to State Dept., April 30 and April 27, 1956, NARA, RG 59, CDF, 1955–1959, box 3358.

27. Phnom Penh to State Dept., May 5, 1956; McClintock to State Dept., May 14, 1956, NARA, RG 59, CDF, 1955–1959, boxes 3356 and 3358.

28. Godley to State Dept., May 19, 1956, NARA, RG 59, CDF, 1955–1959, box 3356.

29. Anschutz interview by Kennedy, July 13, 1992; Bishop interview by Conlon, February 26, 1993.

30. McClintock to State Dept., May 11, 1956, *FRUS, 1955–1957,* XXI, d. 237.

31. McClintock to State Dept., May 3, 1956, NARA, RG 59, CDF, 1955–1959, box 3354.

32. Ibid.

33. OCB, "Progress Report on U.S. Policy towards South Asia," March 30, 1956, *FRUS, 1955–1957,* VIII, d. 1; Lawrence quoted in Dwight Eisenhower to Edgar Eisenhower, February 27, 1956, in Eisenhower, *The Papers of Dwight David Eisenhower,* 16:2032 n.

34. Dwight D. Eisenhower, "The President's News Conference," June 6, 1956, www.presidency.ucsb.edu.

35. Ibid.

36. White House statement, June 7, 1956, www.presidency.ucsb.edu.

37. John Foster Dulles, "The Cost of Peace," *Department of State Bulletin,* June 18, 1956, p. 999.

38. "Nixon's Talk Warning Nations of Perils of Neutralism," *New York Times,* July 4, 1956.

39. Nehru, press conference, July 6, 1956, in Nehru, *SWJN,* 34:425–426.

40. Eric Kocher to Sebald, December 5, 1956, NARA, RG 59, OSAA, Records Relating to Cambodia and Vietnam, 1953–1958, box 2.

41. CIA, *CIB,* June 1, 1956, www.foia.cia.gov.

42. McClintock to State Dept., May 28, 1956, and May 31, 1956, no. 407, NARA, RG 59, CDF, 1955–1959, box 3354; McClintock to State Dept., May 31, 1956, no. 1613, *FRUS, 1955–1957,* XXI, d. 239.

43. State Dept. to McClintock, June 26, 1956, NARA, RG 59, CDF, 1955–1959, box 3361. This document is a complete version of the sanitized cable in *FRUS, 1955–1957,* XXI, d. 241.

44. McClintock to State Dept., July 6, 1956, *FRUS, 1955–1957,* XXI, d. 243.

45. McClintock to Daniel Anderson, August 22, 1956, NARA, RG 84, US Embassy, Saigon, Top Secret Subject Files, 1955–1965, box 1. In this letter, McClintock also observed that Admiral Arthur W. Radford, chairman of the Joint Chiefs of Staff, "was all steamed up when he arrived in Phnom Penh [in late July] about utilizing Dap Chhuon as a means of getting rid of Sihanouk."

46. Ahern, *CIA and the House of Ngo,* p. 83; Charles Kane to the inspector general, CIA, July 5, 1975, www.maryferrell.org. The latter document (also available at NARA, KARC) is an authoritative overview of Lansdale's work for the OSS, CIA, and Pentagon.

47. CIA, "Stenographic Notes of Conversation between DCI and Colonel Lansdale," July 12, 1956, www.foia.cia.gov.

48. Ibid.

49. NSC Meeting, July 12, 1956, DDEL, AWF, NSC Series, box 8.

50. CIA, "Stenographic Notes of Conversation," July 12, 1956.

51. McClintock to State Dept., August 21, 1956, NARA, RG 59, CDF, 1955–1959, box 3358.

52. Kocher to Johnson, July 26, 1956, NARA, RG 59, OSAA, Records Relating to Cambodia and Vietnam, 1953–1958, box 2.

53. W. Robertson to McClintock, August 21, 1956, *FRUS, 1955–1957,* XXI, d. 248.

54. Memorandum of discussion, August 30, 1956, *FRUS, 1955–1957,* XXI, d. 118.

55. Ibid.

56. NSC 5612/1, September 5, 1956, *USVR,* Part-V-B-3d, p. 1086–1092.

57. Dillon Anderson, "US Policy in Southeast Asia," August 29, 1956, DDEL, WHOF, NSC Staff, Disaster File, box 55; NSC 5612/1.

58. NSC 5612/1.

59. C. P. Cabell to J. F. Dulles, September 28, 1956, NARA, RG 59, CDF, 1955–1959, box 3354. This document is a less-sanitized version of the memorandum in *FRUS, 1955–1957,* XXI, d. 249.

60. Ibid.

61. McClintock to State Dept., September 19, 1956, NARA, RG 59, CDF, 1955–1959, box 3354.

62. McClintock to State Dept., August 20, 1956, and Herz to State Dept., October 6, 1956, NARA, RG 59, CDF, 1955–1959, boxes 3354 and 3357.

63. Monireth to the king et al., October 16, 1956, NARA, RG 59, CDF, 1955–1959, box 3354; CIA, biographical sketch of Lon Nol, November 21, 1966, NARA, RG 472, Cambodian Background Files, 1955–1972, box 57.

64. Godley to State Dept., October 22, 1956, NARA, RG 59, CDF, 1955–1959, box 3358.

65. Godley to State Dept., October 20, 1956, and McClintock to State Dept., October 14, 1956, NARA, RG 59, CDF, 1955–1959, box 3357.

66. Herz to State Dept., October 15, 1956, NARA, RG 59, CDF, 1955–1959, box 2511.

67. McClintock to Young, October 11, 1956, NARA, RG 59, CDF, 1955–1959, box 3354.

6. "Many Unpleasant and Difficult Things"

1. Kocher to Sebald, December 3, 1956, NARA, RG 59, CDF, 1955–1959, box 3354.

2. Carl W. Strom to State Dept., January 5, 1957, NARA, RG 59, CDF, 1955–1959, box 3354.

3. Ibid.

4. Ibid.

5. Memorandum of conversation, January 2, 1957, NARA, RG 84, US Embassy, Saigon, Top Secret Subject Files, 1955–1965, box 1. This is the unredacted version of the memorandum reproduced in *FRUS, 1955–1957,* XXI, d. 251.

6. Ibid.

7. Strom to Sebald, January 10, 1957, *FRUS, 1955–1957,* XXI, d. 251.

8. Memorandum of conversation, January 2, 1957.

9. Herz to State Dept., February 14, 1957, and Strom to State Dept., February 4, 1957, NARA, RG 59, CDF, 1955–1959, boxes 3354 and 3358.

10. Strom to W. Robertson, February 14, 1957, *FRUS, 1955–1957,* XXI, d. 252.

11. State Dept. to McClintock, August 9, 1956, NARA, RG 59, CDF, 1955–1959, box 3358.

12. "Cambodia: Corn and Peanuts," *Time,* February 11, 1957.

13. Strom to State Dept., March 11, 1957, NARA, RG 59, CDF, 1955–1959, box 3357.

14. Brinkley, *The Publisher,* pp. 335, 375.

15. Memorandum of conversation, March 7, 1957, NARA, RG 59, OSAA, Records Relating to Cambodia and Vietnam, 1953–1958, box 5.

16. OCB, "Progress Report on U.S. Policy in Mainland Southeast Asia," March 14, 1957, DDEL, WHOF, NSC Series, Policy Papers Subseries, box 18.

17. "Political Power in Cambodia: Possible Alternatives to Leadership of Prince Sihanouk," April 2, 1957, OSAA, Records Relating to Cambodia and Vietnam, 1953–1958, box 2.

18. Ibid; Department of the Army Intelligence Report, August 27, 1957, RG 319, "Who's Who Reports," 1956–1958, box 52.

19. ICC, *Sixth Interim Report,* p. 35.

20. Ibid., pp. 35–36.

21. Ibid., pp. 42, 45.

22. Ibid., p. 46.

23. Bridle, "Canada and the International Commissions in Indochina," p. 441.

24. R. M. MacDonnell to Lester Pearson, May 11, 1956, *DCER,* XXIII, part 2, d. 705; memorandum of conversation, May 9, 1957, *FRUS, 1955–1957,* I, d. 376.

25. Engelbert and Goscha, *Falling out of Touch,* p. 52; Tran, *Tran Bach Dang,* p. 238; CIA, *CIB,* February 28, 1957, and "Cambodia and Communism," May 1972, www.foia.cia.gov.

26. Chandler, *Brother Number One,* Kindle locations 1239–1243.

27. Strom to W. Robertson, April 29, 1957, NARA, RG 59, CDF, 1955–1959, box 3358.

28. Godley to State Dept., May 21, 1957, NARA, RG 59, CDF, 1955–1959, box 3361.

29. Ibid.

30. Memorandum of conversation, March 31, 1957, NARA, RG 59, CDF, 1955–1959, box 3354.

31. Strom to State Dept., May 29, 1957, NARA, RG 59, CDF, 1955–1959, box 3354.

32. Godley to Strom, May 29, 1957, NARA, RG 59, CDF, 1955–1959, box 3354.

33. Ibid; Godley to McClintock, July 26, 1956, RG 59, OSAA, Records Relating to Cambodia and Vietnam, box 2.

34. Godley to Strom, May 29, 1957; Strom to State Dept., May 29, 1957.

35. Robert S. Barrett to State Dept., July 30, 1957, and Strom to State Dept., June 15, 1957, NARA, RG 59, CDF, 1955–1959, boxes 3354 and 3357.

36. Strom to State Dept., July 1 and June 22, 1957, NARA, RG 59, CDF, 1955–1959, boxes 3357 and 3358.

37. "Cambodia: Tearful Time," *Time,* June 10, 1957.

38. Strom to Young, June 24, 1957, OSAA, Records Relating to Cambodia and Vietnam, 1953–1958, box 4.

39. Young to W. Robertson, May 18, 1956, NARA, RG 59, CDF, 1955–1959, box 3361.

40. Strom to W. Robertson, April 29, 1957, NARA, RG 59, CDF, 1955–1959, box 3358.

41. Strom to State Dept., July 1, 1957, NARA, RG 59, CDF, 1955–1959, box 3357.

42. Strom to State Dept., July 29, 1957, NARA, RG 59, CDF, 1955–1959, box 3358.

43. Strom to State Dept., July 19, 1957, NARA, RG 59, CDF, 1955–1959, box 3354.

44. Ibid.

45. Strom to State Dept., July 25 and July 29, 1957, NARA, RG 59, CDF, 1955–1959, boxes 3354 and 3358.

46. Strom to State Dept., July 29, 1957.

47. Strom to State Dept., August 8, 1957, NARA, RG 59, CDF, 1955–1959, box 3355; CIA, *CIB,* July 26, 1957, www.foia.cia.gov.

48. Barrett to State Dept., September 27, 1957, and Strom to State Dept., January 17, 1958, NARA, RG 59, CDF, 1955–1959, boxes 3355 and 2511.

49. Strom to State Dept., August 20, 1957, NARA, RG 59, CDF, 1955–1959, box 3358.

50. Elbridge Durbrow to State Dept., August 20, 1957, NARA, RG 59, CDF, 1955–1959, box 3358.

51. Gordon Heiner to State Dept., January 28, 1958, NARA, RG 59, CDF, 1955–1959, box 3355.

52. Strom to State Dept., September 7, 1957, NARA, RG 59, CDF, 1955–1959, box 3357.

53. Strom to State Dept., October 28, 1957, NARA, RG 59, CDF, 1955–1959, box 3357.

54. CIA, "Subversion," *National Intelligence Survey, Cambodia,* 1965, p. 6.

55. Francis Stuart to External Affairs Dept. (Australia), December 12, 1957, NAA, Cambodia—Foreign Relations and Policy General, 1950–1960.

56. Heiner to State Dept., January 28, 1958; Strom to State Dept., December 10, 1957, NARA, RG 59, CDF, 1955–1959, box 3357.

57. Strom to State Dept., December 23, 1957, NARA, RG 59, CDF, 1955–1959, box 3357.

58. Memorandum of conversation, January 7, 1958, and Strom to State Dept., January 17, 1958, NARA, RG 59, CDF, 1955–1959, boxes 3359 and 2511.

59. Heiner to State Dept., January 28, 1958; Strom to State Dept., January 21, 1958, NARA, RG 59, CDF, 1955–1959, box 3357.

60. "Cambodian Leader Turns against Reds," *New York Times,* January 12, 1958; "Late Wisdom," *Time,* January 20, 1958; Strom to State Dept., February 4, 1958, NARA, RG 59, CDF, 1955–1959, box 3357.

61. "Living on Aid," *Times* (London), March 5, 1958; Henry Norman Brain to FO, April 7, 1958, NAA, Cambodia—Foreign Relations and Policy General, 1950–1960.

62. Sihanouk to Suramarit, March 22, 1958, NARA, RG 59, CDF, 1955–1959, box 3355.

63. Strom to State Dept., March 30, 1958, NARA, RG 59, CDF, 1955–1959, box 3357.

64. "Speech by Prince Sihanouk over National Radio," March 24, 1958, in Heiner to State Dept., NARA, RG 59, CDF, 1955–1959, box 3355.

65. CIA, "Subversion," p. 21.

66. Ibid., pp. 20–21; James C. Thomson Jr. to Johnson, June 14, 1966, *FRUS, 1964–1968,* XXVII, d. 183.

67. Hughes interview by Kennedy, July 7, 1999.

68. James Thomson, "Prince of Peace," *New York Times Book Review,* August 26, 1973.

69. Shawcross, *Sideshow,* p. 122.

70. William E. Colby, testimony, June 4, 1975, US Senate, Select Committee to Study Governmental Operations with Respect to Intelligence Activities, NARA, KARC, CIA, box 239. The "expert" Colby referred to presumably worked in the agency's Technical Services Division.

71. CIA, "Subversion," p. 25.

72. NSC 5809, April 2, 1958, *FRUS, 1958–1960,* XVI, d. 12.

73. Strom to Howard Elting, May 28, 1958, NARA, RG 59, BFEA, OSAA, Cambodia Files, 1958–1963, box 7.

74. Strom to J. Graham Parsons, August 5, 1958, JGPP, box 2.

75. Durbrow to Parsons, July 25, 1958, JGPP, box 2.

76. Ibid.

77. Strom to Parsons, August 5, 1958.

78. Durbrow to Parsons, July 25, 1958.

79. Strom to Kocher, June 20, 1958, NARA, RG 59, BFEA, OSAA, Cambodia Files, 1958–1963, box 7.

7. "Numerous Reports of Plots"

1. ICC, *Seventh Interim Report,* p. 34.

2. Ibid., p. 124.

3. Hugh Cumming to Christian A. Herter, June 25, 1958, *FRUS, 1958–1960,* XVI, MFS, no. 340; Strom to State Dept., July 3, 1958, NARA, RG 59, CDF, 1955–1959, box 3357; and CIA, *CIB,* June 26, 1958, www.foia.cia.gov.

4. Norman Robertson to External Affairs Dept. (Canada), June 30, 1958, *DCER,* XXV, d. 411.

5. State Dept. to Strom, July 1, 1958, *FRUS, 1958–1960,* XVI, d. 72.

6. Stuart to External Affairs Dept. (Australia), July 6, 1958, NAA, Cambodia—Foreign Relations and Policy General, 1950–1960.

7. Strom to State Dept., July 9, 1958, NARA, RG 59, CDF, 1955–1959, box 3357.

8. Durbrow to State Dept., July 5, 1958, NARA, RG 59, CDF, 1955–1959, box 3359.

9. Durbrow to State Dept., July 14, 1958, NARA, RG 59, CDF, 1955–1959, box 2626.

10. Strom to State Dept., July 7, 1958, *FRUS, 1958–1960,* XVI, d. 73.

11. Ibid.

12. Ibid.

13. Durbrow to State Dept., July 9, 1958, *FRUS, 1958–1960,* XVI, d. 74; Durbrow interview by Rust, October 28, 1981.

14. Durbrow to State Dept., July 7, 1958, NARA, RG 59, CDF, 1955–1959, box 3359.

15. Ibid.

16. Sam Rainsy, *We Didn't Start the Fire,* p. 19; John Whitney to State Dept., June 25, 1958, NARA, RG 59, CDF, 1955–1959, box 2321.

17. Strom to State Dept., July 9 and July 8, 1958, NARA, RG 59, CDF, 1955–1959, boxes 3357 and 3355.

18. Ibid.

19. Ibid.

20. Ibid.

21. Strom to State Dept., July 9, 1958, NARA, RG 59, CDF, 1955–1959, box 3355.

22. Ibid.

23. Stuart to External Affairs Dept. (Australia), July 9, 1958, NAA, Cambodia—Foreign Relations and Policy General, 1950–1960.

24. Strom to State Dept., July 10, 1958, no. 52, NARA, RG 59, CDF, 1955–1959, box 2626.

25. Strom to State Dept., July 10, 1958, no. 56, *FRUS, 1958–1960,* XVI, MFS, no. 343.

26. Parsons to Strom, July 10, 1958, *FRUS, 1958–1960,* XVI, d. 75.

27. Ibid.

28. Durbrow to State Dept., July 17, 1958, NARA, RG 59, CDF, 1955–1959, box 2626.

29. Durbrow to State Dept., July 18, 1958, *FRUS, 1958–1960,* XVI, MFS, no. 346.

30. Strom to State Dept., July 21, 1958, NARA, RG 59, CDF, 1955–1959, box 3936.

31. State Dept. to Strom, July 21, 1958, *FRUS, 1958–1960,* XVI, d. 76.

32. Strom to State Dept., July 22, 1958, NARA, RG 59, CDF, 1955–1959, box 3936.

33. Saigon to State Dept., July 23, 1958, NARA, RG 59, CDF, 1955–1959, box 3936.

34. State Dept. to Strom, July 22, 1958, no. 72, NARA, RG 59, CDF, 1955–1959, box 3936.

35. CIA, *CIB,* July 21, 1958, NARA, CREST.

36. State Dept. to Strom, July 22, 1958, no. 72.

37. Ibid.

38. State Dept. to Strom, July 22, 1958, no. 73, *FRUS, 1958–1960,* XVI, d. 76 n.

39. Strom to State Dept., July 25 [*sic*], 1958, *FRUS, 1958–1960*, XVI, d. 77. The reproduction of this document in *FRUS* misstates the date of this cable as "July 25, 1958–4 p.m." The date of the document in the National Archives is "July 24, 1958–4 p.m."

40. Strom to State Dept., July 26, 1958, NARA, RG 59, CDF, 1955–1959, box 3936.

41. Frederick J. Blakeney to External Affairs Dept. (Australia), July 30, 1958, NAA, Cambodia—Relations with South Vietnam, 1958.

42. Durbrow to Parsons, July 25, 1958, JGPP, box 2.

43. Ibid.

44. Ibid.

45. Strom to Parsons, August 5, 1958, JGPP, box 2.

46. Memorandum of conversation, August 5, 1958, *FRUS, 1958–1960*, XVI, d. 78.

47. Clymer, *The United States and Cambodia, 1870–1969*, p. 66.

48. Memorandum of conversation, August 5, 1958. Dap Chhuon's name is redacted in the *FRUS* document. Yet the description of this person—someone who "sent a message to the Ambassador after recognition of Red China that he was loyal to the monarchy and to Sihanouk, but that he was a patriot above all and loved his country more than either of these"—leaves no doubt that the document referred to Dap Chhuon.

49. Ibid.

50. Kocher to W. Robertson, August 12, 1958, NARA, RG 59, BFEA, OSAA, Cambodia Files, 1958–1963, box 6.

51. Alfred Jenkins to W. Robertson, August 21, 1958, NARA, RG 59, BFEA, OSAA, Cambodia Files, 1958–1963, box 6. This document is an unredacted version of the memorandum reproduced in *FRUS, 1958–1960*, XVI, d. 79.

52. Strom to State Dept., December 17, 1957, NARA, RG 59, CDF, 1955–1959, box 3357.

53. CIA, *CIB*, September 9, 1958, www.foia.cia.gov; Kocher to W. Robertson, November 20, 1957, NARA, RG 59, CDF, 1955–1959, box 3909.

54. Johnson to State Dept., September 16, 1958, NARA, RG 59, CDF, 1955–1959, box 3355.

55. Ibid.; Johnson to State Dept., September 26, 1958, NARA, RG 59, CDF, 1955–1959, box 3355.

56. Strom to State Department, September 17, 1958, NARA, RG 59, CDF, 1955–1959, box 3355.

57. Strom to State Dept., September 18, 1958, NARA, RG 59, CDF, 1955–1959, box 3355.

58. Strom to State Dept., September 19, 1958, NARA, RG 59, CDF, 1955–1959, box 3355.

59. State Dept. to Strom, September 23, 1958, *FRUS, 1958–1960*, XVI, MFS, no. 354.

60. Ibid.

61. State Dept. to Johnson, September 23, 1958, *FRUS, 1958–1960,* XVI, MFS, no. 355.

62. Johnson to State Department, September 26, 1958.

63. Memorandum of conversation, August 27, 1958, NARA, RG 59, CDF, 1955–1959, box 3359.

64. Kocher to Strom, March 4, 1958, NARA, RG 59, BFEA, OSAA, Cambodia Files, 1958–1963, box 4.

65. Memorandum of conversation, August 27, 1958.

66. Memorandum of conversation, September 15, 1958, *FRUS, 1958–1960,* XIX, MFS, no. 119.

67. Ibid.

68. Memorandum of conversation, September 16, 1958, *FRUS, 1958–1960,* XIX, d. 98.

69. Strom to State Dept., October 4, 1958, NARA, RG 59, CDF, 1955–1959, box 3357.

70. Memorandum of conversation, September 30, 1958, *FRUS, 1958–1960,* XVI, d. 84 n.; memorandum for the president, September 28, 1958, NARA, RG 59, CDF, 1955–1959, box 3359.

71. W. Robertson to J. F. Dulles, September 29, 1959, *FRUS, 1958–1960,* XVI, MFS, no. 356.

72. Memorandum of conversation, September 30, 1958.

73. Ibid.

74. State Dept. to Strom, October 2, 1958, *FRUS, 1958–1960,* XVI, MFS, no. 357.

8. "A Shady Matter"

1. Strom to W. Robertson, October 20, 1958, *FRUS, 1958–1960,* XVI, MFS, no. 359.

2. Ibid.

3. Ibid.

4. Ibid.

5. W. Robertson to Strom, October 31, 1958, *FRUS, 1958–1960,* XVI, MFS, no. 360.

6. Strom to State Dept., November 8, 1958, *FRUS, 1958–1960,* XVI, d. 86.

7. Durbrow to Cumming, November 20, 1958, *FRUS, 1958–1960,* XVI, d. 88.

8. Ibid.

9. Memorandum of conversation, November 11, 1958, *FRUS, 1958–1960,* I, d. 39.

10. State Dept. to Strom, November 19, 1958, *FRUS, 1958–1960,* XVI, d. 87.

11. Strom to State Dept., December 2, 1958, NARA, RG 59, CDF, 1955–1959, box 3357; memorandum of conversation, December 1, 1958, *FRUS, 1958–1960,* XVI, d. 90.

12. Johnson to State Dept., November 5 and December 4, 1958, NARA, RG 59, CDF, 1955–1959, box 3909.

13. Strom to State Dept., December 2, 1958, NARA, RG 59, CDF, 1955–1959, box 2629.

14. Durbrow to State Dept., November 28, 1958, NARA, RG 59, CDF, 1955–1959, box 3355.

15. CIA, "Subversion," pp. 18–21.

16. Ibid.

17. Taylor, "Prince Sihanouk and the New Order in Southeast Asia," p. 48.

18. William Trimble to State Dept., May 5, 1959, NARA, RG 59, CDF, 1955–1959, box 3355.

19. Taylor, "Prince Sihanouk and the New Order in Southeast Asia," p. 48.

20. Byron E. Byron to State Dept., March 12, 1959, NARA, RG 59, CDF, 1955–1959, box 3362.

21. Strom to State Dept., January 12, 1959, NARA, RG 59, CDF, 1955–1959, box 3355. This document is a less-sanitized version of the cable reproduced in *FRUS, 1958–1960,* XVI, d. 93.

22. Laurin B. Askew, "Tripartite Coordination of Policy in Cambodia," February 4, 1959, NARA, RG 59, BFEA, OSAA, Cambodia Files, 1958–1963, box 6.

23. CIA, *CIB,* January 14, 1959, www.foia.cia.gov.

24. Blakeney to External Affairs Dept. (Australia), January 28, 1959, NAA, Cambodia–Vietnam Relations, 1958–1960.

25. Memorandum of conversation, January 15, 1959, NARA, RG 59, CDF, 1955–1959, box 3359.

26. Stuart to James Plimsoll, January 15, 1959, NAA, South East Asia–Top Secret–Cambodia, 1957–1960.

27. Kocher to W. Robertson, February 6, 1959, NARA, RG 59, BFEA, OSAA, Cambodia Files, 1958–1963, box 6; Clymer, *The United States and Cambodia, 1870–1969,* p. 68.

28. Lansdale to Lionel McGarr, August 11, 1960, *FRUS, 1958–1960,* I, d. 184.

29. McClintock to Daniel Anderson, August 22, 1956, NARA, RG 84, US Embassy, Saigon, Top Secret Subject Files, 1955–1965, box 1.

30. Stuart to External Affairs Dept. (Australia), February 6, 1959, NAA, Intra-regional Relations—Cambodia Relations with Thailand, 1959.

31. Kocher to W. Robertson, January 21, 1958, NARA, RG 59, BFEA, OSAA, Cambodia Files, 1958–1963, box 6.

32. Stuart to External Affairs Dept. (Australia), January 24, 1959, NAA, Intra-regional Relations—Cambodia Relations with Thailand, 1959.

33. Strom to State Dept., February 2, 1959, NARA, RG 59, CDF, 1955–1959, box 3357.

34. Richard P. Peters to Marshall Green, February 3, 1959, NARA, RG 59, CDF, 1955–1959, box 3355.

35. Green to Peters, February 2, 1959, NARA, RG 59, BFEA, Office of the Regional Planning Adviser, Subject Files, 1954–1964, box 1.

36. Matsui obituary, *Virginia Gazette,* April 6, 2012; Lilley interview by Kennedy, May 21, 1998.

37. Trimble to State Dept., October 29, 1961, NARA, RG 59, CDF, 1960–1963, box 1347.

38. Trimble to State Dept., May 5, 1959.

39. Strom to W. Robertson, February 16, 1959, *FRUS, 1958–1960,* XVI, d. 95.

40. W. Robertson to Strom, February 18, 1959, *FRUS, 1958–1960,* XVI, d. 96.

41. Memorandum of conversation, February 18, 1959, *FRUS, 1958–1960,* XVI, MFS, no. 373; Kocher to W. Robertson, February 18, 1959, NARA, RG 59, CDF, 1955–1959, box 2511.

42. Memorandum of conversation, February 18, 1959.

43. Ibid.

44. CIA, *CIB,* February 23, 1959, NARA, CREST.

45. CIA, "Subversion," 1965, p. 18; State Dept. to Phnom Penh, March 4, 1959, NARA, RG 59, CDF, 1955–1959, box 2627.

46. Strom to State Dept., March 3, 1959, NARA, RG 59, CDF, 1955–1959, box 3357.

47. Trimble to State Dept., October 3, 1959, NARA, RG 59, CDF, 1955–1959, box 3356.

48. W. Robertson to Herter, May 7, 1959, NARA, RG 59, CDF, 1955–1959, box 3355.

49. Colby, *Honorable Men,* p. 150.

50. Trimble interview by Kennedy, February 24, 1990.

51. Kennedy–Hilsman conversation, November 20, 1963, JFKL, Telephone Recordings: Dictation Belt 34.

52. Hilsman to Dean Rusk, November 18, 1963, JFKL, NSF, box 320.

53. Lilley interview by Kennedy, May 21, 1998.

54. Taylor, "Prince Sihanouk and the New Order in Southeast Asia," p. 50.

55. CIA, "NSC Briefing," March 11, 1959, NARA, CREST.

56. Rust, *Before the Quagmire,* pp. 144–145. Another example is John M. Allison, the US ambassador to Indonesia in 1957, who was not informed of Washington-authorized CIA assistance to anti-Sukarno rebels (Gardner, *Shared Hopes, Separate Fears,* pp. 136, 141).

57. Trimble interview by Kennedy, February 24, 1990.

58. Trimble to William R. Tyler, October 8, 1959, WCTP, box 3.

59. Herbert Keppand to Ralph Sliffman, February 2, 1959, NARA, RG 59, BFEA, OSAA, Cambodia Files, 1958–1963, box 6, italics added.

60. Strom to Trimble, September 8, 1959, WCTP, box 3.

61. State Dept. to Durbrow, February 23, 1959, *FRUS, 1958–1960,* XVI, d. 101.

62. Ibid.

63. Ibid.

64. Sihanouk to Eisenhower, February 23, 1959, *FRUS, 1958–1960,* XVI, d. 100.

65. Ibid.

66. Ibid.

67. Strom to State Dept., February 26, 1960, *FRUS, 1958–1960,* XVI, d. 103; State Dept. to Saigon, Bangkok, and Phnom Penh, March 2, 1959, DDEL, AWF, Dulles–Herter Series, box 11; State Dept. to Phnom Penh, March 4, 1959.

68. Strom to State Dept., February 23, 1959, *FRUS, 1958–1960,* XVI, MFS, no. 374.

69. Strom to State Dept., February 28, 1959, no. 1139, *FRUS, 1958–1960,* XVI, d. 102 n.; Strom to State Dept., February 28, 1959, no. 1140, NARA, RG 59, CDF, 1955–1959, box 3355 (this document is the unredacted version of the telegram reproduced in *FRUS, 1958–1960,* XVI, d. 104); CIA, *CIB,* March 23, 1959.

70. Strom to State Dept., February 28, 1959, no. 1140.

71. Strom to State Dept., February 26, 1959, *FRUS, 1958–1960,* XVI, d. 104 n.

72. Strom to State Dept., February 28, 1959, no. 1140.

73. Kellogg to State Department, March 9, 1959, NARA, RG 59, CDF, 1955–1959, box 3357.

74. Ibid.; Sihanouk, May 17, 1959, NAA, Cambodia—Foreign Relations and Policy General, 1950–1960.

75. CIA, "Intelligence and Security," p. 56-3; Chandler, *The Tragedy of Cambodian History,* p. 105.

76. Sihanouk, *My War with the CIA,* p. 108; Osborne, *Sihanouk,* p. 111.

77. Kellogg, memorandum for the record, July 9, 1959, NARA, RG 59, BFEA, OSAA, Cambodia Files, 1958–1963, box 5.

78. Strom to State Dept., March 3, 1959, *FRUS, 1958–1960,* XVI, d. 106.

79. Ibid.

80. Osborne, *Sihanouk,* p. 111.

9. "Stupid Moves"

1. State Dept. to Durbrow and Johnson, March 5, 1959, NARA, RG 59, CDF, 1955–1959, box 2627.

2. Johnson to State Dept., March 6, 1959, NARA, RG 59, CDF, 1955–1959, box 2627.

3. Durbrow to State Dept., March 5 and March 6, 1959, NARA, RG 59, CDF, 1955–1959, box 2627.

4. Durbrow to State Dept., March 7, 1959, no. 1868, NARA, RG 59, CDF, 1955–1959, box 2627.

5. Elting to State Dept., March 9, 1957, NARA, RG 59, CDF, 1955–1959, box 2627.

6. Ibid.; Durbrow to State Dept., March 7, 1959, no. 1873, NARA, RG 59, CDF, 1955–1959, box 2627.

7. CIA, *CIB,* March 24, 1959, www.foia.cia.gov.

8. Australian legation, Phnom Penh, to External Affairs Dept. (Australia), March 16, 1959, NAA, South East Asia–Top Secret–Cambodia, 1957–1960.

9. Kellogg to State Dept., March 23, 1959, no. 1248 and no. 1249, NARA, RG 59, CDF, 1955–1959, boxes 3357 and 2627.

10. Kellogg to State Dept., March 31, 1959, and April 3, 1959, NARA, RG 59, CDF, 1955–1959, boxes 2511 and 3357.

11. Eisenhower to Sihanouk, March 28, 1959, *FRUS, 1958–1960,* XVI, d. 108.

12. "Statement from the President to Prince Sihanouk to Be Delivered Orally by Ambassador Trimble," March 28, 1959, WCTP, box 3.

13. W. Robertson to Herter, March 27, 1959, *FRUS, 1958–1960,* XVI, d. 108.

14. Kellogg to State Dept., April 2, 1959, no. 1290, *FRUS, 1958–1960,* XVI, MFS, no. 378.

15. State Dept., "Preliminary Biographical Notes on the Cambodian Delegation," May 11, 1954, NARA, RG 59, Executive Secretariat, Conference Files, 1949–1963, box 48.

16. Kellogg to State Dept., April 2, 1959, no. 1290.

17. CIA, "Stenographic Notes of Conversation between DCI and Colonel Lansdale," July 12, 1956, www.foia.cia.gov. Although Barré's name has been redacted in this document, Lansdale's description of the individual in question leaves little doubt that he was referring to Barré.

18. Kellogg to State Dept., April 2, 1959, no. 1293, NARA, RG 59, CDF, 1955–1959, box 3355.

19. Trimble interview by O'Brien, August 12, 1969.

20. Ibid.; W. Robertson to Loy Henderson, October 13, 1958, JGPP, box 2; memorandum of conversation, July 22, 1960, NARA, RG 59, BFEA, OSAA, Cambodia Files, 1958–1963, box 5.

21. Trimble to State Dept., April 12, 1959, *FRUS, 1958–1960,* XVI, d. 109 n.

22. Parsons to State Dept., April 16, 1959, *FRUS, 1958–1960,* XVI, d. 109; Trimble to Parsons, October 1, 1959, no. 395, NARA, RG 59, CDF, 1955–1959, box 3356.

23. State Dept. to Parsons, April 22, 1959, NARA, RG 59, CDF, 1955–1959, box 3355.

24. Sihanouk to Eisenhower, April 13, 1959, DDEL, AWF, International Series, box 6.

25. Eisenhower to Sihanouk, May 7, 1959, *FRUS, 1958–1960,* XVI, d. 113.

26. W. Robertson to Herter, April 22, 1959, NARA, RG 59, BFEA, OSAA, Cambodia Files, 1958–1963, box 4.

27. W. Robertson to Henry Cabot Lodge, May 5, 1959, and Kocher to W. Robertson, June 10, 1959, NARA, RG 59, BFEA, OSAA, Cambodia Files, 1958–1963, box 4. "Quiet Americans" evidently became Hammarskjöld's preferred euphemism for CIA officers operating in Southeast Asia. Later, in 1959, he told Henry Cabot Lodge, the US representative to the UN, that he was concerned by the presence of "quiet Americans" in Laos (Rust, *Before the Quagmire,* p. 129).

28. Durbrow to State Dept., April 28, 1959, *FRUS, 1958–1960,* I, d. 69; Parsons to State Dept., May 5, 1959, *FRUS, 1958–1960,* XVI, d. 112.

29. Trimble to State Dept., May 5, 1959, NARA, RG 59, CDF, 1955–1959, box 3355; Parsons to State Dept., May 5, 1959, *FRUS, 1958–1960,* XVI, d. 112.

30. Parsons to State Dept., May 5, 1959.

31. Kocher to W. Robertson, May 9, 1959, *FRUS, 1958–1960,* XVI, d. 114.

32. State Dept. to Phnom Penh, June 5, 1959, *FRUS, 1958–1960,* XVI, d. 118.

33. Parsons to State Dept., May 5, 1959.

34. Trimble to State Dept., May 4, 1959, NARA, RG 59, CDF, 1955–1959, box 3355. In the poster that was actually distributed, there was a fourth dog labeled "Chau Bory," referring to a Khmer Serei subordinate of Son Ngoc Thanh.

35. Trimble to State Dept., May 6, 1959, NARA, RG 59, CDF, 1955–1959, box 3355.

36. Trimble to State Dept., May 7, 1959, NARA, RG 59, CDF, 1955–1959, box 3355.

37. Ibid.

38. Durbrow to State Dept., May 10, 1959, *FRUS, 1958–1960,* XVI, MFS, no. 382; Durbrow to State Dept., May 14, 1959, NARA, RG 59, CDF, 1955–1959, box 2627.

39. Johnson to State Dept., February 26, 1959, NARA, RG 59, CDF, 1955–1959, box 3355.

40. Ibid.

41. CIA, *CIB,* May 16, 1959, www.foia.cia.gov; Richard Usher to John Steeves, March 15, 1960, NARA, RG 59, BFEA, OSAA, Cambodia Files, 1958–1963, box 6. This document is the unredacted version of the memorandum reproduced in *FRUS, 1958–1960,* XVI, MFS, no. 397.

42. Trimble to State Dept., June 9, 1959, NARA, RG 59, CDF, 1955–1959, box 2511.

43. Ibid.

44. Stuart to External Affairs Dept. (Australia), June 11, 1959, NAA, Intraregional Relations—Cambodia Relations with Thailand, 1959.

45. Trimble to State Dept., July 2, 1959, and July 8, 1959, NARA, RG 59, CDF, 1955–1959, boxes 2627 and 3357.

46. McClintock to State Dept., August 1, 1956, NARA, RG 59, CDF, 1955–1959, box 3361.

47. Trimble to State Dept., September 29, 1959, NARA, RG 59, CDF, 1955–1959, box 3357.

48. Trimble to Parsons, December 19, 1960, and Trimble to Walter McConaughy, May 18, 1961, WCTP, box 4.

49. Norodom Sihanouk, *Shadow over Angkor* (1968), www.youtube.com. For a discussion of the film, see chapter 11.

50. Daniel Anderson to Parsons, August 13, 1959, *FRUS, 1958–1960,* XVI, MFS, no. 385; CIA, *CIB,* August 13, 1959, www.foia.cia.gov.

51. Trimble to State Dept., September 3 and September 8, 1959, no. 307, NARA, RG 59, CDF, 1955–1959, boxes 3359 and 3357.

52. Trimble to State Dept., September 8, 1959, no. 309, NARA, RG 59, CDF, 1955–1959, box 3359.

53. Memorandum of conversation, September 11, 1959, NARA, RG 59, BFEA, OSAA, Cambodia Files, 1958–1963, box 4.

54. Trimble to State Dept., September 19, 1959, *FRUS, 1958–1960,* XVI, d. 120.

55. "Saving Prince Norodom Sihanouk and Eliminating a Nest of American Spies," translated by Merle Pribbenow, March 1, 2004, www.nhandan.org.vn.

56. Durbrow to State Dept., September 22, 1959, *FRUS, 1958–1960,* XVI, d. 122.

57. Ibid.

58. Ibid.

59. Durbrow to State Dept., September 25, 1959, *FRUS, 1958–1960,* XVI, MFS, no. 389. Also see Durbrow to State Dept., September 26, 1959, NARA, RG 59, CDF, 1955–1959, box 2627.

60. Trimble to State Dept., September 27, 1959, NARA, RG 59, CDF, 1955–1959, box 2627.

61. Trimble to State Dept., October 1, 1959, no. 394, NARA, RG 59, CDF, 1955–1959, box 3356.

62. Trimble to State Dept., October 1, 1959, no. 395, NARA, RG 59, CDF, 1955–1959, box 3356.

63. Trimble to State Dept., October 1, 1959, no. 394.

64. State Dept. to Trimble, October 3, 1959, NARA, RG 59, CDF, 1955–1959, box 3356.

65. Trimble to State Department, October 6, 1959, NARA, RG 59, CDF, 1955–1959, box 3356.

66. Parsons to Trimble, October 8, 1959, NARA, RG 59, CDF, 1955–1959, box 3356.

67. Ibid.; Trimble to State Dept., October 12, 1959, NARA, RG 59, CDF, 1955–1959, box 3357.

68. Trimble to State Dept., October 8, 1959, NARA, RG 59, CDF, 1955–1959, box 3356.

69. Trimble to State Dept., October 10, 1959, NARA, RG 59, CDF, 1955–1959, box 3356.

70. Bangkok to State Dept., October 14, 1959, and Trimble to State Dept., October 14, 1959, NARA, RG 59, CDF, 1955–1959, box 3358.

71. Memorandum of conversation, October 26, 1959, NARA, RG 59, BFEA, OSAA, Cambodia Files, 1958–1963, box 4.

72. Durbrow to State Dept., October 7, 1959, *FRUS, 1958–1960,* XVI, d. 125; Laurin B. Askew, "October 7 Demarche to Diem on Vietnamese Support of Cambodian Dissidents," NARA, RG 59, BFEA, OSAA, Cambodia Files, 1958–1963, box 7.

73. Leonard S. Unger, "Sam Sary and Son Ngoc Thanh," October 15, 1959, NARA, RG 59, BFEA, OSAA, Cambodia Files, 1958–1963, box 6.

74. Ibid.

75. "Memo for Record," undated, c. November 23, 1959, NARA, RG 59, BFEA, OSAA, Cambodia Files, 1958–1963, box 6.

76. Trimble to State Dept., November 28, 1959, NARA, RG 59, CDF, 1955–1959, box 3358.

77. State Dept. to Johnson, January 2, 1960, *FRUS, 1958–1960*, XVI, MFS, no. 394.

78. Trimble diary, December 12, 1959, WCTP, box 8. In a diary entry for December 29, 1959, Trimble wrote: "In all fairness to the little man [Sihanouk], we must assume that his rancor against the Thais is due in part to reports that they have plans to liquidate him."

79. Laurin Askew to Daniel Anderson, January 8, 1960, *FRUS, 1958–1960*, XVI, d. 130; State Dept. to Johnson, January 12, 1960, NARA, RG 59, CDF, 1955–1959, box 1751. The sanitized version of the latter document, reproduced in *FRUS, 1958–1960*, XVI, d. 131, is incorrectly dated January 22, 1960.

80. Australian High Commission (London) to External Affairs Dept. (Australia), January 21, 1960, no. 301 and no. 28, NAA, Thailand–Cambodia Relations, 1960, and Security Council–Thailand–Cambodia Dispute–Question of Phra-Vihar, 1959–1962.

81. James Murray to Frederick Warner, February 21, 1960, UKNA, FO 371/152730.

82. Australian embassy (Washington, DC) to External Affairs Dept. (Australia), NAA, February 3, 1960, Thailand–Cambodian Relations, 1960.

83. Stuart to External Affairs Dept. (Australia), NAA, February 4, 1960, Thai-land–Cambodian Relations, 1960.

84. Trimble to State Dept., February 13, 1960, NARA, RG 59, CDF, 1960–1963, box 1748.

85. Clymer, *The United States and Cambodia, 1870–1969*, p. 78; Australian embassy (Washington, DC) to External Affairs Dept. (Australia), NAA, March 10, 1960, Cambodia–USA Relations, 1960–1966.

86. Trimble to State Dept., January 7, 1961, WCTP, box 4; Durbrow to State Dept., March 21, 1961, NARA, RG 59, CDF, 1960–1963, box 1345.

87. Osborne, *Sihanouk*, p. 109; CIA, "Subversion," p. 24; Sam Rainsy, *We Didn't Start the Fire*, p. 21.

10. "Getting Along with Sihanouk"

1. Trimble to State Dept., February 10, February 11, and February 13, 1960, and John Monjo to State Dept., March 3, 1960, NARA, RG 59, CDF, 1960–1963, box 1751.

2. Trimble to State Dept., February 13, 1960.

3. Trimble to State Dept., February 11, 1960.

4. Sihanouk, *My War with the CIA,* p. 113.

5. Monjo to State Dept., March 3, 1960.

6. Arzac to State Dept., December 13, 1960, NARA, RG 59, CDF, 1960–1963, box 1749.

7. Associated Press, "Cambodia Opposes Allies' Policy of 'Hot Pursuit,'" *Des Moines Register,* April 3, 1970.

8. OCB, "Special Report on Southeast Asia," February 10, 1960, *USVR,* V-B-3d, p. 212; Landon to Bromley Smith, January 27, 1960, DDEL, WHOF, NSC Staff Series, OCB Secretariat Series, box 7.

9. Memorandum of discussion, March 10, 1960, *FRUS, 1958–1960,* XVI, d. 57.

10. Usher to Steeves, March 15, 1960.

11. CIA, *CIB,* April 15, 1960, www.foia.cia.gov.

12. CIA, *CIB,* April 15, 1960, www.foia.cia.gov.

13. Durbrow to State Dept., May 3, 1960, *FRUS, 1958–1960,* I, d. 150.

14. Ibid.

15. Memorandum, May 4, 1960, *FRUS, 1958–1960,* I, d. 153. This document was unsigned, but a cover note, not to mention the memorandum's idiosyncratic rhetoric, identifies Lansdale as the author.

16. Ibid.

17. State Dept. to Durbrow, May 9, 1960, *FRUS, 1958–1960,* I, d. 157.

18. Durbrow to State Dept., May 15, 1960, NARA, RG 59, CDF, 1960–1963, box 1345; Durbrow to State Dept., May 13, 1960, *FRUS, 1958–1960,* I, d. 160.

19. Tillman Durdin, "In Asia: The Response Is Generally Favorable Despite Concern in Authoritarian Regimes," *New York Times,* May 1, 1960.

20. Herz, *A Short History of Cambodia,* p. 83.

21. Parsons to Trimble, January 2, 1959, JGPP, box 3.

22. Trimble to State Dept., May 23, 1960.

23. C. Robert Moore to State Dept., May 23, 1960, *FRUS, 1958–1960,* XVI, MFS, no. 403.

24. Trimble to State Dept., May 24, 1960, *FRUS, 1958–1960,* XVI, MFS, no. 401.

25. Moore to State Dept., May 30, 1960, *FRUS, 1958–1960,* XVI, MFS, no. 404.

26. Daniel Anderson to Parsons, June 1, 1960, *FRUS, 1958–1960,* XVI, d. 136; State Dept. to Phnom Penh, June 11, 1960, NARA, RG 59, CDF, 1960–1963, box 1751.

27. Moore to State Dept., June 16, 1960, *FRUS, 1958–1960,* XVI, MFS, no. 407.

28. Moore to State Dept., June 16, 1960; Steeves to Herter, June 18, 1960, NARA, RG 59, BFEA, OSAA, Cambodia Files, 1958–1963, box 4 (this document is the unredacted version of the memorandum reproduced in *FRUS, 1958–1960,* XVI, d. 137); CIA, "Intelligence and Security," p. 56-3.

29. CIA, *CIB*, May 20, 1960, www.foia.cia.gov.

30. Steeves to Herter, June 18, 1960.

31. Steeves to Herter, June 30, 1960, NARA, RG 59, ESRCOF, 1953–1961, box 16; State Dept. to Moore, June 24, 1960, *FRUS, 1958–1960*, XVI, d. 141n.

32. David Chandler, "Coming to Cambodia," in Hansen and Ledgerwood, eds., *At the Edge of the Forest*, p. 22.

33. Memorandum of conversation, June 29, 1960, NARA, RG 59, CDF, 1960–1963, box 1749.

34. Phnom Penh to State Dept., "Cambodian Request for Expanded Military and Police Aid," September 28, 1960, NARA, RG 59, CDF, 1960–1963, box 1753; memorandum of conversation, June 29, 1960.

35. Cumming to Herter, June 22, 1960, *FRUS, 1958–1960*, XVI, d. 138.

36. Dennis Bloodworth, "Cambodia Threatens the West," *Observer* (London), July 3, 1960.

37. Ibid.

38. Herter to Eisenhower, July 13, 1960, *FRUS, 1958–1960*, XVI, MFS, no. 410.

39. Ibid.

40. Moore to State Dept., July 13, 1960, NARA, RG 59, CDF, 1960–1963, box 1749.

41. Memorandum of conversation, July 22, 1960, NARA, RG 59, BFEA, OSAA, Cambodia Files, 1958–1963, box 5.

42. Samuel E. Belk, "Briefing Note for NSC Meeting," July 20, 1960, DDEL, AWF, NSC Series, box 12; memorandum of conversation, July 21, 1960, *FRUS*, XVI, d. 64.

43. Memorandum of conversation, July 21, 1960.

44. Ibid.; memorandum of conversation, July 2, 1960, DDEL, Christian A. Herter Papers, box 17.

45. Herter interview by Challener, August 31, 1964; Parsons, unpublished memoir, JGPP, box 12.

46. Memorandum of conversation, July 21, 1960.

47. NSC 6012, July 25, 1960, *USVR*, V-B-3d, p. 1292.

48. For a discussion of Eisenhower's lack of attention to Vietnam at the end of his presidency, see Anderson, *Trapped by Success*, pp. 202–204; for Laos, see Rust, *Before the Quagmire*, pp. 217–218.

49. Memorandum of conversation, July 27, 1960, DDEL, WHOF, Office of the Special Assistant for National Security Affairs, Special Assistant Series, Presidential Subseries, box 5.

50. Memorandum of conversation, August 10, 1960, NARA, RG 59, CDF, 1960–1963, box 1751.

51. Ibid.

52. Ibid.

53. Ibid.

54. Australian embassy, London, to External Affairs Dept. (Australia), August 24, 1960, NAA, Security Council—Thailand—Cambodia Dispute—Question of Phra-Vihar, 1959–1962.

55. Moore to State Dept., August 14, 1960, *FRUS, 1958–1960,* XVI, MFS, no. 412.

56. Memorandum of conversation, August 8, 1960, NARA, RG 59, CDF, 1960–1963, box 1749.

57. Ibid.

58. Robert Ballantyne to State Dept., August 16, 1960, NARA, RG 59, CDF, 1960–1963, box 1749.

59. Trimble to State Dept., September 3, 1960, *FRUS, 1958–1960,* XVI, d. 146.

60. Ibid.

61. Trimble to State Dept., September 5, 1960, *FRUS, 1958–1960,* XVI, MFS, no. 414; Trimble to Parsons, September 15, 1960, NARA, RG 59, BFEA, OSAA, Cambodia Files, 1958–1963, box 4.

62. Trimble to State Dept., September 9, 1960, and memorandum of conversation, September 20, 1960, NARA, RG 59, CDF, 1960–1963, box 1751.

63. Steeves, memorandum of conversation, September 27, 1960, NARA, RG 59, CDF, 1960–1963, box 1751.

64. John Eisenhower, memorandum of conversation, September 27, 1960, *FRUS, 1958–1960,* XVI, d. 147.

65. Sihanouk, statement to the UN General Assembly, September 29, 1960, NARA, RG 59, BFEA, OSAA, Laos Files, 1954–1961, box 13.

66. Ibid.

67. "Cambodia: The Neutral Harvest," *Time,* September 12, 1960.

68. Sihanouk, statement to the UN General Assembly, September 29, 1960.

69. Trimble to State Dept., November 2, 1960, *FRUS, 1958–1960,* XVI, d. 150.

70. Trimble to State Dept., August 24, 1960, NARA, RG 59, CDF, 1960–1963, box 1751.

71. Chandler, *Brother Number One,* Kindle location 1357.

72. Nguyen, *Hanoi's War,* p. 52.

73. Kiernan, *How Pol Pot Came to Power,* p. 191.

74. Heder, *Cambodian Communism,* p. 68.

11. "Definite Political Problems"

1. Trimble to State Dept., October 1, 1960, *FRUS, 1958–1960,* XVI, MFS, d. 415; Phnom Penh embassy despatch 93, September 28, 1960, NARA, RG 59, CDF, 1960–1963, box 1753.

2. John O. Bell to Steeves, October 17, 1960, NARA, RG 59, CDF, 1960–1963, box 1753.

3. Parsons to State Dept., October 23, 1960, *FRUS, 1958–1960,* XVI, d. 149. Ironically, Parsons's insight about US policymakers echoed an observation made by a State Department official during Sihanouk's "crusade" for independence in 1953:

"Is it possible [that the] French are being unduly influenced by [the] admittedly highly irritating Cambodian tactics?" (Bonsal to Heath, October 2, 1953, NARA, RG 59, CDF, 1950–54, box 2924).

4. Parsons to State Dept., October 16, 1960, *FRUS, 1958–1960,* XVI, d. 430. For a more complete discussion of the Parsons–Irwin–Riley visit to Laos, see Rust, *Before the Quagmire,* pp. 218–225.

5. Julian Fromer, "Sihanouk Proposal for Neutralization of Cambodia and Laos," November 29, 1960, NARA, RG 59, CDF, 1960–1963, box 1344.

6. Parsons, unpublished memoir, JGPP, box 12.

7. Parsons to Dillon, October 29, 1960, NARA, RG 59, CDF, 1960–1963, box 1753.

8. Ibid.

9. Memorandum of conversation, August 8, 1960, NARA, RG 59, CDF, 1960–1963, box 1749; Parsons to State Dept., October 23, 1960.

10. L. H. McKenzie, "Report on CINCPAC Weapons Demonstration, 1959," January 8, 1960, WCTP, box 3.

11. Defense Dept., "Memorandum for Mr. Irwin," October 31, 1960, *FRUS, 1958–1960,* XVI, MFS, no. 416; Robert Cleveland to Steeves, November 1, 1960, NARA, RG 59, BFEA, OSAA, Cambodia Files, 1958–1963, box 4.

12. Memorandum of conversation, November 2, 1960, *FRUS, 1958–1960,* XVI, MFS, no. 417.

13. Joseph V. Charyk to Thomas S. Gates Jr., November 4, 1960, *FRUS, 1958–1960,* XVI, MFS, no. 418.

14. OCB report, November 7, 1960, DDEL, WHOF, NSC Staff, OCB Secretariat Series, box 7.

15. Steeves to Livingston Merchant, November 8, 1960, and Charles Rogers, OCB notes, November 11, 1960, *FRUS, 1958–1960,* XVI, d. 152 and d. 153.

16. Gates interview by Challener, July 13, 1965; memorandum of telephone conversation, November 11, 1960, *FRUS, 1958–1960,* XVI, d. 155.

17. Memorandum of telephone conversation, November 11, 1960; memorandum for the record, November 11, 1960, *FRUS, 1958–1960,* XVI, d. 156.

18. Memorandum of conversation, November 12, 1960, *FRUS, 1958–1960,* XVI, MFS, no. 420.

19. Ibid.

20. William Thomas, "Prince Sihanouk's Speech to the Cambodian Students in Paris, November 19, 1960," NARA, RG 59, CDF, 1960–1963, box 1749. On January 9, 1961, Sihanouk told Ambassador Trimble that he was "content" with the additional US military and police aid (Trimble to State Dept., January 10, 1961, WCTP, box 4). On December 7, 1961, MAAG formally turned over four unarmed T-37 jet trainers to the Cambodian air force.

21. Trimble to Louis Springer, January 19, 1961, WCTP, box 4.

22. Trimble to Felt, March 17, 1961, WCTP, box 4.

23. US Department of Defense, "Summary and Historical Analysis of the Laos Incident," p. 156.

24. Rust, *Before the Quagmire,* pp. 231–241.

25. State Dept. to United States Mission at the United Nations, November 26, 1960, NARA, RG 59, CDF, 1960–1963, box 1749.

26. Major General John M. Willems to Cumming, December 8, 1960, NARA, RG 59, BFEA, OSSA, Laos Files, 1954–1961, box 11.

27. Brown interview by Hackman, February 1, 1968.

28. For a more complete discussion of the battle of Vientiane, see Rust, *Before the Quagmire,* pp. 244–246.

29. Trimble to State Dept., December 24, 1960, *FRUS, 1958–1960,* XVI, MFS, no. 423.

30. CIA, *CIWS,* December 8, 1960, NARA, CREST.

31. Trimble to State Dept., December 23, 1960, *FRUS, 1958–1960,* XVI, d. 158.

32. Phnom Penh embassy despatch 241, February 15, 1961, NARA, RG 59, CDF, 1960–1963, box 1347; Trimble to State Dept., December 23, 1960.

33. Trimble to State Dept., December 28, 1960, NARA, RG 59, CDF, 1960–1963, box 1751.

34. Trimble to State Dept., January 3, 1961, DDEL, AWF, International Series, box 5.

35. Memorandum of conversation, January 17, 1961, *FRUS, 1961–1963,* XXIV, d. 6.

36. Herter to Eisenhower, January 13, 1960, and State Dept. to Trimble, January 17, 1960, DDEL, AWF, International Series, box 5.

37. Immerman, *The Hidden Hand,* p. 50.

38. *FRUS, 1958–1960,* volume XVII, provides a relatively candid documentary depiction of covert US support for the rebellion in 1958. For more details about the plots against Souvanna and Phoui, see Rust, *Before the Quagmire.*

39. Immerman, *The Hidden Hand,* p. 47.

40. Gordon Gray, memorandum for the record, January 7, 1959, DDEL, NSC Presidential Records, Intelligence Files, box 1.

41. John E. Hull to Eisenhower, January 5, 1961, *FRUS, 1961–1963,* XXV, d. 82.

42. Rusk to Kennedy, May 19, 1961, *FRUS, 1961–1963,* XXIV, d. 95.

43. Memorandum of conversation, January 2, 1958, *FRUS, 1958–1960,* XVII, d. 2; George Ball to Lyndon Johnson, March 16, 1965, quoted in Gardner, *Shared Hopes, Separate Fears,* p. 191; Bissell, April 21, 1975, quoted in Weber, *Spymasters,* p. 72.

44. Sihanouk, *Shadow over Angkor* (1968), www.youtube.com.

45. Ibid. Although *Shadow over Angkor* was a film of dubious dramatic quality, Sihanouk later claimed, with some justification, that his movies were significant records of Cambodia's archaeology, arts, and culture.

46. Osborne, *Sihanouk,* p. 183.

47. "Cambodia: Lights . . . Camera . . . Sihanouk," *Time,* December 6, 1968; Sihanouk, *My War with the CIA,* p. 111.

Epilogue

1. "Summary of President Kennedy's Remarks to the 496th Meeting of the National Security Council," January 18, 1962, *FRUS, 1961–1963,* VIII, d. 69; "Cambodia: Department of State Guidelines for Policy and Operations," January 1962, JFKL, James C. Thomson Papers, box 21.

2. Frederick E. Nolting Jr. to State Dept., June 15, 1961, *FRUS, 1961–1963,* XXIII, d. 71. Cambodia released the C-47 to South Vietnam in October 1962.

3. Memorandum of conversation, September 25, 1961, *FRUS, 1961–1963,* XXIII, d. 74.

4. Rostow to Kennedy, September 23, 1961, *FRUS, 1961–1963,* XXIII, d. 73; State Dept., biographical sketch of Sihanouk, September 21, 1961, NARA, RG 59, ESRCOF, 1953–1961, box 16.

5. Memorandum of conversation, September 25, 1961.

6. Bangkok to State Dept., October 20, 1961, NARA, RG 59, CDF, 1960–1963, box 1347; Steeves to Rusk, October 24, 1961, NARA, RG 59, ASFEA, Subject Files, 1960–1963, box 4.

7. Trimble to State Dept., November 5, 1961, WCTP, box 4.

8. "The Thai–Cambodian Dispute," *New York Times,* October 25, 1961.

9. "Translation of Prince Sihanouk's Speech of October 26" and Trimble to State Dept., October 27, 1961, WCTP, boxes 8 and 4.

10. State Dept. to Phnom Penh, October 28, 1961, JFKL, NSF, box 16.

11. Trimble to State Dept., October 29, 1961, no. 233, NARA, RG 59, CDF, 1960–1963, box 1347.

12. Ibid.

13. Ibid.

14. Trimble to State Dept., October 29, 1961, no. 234, NARA, RG 59, CDF, 1960–1963, box 1347.

15. Trimble to State Dept., October 30, 1961, WCTP, box 4.

16. Trimble to State Dept., November 2, 1961, WCTP, box 4.

17. Memorandum of conversation, November 3, 1961, JFKL, George W. Ball Papers, box 2.

18. State Dept. to United States Mission at the United Nations, December 7, 1961, NARA, RG 59, CDF, 1960–1963, box 1347.

19. Herbert Gordon to State Dept., March 8, 1962, NARA, RG 59, CDF, 1960–1963, box 1348; Taylor, "Prince Sihanouk and the New Order in Southeast Asia," p. 87. Diem was, in fact, at the presidential palace during the bombing.

20. CIA, *CIB,* April 27, 1962, www.foia.cia.gov; State Dept. to Nolting, May 10, 1962, NARA, RG 59, CDF, 1960–1963, box 1345.

21. State Dept. to Trimble, June 1, 1962, *FRUS, 1961–1963,* XXIII, d. 84; CIA, "Covert Annex to Status Report of Task Force Vietnam," May 16, 1962, and CIA, *CIB,* July 14, 1962, both at www.foia.cia.gov.

22. Memorandum of conversation, May 22, 1962, NARA, RG 59, BFEA, OSAA, Thailand, 1960–1963, box 4.

23. State Dept. to Trimble, June 1, 1962.

24. Trimble to State Dept., June 4, 1962, NARA, RG 59, CDF, 1960–1963, box 1345.

25. Ibid.

26. Ibid.

27. Trimble to State Dept., June 5, 1962, *FRUS, 1961–1963,* XXIII, d. 85.

28. Moore to State Dept., July 13, 1962, nos. 20 and 22, NARA, RG 59, CDF, 1960–1963, box 1347.

29. Nolting to State Dept., June 6, 1962, NARA, RG 59, CDF, 1960–1963, box 1750.

30. Trimble to State Dept., June 7, 1962, NARA, RG 59, CDF, 1960–1963, box 1345; Nolting to State Dept., June 22, 1962, *FRUS, 1961–1963,* XXIII, d. 86.

31. Nolting to State Dept., June 22, 1962.

32. CIA, "Plan to Overthrow Sihanouk Government," June 13, 1962, JFKL, NSF, box 16A.

33. Nolting to State Dept., June 22, 1962.

34. Young to State Dept., June 21, 1962, NARA, RG 59, CDF, 1960–1963, box 1347.

35. CIA, *CIB,* July 14, 1962, www.foia.cia.gov; CIA, *President's Intelligence Check List,* July 14, 1962, www.jfklibrary.org; John McCone, "Memorandum for the Special Group," July 25, 1962, www.foia.cia.gov.

36. State Dept. to Bangkok, August 13, 1962, NARA, RG 59, CDF, 1960–1963, box 1750.

37. Nolting to State Department, August 20, 1962, NARA, RG 59, CDF, 1960–1963, box 1346; Young to State Dept., August 17 and August 18, 1962, NARA, RG 59, CDF, 1960–1963, box 1347.

38. Sprouse interview by Fuchs, February 11, 1974. In an interview by Dennis O'Brien on June 24, 1969, Sprouse acknowledged that China specialist Horace H. Smith had been appointed ambassador to Laos in 1958.

39. Memorandum of conversation, December 14, 1963, *FRUS, 1961–1963,* XXIII, d. 136. During this phone call with David E. Bell, director of the Agency for International Development, Harriman observed that Sihanouk was "a sucker for black propaganda"—that is false information planted by an intelligence service. It is unclear whether Harriman was referring to communist or US black propaganda—or both.

40. Sprouse to State Dept., August 13 and August 15, 1962, JFKL, NSF, box 16A; Citadel Alumni Association, "Samuel B. H. Hopler, '50," www.citadelalumni.org.

41. Cleveland to W. Averell Harriman, August 16, 1962, NARA, RG 59, BFEA, ASFEA, Subject Files, 1960–1963, box 11.

42. Ibid.

43. State Dept. to Sprouse, August 16, 1962, JFKL, NSF, box 16A; Cleveland to Harriman, August 20, 1962, NARA, RG 59, BFEA, ASFEA, Subject Files, 1960–1963, box 11.

44. Sprouse to State Dept., August 21, 1962, JFKL, NSF, box 16A.

45. Lilley interview by Kennedy, May 21, 1998.

46. Sprouse to State Dept., August 27, 1962, NARA, RG 59, CDF, 1960–1963, box 1750.

47. State Dept. to Phnom Penh, August 18, 1962, NARA, RG 59, CDF, 1960–1963, box 1347.

48. CIA, *CIB,* October 31, 1962, www.foia.cia.gov.

49. Sprouse to State Dept., October 5, 1962, NARA, RG 59, CDF, 1960–1963, box 1752.

50. Nolting to State Dept., November 17, 1962, and Young to State Dept., November 22, 1962, NARA, RG 59, CDF, 1960–1963, box 1347.

51. Harriman to Rusk, December 8, 1962, NARA, RG 59, Entry 5415-A, box 1.

52. State Dept. to Sprouse, December 6, 1962, *FRUS, 1961–1963,* XXIII, d. 99.

53. Harriman to Rusk, December 8, 1962; CIA, *CIB,* January 3, 1963, www.foia.cia.gov.

54. Henry L. T. Koren to Harriman, November 10, 1962, NARA, RG 59, Entry 5415-A, box 1.

55. Gordon to State Dept., March 7, 1963, NARA, RG 59, CFPF, 1963, box 3847; Sprouse to State Dept., March 4, 1963, *FRUS, 1961–1963,* XXIII, d. 102 n.

56. Sprouse to State Dept., March 4, 1963; Gordon to State Dept., March 7, 1963.

57. State Dept. to Nolting, March 8, 1963, *FRUS, 1961–1963,* XXIII, d. 103.

58. Nolting to State Dept., March 13, 1963, *FRUS, 1961–1963,* XXIII, d. 103 n.

59. Ibid.

60. CIA, "Subversion," p. 20.

61. William Colby to B. Chalmers Wood, "Manpower Utilization in South Vietnam," February 13, 1963, www.foia.cia.gov.

62. Clymer, *The United States and Cambodia, 1870–1969,* p. 108.

63. H. H. Knight to Rollen H. Anthis, December 11, 1964, NARA, KARC, Earle Wheeler Papers, box 43.

64. Sihanouk to Kennedy, June 14, 1963, JFKL, NSF, box 17.

65. CIA, "Subversion," p. 19.

66. Gordon to State Dept., August 29, 1963, NARA, RG 59, CFPF, 1963, box 3847; Sprouse to State Dept., October 12, 1963, *FRUS, 1961–1963,* XXIII, d. 108. The Cambodian National Assembly formally severed relations with South Vietnam on August 27.

67. Memorandum of conversation, October 21, 1963, NARA, RG 59, CFPF, 1963, box 3850.

68. Memorandum of conversation, October 28, 1963, NARA, RG 59, CFPF, 1963, box 3850.

69. State Department, "Chronology of Events in Cambodia," undated, c. December 15, 1963, LOC, WAHP, box 441.

70. Ibid.; Thomas Hughes to Rusk, December 19, 1963, JFKL, James C. Thomson Papers, box 21.

71. State Dept. to Sprouse, November 16, 1963, *FRUS, 1961–1963,* XXIII, d. 114 n; memorandum of conversation, November 6, 1963, NARA, RG 59, CFPF, 1963, box 3850.

72. Lodge to State Dept., November 8, 1963, JFKL, NSF, box 17; Lodge to State Dept., November 30, 1963, *FRUS, 1961–1963,* IV, d. 334.

73. Lodge to State Dept., November 18, 1963, and November 19, 1963, NARA, RG 59, CFPF, 1963, box 3850.

74. CIA, *CIB,* November 20, 1963, www.foia.cia.gov, and State Department, "Chronology of Events in Cambodia."

75. State Dept. to Sprouse, November 20, 1963, *FRUS, 1961–1963,* XXIII, d. 117 n.; Kennedy–Hilsman conversation, November 20, 1963, JFKL, Telephone Recordings: Dictation Belt 34.

76. CIA, "Current Intelligence Memorandum," December 19, 1963, *FRUS, 1961–1963,* XXIII, d. 139.

77. Sprouse to State Dept., November 21, 1963, JFKL, NSF, box 17A.

78. Ibid.

Bibliography

Archival Sources

American Presidency Project, University of California, Santa Barbara. www
.presidency.ucsb.edu.

Central Intelligence Agency, Freedom of Information Act Electronic Reading
Room. www.foia.cia.gov.

Dwight D. Eisenhower Presidential Library (DDEL), Abilene, KS.
  Christian A. Herter Papers
  Dwight D. Eisenhower Oral History Program (DDEOHP)
  John Foster Dulles Papers
  Papers as President/Ann Whitman File
  White House Office Files

Foreign Affairs Oral History Collection of the Association for Diplomatic Studies
  and Training (FAOHC). Library of Congress, Washington, DC. http://memory
  .loc.gov/ammem/collections/diplomacy/index.html. Also Jimmy Carter Library,
  Atlanta, GA.

Georgetown University, Special Collections Research Center, Washington, DC.
  J. Graham Parsons Papers

George Washington University, National Security Archives. www2.gwu.edu/
  ~nsarchiv/.

Harry S. Truman Presidential Library, Independence, MO. www.trumanlibrary
  .org.

John F. Kennedy Presidential Library, Boston.
  George W. Ball Papers
  James C. Thomson Papers
  JFK Oral History Program (JFKOHP)
  National Security Files
  Presidential Office Files
  Presidential Recordings
  Roger Hilsman Papers

Library of Congress, Washington, DC.
  W. Averell Harriman Papers

National Archives, United Kingdom, Surrey. www.nationalarchives.gov.uk.
  Foreign Office (FO) 371, Political Departments, General Correspondence
  1906–1966

National Archives and Records Administration (NARA), College Park, MD.
  Central Intelligence Agency Records Search Tool
  Kennedy Assassination Records Collection
  Record Group (RG) 59, General Records of the Department of State
  RG 84, Records of the Foreign Service Posts of the Department of State, 1788–1990
  RG 319, Records of the Army Staff
  RG 469, Records of the US Foreign Assistance Agencies, 1948–1961
  RG 472, Records of the US Forces in Southeast Asia, 1950–1976
National Archives of Australia. www.naa.gov.au.
Princeton University, Department of Rare Books and Special Collections, Princeton, NJ.
  John Foster Dulles Oral History Program
  William C. Trimble Papers
  Texas Tech University, Virtual Vietnam Archive. www.vietnam.ttu.edu.
University of Virginia, Miller Center. www.millercenter.org.
University of Wisconsin Digital Collections. http://uwdc.library.wisc.edu.
US Department of State, Office of the Historian. http://history.state.gov/historicaldocuments.
Wilson Center Digital Archive. http://digitalarchive.wilsoncenter.org.

Documentary Sources and Government Histories

Ahern, Thomas L., Jr. *CIA and the House of Ngo: Covert Action in South Vietnam, 1954–1963.* Washington, DC: Central Intelligence Agency, 2000.
Canadian Department of Foreign Affairs and International Trade. *Documents on Canadian External Relations.* Vol. XX: *1954.* Ottawa: Canadian Government Printing Office, 1997.
———. *Documents on Canadian External Relations.* Vol. XXI: *1955.* Ottawa: Canadian Government Printing Office, 1999.
———. *Documents on Canadian External Relations.* Vol. XXIII: *1956–1957, Part 2.* Ottawa: Canadian Government Printing Office, 2002.
———. *Documents on Canadian External Relations.* Vol. XXV: *1957–1958.* Ottawa: Canadian Government Printing Office, 2004.
Central Intelligence Agency (CIA). "Communism and Cambodia." Intelligence report. February and May 1972. www.foia.cia.gov.
———. "Intelligence and Security." *National Intelligence Survey, Cambodia.* 1960. NARA, RG 472, Cambodian Background Files, 1955–1972, Box 57.
———. "Political Dynamics." *National Intelligence Survey, Cambodia.* 1955. NARA, RG 472, Cambodian Background Files, 1955–1972, Box 57.
———. "Subversion." *National Intelligence Survey, Cambodia.* 1965. NARA, RG 472, Cambodian Background Files, 1955–1972, Box 57.
Eisenhower, Dwight D. *The Papers of Dwight David Eisenhower.* Vols. 14–17: *The*

Presidency: The Middle Way. Online ed. Baltimore: Johns Hopkins University Press, 2003. https://eisenhower.press.jhu.edu.

———. *The Papers of Dwight David Eisenhower.* Vols. 18–21: *The Presidency: Keeping the Peace.* Online ed. Baltimore: Johns Hopkins University Press, 2003. https://eisenhower.press.jhu.edu.

International Commission for Supervision and Control (ICC). *Fifth Interim Report of the International Commission for Supervision and Control in Cambodia for the Period October 1, 1955 to December 31, 1956.* London: Her Majesty's Stationary Office, September 1957.

———. *First Progress Report of the International Commission for Supervision and Control in Cambodia for the Period Ending December 31, 1954.* London: Her Majesty's Stationary Office, May 1955.

———. *Fourth Interim Report of the International Commission for Supervision and Control in Cambodia for the Period April 1 to September 30, 1955.* London: Her Majesty's Stationary Office, January 1956.

———. *Second Progress Report of the International Commission for Supervision and Control in Cambodia for the Period January 1 to March 31, 1955.* London: Her Majesty's Stationary Office, July 1955.

———. *Seventh Interim Report of the International Commission for Supervision and Control in Cambodia for the Period January 1, 1958 to December 31, 1958.* London: Her Majesty's Stationary Office, November 1959.

———. *Sixth Interim Report of the International Commission for Supervision and Control in Cambodia for the Period January 1, 1957 to December 31, 1957.* London: Her Majesty's Stationary Office, September 1957.

———. *Third Interim Report of the International Commission for Supervision and Control in Cambodia for the Period April 1 to July 28, 1955.* London: Her Majesty's Stationary Office, October 1955.

International Cooperation Administration. *U.S. Economic Aid Program to Cambodia, 1955–1960.* Phnom Penh: United States Operations Mission to Cambodia, January 1960.

Mansfield, Mike. *Report of Senator Mike Mansfield on a Study Mission to the Associated States of Indochina.* Washington, DC: US Government Printing Office, 1953.

———. *Report on Indochina.* Washington, DC: US Government Printing Office, 1954.

Nehru, Jawaharlal. *Letters to Chief Ministers.* Vol. 4: *1954–1957.* London: Oxford University Press, 1988.

———. *Selected Works of Jawaharlal Nehru, Series 2.* Vol. 27: *1 October 1954–31 January 1955.* London: Oxford University Press, 2000.

———. *Selected Works of Jawaharlal Nehru, Series 2.* Vol. 28: *1 February 1955–31 May 1955.* London: Oxford University Press, 2001.

———. *Selected Works of Jawaharlal Nehru, Series 2.* Vol. 29: *1 June 1955–31 August 1955.* London: Oxford University Press, 2001.

———. *Selected Works of Jawaharlal Nehru, Series 2.* Vol. 31: *1 February 1956–30 April 1956.* London: Oxford University Press, 2003.

———. *Selected Works of Jawaharlal Nehru, Series 2.* Vol. 34: *21 June 1956–31 August 1956.* London: Oxford University Press, 2005.

Taylor, John M. "Prince Sihanouk and the New Order in Southeast Asia." Central Intelligence Agency, 1964. www.foia.cia.gov.

US Department of Defense. *The Pentagon Papers: The Defense Department History of United States Decisionmaking on Vietnam.* Gravel ed. Boston: Beacon Press, 1971.

———. "Summary and Historical Analysis of the Laos Incident, August 1960 to May 1961, Part I." Weapons Systems Evaluation Group, 1962. http://www.dod.mil/pubs/foi.

———. *United States–Vietnam Relations, 1945–1967.* Washington, DC: US Department of Defense, 1969. http://www.archives.gov.

US Department of State. *American Foreign Policy: Current Documents 1962.* Washington, DC: US Government Printing Office, 1966.

———. *Foreign Relations of the United States, 1945.* Vol. VI: *The British Commonwealth and the Far East.* Washington, DC: US Government Printing Office, 1969.

———. *Foreign Relations of the United States, 1946.* Vol. VIII: *The Far East.* Washington, DC: US Government Printing Office, 1971.

———. *Foreign Relations of the United States, 1947.* Vol. VI: *The Far East.* Washington, DC: US Government Printing Office, 1972.

———. *Foreign Relations of the United States, 1948.* Vol. VI: *The Far East and Australasia.* Washington, DC: US Government Printing Office, 1974.

———. *Foreign Relations of the United States, 1949.* Vol. VII: *The Far East and Australasia, Part 1.* Washington, DC: US Government Printing Office, 1975.

———. *Foreign Relations of the United States, 1950.* Vol. VI: *East Asia and the Pacific.* Washington, DC: US Government Printing Office, 1976.

———. *Foreign Relations of the United States, 1951.* Vol. VI: *Asia and the Pacific, Part 1.* Washington, DC: US Government Printing Office, 1977.

———. *Foreign Relations of the United States, 1952–1954.* Vol. XII: *East Asia and Pacific.* Washington, DC: US Government Printing Office, 1984.

———. *Foreign Relations of the United States, 1952–1954.* Vol. XIII: *Indochina.* Washington, DC: US Government Printing Office, 1982.

———. *Foreign Relations of the United States, 1952–1954.* Vol. XIV: *China and Japan.* Washington, DC: US Government Printing Office, 1985.

———. *Foreign Relations of the United States, 1952–1954.* Vol. XVI: *The Geneva Conference: Korea and Indochina.* Washington, DC: US Government Printing Office, 1981.

———. *Foreign Relations of the United States, 1955–1957.* Vol. I: *Vietnam.* Washington, DC: US Government Printing Office, 1985.

———. *Foreign Relations of the United States, 1955–1957.* Vol. II: *China.* Washington, DC: US Government Printing Office, 1986.

———. *Foreign Relations of the United States, 1955–1957.* Vol. VIII: *South Asia.* Washington, DC: US Government Printing Office, 1987.

———. *Foreign Relations of the United States, 1955–1957.* Vol. X: *Foreign Aid and Economic Defense Policy.* Washington, DC: US Government Printing Office, 1989.

———. *Foreign Relations of the United States, 1955–1957.* Vol. XXI: *East Asian Security; Laos; Cambodia.* Washington, DC: US Government Printing Office, 1990.

———. *Foreign Relations of the United States, 1955–1957.* Vol. XXII: *Southeast Asia.* Washington, DC: US Government Printing Office, 1989.

———. *Foreign Relations of the United States, 1958–1960.* Vol. I: *Vietnam.* Washington, DC: US Government Printing Office, 1986.

———. *Foreign Relations of the United States, 1958–1960.* Vol. XVI: *East Asia–Pacific Region, Cambodia; Laos.* Washington, DC: US Government Printing Office, 1992.

———. *Foreign Relations of the United States, 1958–1960.* Vol. XVI: *East Asia–Pacific Region, Cambodia, Laos.* Microfiche Supplement. Washington, DC: US Government Printing Office, 1992.

———. *Foreign Relations of the United States, 1958–1960.* Vol. XVII: *Indonesia.* Washington, DC: US Government Printing Office, 1994.

———. *Foreign Relations of the United States, 1958–1960.* Vol. XIX: *China.* Washington, DC: US Government Printing Office, 1996.

———. *Foreign Relations of the United States, 1958–1960.* Vol. XIX: *China.* Microfiche Supplement. Washington, DC: US Government Printing Office, 1996.

———. *Foreign Relations of the United States, 1961–1963.* Vol. I: *Vietnam.* Washington, DC: US Government Printing Office, 1988.

———. *Foreign Relations of the United States, 1961–1963.* Vol. II: *Vietnam.* Washington, DC: US Government Printing Office, 1990.

———. *Foreign Relations of the United States, 1961–1963.* Vol. III: *Vietnam.* Washington, DC: US Government Printing Office, 1991.

———. *Foreign Relations of the United States, 1961–1963.* Vol. IV: *Vietnam.* Washington, DC: US Government Printing Office, 1991.

———. *Foreign Relations of the United States, 1961–1963.* Vol. VIII: *National Security Policy.* Washington, DC: US Government Printing Office, 1996.

———. *Foreign Relations of the United States, 1961–1963.* Vol. XXIII: *Southeast Asia.* Washington, DC: US Government Printing Office, 1994.

———. *Foreign Relations of the United States, 1961–1963.* Vol. XXIV: *Laos Crisis.* Washington, DC: US Government Printing Office, 1994.

———. *Foreign Relations of the United States, 1961–1963.* Vol. XXV: *Organization of Foreign Policy; Information Policy; United Nations; Scientific Matters.* Washington, DC: US Government Printing Office, 2002.

———. *Foreign Relations of the United States, 1964–1968.* Vol. XXVII: *Mainland Southeast Asia; Regional Affairs.* Washington, DC: US Government Printing Office, 2000.

————. *Foreign Relations of the United States: The Intelligence Community, 1950–1955*. Washington, DC: US Government Printing Office, 2007.

US Senate, Select Committee to Study Governmental Operations. *Alleged Assassination Plots Involving Foreign Leaders*. Washington, DC: U.S. Government Printing Office, 1975.

Oral Histories and Interviews

Anschutz, Norbert L. Interview by Charles Stuart Kennedy. July 13, 1992. FAOHC, Library of Congress.

Bishop, Max W. Interview by Thomas F. Conlon. February 26, 1993. FAOHC, Library of Congress.

Brown, Winthrop G. Interview by Larry J. Hackman. February 1, 1968. JFKOHP.

Clark, William, Jr. Interview by Thomas Stern. January 11, 1994. FAOHC, Library of Congress.

Cunningham, William J. Interview by Charles Stuart Kennedy. March 17, 1997. FAOHC, Library of Congress.

Dean, John Gunther. Interview by Charles Stuart Kennedy. September 6, 2000. FAOHC, Jimmy Carter Library, Atlanta, GA.

Draper, Morris. Interview by Charles Stuart Kennedy. February 27, 1991. FAOHC, Library of Congress.

Durbrow, Elbridge. Interview by William J. Rust. October 28, 1981. Washington, DC.

Erickson, Elden B. Interview by Charles Stuart Kennedy. June 25, 1992. FAOHC, Library of Congress.

Gates, Thomas S. Interview by Richard D. Challener. July 13, 1965. John Foster Dulles Oral History Program. Princeton University, Department of Rare Books and Special Collections, Princeton, NJ.

Green, Marshall. Interview by Charles Stuart Kennedy. March 17, 1995. FAOHC, Library of Congress.

Harr, Karl G. Interview by Paul Hopper. April 27, 1967. DDEOHP, DDEL .

Haverkamp, Roy T. Interview by Charles Stuart Kennedy. April 11, 1994. FAOHC, Library of Congress.

Heavner, Theodore J. C. Interview by Charles Stuart Kennedy. May 28, 1997. FAOHC, Library of Congress.

Herter, Christian A. Interview by Richard D. Challener. August 31, 1964. John Foster Dulles Oral History Program. Princeton University, Department of Rare Books and Special Collections, Princeton, NJ.

Howland, Richard C. Interview by Charles Stuart Kennedy. January 26, 1999. FAOHC, Library of Congress.

Hughes, Thomas L. Interview by Charles Stuart Kennedy. July 7, 1999. FAOHC, Library of Congress.

Jenkins, Kempton B. Interview by William Rust. June 23, 2010. Washington, DC.

Josif, Harold G. Interview by Charles Stuart Kennedy. October 4, 1999. FAOHC, Library of Congress.

Kidder, Randolph A. Interview by Charles Stuart Kennedy. December 13, 1989. FAOHC, Library of Congress.
Lilley, James R. Interview by Charles Stuart Kennedy. May 21, 1998. FAOHC, Library of Congress.
MacArthur, Douglas II. Interview by Mack Teasly. August 6, 1990. DDEOHP, DDEL.
Melby, John F. Interview by Robert Accinelli. November 14, 1986. Harry S. Truman Oral History Program, DDEL.
Mendenhall, Joseph. Interview by Horace Torbert. February 11, 1991. FAOHC, Library of Congress.
Moore, C. Robert. Interview by Dayton Mak. May 1988. FAOHC, Library of Congress.
Rives, L. Michael. Interview by Charles Stuart Kennedy. July 25, 1995. FAOHC, Library of Congress.
Robertson, Walter S. Interview by Ed Edwin. April 18–19, 1967. DDEOHP, DDEL.
Saccio, Leonard J. Interview by Melbourne Spector. September 30, 1990. FAOHC, Library of Congress.
Sprouse, Philip D. Interview by Dennis O'Brien. June 24, 1969. JFKOHP.
———. Interview by James R. Fuchs. February 11, 1974. Harry S. Truman Oral History Program, DDEL.
Steeves, John M. Interview by Dennis J. O'Brien. September 5, 1969. JFKOHP.
Stutesman, John H. Interview by William Burr. June 22, 1988. FAOHC, Library of Congress.
Trimble, William C. Interview by Charles Stuart Kennedy. February 24, 1990. FAOHC, Library of Congress.
———. Interview by Dennis J. O'Brien. August 12, 1969. JFKOHP.
Valeo, Francis R. Interview by Donald A. Ritchie. July 3, 1985, US Senate Historical Office. www.senate.gov.
Young, Kenneth T. Interview by Dennis J. O'Brien. February 25, 1969. JFKOHP.

Memoirs

Acheson, Dean. *Present at the Creation: My Years in the State Department.* New York: Norton, 1969.
Allison, John M. *Ambassador from the Prairie: Or Allison Wonderland.* Boston: Houghton Mifflin, 1973.
Blanchette, Arthur E. "Indochina: From Desk Officer to Acting Commissioner." In *Special Trust and Confidence: Envoy Essays in Canadian Diplomacy,* edited by David Reece. Carleton University Press, 1996.
Bridle, Paul. "Canada and the International Commissions in Indochina." In *Conflict and Stability in Southeast Asia,* edited by Mark W. Zacher and R. Stephen Milne. Garden City, NY: Anchor Books, 1974.
Cable, James E. *The Geneva Conference of 1954 on Indochina.* London: Macmillan, 1986.

Colby, William. *Honorable Men: My Life in the CIA*. New York: Simon and Schuster, 1978.

Dean, John Gunther. *Danger Zones: A Diplomat's Fight for America's Interest*. Washington, DC: New Academia, 2009.

Eden, Anthony. *Full Circle: The Memoirs of Anthony Eden*. Boston: Houghton Mifflin, 1960.

Eisenhower, Dwight D. *The White House Years: Mandate for Change, 1953–1956*. New York: Doubleday, 1963.

———. *The White House Years: Waging Peace, 1956–1961*. New York: Doubleday, 1965.

Jenkins, Kempton B. *Cold War Saga*. Ann Arbor, MI: Nimble Books, 2010.

Johnson, U. Alexis. *The Right Hand of Power: The Memoirs of an American Diplomat*. Englewood Cliffs, NJ: Prentice-Hall, 1984.

Nixon, Richard M. *The Memoirs of Richard Nixon*. New York: Grosset & Dunlap, 1978.

Norodom Sihanouk. "Cambodia Neutral: The Dictate of Necessity." *Foreign Affairs*, July 1958.

———. *My War with the CIA: The Memoirs of Prince Norodom Sihanouk*. New York: Pantheon Books, 1972.

———. *War and Hope: The Case for Cambodia*. New York: Pantheon Books, 1980.

Parsons, J. Graham. Unpublished manuscript. J. Graham Parsons Papers, Georgetown University, Washington, DC.

Radford, Arthur W. *From Pearl Harbor to Vietnam*. Stanford, CA: Hoover Institution Press, 1980.

Sam Rainsy. *We Didn't Start the Fire: My Struggle for Democracy in Cambodia*. Chiang Mai, Thailand: Silkworm Books, 2013.

Shuckburgh, Evelyn. *Descent to Suez: Diaries 1951–56*. London: Weidenfeld and Nicolson, 1986.

Smith, Russell Jack. *The Unknown CIA: My Three Decades with the Agency*. Washington, DC: Pergamon-Brassey's International Defense, 1989.

Tran Bach Dang. *Tran Bach Dang: Life and Memories*. Translated by Merle L. Pribbenow II. Ho Chi Minh City, Vietnam: Tre Publishing House, 2006.

Secondary Sources

Ambrose, Stephen E. *Eisenhower: The President*. New York: Simon and Schuster, 1984.

Anderson, David L. *Trapped by Success: The Eisenhower Administration and Vietnam, 1953–61*. New York: Columbia University Press, 1991.

Ang, Cheng Guan. "The Bandung Conference and the Cold War International History of Southeast Asia." In *Bandung Revisited: The Legacy of the 1955 Asian–African Conference*, edited by Sang Tang and Amitav Acharya. Singapore: National University of Singapore Press, 2008.

———. *Vietnamese Communists' Relations with China and the Second Indochina Conflict, 1956–1962*. Jefferson, NC: McFarland, 1997.

Barnett, A. Doak. "Asia and Africa in Session: Random Notes on the Asian–African Conference." American Universities Field Staff, May 18, 1955. www.icwa.org.

Brands, H. W. *The Specter of Neutralism: The United States and the Emergence of the Third World, 1947–1960.* New York: Columbia University Press, 1989.

Brinkley, Alan. "A President for Certain Seasons." *Wilson Quarterly,* Spring 1990.

———. *The Publisher: Henry Luce and His American Century.* New York: Knopf, 2010.

Brocheux, Pierre, and Daniel Hémery. *Indochina: An Ambiguous Colonization, 1858–1954.* Berkeley: University of California Press, 2009.

Chandler, David P. *Brother Number One: A Political Biography of Pol Pot.* Rev. ed. Boulder, CO: Westview Press, 1999.

———. "Coming to Cambodia." In *At the Edge of the Forest: Essays on Cambodia, History, and Narrative in Honor of David Chandler,* edited by Ruth H. Hansen and Judy Ledgerwood. Ithaca, NY: Southeast Asia Program, Cornell University, 2008.

———. *The Tragedy of Cambodian History: Politics, War, and Revolution since 1945.* New Haven, CT: Yale University Press, 1991.

Chapman, Jessica M. *Cauldron of Resistance: Ngo Dinh Diem, the United States, and 1950s Southern Vietnam.* Ithaca, NY: Cornell University Press, 2013.

Clymer, Kenton. "Ambassador William Cattell Trimble and Cambodia, 1959–1962." In *The Human Tradition in the Vietnam Era,* edited by David L. Anderson. Wilmington, DE: Scholarly Resources, 2000.

———. *Troubled Relations: The United States and Cambodia since 1870.* Dekalb: Northern Illinois University Press, 2007.

———. *The United States and Cambodia, 1870–1969: From Curiosity to Confrontation.* New York: RoutledgeCurzon, 2004.

———. *The United States and Cambodia, 1969–2000: A Troubled Relationship.* New York: RoutledgeCurzon, 2004.

Crosswell, D. K. R. *Beetle: The Life of General Walter Bedell Smith.* Lexington: University Press of Kentucky, 2010.

Currey, Cecil B. *Edward Lansdale: The Unquiet American.* Washington, DC: Brassey's, 1998.

Dai, Poeliu. "Canada's Role in the International Commission for Supervision and Control in Cambodia." In *Canadian Yearbook of International Law, 1970.* Vancouver: Publications Centre, University of British Columbia, 1971.

Dommen, Arthur J. *The Indochinese Experience of the French and the Americans: Nationalism and Communism in Cambodia, Laos, and Vietnam.* Bloomington: Indiana University Press, 2001.

Edwards, Philip K. "The President's Board: 1956–1960." *Studies in Intelligence,* Summer 1969. www.foia.cia.gov.

Engelbert, Thomas, and Christopher E. Goscha. *Falling out of Touch: A Study on Vietnamese Communist Policy towards an Emerging Cambodian Communist Movement, 1930–1975.* Clayton, Canada: Monash University, 1995.

Fineman, Daniel. *A Special Relationship: The United States and Military Government in Thailand, 1947–1958*. Honolulu: University of Hawaii Press, 1997.

Fursenko, Aleksandr, and Timothy Naftali. *Khrushchev's Cold War: The Inside Story of an American Adversary*. New York: Norton, 2007.

Gaiduk, Ilya V. *Confronting Vietnam: Soviet Policy toward the Indochina Conflict, 1954–1963*. Washington, DC: Woodrow Wilson Center Press, 2003.

Gardner, Paul F. *Shared Hopes, Separate Fears: Fifty Years of U.S.–Indonesian Relations*. Boulder, CO: Westview Press, 1997.

Gnoinska, Margaret K. "Poland and the Cold War in East and Southeast Asia, 1949–1965." PhD diss., George Washington University, 2010.

Goscha, Christopher E. *Thailand and the Southeast Asian Networks of the Vietnamese Revolution, 1885–1954*. New York: Routledge, 1999.

———. "Vietnam and the World Outside: The Case of Vietnamese Communist Advisers in Laos (1948–62)." *South East Asia Research* 12, no. 2 (July 2004).

Greenstein, Fred I. *The Hidden-Hand Presidency: Eisenhower as Leader*. Baltimore: Johns Hopkins University Press, 1994.

Grose, Peter. *Gentleman Spy: The Life and Times of Allen Dulles*. Boston: Houghton Mifflin, 1994.

Hansen, Ruth H., and Judy Ledgerwood, eds. *At the Edge of the Forest: Essays on Cambodia, History, and Narrative in Honor of David Chandler*. Ithaca, NY: Southeast Asia Program, Cornell University, 2008.

Heder, Steve. *Cambodian Communism and the Vietnamese Model*. Vol. 1: *Imitation and Independence, 1930–1975*. Bangkok: White Lotus, 2004.

Herz, Martin F. *A Short History of Cambodia: From the Days of Angkor to the Present*. New York: Praeger, 1958.

Immerman, Richard H. *The Hidden Hand: A Brief History of the CIA*. Hoboken, NJ: Wiley, 2014.

———. *John Foster Dulles: Piety, Pragmatism, and Power in U.S. Foreign Policy*. Wilmington, DE: Scholarly Resources, 1999.

———. "The United States and the Geneva Conference of 1954: A New Look." *Diplomatic History* 14, no. 1 (January 1990).

Jones, Matthew. *Conflict and Confrontation in Southeast Asia, 1961–1965: Britain, the United States, Indonesia, and the Creation of Malaysia*. Cambridge: Cambridge University Press, 2002.

Kahin, Audrey R., and George McT. Kahin. *Subversion as Foreign Policy: The Secret Eisenhower and Dulles Debacle in Indonesia*. New York: New Press, 1995.

Kahin, George McT. *The Asian–African Conference: Bandung, Indonesia, April 1955*. Ithaca, NY: Cornell University Press, 1956.

———. *Southeast Asia: A Testament*. London: RoutledgeCurzon, 2003.

Kerr, Jeffrey L. "'Honest Brokers'? Canada and the International Commission for Supervision and Control, Cambodia, 1954 to 1964." MA thesis, Carleton University, 1997.

Kiernan, Ben. *How Pol Pot Came to Power: Colonialism, Nationalism, and Commu-

nism in Cambodia, 1930–1975. 2nd ed. New Haven, CT: Yale University Press, 2004.

Kislenko, Arne. "A Not So Silent Partner: Thailand's Role in Covert Operations, Counter-insurgency, and the Wars in Indochina." *Journal of Conflict Studies,* Summer 2004. http://journals.hil.unb.ca.

Kurlantzick, Joshua. *The Ideal Man: The Tragedy of Jim Thompson and the American Way of War.* Hoboken, NJ: Wiley, 2011.

Kux, Dennis. *India and the United States: Estranged Democracies, 1941–1991.* Washington, DC: National Defense University Press, 1993.

Logevall, Fredrik. *Embers of War: The Fall of an Empire and the Making of America's Vietnam.* New York: Random House, 2012.

Nguyen, Lien-Hang T. *Hanoi's War: An International History of the War for Peace in Vietnam.* Chapel Hill: University of North Carolina Press, 2012.

Oberdorfer, Don. *Senator Mansfield: The Extraordinary Life of a Great American Statesman and Diplomat.* Washington, DC: Smithsonian Books, 2003.

Osborne, Milton. "The Complex Legacy of Norodom Sihanouk." *Phnom Penh Post,* October 17, 2012.

———. *Sihanouk: Prince of Light, Prince of Darkness.* Honolulu: University of Hawaii Press, 1994.

Petraeus, David H. "Korea, the Never-Again Club, and Indochina." *Parameters,* December 1987.

Rabe, Stephen G. "Eisenhower Revisionism: A Decade of Scholarship." *Diplomatic History,* January 1993.

Rust, William J. *Before the Quagmire: American Intervention in Laos, 1954–1961.* Lexington: University Press of Kentucky, 2012.

Sanger, Clyde. *Malcolm MacDonald: Bringing an End to Empire.* Montreal: McGill-Queen's University Press, 1995.

SarDesai, D. R. *Indian Foreign Policy in Cambodia, Laos, and Vietnam, 1947–1961.* Berkeley: University of California Press, 1968.

Scott-Smith, Giles. "Building a Community around the Pax Americana: The US Government and Exchange Programmes during the 1950s." In *The US Government, Citizen Groups, and the Cold War: The State–Private Network,* edited by Helen Laville and Hugh Wilford. New York: Routledge, 2006.

Shawcross, William. *Sideshow: Nixon, Kissinger, and the Destruction of Cambodia.* New York: Simon and Schuster, 1979.

Statler, Kathryn N. *Replacing France: The Origins of American Intervention in Vietnam.* Lexington: University Press of Kentucky, 2007.

Tarling, Nicholas. *Britain and Sihanouk's Cambodia.* Singapore: National University of Singapore Press, 2014.

Trachtenberg, Marc. "Audience Costs in 1954?" H-Diplo/International Security Studies Forum. www.h-net.org/~diplo.

Tucker, Nancy Bernkopf, ed. *China Confidential: American Diplomats and Sino–American Relations, 1945–1996.* New York: Columbia University Press, 2001.

Turkoly-Joczik, Robert L. "Cambodia's Khmer Serei Movement." *Asian Affairs* 15, no. 1 (1988).

Waller, Douglas. *Wild Bill Donovan: The Spymaster Who Created the OSS and Modern American Espionage.* New York: Free Press, 2011.

Weber, Ralph E. *Spymasters: Ten CIA Officers in Their Own Words.* Wilmington, DE: Scholarly Resources, 1999.

Zhai, Qiang. *China and the Vietnam Wars, 1950–1975.* Chapel Hill: University of North Carolina Press, 2000.

Index